THE GENERAL AND
THE JOURNALISTS

For Gib and Sarita —
With warm regards and
lasting friendship!

Harry 1/12/99

Also by Harry J. Maihafer

From the Hudson to the Yalu:
West Point '49 in the Korean War

Oblivion:
The Mystery of West Point Cadet Richard Cox

Brave Decisions:
Moral Courage from the Revolutionary War to Desert Storm

THE GENERAL AND THE JOURNALISTS

ULYSSES S. GRANT, HORACE GREELEY, AND CHARLES DANA

HARRY J. MAIHAFER

Brassey's

Washington • London

Jacket photo of Grant courtesy of National Archives
   Insert photo left (Greeley) courtesy of National Archives
   Insert photo right (Dana) courtesy of U.S. Army Military History Institute/
   Massachusetts Commanding Military Order of the Loyal Legion

Editorial Offices: Order Department:
22883 Quicksilver Drive   P.O. Box 960
Dulles, VA 20166   Herndon, VA 20172

Brassey's books are available at special discounts for bulk purchases for sales
promotions, premiums, fund-raising, or education use.

Library of Congress Cataloging-in-Publication Data

Maihafer, Harry J. (Harry James), 1924-
   The general and the journalists : Ulysses S. Grant, Horace
Greeley, and Charles Dana / Harry J. Maihafer.
      p. cm.
   Includes bibliographical references and index.
   ISBN 1-57488-105-1
   1. Grant, Ulysses S. (Ulysses Simpson), 1822–1885—Relations with
journalists. 2. Greeley, Horace, 1811–1872. 3. Dana, Charles A.
(Charles Anderson), 1819–1897. 4. Presidents—United States—Biography.
6. United States—Politics and government—1869–1877. 7. United States—
History—Civil War, 1861–1865—Journalists. 8. Press and politics—
United States—History—19th century. I. Title.
E672.M126 1998
973.8'2'092—dc21   98-19351
                                                           CIP

First Edition

10 9 8 7 6 5 4 3 2 1
Printed in Canada

For George and Loyola

CONTENTS

LIST OF MAPS

Grant is one of the most remarkable men I have ever met. He does not seem to be aware of his powers, but in the future he will undoubtedly exert a controlling influence in shaping the destinies of the country.

—Alexander Stephens, Vice President,
Confederate States of America

Horace Greeley would be the greatest journalist in America if he did not aim to be the leading politician in America.

—John Russell Young, former managing editor,
New York Tribune

As a journalist and as Assistant Secretary of War, Charles Dana was one of the most influential men of his time. . . . he must be considered as the first of American editors.

—James Harrison Wilson, Major General,
U.S. Army (Retired)

FOREWORD

At this advanced stage in Civil War historiography, it is indeed refreshing to find a book that deals with the complex subject of relationships of prominent military participants with lesser known contemporaries, especially those in other professions. In *The General and the Journalists,* Harry Maihafer has written an important book that fills a previously overlooked gap. In the process, he manages to blend three life stories with the precision of a juggler and the assurance of a surgeon.

For all the hours I've logged reading about Ulysses S. Grant, I'd never comprehended how much—in different but significant ways—Horace Greeley and Charles Dana contributed to his selection by the Lincoln administration as the general who might finally win the war. But as I read chapter after chapter (I defy anyone to read just one), I found myself conceding, I didn't know that! As Maihafer makes clear, Dana rose to prominence as managing editor of Horace Greeley's *New York Tribune.* This led to his becoming an assistant secretary of war, a position from which he telegraphed Washington repeatedly throughout the Vicksburg Campaign and convinced the Union's war managers to set aside derogatory rumors and rely on soldier's soldier Grant.

Studies of Civil War era figures' relationships, their development and fluctuation, and most of all their consequences, are rare. They are also too instructive and too fascinating to be so neglected. Harry Maihafer has gone a long way toward correcting this. Particularly interesting, in my opinion, is the coverage he gives to the trio's linkages—and ruptures—in the years of Grant's presidency and beyond. Greeley and Dana supported him initially, but at times they were also his detractors as well as enemies of each other. Best of all, Maihafer combines solid research with readability, seasoned with irony and flashes of wit. His readers will quickly recall that these are the characteristics of his earlier books, about his West Point classmates in the Korean War, the strange mystery of Cadet Richard Cox, and the moral courage displayed by military decision-makers from the Revolutionary War through the Gulf War. They ought to attract more fans to this new one. Query: How many Civil War authors can you think of who have his versatility, as well as his ability to write with competence and enviable style?

Booksellers are well advised to go beyond assigning this book only to their Civil War shelves. The stories told in these pages are of the kind William Faulkner declared the only ones worth telling, the ones reminding us of the "courage and honor and hope and pride and compassion and pity and sacrifice" that have been the glory of our past. *The General and the Journalists* is a worthy addition to Harry Maihafer's shelf. He will have to reach mighty far to turn out a better book.

—Curt Anders

PREFACE

GREELEY, GRANT, AND DANA. If by some magic I could visit the 19th century, these are three men I'd want to meet. I might start with Greeley, for he could fill me in on events of the day—or at least his version of them. Hearing his name today, people tend to think of "Go West, Young Man." Well, he *did* say that, or at least something close to it. But he said, and wrote, countless other things in what was arguably the most prolific, influential life in the annals of American journalism.

A conversation with Greeley would be not only a good place to start, it would also be highly enjoyable. Although he was opinionated, eccentric, and overly concerned with political wheeling and dealing, he was also an eloquent conversationalist and a true crusader. He had a multitude of causes, each of which he promoted with passionate conviction. In modern terms, we might think of him as a combined *Washington Post*, *New York Times*, major television network, and for good measure, a bit of Rush Limbaugh. In Greeley's heyday, there were few discussions that weren't influenced by "what Uncle Horace has to say on the subject."

Talking with Charles Dana, however, would be quite a different matter. First of all, he might give us a choice of languages; he was fluent in a half dozen. In addition, much would depend on Dana's age when we met. The young Dana would come across as a bright, idealistic scholar, thirsty for knowledge, full of ambition, and possessed of great personal charm. An older Dana, by contrast, would be a crusty, affluent businessman, a connoisseur of fine wine, a world traveler, and above all a confirmed cynic. His conversation would still sparkle, but his wit would be full of barbs, often targeted at what today we call the "establishment."

Probably my greatest challenge would come as I tried to engage Ulysses Grant, the legendary "quiet man," in conversation. In social gatherings, Grant usually sat rather silently, perhaps puffing on a cigar, taking in what others were saying but volunteering little himself. In a small group, however, especially with trusted friends, he would open up. When he did, people listened, for his words were thoughtful and full of good-natured common sense. I would hope that, when he learned I was a fellow infantry officer, I'd be one of the ones with whom he'd relax.

This, then, is a tale of three distinguished Americans. Our story touches on the Civil War, Grant's presidency, and 19th-century journalism, but it is above all an effort to describe three remarkable lives, emphasizing how those lives became interwoven, influenced each other, and in turn affected the course of American history. Since each of our subjects was a man of strong will, we might expect their relationships to have been complex, and we'd be right. The Greeley/Dana relationship, for example, went from positive to negative, then back to positive. When Greeley hired Dana as managing editor of his *New York Tribune*, Greeley became both a mentor and a colleague for Dana. After their falling out, however, the two became, if not enemies, at least rivals. Then, in later life, Dana became one of Greeley's staunchest supporters.

The Greeley/Grant relationship also shifted over time. Early in the war, the pacifist Greeley was outspoken in his criticism of West Pointers, and after Shiloh, much of that criticism was directed at Grant. Later, when Grant showed his true worth as a commander, Greeley sang his praises, even proposing him as a presidential candidate in place of Lincoln. Then, in 1872, Horace Greeley, despite being a co-founder of the Republican Party, paradoxically ran for president against the Republican candidate, Ulysses Grant.

The Dana/Grant relationship probably underwent the most dramatic shifts of all. Dana, as a War Department observer sent to report on Grant, was a major player in the general's rise to military prominence. A few years later, as editor of the *New York Sun*, Dana became the country's most vicious critic of Grant's administration. Eventually, however, when he wrote his Civil War *Recollections*, a mellowing Dana spoke of Grant with respect and affection.

For anyone interested in human nature, and who is not, these changing relationships can be fascinating. They may also help explain why Ulysses Grant has come down to us wrapped in such a puzzling dichotomy, that of very good general/very bad president. Obviously the press played a major role in creating each of those overly simplistic portraits.

In the lives of Greeley, Dana, and Grant, we can find more than a few flaws. For each man, however, there is far more to admire than to criticize. Perhaps the reader, while sensing my respect for all three, will also understand my partiality for Ulysses Grant. "I would like to see truthful history written," a dying Grant wrote in his *Memoirs*. I hope he would approve of this book.

1

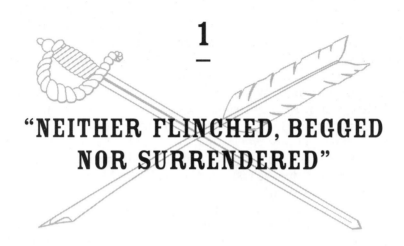

"NEITHER FLINCHED, BEGGED NOR SURRENDERED"

IN TINY Georgetown, Ohio, nestled in the valley of White Oak Creek just north of Kentucky, people all knew their neighbors. Holidays were a time for gathering, and on this July 4, 1837, the air was festive.

Flags were whipping in the breeze, the sun was shining, and smiling villagers circled the courthouse square, watching the local militia company wheel and turn in close-order drill. Nervous, sweaty young men, wanting to show off for families and sweethearts, were stepping off smartly, responding to the crisp commands of a martial-looking visitor, a 30-year-old lieutenant of artillery.

The unit came to a halt, executed "Present arms," and the lieutenant sang out, "Company . . . dismissed!"

Bystanders applauded. They were impressed, not only by their militiamen sons but by the visiting drillmaster, a local boy, Jake Ammen—a West Pointer, no less. Home on vacation, Ammen had been persuaded, albeit reluctantly, to lead the drill and "show how the regular army did it."

Nearly everyone knew Lieutenant Ammen, whose father, David, edited the *Georgetown Castigator*. Six years earlier, young Jake had graduated from West Point; his neighbors were proud of him, proud also of the fact that for these past 4 years he'd been stationed at the Military Academy teaching cadets both mathematics and philosophy.[1]

As the drill ended and the crowd began to disperse, a tall, thin, plainly dressed civilian stepped forward and asked Ammen if they could talk for a moment. Ammen recognized the man as Jesse Grant, the 43-year-old owner of the local tannery. No introductions were necessary. Before he left for West Point, Jake had worked for his father, and he remembered Grant, who often wrote political articles for the paper, as a frequent visitor to the *Castigator* office. Once a Jacksonian Democrat, Grant had changed parties several years earlier. Now, like David Ammen, he was an ardent Whig, an admirer of the great statesman and orator Henry Clay. As they began talking, Grant might well have asked the lieutenant about Henry Clay's son, Ammen's West Point classmate. In turn, Ammen perhaps congratulated Grant for having recently been elected to a term as Georgetown's mayor, maybe saying it proved that even a dedicated Whig, if respected enough, could win an election in Democratic Georgetown![2]

Soon, however, Jesse Grant, always a no-nonsense person, came to the point. His son Ulysses, he said, was now 15. The boy was bright —in Jesse's opinion, even exceptional—and he needed to be thinking about higher schooling. What about West Point? Jesse had heard a man could not only get a good education there but could do so at government expense.

That was true, Ammen said, and not only that, after a graduate put in his time, he could resign from the army and find a good position on the outside, perhaps as a teacher or an engineer. West Point, as a matter of fact, was one of only two colleges in the country turning out civil engineers; the other was the newly founded Rensselaer Polytechnic Institute in Troy, New York, and its graduates were only now beginning to appear.[3]

But Jesse wondered whether people wouldn't resent a man who turned in his resignation after he'd been educated at government expense. Ammen assured him that West Pointers would always be ready to serve when the country needed them, but the army understood that graduates might seek more lucrative civilian careers during peacetime. As a matter of fact, next fall Ammen himself would be taking off the uniform to become a mathematics professor at a small Kentucky college. When he did, he'd be the 23rd member of his class to resign, leaving only nine of his classmates still on active duty.[4]

That clinched it. As the conversation ended, a nearby bystander, one of the *Castigator*'s printers, heard Jesse say, "I am determined that Ulysses shall go to West Point."[5]

It was understandable for Jesse Grant to be ambitious for his eldest child, for Jesse himself had always been driven by ambition, his life marked by hard work and a burning desire to get ahead. It hadn't been easy. His father, Capt. Noah Grant, Revolutionary War veteran, hard drinker, and aimless ne'er-do-well, had been better at siring children than providing for them.

Jesse's mother, Rachel, Noah's second wife, had given birth to seven children in 11 years and had moved twice with her restless husband, all the way to a cabin on the rough Ohio frontier. Then she had died, and Noah, just as he'd done when his first wife passed away, had broken up the home. The two oldest children, Susan and Jesse, 13 and 11, set out on their own; the next three in age were taken in by neighbors and relatives; the youngest two went with their father to live with Peter Grant, a son from Noah's first marriage who owned a prosperous tannery in Kentucky.[6]

Young Jesse began working for bed and board at some of the neighboring farms. Three years later, at age 14, he had the good fortune to end up with a family named Tod, kindly people who cared about his future. Although the Tods were far from rich, they were comfortably well off, enough to make Jesse appreciate what it meant to be a person of means.[7] By the time he was 16, young Jesse had set himself a series of goals. He would learn a trade, acquire his own business, and by age 25 have enough money to afford a wife and a home of his own. The trade he decided upon was that of a tanner. Harnesses, saddles, shoes, boots—in Kentucky and neighboring Ohio, there would always be a demand for good leather.

After leaving the Tods and working for a time in a local tannery, Jesse decided he'd have a better opportunity by apprenticing himself to his half-brother Peter. For 5 years, he worked for Peter in Maysfield, Kentucky, toiling hard by day and studying hard by night, reading everything he could get his hands on.[8]

At age 21, having worked off his apprenticeship, Jesse moved back to Ohio. He'd later say he left slave state Kentucky because "I would not own slaves and I would not live where there were slaves and not own them."[9]

The first tannery Jesse worked for in Ohio was run by an abolitionist, Owen Brown, who maintained a station on the underground railroad. Owen's son John would later become either famous or infamous, depending on one's point of view, especially after his body "lay mouldering in the grave."[10]

After a year with the Browns, Jesse moved to Ravenna, Ohio, where a local tanner, John F. Wells, took him in as a partner. Once again he worked hard and saved his money. By the time he was 25 he was financially secure, meeting the schedule he'd set for himself as a teen-ager.

When an epidemic of malaria swept through Ravenna, Jesse became seriously ill. For a year he was unable to work. His cash vanished, creditors took over his share of the business, and he had to start over, this time in Point Pleasant, Ohio. At Point Pleasant, although in his words he was "without one dollar to his name," people soon recognized his industry and determination.[11] That helped when he went looking for a wife.

The girl he found was 23-year-old Hannah Simpson, whom Jesse would later describe as a "plain unpretending country girl, handsome but not vain."[12] Her father, John, owned a 600-acre farm, and the family, originally from Pennsylvania, was solid, respected, and deeply religious. Jesse was particularly impressed by Hannah's mother, who loved talking to him about books.

Hannah herself, according to the neighbors, was quiet to the extreme, speaking only when spoken to and then only in monosyllables. She was the type of person, they said, who "thought nothing you could do would entitle you to praise . . . you ought to praise the Lord for giving you an opportunity to do it."[13] Hannah might have been unemotional, humor-less, and lacking in warmth, but she had common sense, was hardwork-ing, and came from a good family. Jesse liked what he saw, proposed, and the two were married on June 24, 1821.[14]

Jesse brought Hannah back to a sturdy frame house he'd rented in Point Pleasant, next door to the tannery. Its best feature was the view. Their home stood high on a bluff, and down the slope, 100 yards away, ran the broad Ohio. On its blue waters ships were constantly passing, carrying people and goods along one of the nation's great thorough-fares. The house's worst feature, on the other hand, was its proximity to the tannery, where bloody hides were forever being scraped and treated. The resultant smells of dried blood, wet leather, and decaying flesh could not have been pleasant, especially for a young bride who was soon pregnant.

Jesse and Hannah's first child, a boy, was born on April 27, 1822. Naming him was to be a family affair, involving all the Simpsons. Hannah suggested "Albert," her sister Anne came up with "Theodore," and her father offered "Hiram," which he considered "quite handsome a name." Hannah's mother, however, more romantic than any of them, said she'd been reading the classics, and with Jesse's strong support, she argued for the name of a great Greek hero, "Ulysses."

Names were written on slips of paper, placed in a hat, and Anne, the youngest, drew out the name "Ulysses." At this, the diplomatic Jesse, wanting to accommodate both his wife's parents, stopped the proceedings and declared it was settled: the boy would be called "Hiram," his grandfather's suggestion, and have for a middle name "Ulysses," admired by both his grandmother and his proud father.[15] Although he was "Hiram Ulysses," once he was home the "handsome" name of "Hiram" was seldom used. To friends and family he was mostly "Ulysses" or "'Lyss."

Before the year was out, the ever-ambitious Jesse, wanting a tannery of his own, decided Point Pleasant wasn't growing fast enough to suit him. He found a likely spot 25 miles to the east, in the newly formed but promising village of Georgetown. He bought a site, cleared the land, started a tannery, and built a small two-story brick house for Hannah and the baby. The house itself might have been unimaginative, but thanks to the Simpson family and Jesse's love of education, there were 30 books on hand, at the time a remarkable home library for the area.

From the beginning, Jesse doted on his baby son. Whenever he could induce a neighbor to listen, he'd brag about how quickly the youngster learned things and how amazing he was with horses. By the time Ulysses was 5, his father would let him ride the workhorses down to the creek for watering, and Jesse would beam with pride as a horse came back with Ulysses standing upright on its back, balancing himself with the reins.[16]

Jesse was determined that his "exceptional" son would get the education he himself had never received. When Ulysses was 5 or 6, he was enrolled in the town's only school. He'd later write: "I never missed a quarter from school from the time I was old enough to attend till the time of leaving home." However, he'd also admit he "was not studious in habit."[17]

The schoolhouse was a primitive, one-room affair and, typical of its time, a place where the teacher kept order by the liberal use of corporal punishment. Only once, though, did his schoolmates remember Ulysses being punished. "Some of the boys," according to the story, "attempted to take his knife away from him and the teacher, coming upon the fracas, ordered 'Lyss to hand it over." He refused, and although the teacher switched him, "he neither flinched, begged nor surrendered, and kept the knife."[18]

One of Jesse's favorite stories dated from the time Ulysses was 6. As the proud father told it: "I had gone away from home, to Ripley, 12 miles off. I went in the morning and did not get back until night. I owned at the time a 3-year-old colt, which had been ridden under a saddle to carry the mail, but had never had a collar on. While I was gone, Ulysses got the colt and put a collar and a harness on him, and drove off, and loaded up the sled with brush and came back again. He kept at it, hauling successive loads, all day, and when I came home at night, he had a pile of brush as big as a cabin. He used to harness horses when he had to get up in the manger to put the bridle and collar on, and then turn the half-bushel over and stand on that, to throw the harness on."[19] Understandably, by the time Ulysses was 8, he was a regular driver for the tannery.

Any son of Jesse's, of course, was also expected to handle his share of the more mundane chores. From an early age, Ulysses worked hard on the farm Jesse had acquired—particularly, he later reported, "all the work done with horses, such as breaking up the land, furrowing, ploughing corn and potatoes, bringing in the crops when harvested, hauling all the wood, besides tending two or three horses, a cow or two, and sawing wood for stoves, etc., while still attending school."[20]

As each year passed, Jesse Grant kept adding more stories about his precocious son. When Ulysses was 12, the enterprising Jesse took on a contract to build a new county jail on the Georgetown square. It involved cutting and hauling huge logs. Ulysses, according to Jesse, said he'd do the hauling if they could buy a certain powerful horse, Dave, he had long wanted.

Jesse agreed but later said he doubted Ulysses could "hold out for over a week—he was such a little bit of a fellow." Consequently, Jesse hired a man to go along on the job to give Ulysses a hand. A week later, Jesse said, the man came to say there was no use in his being there, that the boy "understands the team and can manage it as well as I can, and better, too!"

Jesse's story continued. One day Ulysses came home with a load and said there was no use going back, since the woodchoppers weren't working that day. Then how, Jesse wondered, had he managed to load the logs if no one was working?

"Oh, Dave and I did it," was the answer. Jesse asked what he meant; how could he have lifted such huge logs into the wagon?

Ulysses explained: "Dave and I loaded. I took a chain and hitched it to the end of the logs and we managed to get them in." He then told how he had found a half-fallen tree, lying at a slant, up which the logs could be dragged. They were then slipped off onto the wagon when he backed it underneath.

"There was much talk of it in the neighborhood," said Jesse, "as it was considered a great achievement for a boy his size."[21]

Not so flattering was the story of the horse trade. As Ulysses remembered it years later: "There was a Mr. Ralston living within a few miles of the village, who owned a colt which I very much wanted. My father had offered twenty dollars for it, but Ralston wanted twenty-five. I was so anxious to have the colt, that after the owner left, I begged to be allowed to take him at the price demanded. My father yielded, but said twenty dollars was all the horse was worth, and told me to offer that price; if it was not accepted, to offer twenty-two-and-a-half, and if that would not get him, to give the twenty-five. I at once mounted a horse and went for the colt. When I got to Mr. Ralston's house, I said to him, 'Papa says I may offer you twenty dollars for the colt, and if you won't take that I am to offer you twenty-two-and-a-half, and if you won't take that, to give you twenty five.'" Needless to say, the practical Mr. Ralston set his price.

"The story got out among the boys in the village," Ulysses would write, "and it was a long time before I heard the last of it."[22] Young boys love to tease, and this was a story providing lots of ammunition. Similarly, they might have teased after hearing their parents chuckle over Jesse's boasts about his "remarkable" son. It was only natural to seek ways to show that Ulysses wasn't nearly as precocious as Jesse maintained. In any case—and the teasing might have helped—by the age of 12 Ulysses was painfully shy, taking after his quiet mother rather than his outspoken father. His habitual silence even made those who saw him but casually sometimes suspect that Jesse's boy might be "backward."[23]

Nevertheless, young Ulysses had his share of friends and enjoyed the usual activities of a healthy boyhood: fishing, swimming, or ice-skating in winter. The only exception was when it came to hunting. Although he'd learned to shoot and was even a good marksman, he refused to shoot game. In later years, a friend would say, "He was unusually sensitive to pain, and his aversion to taking any form of life was so great that he would not hunt."[24]

At the schoolhouse, meanwhile, Ulysses was only an average student. Thomas Upham, who taught the village school for 2 years, would later say his pupil's "standing in arithmetic was unusually good, but that he had no taste for grammar, geography, and spelling, although he was not noticeably dull in any of these studies."[25]

While the bashful Ulysses accepted school, although with little enthusiasm, he had a downright hatred of it when it involved public speaking. Upham, who periodically required student declamations, said this "was unbearable to young Grant," who simply "could not bear to get up and face a whole room full of boys and girls." When called on to recite Washington's Farewell Address, Upham remembered, Ulysses "made fearful work of it, and after school said he would 'never speak there again, no matter what happened.'"[26]

It was about this time that Jesse asked Ulysses what he wanted to be when he grew up. Ulysses wasn't sure; he was only certain of one thing—he did *not* want to work in his father's tannery, where the sight and stench of bloody hides almost made him physically ill.

"If you want me to," he told his father, "I'll work at the tannery until I'm twenty-one, but you may depend on it, I'll never work a day at it after that."

"No, I don't want you to work at it, now, if you don't like it and mean to stick to it," Jesse said. "Now, what do you think you *would* like?"

Ulysses, who hadn't given much thought to the matter, said he might like to be a farmer, or perhaps a trader working down the river. Jesse said he didn't own enough acreage to set Ulysses up as a farmer, and he disapproved of the vulgar, brawling life on the river. It seemed to him, he said, that the best course for Ulysses would be to acquire more education, thereby opening up all sorts of opportunities.[27]

Accordingly, in the fall of 1836, when Ulysses was 14, Jesse decided that Georgetown schools were inadequate for his talented son. Ulysses was enrolled in Richeson and Rand's Academy in neighboring Maysville, Kentucky.

Although Jesse Grant was one of Georgetown's leading businessmen, sending Ulysses off to a private school was something of a financial strain. By this time there were four other children at home to support. Also, throughout the nation there were growing signs of falling prices and financial uneasiness. Whatever the cost, though, a private school it would be.

Ulysses, who appreciated his father's financial sacrifice, later wrote with a touch of embarrassment, "I was not studious in habit, and probably did not make progress enough to compensate for the outlay for board and tuition." Classmates, on the other hand, remembered him as a serious student, mostly quiet, but one who was "there for business," frequently breaking his silence to pose questions to the teacher as if determined to get his money's worth.

Richeson and Rand's, although good enough in its way, in truth wasn't much better than the schools of Georgetown. Ulysses later said he spent time "going over the same old arithmetic which I knew every word of before." And with the rote learning practiced at Richeson's, he had to keep repeating "a noun is the name of a thing" until, as he said drolly, "I had come to believe it."[28]

It began in New York in the spring of 1837, and within a very short time it had spread to every corner of the nation—a financial crisis disrupting every element of American society. They called it the Panic of '37; nearly everyone was affected; and no one fully understood it. Some blamed it on reckless banking practices. Others said it stemmed from a series of shady and greedy financial conspiracies. Whatever the cause, the effects were devastating. Unemployment soared, banks began calling in their loans, and even in out-of-the-way Georgetown, Ohio, money became scarce and credit impossible to obtain.

Like many other small businessmen, Jesse Grant was affected by the '37 crisis. Regretfully, he told his son he'd have to drop out of school and return home. That was fine by Ulysses, who would remember the following months as among the happiest of his life.

That happiness, unfortunately, was mostly obtained outside the home, for in the Grant household there wasn't much by way of communication. Mother Hannah was invariably withdrawn. Father Jesse, concerned with his struggling business, now talked to people very little. When he did, he tended to put everything in the form of an undisputable pronouncement. That was especially true when it came to politics. A few years earlier, in fact, his hardheadedness had cost him the friendship of Tom Hamer, a man he'd known and liked for years. He and Hamer had disagreed over Andrew Jackson's withdrawal of funds from the United States Bank, which Jesse considered a risky endangerment of the country's financial structure. Jesse therefore turned from the Jacksonian Democrats to the newly formed Whig Party of Henry Clay, which he considered more favorable to businessmen like himself. Consequently, in 1832, when Democrat Hamer ran successfully for Congress, Jesse supported his Whig opponent. As their political disagreement turned personal, each man stuck to his position, unwilling to give an inch. Eventually they stopped speaking. Deep down, each man probably regretted the lost friendship, but neither was willing to be the first to admit it.[29]

Unlike his father, Ulysses had little interest in politics or newspapers. Jesse, of course, was an avid reader of newspapers and a frequent contributor to the local *Castigator*. Moreover, even Ulysses's young brother Simpson, when he wasn't in school, was now working for the *Castigator* as a printer's helper.

Back in Georgetown, meanwhile, people saw Ulysses' eyes light up only when he was working with horses. His skill along those lines was by this time well-known, and neighbors often hired him to turn a colt into a pacer or to work with and tame an unruly mount. On the latter occasions, the people of Georgetown saw the normally shy lad shed his bashfulness. He even seemed to enjoy all the attention when people gathered on the village square to watch him break some fiery, plunging colt.

The carefree days of youth were winding down all too soon. Before many months had passed, Jesse told Ulysses he was enrolling him in the new Presbyterian Academy at Ripley, Ohio. Great things were expected of the place, whose president, the Reverend John Rankin, had an outstanding scholarly reputation.[30] All this, of course, fitted in with Jesse's long-range plan: qualifying Ulysses for an appointment to West Point, where he could obtain a fine education—and at no cost to Jesse.

Ulysses, who had never shown the slightest interest in anything military, might or might not have known what his father had in mind for him. Perhaps at this point it was just as well that he did not.

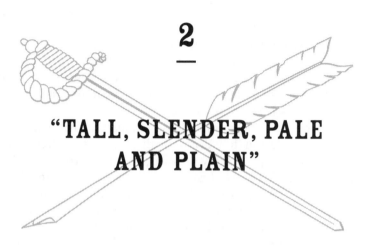

2

"TALL, SLENDER, PALE
AND PLAIN"

AS IT WAS for the Grants, 1837, the year of the Panic, was also crucial for a 26-year-old printer named Horace Greeley.

In the first 3 years of its existence, Greeley's weekly *New Yorker* had shown phenomenal growth. Beginning with just 50 subscribers, it had a circulation of 7,000 by the end of its second year, and now, a year later, the number had grown to 9,000. Readers had first smirked at the paper's pretentiousness, particularly its claim to be a journal of "general literature, news and comment." Soon, however, they were looking forward to its stories and sketches, some submitted by an Englishman who signed his work "Boz" and who later turned out to be Charles Dickens.[1] Readers also had come to enjoy the paper's outspoken pronouncements, especially those written by Greeley himself. The brash young journalist, witty, opinionated, wide-ranging in his subjects, was nothing if not entertaining.

The paper's growth, and Greeley's resultant prosperity, reflected that of the country as a whole. Business was booming, and in this spring of 1837, Greeley ignored the prudent voices that warned of speculation's hollow, phantom profits. In the *New Yorker*, Greeley applauded the news that one parcel of New York City lots, sold for $93,000 a year earlier, had just been resold for $750,000. Cheerfully, he told his readers: "Speculation, in its broadest sense, is not an evil in itself, but the contrary, and relieves public distress far oftener than it creates it."[2]

11

A month after Greeley wrote so optimistically, the calamitous Panic of '37 struck with full force. Banks and brokerage houses, overextended in western land deals and awash in inflated paper schemes, began to collapse. One after another, businesses began closing their doors. In New York, armies of unemployed roamed the streets looking for work. Wherever one looked, there was hunger and misery. The once-confident Greeley, now badly shaken, wrote: "Times can hardly be worse than they are now. . . . Where will this end?"[3]

Inevitably, one of the victims of the financial crisis was the *New Yorker* itself. Circulation fell dramatically, debts mounted, and subscribers failed to pay up. Greeley pleaded, cajoled, threatened: "Friends of the *New Yorker*! We appeal to you, not for charity, but for justice. Whoever among you is in our debt, no matter how small the sum, is guilty of a moral wrong in withholding the payment. . . ."[4] Despite his best efforts, the paper continued to lose money.

And what of his urban readers, whose jobs had disappeared and for whom no relief was in sight? Greeley offered some emotional words of advice, based more on panic than on hope: "We say to the unemployed, you who are able to leave the cities should do so without delay. You have a winter in prospect of fearful, unexampled severity. Do not wait to share its horrors. Fly—scatter through the land—go to the Great West. . . ."[5]

"Go West" was a cry that would ever after be linked to his name.

Horace Greeley, like Jesse Grant, had a restless father given to drink, a man forever moving, forever hoping, and never quite succeeding.

Greeley was born in Amherst, New Hampshire, on February 3, 1811, the third child, and first to survive, of Zaccheus (Zac) Greeley and the former Mary Woodburn. Childhood memories were basically happy ones, thanks in large part to a loving mother who read to him, sang to him, and charmed him with tales handed down from her Scotch-Irish Woodburn ancestors.

As far back as anyone could remember, the boy was a prodigy: sent to school at 3; at 4 beating boys twice his age in spelling bees; at 5 allegedly reading the Bible with ease. During the school year, mother Mary would send him to stay at her father's large farm, near Londonderry, which was closer to a school. In the springtime, however, father Zac would summon him home to help with the planting, and Horace, from birth a frail, sickly child, would have poignant memories of riding a plow horse at age 5, when "occasionally the plow would strike a fast stone and bring up the team all standing, pitching me over the horse's head and landing three to five feet in front."[6]

Greeley would describe his father as "poor and hard-working, struggling to pay off the debt he had incurred in buying his high-priced farm." Unfortunately, Zac's land proved rocky and unproductive, with crops that grew slowly "while burrowing insects fed and fattened on them."[7] Unable to put the farm on a paying basis, Zac fell further and further behind. At age 9, young Horace saw creditors taking over all the family possessions while his father fled to avoid being arrested for debt.[8]

Zac returned a few months later, loaded his dispossessed family on a sleigh, and moved them through the snows of New England to a far corner of neighboring Vermont. There Zac hired himself out as a farm laborer, but once again he was fighting a losing battle. Local farms were barely scratching out a living, and for the Greeleys, each season presented new challenges and new fears. When a crop failed to make a profit, Zac would be out of a job—and often out of any back pay. The Greeleys drifted from place to place, all without success. By the time Horace was 15, his father determined once again to drift westward, this time to Pennsylvania.

Horace would not accompany the family; he had decided it was time to strike out on his own. In the nearby Vermont town of East Poultney, after demonstrating an agile wit and a retentive memory, he convinced Amos Bliss, owner of the *Northern Spectator*, to take him on as an apprentice printer. It would mean a 4-year commitment, with wages barely enough to cover room and board, but at least he'd be learning a trade. Also, by making full use of reading material in the newspaper office and the East Poultney town library, he could further his education. Soon the residents of East Poultney came to know Greeley as a well-informed teenager, an active member of the town's debating society, and a lad who was always ready to pass on the latest news or offer an opinion on just about anything.

One of the *Northern Spectator* editors hired by Bliss was also a Baptist preacher. Little by little, with the preacher often away tending his scattered flocks, Greeley assumed full responsibility for the paper. About the time his apprenticeship ended, however, the paper, which had been losing money for years, finally went out of business.[9]

Discouraged, Greeley went back to his family in Pennsylvania, only to find they were as hard up as ever. To help them along, he found a series of jobs as a journeyman printer in Jamestown and Lodi, New York, and in Erie, Pennsylvania. After several months of this, as he later wrote, "work failed." He went from town to town, talked to one editor after another, but was unable to find another position.

His last job had been on the *Erie Gazette*. Erie, however, like the other towns where he'd lived and worked, seemed to hold little promise; he'd later remember it as "a place which started with too sanguine expectations," ones he suspected would never be realized.[10] It was time to move on.

Up to this point, he'd looked for opportunity only in small country towns. With his religious, rural upbringing, New York City—the "Commercial Emporium," as he called it—had always seemed intimidating. Each year, he knew, some 40,000 immigrants were landing on its doorstep; most of them soon disappeared into the city's festering slums, many to become victims of crime or disease. Nevertheless, New York would be his goal. The man who would later tell others "Go West" would now head east to seek his fortune.

He made a final visit to his family, and knowing the next absence would be a long one, he gave his father half the money he'd saved from his earnings on the *Erie Gazette*. Then, pocketing the remaining $25 and with his personal possessions tied in a handkerchief, he started walking east, past Buffalo and along a towpath of the Erie Canal.

Toward dawn, Greeley hailed an eastbound barge. He climbed aboard, and after paying his fare was greeted by rowdy passengers, still drinking on the cabin roof. They jokingly asked why he was up so early. Had he spent the night on the bank "sparking" some lady friend? Young Greeley, embarrassed, hastened below and tried to sleep.[11]

Next morning he awoke to the sound of creaking lines and the soft, steady clump of a plodding towhorse. Throughout the day, as Greeley watched in fascination, they loaded and unloaded, paused for locks to operate, and glided past the rough, growing towns of Rochester, Syracuse, and Utica. Then, at Schenectady, he left the boat and walked overland to Albany. After spending the night in a "hospitable" tavern, at 10 the next morning he found a Hudson River boat headed for New York.

He later described himself at this stage as "tall, slender, pale and plain," with an "unmistakably rustic manner and address" and armed only with ambition and "so much of the art of printing as a boy will usually learn in the office of a country newspaper."[12]

During that summer of 1831, New York was raw, vulgar, crowded, even dangerous, but for one used to rural life, highly exhilarating. Thanks to the canal, the city bustled with newfound importance, growing exponentially as it received the corn, wheat, oats, hides, and lumber of the Midwest that 5 years earlier might have gone down the Ohio and the Mississippi to New Orleans.

Greeley was happy to see that the city had a variety of newspapers, although generally of poor quality. They were mostly unattractive four-pagers with advertising, market and ship-movement information, extracts from foreign papers, but very little actual news.

Soon Greeley found work at a dreary job most printers would have shunned—setting narrow columns of small type for a pocket-sized New Testament.[13] Once the project was completed, however, he again found himself unemployed. After several weeks of drifting and working odd jobs, he was hired to set type for a new sporting and betting weekly called the *Spirit of the Times*. Launching a new publication was chancy, and a few months later, almost predictably, the *Spirit* went out of business. To make matters worse, the city was in the throes of a cholera epidemic. Greeley described New York that summer as a place where "the season was sultry, the city filthy, and the water we drank such as should breed a pestilence at any time."[14]

Greeley once more went looking—this time, however, for something that would let him be his own boss. Early in 1833, he entered into a partnership with a friend named Francis Story. Before long the firm of Greeley & Story, at 54 Liberty Street, in the lower east side of Manhattan, was soliciting any and all kinds of printing business, to include handbills, periodicals, or even lottery tickets.[15]

Meanwhile, Greeley was considering a new kind of publication, one geared to the masses, especially the recent immigrants, many of whom were just learning to read English, but all of whom were thirsting for information about their new homeland. He wanted mostly to print such a paper, but he also knew that many printers soon became editors in their own right.

Greeley and Story, together with a partner, H. S. Shepard, came out with a cheap daily they called the *Morning Post*, which had little to recommend it other than its cost—one penny per copy. It lasted only a few weeks, leaving Greeley and Story, as Greeley put it, "hard aground on a lee shore, with little prospect of getting off."[16]

Undeterred, the nimble Greeley determined to put into practice a far different concept, one he'd been turning over in his mind for the past few months. He would publish and edit a distinctive weekly journal. Others might deal in sensationalism, with their ghost stories, backstairs scandals, and titillating tales of fallen servant girls; *his* paper would contain worthwhile literature, news, and opinions. Moreover, it would be attractive in appearance, meaning that Greeley himself would do much of the writing and supervise the typesetting.

By living frugally, Greeley had saved $1,500 from money he'd earned in the printing business. With this as start-up capital, he approached the new project with characteristic zeal, ignoring the contrast between a one-penny daily and a weekly with literary pretensions. Greeley, then as in later years, could adopt a new project or a new point of view and go full speed ahead without looking back.

Sadly, his former partner and good friend Francis Story had drowned while swimming in the East River. For this new venture, Greeley linked up with Jonas Winchester, a promoter who would see to the business end of things, including the handling of subscriptions, buying of supplies, and hiring of the pressroom workers. For his part, Greeley would be assembling material for each week's edition of his *New Yorker*.

In a second-floor office at 20 Nassau Street, in lower Manhattan, Greeley began turning out copy, much of it lifted bodily and unashamedly from English monthlies. There were travel letters, moral essays, miscellaneous items about life in general, and vast quantities of mediocre poetry, much of it trite and gushing, some by romantic ladies who signed themselves "Eloisa," "Clarice," or "Lutetia," and some, equally romantic, by Greeley himself.

At this stage of his life, the idealistic Greeley believed that writing poetry was perhaps the noblest of all endeavors. He wrote a friend: "As to Prose, it is not worth writing, except for bread; to live, it must be Poetry." So far he had been much too busy to think about love or even to have a female friend. Now, however, he composed a poem of boyish romanticism addressed to some mythical loved one yet to appear:

Fantasies

They deem me cold, the thoughtless and light hearted,
    In that I worship not at beauty's shrine;
They deem me cold, that through the years departed,
    I ne'er have bowed me to some form divine.
They deem me proud, that, where the world hath flattered,
    I ne'er have knelt to languish or adore;
They think not that the homage idly scattered
    Leaves the heart bankrupt, ere its spring is o'er.

No! in my soul there glows but one bright vision
    And o'er my heart there rules but one fond spell,
Bright'ning my hours of sleep with dreams Elysian
    Of one unseen, yet loved, aye cherished well;
Unseen? Ah! no; her presence round me lingers,
    Chasing each wayward thought that tempts to rove;

Weaving Affection's web with fairy fingers,
And waking thoughts of purity and love.[17]

Mercifully, Greeley matured, as did his weekly journal. It began carrying items of greater practicality: stories describing an improved plow, a new type of fertilizer, or perhaps that week's attractions at the American Museum on Broadway. Soon he acquired another interest, one that would dominate the rest of his life: politics.

Most papers of the day were blatantly partisan in their political reporting. Greeley determined to set himself apart by writing evenly and accurately. He began with the local scene, attending city council meetings and scrupulously reporting what transpired. After an election day, he would come out with carefully checked voting tabulations. Then, moving beyond the local scene, he shifted his attention to state and national affairs, persuading legislators in Albany and Washington to send him advance copies of their bills and speeches, which he then printed quickly and accurately. During the presidential election of 1836, when Martin Van Buren easily defeated Daniel Webster and William Henry Harrison, Greeley printed accurate, early returns and chided the dailies that had published misinformation, lecturing them about "undermining their credit with the public" and saying: "They must mind their manners."[18]

Horace Greeley was feeling his oats. With increasing self-confidence, he started to write editorials on wide-ranging subjects, always with the air of an all-knowing crusader: calling for cleaner streets, condemning the spread of prostitution, explaining the essence of Christianity or the problems with a national bank. When certain readers complained that he presumed too much, especially in voicing his political opinions, Greeley answered: "We shall pursue unwaveringly the even tenor of our way."[19]

Readership continued to grow. People seemed to enjoy young Greeley's pompous self-assurance; they even liked it when he put down his competitors: "The *Knickerbocker* is but fair this month. . . ."; "We do not like the February number of the *American Monthly Magazine* at all. . . ."[20]

About this time, the teetotaling Greeley began boarding at a place uniquely appealing to one with an active interest in personal health. The house was run by Dr. Sylvester Graham, a health food fanatic now best remembered for the cracker bearing his name. Graham condemned tea, coffee, tobacco, and alcohol. He also, Greeley noted, "disapproved of all spices and condiments save (grudgingly) a very little salt; and he held that more suitable and wholesome food for human beings than the flesh of animals can almost always be found, and should be preferred."[21]

It was at Graham's boardinghouse that Greeley met dark-eyed Mary Cheney. In his "Fantasies" poem, he'd revealed an almost desperate longing for romance. Now he found it, in the person of Mary, a high-spirited former schoolteacher and fellow poetry lover. They were married on July 5, 1836. In later years, the marriage brought little happiness to either of them. Greeley was never able to understand what went wrong. Perhaps the fault lay with his total dedication to work, with little time left for family. For her part, Mary became a sharp-tongued, complaining wife, bearing little resemblance to the girl about whom the youthful Greeley had fantasized.

Meanwhile, the *New Yorker* was growing steadily in importance and circulation. Then came the Panic of '37. Week after week, subscribers failed to pay what they owed, and bills for labor and supplies continued to mount. Greeley wondered if the paper could survive.

Suddenly a lifeline was thrown by certain New York politicians, including the powerful Whig editor of the *Albany Evening Journal*, Thurlow Weed. For some time, prominent Whigs had felt the need for a statewide house organ to counter the noisy supporters of the Jacksonian Democrats such as William Cullen Bryant's *Evening Post*. It was suggested that Greeley, already known to have Whig leanings, print a weekly paper favorable to the party. It needn't take all his time; he could do it while continuing with his own *New Yorker*. Would he be willing to print such a journal if they were to subsidize it?

Greeley, although young, was not naive. He knew Thurlow Weed's reputation as a manipulative, unprincipled power broker. However, since his pockets were empty, he saw this as a heaven-sent opportunity, especially since it included a salary of $1,000 per year, enough to keep afloat his sagging *New Yorker*.

Splitting his time between New York and Albany, Greeley began putting out a paper he shrewdly called the *Jeffersonian*.[22] The name deliberately challenged the Democrats' claim to be the sainted Jefferson's sole heirs. Equally shrewd was Greeley's decision, while he was espousing Whig principles and supporting Whig candidates, not to let on that it was Whig politicians who were paying his salary. He began, in fact, by writing that the *Jeffersonian* would not be "a party paper in the ordinary acceptation of that term."[23]

During its 1-year existence, the *Jeffersonian*, subtly advancing Whig arguments without mentioning the word *Whig*, was highly effective. When State Senator William H. Seward, a rising Whig star, became the first non-Democrat in 40 years to be elected New York's governor, he gave much of the credit to Weed and Greeley. At year's end, the political triumvirate of Seward, Weed, and Greeley was firmly in place.

Back in the city, the *New Yorker*, suffocating under its heavy load of debt, continued to struggle. By early 1840, Greeley was making a few extra dollars by writing articles for various eastern papers. Everything he could scrape up went into sustaining his *New Yorker*. It was a week-to-week challenge. At one point he wrote a friend, "I owe $40 personal now, and must borrow $50 more to pay board, etc., tomorrow. . . ."[24]

All this time Greeley had retained a passion for politics, so when Weed invited him to the 1840 Whig political convention, he quickly accepted. Personally, Greeley would have liked Henry Clay to be the Whig nominee. The party bosses, however, believed Clay was not only unelectable but, even if elected, would be hard to "control." Strictly for his vote-getting appeal, they chose the popular, and presumably "amiable," military hero of Tippecanoe, William Henry Harrison. At first Greeley found this hard to swallow; as an inherent pacifist, he distrusted all soldiers. He knew, however, that the first goal of practical politics was to win.

Remembering the successful *Jeffersonian*, Weed now proposed that Greeley publish a journal supporting Harrison. Earlier, a Democratic newspaper had ridiculed Harrison as a backwoodsman who'd be happiest in a log cabin. The Whigs joyfully agreed, calling Harrison the poor man's candidate who *would* be at home in a log cabin and using the cabin as a campaign theme. Cleverly, Greeley named his campaign newspaper the *Log Cabin*. It was wildly successful, with a circulation that reached 80,000 and could have been more if Greeley had had the mailing capacity. Cynically, he would later write: "Our opponents struggled manfully, desperately; but wind and tide were against them. They had campaign and other papers, good speakers, and large meetings; but we were far ahead of them in singing and in electioneering emblems and mottoes which appealed to popular sympathies."[25] Harrison and his running mate, John Tyler, won in a landslide.

The *Log Cabin*'s popularity gave Greeley added prominence and provided a leg up the following spring when he started a new daily paper, the *New York Tribune*. The *Tribune*, like the phrase "Go West, young man," would ever be associated with Horace Greeley. Of the city's papers then in existence, most successful by far was the *Herald* of James Gordon Bennett. Bennett might have been a peddler of sensationalism, but he was a true journalistic pioneer, a man who sensed what people wanted to read. Others might overlook the lurid murder, the story of a lost child, the description of a calamitous fire, a scandal, or the gowns worn at a society ball. Bennett printed such things in full detail, and his readers loved it.

The moralistic Greeley, while deploring much of Bennett's subject matter, appreciated his journalistic talent. Greeley resolved to do many of the same things but to do so in a principled manner. As he later wrote, he would "embody in a single sheet the information daily required by all those who aim to keep 'posted.'"[26] Also, since this was a wicked world, he would help reform it by by setting a high moral tone for the public, even lecturing to them about what he considered to be proper behavior. Simultaneously, building on the well-known *Log Cabin* and the *New Yorker*, both of which he'd later merge into the *Tribune*, he would become the main voice of the newly powerful Whig Party.

Putting out a daily paper was no easy thing. Greeley would need a vast amount of new copy each day if he hoped to compete with Bennett. He would also have to react quickly to current events. This would require a news-gathering staff, which the fledgling paper simply didn't have.

The *Tribune* got off to a stumbling start. On April 10, 1841, when the first issue hit the streets, it failed even to mention the big news of the day: President William Henry Harrison, a mere month after his inauguration, had died of penumonia. In time, however, the paper managed not only to improve but also to prosper, thanks in large part to a suggestion from Thomas McElrath, a *Tribune* investor. It was his idea to publish a weekly edition aimed at rural upstate and western audiences, people living beyond the reach of eastern dailies. Eventually the far-flung weekly edition would contribute more than the local daily to making Greeley rich and famous. He would later write: "The transition from my four preceding years of incessant pecuniary anxiety, if not absolute embarrassment, was like escaping from the dungeon and the rack to freedom and sympathy."[27]

The *Tribune*'s popularity was due to a variety of practices, not the least of which were its blistering attacks on the *Herald*, which, according to Greeley, should be circulating mainly "in houses of infamy . . . and drinking saloons of the lowest order."[28] Businessmen, he implied, would dirty their hands by associating with such a publication. On the other hand, an advertisement in *his* paper would lend a product a certain air of respectability!

Greeley's growing influence let him give free rein to ever-widening interests. On a given day, he might be crusading for temperance, for pacifism, or for a new socialistic, utopian philosophy being advanced by Albert Brisbane, George Ripley, and Charles Fourier.

The latter movement, called Fourierism, preached the benefits of communal associations. It was held that liberal, intelligent persons, living and working together, could lead a healthier, better, and more productive existence if they combined their efforts in an atmosphere free from the pressures of competitive life.

Under this idealistic concept, communities, or "phalanxes," would be set up to replace the oppressive monotony of industrial labor by harmonious, classless teams in which all would share equally. Greeley, who sensed the impracticality of such schemes and communities, was nevertheless fascinated by them. He took particular interest in one such place, Brook Farm, some 8 miles from Boston, which he occasionally visited.

At some point it was decided that Brook Farm would be an ideal place for Greeley's ailing wife, Mary, to spend some time. On August 29, 1842, Greeley wrote a Brook Farm representative: "I received yours of the 24th on Saturday evening, at Albany, having spent Friday and Saturday there on business. I take the very first opportunity to thank you and the community for your kindness. I shall write to Mrs. Greeley today, and presume you will hear from her directly—probably in the course of a week. I cannot doubt that she will be very happy to accept your obliging offer. . . . With you she will find all she needs, and I hope her recovery to health and vision will be sure and rapid. It will be a great satisfaction to me in every way to know that she is with you, not only on her account, but my own, as I hope sometime to be able to steal two or three days from my distracting, harassing occupation to pay her a visit, and yours is just the place that I should like to find her. . . ."[29]

Greeley addressed the letter to the young man who had made the "obliging" offer. His name was Charles A. Dana, and evidently this was their initial contact. In the years to come, each man would have a profound effect upon the other's life.

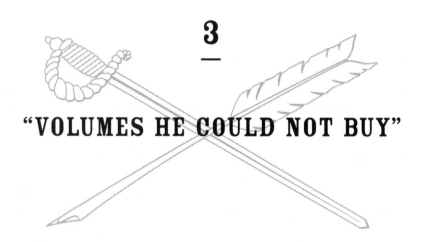

3

"VOLUMES HE COULD NOT BUY"

THE FINANCIAL PANIC that hurt Jesse Grant's tannery and Horace Greeley's newspaper also affected 18-year-old Charles Dana, who in 1837 was working in Buffalo at his uncle's general store. As the crisis worsened, the firm of Staats and Dana, with young Charles doing his best to help, fought bravely to stay afloat. Nevertheless, money stopped coming in and debts continued to mount. Finally the store was forced to close its doors and discharge its clerks. That included Dana. Despite being an owner's nephew, he was now unemployed.[1]

Charles Anderson Dana was the eldest child of Anderson Dana and his first wife, Ann Denison. He was born on August 8, 1819, in Hinsdale, a small town in western New Hampshire, where his father was said to be "a merchant in a modest way."[2] Dana's family, like Horace Greeley's, found middle-class survival to be a never-ending struggle. When Charles was very young, Anderson Dana's business failed and the family moved to the village of Gaines, in upstate New York. For a time, the elder Dana had charge of a warehouse on the banks of the Erie Canal, but he soon gave that up to cultivate a small nearby farm he had bought.

When Charles was 9, his mother died, leaving his father with four small children. The family was split up, and Charles, the oldest, went to live with an uncle, David Denison, in northeastern Vermont. There he attended a local school, where a perceptive teacher recognized that he was an uncommonly bright student; by the time he was 10, he was being classified with boys 6 or 8 years older. When he reached the age of 12, however, his uncle decided he'd had enough of the "three R's." It was time to start earning his own living. Dana was packed off to Buffalo, where he began working as a clerk in his uncle William's store.

Back in Vermont, Dana had acquired a Latin grammar book. He continued to study it on his own, and within a short time he was reading the Latin classics. It was the start of a lifelong fascination for languages. A fellow clerk during this period described Dana as "a quiet, studious boy who loved nature and books, and although a good salesman, rather prone to spend too much time in the adjoining book-store looking over volumes he could not buy."[3]

At this stage of his life, Dana didn't know where his ambition would take him. He *did* know, however, that he had a burning thirst for knowledge, whether it be of literature, languages, history, or commerce. Late in life, he told a friend that "the best days of his life, as regards health and happiness, were spent in Buffalo."[4] He found joy in fishing and hunting, in "hobnobbing" with Indians at the nearby reservation, in taking long walks in the country. He also thrived on programs of study, ones he designed for himself and adhered to scrupulously.

After his uncle's store closed, Dana eventually found work at another Buffalo establishment. It was only temporary; by now he had his heart set on college. He had saved a little money, enough at least for initial tuition. When that ran out, he'd somehow scrape together enough to keep going.

Dana, now 20, applied to Harvard. Even though his formal education had ended when he was 12, at Cambridge the entrance examiners found his self-study had made him proficient in both Latin and Greek. He was admitted to Harvard in September 1839 and was soon intoxicated by campus life and the intellectual world he saw opening before him. After hearing lectures by the famed Ralph Waldo Emerson, Dana wrote: "Their great merit appears to me to be their suggestive character; they make me think."[5]

The following March, Dana would tell a friend: "I have been at Cambridge one term, half a year, and have never passed time so pleasantly and profitably to myself."[6] Studies were going well, and at term's end, he stood seventh in a class of 74.

Students of every era are often aroused by idealism, a need to change the world. Dana was no exception. Harvard that year was awash in discussions of transcendentalism, a philosophical belief in the ability to gain ultimate insights through the power of the human mind. Dana wrote a friend that "to tell the truth, I take to it rather kindly though I stumble sadly at some notions. But there is certainly a movement going on in philosophy which must produce a revolution in politics, morals, and religion, sooner or later. The tendency of the age is spiritual, and though the immediate reaction of the mind may be somewhat ultra, it is cheering to know that a genuine earnest action of some sort is in progress."

By November 1840, Dana was strapped for funds. Taking a leave of absence from Harvard, he accepted a job teaching school. To his mind, the absence was only temporary, and on his own he continued to study, often reading by candlelight far into the night. Soon his eyesight began to fail; his financial problems were now matched by physical ones.

Nevertheless, Harvard records show Dana completing his sophomore year. There is evidence he might have been helped by understanding professors who, recognizing a brilliant student, overlooked attendance records and granted credits based on demonstrated knowledge. Still, because of failing funds and failing eyes, sophomore year was it as far as Harvard was concerned.

"In those days," Dana later said, "when a person broke down his eyes he had to try farming or else to go to sea."[7] His cousin, Richard Henry Dana, writer of the classic *Two Years Before the Mast*, had chosen the sea because of failing eyes. For Charles, it would be farming, but farming with a difference.

At the end of the summer, Dana was accepted as a member by the recently formed Brook Farm Association. On September 17, 1841, he wrote his sister: ". . . as my eyes are not fully restored, although they are considerably improved, I have not returned to college. I am living with some friends who have associated themselves together for the purpose of living purely and justly and of acting from higher principles than the world recognizes. I study but little—only as much as my eyes will permit. I pay for my board by labor upon the farm and by giving instruction in whatever lies within my capacity."[8]

He had little money, he was a hard worker, and he wanted to use his mind—a mind hungry for knowledge. For Dana, Brook Farm was a perfect fit. If he'd been European, he would have been drawn to philosophical coffeehouse discussions; in America, the closest parallel was Brook Farm, with its assemblage of well-meaning but often naive intellectuals. As an added benefit, Brook Farm was devoted to improving the body as well as the mind. Scholars, said the transcendentalists, should not be confined to musty classrooms. They should instead spend time in the open, preferably doing honorable, everyday farm labor.

The founders of Brook Farm preached the equality of man. There should be no masters and no servants, only an uplifting association in which everyone helped everyone else in a spirit of selflessness. Trying to describe these beliefs years later, Dana said: "The Transcendentalists maintained the doctrine of the original intuitions of the mind, and that the soul communes with regions that lie beyond the senses, and has intimations of divine truth that the senses cannot reveal."[9]

A thousand people, said Albert Brisbane and others, could live much more cheaply in one great socialist household than when each family had its own separate dwelling. Critics such as Henry Raymond of the *New York Times* were quick to point out the scheme's impracticality, saying if such associations became successful, those who worked the hardest would soon become annoyed with those who shirked but still wanted to share equally in the benefits.

Responding to the critics, the idealistic crusader Horace Greeley wrote in the *Tribune* that he didn't profess to understand the philosophical theories of Fourier. He still believed, however, that there were great advantages in democratic associations that served to advance the spirit of true Christianity. To prove his sincerity, he had the *Tribune*, on a regular basis, carry the essays of Brook Farm enthusiast Albert Brisbane.[10]

Eventually, however, Greeley came to agree with the critics. Years later, in his book, *Recollections of a Busy Life*, he would write: "I cannot conceive it just, that an associate who invests $100,000 should stand on an equal footing, so far as property is concerned, with one who brings nothing to the common fund; nor can I see why an ingenious, efficient mechanic, whose services are worth $5 per day, should receive no more of the annual product than an ignorant ditcher, who can at best earn but $2 per day."

Then, speaking as one who by this time had become personally affluent, he added: "Credit me on the books with what I invested, and what I have since earned or otherwise added to the common wealth; and, if I choose to spend my day with a visiting friend, or go off for a week's fishing, it is no one's business but my own. But, say that all we have and all we make are common property, wherein each has rightfully an equal interest, and I shall feel morally bound to do my share of the work, and shall be dissatisfied when others palpably do less than I do."[11]

Charles Dana probably reached the same conclusion much earlier than Greeley did; he never seems to have accepted Fourierism and Transcendentalism wholeheartedly, and his pragmatic mind doubtless saw the fallacies of a socialist utopia.[12] Still, he entered fully into the Farm's activities, and with a happy heart.

Dana milked cows; he waited on tables at the communal dining hall; in the evenings he taught classes in both Greek and German. He also began writing essays for a Brook Farm publication, *Harbinger*. As time went on, his writing expanded to include editorials, poems, book reviews, and bright, clever notes on a variety of subjects.[13]

The talented Dana, having become a prominent Brook Farm figure as well as a trustee, was also making what in a later day might be called "connections." Emerson was a frequent Farm visitor, as were other New England literati. So was the gifted Nathaniel Hawthorne, who cut quite a figure as he pitched hay in his bright yellow pantaloons. However, like Greeley and Dana, and despite having invested in the Farm and living there several months, Hawthorne was too skeptical to place much confidence in utopian idealism, and ideology was not to his taste.[14]

Meanwhile, Horace Greeley was keeping in touch, both in person and through his paper. Once, when Dana was traveling on business, he received a letter from the Farm written by George Ripley, who later became Greeley's literary editor. In the letter, Ripley spoke of finding accommodations at the Farm for Greeley's wife, then added: "We are very glad to get the *Tribune* every week, as we do from Mr. Greeley; it is as pleasant an avenue as we could have wherewith to communicate with the Babel world it comes from."[15]

Some said the Brook Farm members were intellectuals trying to escape urban life while maintaining the urbanities. This wasn't entirely true. As Dana later described the colony: "A large majority of the Brook Farmers were literary people or of literary associations, but there were people of other callings among them, too. There was a pressman and a grocer, each with his family. Several had been farmers' hired men. There was an English girl who had been a domestic, and a very superior woman she was." In short, Dana said with a touch of pride, "There was no social differentiation at Brook Farm."[16]

During the 5 years Dana spent at the Farm, he met many people and acquired many friends, including a widow named McDaniel who had come there with her three children, a son and two daughters. In this case, however, Dana's interest was centered on Eunice, the younger daughter, an attractive, bright, spirited girl with black, sparkling eyes. They fell in love and on March 2, 1846, were married in New York City. It was the beginning of a long, successful marriage. With typical 19th-century male chauvinism, James Harrison Wilson, Dana's biographer, later gave Eunice something of a left-handed compliment: "If her mind had dwelt in the form of a man," Wilson wrote, "it must have been regarded as a notable one."[17]

While the new bridegroom was still in New York, Dana received word of a Brook Farm calamity. Fire had broken out and the main building had burned to the ground. Years later, he ruefully spoke of the fire, saying they put into the new building "the last cent we had. Well, one night the whole thing took fire and burned up . . . and the one thing that we were most ashamed of was that the insurance expired the day before the fire and hadn't been renewed. But the faith of the majority of the members was not shaken."[18]

The faith might not have been shaken, but the bank account was. Brook Farm had never been able to sustain itself financially, and the fire marked the beginning of the end. Dana and his wife returned to the Farm and stayed a few more months. It was obvious, however, that he could no longer depend on the place for a living.

In addition to writing for the Brook Farm *Harbinger*, Dana had been supplementing his income by selling articles to various New England journals. One of these was the *Boston Chronotype*, a religious publication supported by the Congregationalist ministers of Massachusetts. With Brook Farm now on its last legs, Dana accepted a job as assistant editor of the *Chronotype*. The paper was too poor to pay much, and although Dana was expected to serve as editor when the principal editor was absent, it was with no addition to his pay of $4 a week.

Dana, like Emerson, was something of a Unitarian liberal, ill attuned to gloomy Congregationalist doctrines. Once, when the editor was away, Dana showed his independence, and perhaps his sense of humor, by deriding the concept of hell, thereby shocking both the paper's subscribers and the responsible editor, Elizur Wright.

Years later, when Dana had become famous, Wright enjoyed telling about it. Dana, he said, "came out mighty strong against hell," and at the time it caused Wright a great deal of trouble, obliging him to write a letter to every Congregationalist minister in Massachusetts saying the paper's doctrinal lapse was due to no change of faith on his own part but to having been left temporarily in charge of "a young man without journalistic experience."[19]

Dana might have been a talented writer, might even have had great promise as an editor. In the future, however, whatever he wrote would be carefully scrutinized by dour ministerial eyes. To say the least, Dana and the *Boston Chronotype* were not a happy match. Thinking it over, and after discussing the situation with Eunice, Dana decided his opportunities in Boston were surely limited. New York was the place to be.

During those years at Brook Farm, the ambitious Dana had been developing contacts. It was time to take advantage of them. Well, who might he talk to? The first name that came to mind was that of Horace Greeley, who along with his wife had always been sympathetic, not only to Brook Farm but to Dana personally.

The rapidly expanding *New York Tribune*, now in its own five-story building at the corner of Nassau and Spruce, was nearly 6 years old, and editor Greeley was one of the most influential men in the country. At the same time, Greeley had acquired a reputation as something of an eccentric in his dress and personal habits. James Watson Webb, editor of the *Courier and Enquirer*, undoubtedly jealous of Greeley, had written: "The editor of the Tribune seeks for notoriety by the strangeness of his theories and practices. . . . He lays claim to greatness by wandering through the streets with a hat double the size of his head, a coat after the fashion of Jacob's of old, with one leg of his pantaloons inside and the other outside of his boot, and with boots all bespattered with mud. . . ."[20]

Greeley actually seems to have enjoyed Webb's unflattering description. It was the old story of "say what you will about me, as long as you get my name right." Moreover, it was not half as bad as what Greeley was saying about Webb and others, all in the interest of spicing up the *Tribune* and adding to its circulation. To Mordecai Noah of the *Union*, Greeley wrote: "Major Noah! Why won't you tell the truth once in a century, for the variety of it?" Brashly, he even told the literary and cultivated William Cullen Bryant of the *Evening Post*: "You lie, you old villain!"[21]

In reality, Webb's description of Greeley wasn't that far off the mark. One trouser leg *did* often hang outside his boot. His collar and string necktie had a way of slipping off to one side; his spectacles normally drooped; his frayed jacket inevitably bulged with clippings, letters, and manuscripts. On the street, he wore a bleached white duster crammed with still more odds and ends. Somewhere he had acquired an unattractive, wide-brimmed, low-crowned hat that was pushed back on his head as he moved along, shuffling rather than walking, perhaps stopping to talk with someone in his high, squeaky, nasal voice. Always he seemed oblivious to how society expected a successful businessman to look and act. No one could be sure—was it merely indifference, or was it a deliberate attempt to cultivate an "image"? Perhaps it was a bit of both.

Truly, Greeley was fair game for criticism, both personal and professional. The witty reporter, Henry Clapp Jr., called him "a self-made man who worships his creator."[22] Say what one would, however, he was respected, and that in itself was unusual. His rival editor, William Cullen Bryant, describing the public's attitude toward editors, said, "contempt is too harsh a word for it, perhaps, but it is far below respect."[23]

As he arrived in New York, Dana knew all this, but he also knew that, for the right man, there was a real opportunity at Horace Greeley's journal. He proceeded to the "immense dry-goods box, surmounted by a flagstaff," which was the *Tribune*. Up the stairs he went, to the third floor and to a sign reading: EDITORIAL ROOMS: RING THE BELL. People never did, he had been told; go right in.

Dana entered Greeley's dusty office overlooking City Hall Park. On the floor was a thin green carpet; on the wall was a crooked engraving called "The Landing of the Pilgrim Fathers." Every piece of furniture—the sofa, the bookcase, the cane-bottomed chairs—was piled high with directories, almanacs, or old newspapers. Greeley, sitting behind an equally cluttered desk, told Dana to clear off one of the chairs and take a seat.[24]

The conversation apparently went well. When it ended, Dana was offered the position of *Tribune* city editor at a salary of $10 a week. He began work in February 1847.

Before the end of the year, Dana felt valuable enough, and secure enough, to tell Greeley he needed more money. He was promoted to managing editor; his salary was raised to $14 per week. Greeley no doubt grumbled that his *own* salary was only $15!

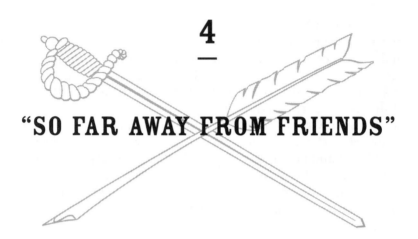

4

"SO FAR AWAY FROM FRIENDS"

JESSE GRANT had not forgotten his plan. He fully intended for his "remarkable" son to attend West Point and be educated at government expense. In the fall of 1838, Jesse approached Ohio Senator Tom Morris, whom he'd supported when Morris ran for Congress against Tom Hamer. That support, understandably enough, had exacerbated the early political quarrel between Jesse and Hamer. Accordingly, it was to Senator Morris, not Representative Hamer, that Jesse wrote asking a favor: What about an appointment to the Military Academy for Ulysses?

Sorry, Morris told him, at the moment he had no appointment to give. However, there *was* an opening coming up in Jesse's district. It was controlled by Tom Hamer, and Morris suggested that Jesse write him. Jesse hesitated. He and Hamer still weren't speaking. It sure would mean swallowing his pride, and who knew how Hamer would react? Well, so be it; he'd give it a try.

Jesse wrote Hamer a polite, formal letter, saying that at Morris's suggestion, he had applied to the War Department for an appointment for his son, H. Ulysses. However, he had learned that only Hamer had an appointment to give. Therefore, he wrote Hamer, "I have thought it advisable to consult you on the subject. And if you have no other person in view for the appointment & feel willing to consent to the appointment of Ulysses, you will please signafy [*sic*] that consent to the department."[1]

Hamer evidently was happy for a chance to mend an old and valued friendship. Not only would he grant the appointment at once, he even asked, "Why didn't you write sooner?" Hamer knew that Jesse's boy was called "Ulysses," and he assumed a middle name came from the mother's Simpson family. When he filled out the papers, Hamer mistakenly omitted the "Hiram" and instead gave the candidate's name as "U. S. Grant."[2]

"Well," Jesse told his son, "I believe you are going to receive the appointment."

"What appointment?"

"To West Point. I have applied for it."

"But I won't go!"

As Ulysses later recalled the conversation: "He said he thought I would, *and I thought so too, if he did*."[3]

That summer, Ulysses started packing his trunk. On it were brass tacks spelling "H. U. G." for "Hiram Ulysses Grant." For the shy boy who hated teasing, that was asking for trouble. He switched tacks; they now read "U. H. G."[4]

Off he went, first by boat, then by rail, riding the first train he'd ever seen. As it zipped along at what seemed a breathtaking 18 miles per hour, he felt they were "annihilating space."[5]

Grant was hardly a picture of enthusiasm. "Military life had no charms for me," he later would write, and he wished something would give him an excuse not to report, even "a steamboat or railroad collision, or any other accident . . . by which I might have received a temporary injury sufficient to make me ineligible, for a time, to enter the Academy."[6]

He dragged out the trip from Ohio to West Point as long as possible, and despite his apprehension about the Military Academy, the journey itself proved rather enjoyable. Eventually he'd describe it with a touch of nostalgia: "There were no telegraphs in those days to disseminate news rapidly, no railroads west of the Alleghanies, and but few east." To this he added a wry comment reflecting his later life: "Above all, there were no reporters prying into other people's private affairs."[7]

At this point, of course, Grant gave little heed to the press, and in New York, where he lingered long enough to see the sights, he might not have bothered with a newspaper. Even if he had, it probably wouldn't have been Greeley's *New Yorker*, which at the moment was barely solvent. A more likely candidate would have been the *Herald*. That spring, James Gordon Bennett was boasting, particularly to advertisers, that *his* paper was the one that mattered.

"It is important," Bennett wrote, "for dealers and importers here to give the choicest publicity to their assortments and stocks of goods. . . . Now, as a channel for conveying this information to every part of the country, no journal in New York possesses such facilities as THE HERALD."[8]

Finally, reluctantly, Grant boarded a Hudson River boat for the last leg of his journey. Then came a surprise: When he arrived at the Academy, he was told there was no record of an appointment for any "Hiram Ulysses Grant." There was one, though, for a "Ulysses S. Grant." With a shrug, Grant said it made little difference. If the army wanted him to be "Ulysses S.," that's who he'd be.

When the name "U. S. Grant" appeared on the roster of incoming plebes, hovering upperclassmen began making jokes. The "U. S." must stand for "United States," said one.

"No," said a senior cadet from Ohio, William T. Sherman, "it stands for 'Uncle Sam.'" The nickname would stick, and to friends from West Point days, he'd always be "Sam" Grant.

Sherman would remember his first sight of Grant. The young newcomer was small, round-faced, innocent looking. "A more unpromising boy never entered the Military Academy," Sherman would write.[9] Similarly, Rufus Ingalls of Maine, Grant's roommate that first year, remembered him as a somewhat indifferent student: "Instead of studying a lesson, he would merely read it over once or twice; but he was so quick in his perceptions that he usually made very fair recitations even with so little preparation. . . . His memory was not at all good in an attempt to learn anything by heart accurately, and this made his grade low in those branches of study which required a special effort of memory."[10]

Like every new cadet in West Point history, Grant hated life as a plebe, with the drilling, the hazing, the need to respond immediately and unquestioningly to the harsh orders of an upperclassman or the blaring sounds of a bugle.

Midway through that first year, a bill was introduced in Congress to abolish the Military Academy. Grant hoped it would pass, since he saw it as "an honorable way to obtain a discharge." Nothing came of it, however, and a year later, by which time he had adjusted to the Academy routine and was no longer a harassed plebe "animal," he was glad the bill had failed.[11]

Military life still held no attraction for Grant. Looking ahead, he suspected he'd fulfill his obligation to the army, resign as soon as it was permitted, and then take a job teaching mathematics at some small school or college. Despite all that, he'd always remember a moment when he saw it differently. It came when the head of the army, the imposing Gen. Winfield Scott, with his "colossal size and showy uniform," was at West Point reviewing the cadets. Grant said Scott was "the finest specimen of manhood my eyes had ever beheld, and the most to be envied. I could never resemble him in appearance, but I believe I did have a presentiment for a moment that some day I should occupy his place on review." Fearing ridicule, Grant never told anyone about this, even his "most intimate chum."[12]

Although he'd been concerned about coping with the Academy's stiff academic program, Grant was able to handle his studies without too much difficulty. He did well in math, less well in science, amassed a fair number of demerits, but nothing excessive, and soon settled in around the middle of the class, where he'd stay for the next 4 years.

All in all, Grant was but a mediocre cadet. Among other things, he was tone-deaf and a stranger to rhythm, making him constantly out of step during parades, which were managed by bugle calls and drumbeats. (When he was temporarily made a cadet sergeant, his friends claimed it was only because the tactical officers couldn't stand seeing him march in column; it was too horrid a sight.)[13]

Grant's finest day at West Point came just before graduation, when, thanks to his superb horsemanship, he was called on to give a riding exhibition. Mounted on York, a horse only he seemed able to control, Grant cantered into the riding hall as the entire Corps of Cadets looked on. A soldier held a pole high over his head, with the other end of the pole against a wall. Grant came galloping full speed; it seemed as if horse and rider were welded together. With a mighty leap, York and his rider soared into the air, clearing the bar with inches to spare.

"Very well done, sir!" said the sergeant-instructor.[14] A few days later came graduation. When the final order of merit was announced, Grant stood 21st in a class of 39.

Now a lieutenant of infantry and back home on leave, Grant was eager to show off in his splendid new uniform. As he later wrote, he wanted "my old schoolmates, particularly the girls, to see me in it." Soon after he donned that uniform, however, he was deflated by a mocking street urchin who called out, "Soldier, will you work? No siree, I'll sell my shirt first!" Further deflation took place when a drunk at the local stagecoach tavern mocked him by strutting around barefoot in military fashion while wearing ragged trousers of infantry blue with strips of cotton sewn down the side to resemble braid.[15] For the rest of his life, Grant would remember those moments. Never again would he try to impress anyone with military glitter. His dress, like his conversation, would remain simple, functional, and unadorned.

At the Academy, politics had been taboo. Now, back in Georgetown, Ulysses heard his father, Jesse, preaching the Whig gospel as spread over the country by Horace Greeley's *New York Tribune*. Under Greeley's influence (as well as his father's), Ulysses for the first time began developing his own political convictions, basically those of the Whig Party, which included opposition to the annexation of Texas, called by Greeley a "conspiracy" by the slave states for purely sectional advantage.[16]

"Sam" Grant's initial assignment was to the Fourth Infantry Regiment, at Jefferson Barracks outside St. Louis. Nearby, only 5 miles from the Barracks, was White Haven, the home of Frederick Dent, Grant's roommate during their final year. Soon Grant rode over to call on the Dent family, and over the next few months his calls became increasingly frequent. For the first time in his life, Grant was in love. The object of his affection was the Dents' oldest daughter, Julia.

At White Haven, the young lieutenant was becoming everyone's favorite, with the possible exception of Julia's father. The senior Dent, called "Colonel" by courtesy, was a strong Jacksonian Democrat, strongly in favor of Texas annexation, and far from sympathetic to Grant's Whig leanings.

In May 1844, the Fourth Infantry was alerted for shipment to Louisiana. According to the administration in Washington, it was to prevent "filibustering" into Texas. Grant recognized this as sheer hypocrisy; everyone knew this was a warning to Mexico to submit peacefully if and when Texas was annexed. The move, of course, would mean separation from Julia, and Grant suddenly discovered how painful that would be. Before leaving, he "mustered up courage" to propose, as he said, "in the most awkward way imaginable."[17] Awkward or not, it sufficed. Julia consented but said that for now the engagement must be kept secret from her father. The Colonel, although he liked Grant well enough, had seen the folly of delicately bred girls marrying poorly paid officers.

That same month, in Baltimore, amid bitter wrangling and after nine hard-fought ballots, the Democratic Party nominated James K. Polk of Tennessee for president. As a Free-Soiler opposed to the extension of slavery, Horace Greeley would have preferred the northerner, Martin Van Buren. Seeing the Democrats' action as a victory for annexation of Texas and hence for slavery, he wrote disdainfully: "Mr. Polk had been an early, and was a zealous, champion of Annexation, as always of every proposition or project calculated to aggrandize the Slave Power."[18]

Grant and Julia said their loving farewells, and then he was off for Louisiana to join his regiment. It was a pleasant trip, down the Mississippi to New Orleans, back up the Mississippi to the Red River, and then up that waterway to Camp Salubrity, near the town of Natchitoches.

Soon the camp was buzzing over the arrival of a new commander, Gen. Zachary Taylor. Surely this meant action, for Taylor's reputation was that of a fighter. The popular new general, unlike old "Fuss and Feathers" Winfield Scott, cared little for military pomp. Each day the troops saw him wandering through the camp, noting everything with a practiced eye, but meanwhile dressed casually in jeans, a flapping linen coat, and a broad, almost comical, palmetto hat.

Grant went about his duties with quiet confidence. He and the other junior officers, thrown together over this extended period, had a chance to size each other up. James "Pete" Longstreet, perhaps his closest friend, said that Sam was the "soul of honor," a man whose "hatred of guile was pronounced," and whose "detestation of tale bearers was absolute."[19]

In September, Grant got up the nerve to write Colonel Dent asking for Julia's hand in marriage. Dent, telling Julia she was too young and Grant was too poor, never bothered to answer the letter. Perhaps it was just as well; whatever Dent's response, the engagement would have to be a long one. In November 1844, Polk won the presidential election over the Whig candidate, Henry Clay, a man both Greeley and Grant preferred. During the campaign, Polk had promised war with Mexico unless "American rights were respected." To Grant it now appeared that war was imminent. Nevertheless, month after month went by, and to the army, matters seemed at a standstill. Was it the same at home? Or were the newspapers trying to alarm people?

Writing to Julia in September 1845, Grant asked, "Do you hear much about War with Mexico? From the accounts we get here, one would suppose that you all thought the Mexicans were devouring us."[20]

By the following February, his feelings about newspaper accuracy were even more pronounced: "The extract from some newspapers you sent me is a gross exaggeration of the morals and health of Corpus Christi. I do not believe that there is a more healthy spot in the world."[21]

Horace Greeley, writing of this time, gave credit to Zachary Taylor for ignoring those politicians who, wanting to provoke Mexico, urged him to move aggressively into disputed territory. Taylor stood pat, refusing to allow Washington to play the "deniability" game if something went amiss. Finally he received orders to advance, and as he'd insisted, they were in writing.[22] Grant sensed what was happening. "We were sent to provoke a fight," he'd say, "but it was essential that Mexico should commence it."[23]

When the army left Corpus Christi to confront the Mexicans at Matamoros, strict orders were issued against plundering. Grant believed that Taylor's resentment toward American policy was partly responsible. "I doubt not," he would write, "he looked upon the enemy as the aggrieved party and was not willing to injure them further than his instructions from Washington demanded."[24]

In April, as the army moved across disputed territory, Mexico declared war. Then, on May 8 at Palo Alto, Taylor's army had its first real fight. When they formed for battle, Grant was thinking not just of himself: "As I looked down that long line of about three thousand armed men, advancing toward a larger force also armed, I thought what a fearful responsibility General Taylor must feel, commanding such a host, and so far away from friends."[25]

The American army, perhaps for the first time, but sadly not the last, was going to war without full public support. For Grant, it was a time of mixed emotions. Like Greeley, he considered this an "unholy" war. Nevertheless, he would do his duty to the full limit of his ability. Moreover, after the actions at Palo Alto and Resaca de la Palma, he would brag to Julia about how well the army was performing: "After two hard fought battles against a force far superior to our own in numbers, Gen. Taylor has got possession of the Enemy's camp and now I am writing on the head of one of the captured drums. . . . The victory for us has been a very great one. No doubt you will see accounts enough of it in the papers."[26]

And what *were* the papers saying? Some, like Bennett's *Herald*, were enthusiastic in their support. Others, especially Greeley's powerful *New York Tribune*, continued to speak out, both loudly and often, against administration policy. In Washington, meanwhile, Whig leader Henry Clay remained staunchly opposed to the war, as did a freshman Whig congressman from Illinois named Abraham Lincoln. Obviously, for Grant and his Whig father, any celebration of American victories would be tempered by misgivings.

That summer, Grant was made regimental quartermaster. He had known the business of transportation from boyhood, so he should be well able to manage the horse and mule trains. Too, as the son of a successful businessman, he was a logical person to requisition equipment and keep records. Grant protested, saying he objected "to a duty which removes me from sharing in the dangers and honors of service with my company at the front."[27] The reply, in effect, was to keep quiet and do as he was told.

As quartermaster, Grant supervised the soldiers who loaded and drove the wagons allotted to the Fourth Infantry. Writing of those days, he described mules that kicked up their heels to scatter their loads while others simply lay on their backs, refusing to move. Grant said that although personally he never used profanity, he surely could "excuse those who may have done so, if they were in charge of a train of Mexican pack mules at the time."[28]

The next battle, which proved to be a particularly bloody one, was for the strongly defended city of Monterey. When his unit began to advance, Quartermaster Grant was left behind with a company of men to guard the camp. Finally he could stand it no longer. "My curiosity got the better of me," he wrote, deprecatingly, years later, "and I . . . rode to the front to see what was going on." He arrived just as the unit was ordered to charge, and "lacking the moral courage to return to camp—where I had been ordered to stay—I charged with the regiment."[29]

Among those killed was a friend of Grant, Lt. Charles Hoskins, the regimental adjutant. Grant was named to succeed him temporarily. The next day, Grant was again in the thick of things instead of at his place in the rear. City fighting became intense, ammunition was running low, and the unit commander needed someone to ride for help. Grant volunteered to go, despite the blistering fire that covered every intersection. He hooked one foot around the cantle of his saddle, one arm around the neck of his horse, and with his body hanging down the sheltered side of the animal, Indian fashion, he galloped off. The message got through.[30] Later, Grant claimed it had been nothing special, that only the far side of his horse had been endangered.

That night, in a pouring rain, Lt. Cal Benjamin wandered through the darkness, trying to locate any wounded men he might help. On the recent battlefield, he came upon three figures, one dead, one wounded, one uninjured. The last was holding the head of the second and, as Benjamin wrote home, "giving him water from a canteen and wiping his face with a moistened handkerchief." The Samaritan, Benjamin wrote, was "my dear friend, Lieutenant Grant," who had come looking for his fallen comrade and friend Adjutant Hoskins. After finding Hoskins's body and straightening the limbs, he had then tended to the wounded man he found lying close by.[31]

Among those distinguishing themselves at Monterey was Brig. Gen. Tom Hamer, who as a congressman had appointed Grant to the Military Academy. Hamer, a "political general," but a good one, had seen Grant frequently. Writing home about Jesse Grant's son, Hamer had called him "a most remarkable and valuable young soldier," adding, "I anticipate for him a brilliant future."[32] Then, as 1846 drew to a close, Hamer became seriously ill with dysentery. In the next few weeks, he grew increasingly weak, and on December 2, he breathed his last. A mournful Grant wrote that Hamer's death was a "loss to me which no words can express."[33]

After Monterey, Grant's unit was detached from Taylor's army so as to join Winfield Scott's, now preparing to land at Vera Cruz for a direct thrust at Mexico City. By February 1847, they were at sea, heading for a rendezvous with other members of Scott's expedition.

That same month, back in New York, Charles Dana was arriving at Greeley's *Tribune* office and assuming the duties of city editor. Needless to say, Greeley was still speaking out vehemently against the "unholy" invasion of Mexico. This, however, was but one of his many crusades. Tirelessly, he continued to remind his readers about the evils of slavery, the need for agrarian reform, the plight of the urban poor, and the superiority of Henry Clay and the Whig Party.

Greeley's idealism was very real and very sincere. At the same time, he was well aware of his growing personal influence and the inviting possibilities of that influence. What about a political position? He had done many favors for Thurlow Weed and William Seward, the other members of his political triumvirate and now the unquestioned Whig leaders of New York State. Perhaps it was payback time. All the same, he didn't want to sound too eager.

So far Greeley had played his cards close to the vest. "I shall never comprehend Greeley," Weed had told Seward, "for I can never discern the personal considerations which sway and govern him."[34]

Things became clearer when Weed received a letter from Greeley quoting a man in Albany who "had talked with several (I can't imagine who) and had gone home resolved to defy my entreaties and propose my name for Governor." Greeley had underlined the word, as though he was completely *shocked* at the suggestion. He then added that he'd told this man that "this would be the maddest foolery ever started. . . .

I told him finally that if he would let me off on the Governor, he might use my name for Lieutenant Governor."[35]

The letter was far from subtle, and to the cynical Weed, the hint was obvious. Greeley, like others who played the political game and were willing to scratch backs, simply wanted to be scratched in return. For the moment, Weed offered no encouragement. However, he'd keep Greeley in mind for any future opportunity. Horace Greeley's value to the party was well-known. He would not go unrewarded.

5

"REPORTS ARE SOMEWHAT EXAGGERATED"

IN MARCH 1847, Winfield Scott's army, after making a lightly opposed amphibious landing, began laying siege to Vera Cruz. Following a 3-day bombardment, the city capitulated, and as the bands played "Yankee Doodle," proud troops marched in to take possession. Modestly, Quartermaster Grant said that "during the siege, I had little to do except to see to having the Pork and Beans rolled about."[1]

North of Buena Vista, Zachary Taylor's army had also won a victory, but not without cost. Among those killed was Henry Clay Jr., West Point class of 1831, son of the great Speaker of the House and leading opponent of the war.[2]

Soon, Grant and the rest of Scott's men were heading for Mexico City, marching along sandy roads in sweltering heat, scratching their way through clouds of mosquitoes and following the trail marked by Mexico's first conqueror, Hernando Cortés.

In April, Scott was temporarily blocked at Cerro Gordo by the army of Gen. Antonio López de Santa Anna. However, after executing a skillful flanking maneuver, the Americans routed the enemy forces and continued their advance. Contributing to the victory was a brilliant personal reconnaissance by a captain of engineers named Robert E. Lee.

In Grant's opinion, "the surprise of the enemy was complete, the victory overwhelming."[3] Nevertheless, the wily Santa Anna, who'd managed to escape with a handful of troops, was soon back at Mexico City, strengthening fortifications and raising another army.

American soldiers in Mexico, like their countrymen of every war, not only wanted to read about themselves, they also yearned to know what the folks back home were thinking. Young Lt. Ralph Kirkham, who'd graduated from the Military Academy a year before Grant, was quite typical. He wrote his wife, Kate, again and again, asking her to send him newspapers. Even so, he cautioned "that reports are somewhat exaggerated."[4]

Earlier, from Santa Cruz, Kirkham had written his "dear little Kate" of getting the news of Cerro Gordo from Kendall's *Express*, which he said was ahead of the government reports. When the full story became known, however, it turned out that official reports were far more accurate than those written by Kendall.[5] By the same token, after getting a letter from Kate, Kirkham complained to his diary that "all the papers have been filled with incorrect stories of battles, etc., and her mind has been constantly agitated by hope and fear."[6]

In like manner, Grant would write Julia: "One bit of credit need not be given to accounts that are given except those taken from the reports of different commanders."[7]

As for Mexico, Grant seemed to agree with the traveler quoted in the *American Star* who said, "There is no country for which God has done so much and man so little as Mexico."[8] From Puebla, Grant wrote: "Of all the countries and all the climates on Earth, no other people are so blessed by Nature." Toward the Mexican soldier, meanwhile, he felt mostly pity, saying, "They fight and simply quit. Poor fellows; if they were well drilled, well fed, and well paid, no doubt they would fight and persist in it; but as it is, they are put to the slaughter without avail."[9]

On August 4, Grant wrote Julia, perhaps apprehensively: "Tomorrow we start for the City of Mexico, where no doubt we will have another big battle."[10] He was right. Soon Scott's army was at the outskirts of the city, storming the guardian fortress of Chapultepec. After Chapultepec fell, the enemy took up new positions behind low stone walls. Grant noticed a church whose belfry seemed to overlook the enemy lines. He gathered together a few men and a disassembled mountain howitzer. Then, wading through waist-deep water, he led his party forward.

Grant knocked on the door of the church and informed the priest who answered that they needed to enter. The outraged padre refused admission, whereupon Grant said they intended to go in whether he consented or not. At this point, Grant said, "He began to see his duty in the same light that I did, and opened the door, though he did not look as if it gave him special pleasure to do so."[11] Piece by piece, the howitzer was carried to the belfry, where it was reassembled. Soon they began firing on the enemy with good results. A nearby American general, pleased by the action, sent for Grant and said he was sending a second howitzer for him to take back to the church. Grant kept quiet. He knew there was no room for another gun in the belfry, but he didn't think a prudent second lieutenant should appear to be contradicting a general.[12]

After Chapultepec, and more fighting at San Cosme (where Grant again distinguished himself), Santa Anna realized further resistance was useless. Mexico City surrendered on September 14, Santa Anna fled to the hills, and peace negotiations were initiated.

For Grant, it was taking far too long to wrap things up. Although the Fourth Infantry was now quartered in Mexico City, where life became unhurried and rather pleasant, he could think only of returning to his beloved Julia.

While the army in Mexico waited impatiently for peace to become final, the year 1847 drew to a close. Meanwhile, despite the war (to most people but a minor distraction), the nation had not been standing still. During recent months it had been full speed ahead for commerce, industry, and the *New York Tribune*. In Chicago, for example, where the *Tribune* had recently printed 400 copies of its first local edition, hundreds of businessmen had gathered for an ambitious river-and-harbor convention. On hand to observe were Illinois Congressman Abraham Lincoln, New York politician Thurlow Weed, and the ubiquitous journalist Horace Greeley.[13]

As 1848 began in Mexico City, Quartermaster Grant, in addition to fulfilling his other functions, started a highly successful bakery. After taking care of his own regiment, he even built up the unit fund by selling extra supplies to the chief army commissary. As behooved a son of Jesse, he would say, "In two months I made more money for the fund than my pay amounted to during the entire war."[14] Despite all he'd done during the course of the conflict, this was about as close as he'd ever come to boasting.

Finally, on May 30, 1848, after what seemed to the army an eternity of waiting, the Treaty of Guadalupe Hidalgo was ratified. The Mexican War was history, and the United States acquired vast new lands reaching from the fertile Oklahoma panhandle to the blue Pacific.

On June 23, the Fourth Infantry landed at Pascagoula, Mississippi. Grant was on his way home. "My experience in the war was of great advantage to me afterwards," he would write, citing the many officers he'd come to know who later became senior leaders of either the Union or the Confederacy.[15] That wasn't all he'd learned. For example, he had seen the devastating effects of disease. For every man killed in action in Mexico, six had died from some form of illness. Then, as quartermaster, although he'd chafed at the assignment, he had learned valuable lessons about keeping an army supplied. Significantly, he also had seen the great ability of the American volunteer soldier, especially when given proper leadership, which unfortunately was not always provided. He recalled an incident involving Gen. William J. Worth, when men, after a full day's march, had been in camp preparing their food. Worth, for no good reason, had made them pack up, strike their tents, and set out again in the darkness. "Some commanders," Grant said, "can move troops so as to get the maximum distance out of them without fatigue, while others can wear them out in a few days without accomplishing so much. General Worth belonged in this latter class."[16]

On the other hand, Grant had a positive role model in the person of Zachary Taylor, the straightforward, unpretentious leader who wrote orders clearly "without reference to how they would read in history."[17] He was also to be admired, in Grant's opinion, for granting generous terms to the defeated Gen. Pedro de Ampudia after the fall of Monterey—even though his leniency brought howls from vengeful congressmen. Grant believed that Taylor's chivalry to a defeated foe had helped to ensure a lasting peace.

Grant also saw that Taylor was a "make-do" person, "not an officer to trouble the Administration much with his demands . . . inclined to do the best he could with the means given him."[18] Many years later, hardly by coincidence, similar words would be written of Grant: "Through him something was always accomplished. There was an absence of excuse, complaint, or delay; always the report of a task performed. If his means or supplies were imperfect, he found or improvised the best available substitute. If he could not execute the full requirement, he performed so much of it as was possible."[19]

At war's end, although he was thankful for America's victory, Grant continued to believe, as did Greeley and Dana, that his country's cause had not been just. He would write: "The Mexican war was a political war, and the administration conducting it desired to make party capital out of it."[20] In his opinion, the Polk administration, not wanting either Taylor or Scott, both Whigs, to become a political threat, had done much to thwart them, including the withholding of troops and the naming of subordinate generals from the "correct" party. Those subordinates, violating all decent military protocol, had openly criticized Scott and Taylor and had tried to take credit themselves for American victories. Fortunately neither the army nor the American public had been fooled. Ironically, Grant noted, the obvious efforts to tear down two able men had turned each of them into a formidable presidential candidate.

Finally, Grant had learned much about the workings of the free American press. He acknowledged its presence, knew it might often be inaccurate, but also knew it was a blessing and a necessity, for the army as well as the nation.

Charles Dana was now the *Tribune*'s managing editor, and a good one, growing steadily in professionalism, self-confidence, and personal reputation. Much of this he owed to Horace Greeley and to a policy that tolerated no factual errors or technical blunders but allowed free expressions of opinion, even opinions directly counter to Greeley's own.

To his lasting credit, Greeley was building a team and doing it in the right way. Once, when praising a talented staff member for a piece he'd written, he said: "I wish you would resolve henceforth to write one such article per week, and sign your own initials at the bottom. I want everybody connected with the *Tribune* to become known to the public (in some unobtrusive way) as doing what he does."[21]

Greeley, said a biographer, "was wholly different from the dictatorial Bennett over at the *Herald*, who saw everything and ran everything himself. The peremptory, commanding manner which Greeley cultivated was largely for show; actually, he steered the *Tribune* with relaxed, easy reins, and enjoyed giving his men their head."[22]

In the spring of 1848, as American troops were returning from Mexico, Charles Dana, despite his growing influence at the *Tribune*, still thought of himself as a scholar, one who found his greatest pleasure in the pursuit of knowledge. All his life he had wanted to visit Europe and see firsthand the countries whose literature, language, and philosophy fascinated him. Then, too, he wanted to make practical use of the languages he'd acquired. Not only did he know Latin, Greek, and German from his school years, on his own he'd also become fluent in French, Spanish, and Italian. Now, to make Europe even more intriguing, a revolution had broken out in France that would lead to the establishment of a new republic. Social turmoil also prevailed on the rest of the continent. Wanting to see these events with his own eyes, Dana asked to go abroad and report on European affairs. Greeley, as

Dana remembered it, said, "that would be no use, as I did not know anything about European matters, and would have to learn everything before I could write anything worthwhile." Undaunted, Dana said he'd like to try and asked how much Greeley would pay for a letter a week.

"Ten dollars," Greeley said.

"On this I went," said Dana, "and wrote one letter a week to the *Tribune* for ten, one to McMichael's *Philadelphia American* for ten, one to the New York *Commercial Advertiser* for ten, one for the *Harbinger* at five, and one for the *Chronotype* at five. That gave me forty dollars a week . . ." It was far more than he had been making as *Tribune* managing editor—more, in fact, than he'd made in his whole life.[23]

It was a remarkable performance. By combining wit, hard work, and personality, Dana established himself on the continent. By June he was writing knowledgeable letters on a broad range of affairs—and often earning from Greeley even *more* than the agreed-on $10. On October 7, for example, the *Tribune* had two articles signed "C.A.D.," both displayed prominently on the front page. One concerned discussions in the French Assembly on "the right to labor." The other, headed POLITI-CAL ASPECTS IN EUROPE, had an impressive potpourri of subheads: "Threatened Revolution in Prussia, Excitement in Berlin, The Constituent Assembly, The King a Cypher, The Danish Armistice, Petition for the Rejection, Can the Austrian Emperor Dissolve the Assembly, Progress in Hungary, Defiance of the Emperor, Movement Toward Independence, The Croats, Rumored Battle, State of Italy, etc."[24]

Dana's letters kept rolling in. As people read in-depth reporting with significant analysis, the whole nature of journalism was changing. Thanks to men like Greeley, Bennett, and Dana, papers now carried a greater percentage of actual news as opposed to items of general culture and education. Even so, one might still find on the *Tribune* front page a lengthy sermon by Henry Ward Beecher with pious admonitions such as: "No man can be happy who confers *un*happiness. Benevolence alone is the faculty whose action harmonizes with itself every other faculty of the mind."[25]

Of course, while the *Tribune* might preach benevolence, Greeley himself continued to speak his mind and lash out uncharitably whenever the spirit moved him. When the *Express* dismissed a weighty Greeley argument by saying only "Bah," Greeley responded, "We are quite willing that every animal shall express its emotions in the language natural to it."[26]

Also, Greeley was not one to forgive and forget. He had warned, when Texas was annexed and war with Mexico was on the horizon: "We have adopted a war ready-made, and taken upon ourselves its prosecution to the end. We are to furnish the bodies to fill trenches and the cash to defray its enormous expense."[27] As late as September 1848, when the war had been won and annexation was an accomplished fact, he still referred to that annexation as a "gross political mistake, as well as crime."[28]

In Europe, meanwhile, Charles Dana, although not yet 30, had shed whatever remained of his youthful idealism. While deep down he still believed that some form of cooperative endeavor was man's best hope, he was no longer the starry-eyed optimist of Brook Farm. As he traveled widely and talked to national leaders and to commoners, he was struck both by the poverty of the masses and by the seeming insensitivity of those in authority. In his letters to the *Tribune*, he implied that France and other European countries needed superior, high-minded individuals to step forward, perhaps to install a system of benevolent socialism. However, as he saw the inherent selfishness of mankind, he was not hopeful. From Paris he wrote: "This age seems poorer in individual greatness than other ages, because its necessities and perils are more gigantic, and individuals cannot tower above them."[29]

For nearly 3 months, Dana attended sessions of the French Assembly as it carved out a new constitution. He listened to impassioned speeches by notables such as Alexis de Tocqueville and Victor Hugo and took ample notes of all he saw and heard. Even when he admired the oratory, he noted its impracticality. Of one speaker he wrote: "It is not the reason he addresses, and logic is not one of his weapons, but there is something electric, something inspired in his words which makes you forget reason, forget everything. . . . His oratory absorbs you, carries you away, magnetizes and delights you." Then, after praising the man's fervent plea for workingmen's rights, he pointed out that there were no intelligible ideas as to how those rights were to be secured.[30]

After France, Dana traveled to other major European countries, and from each he sent back lengthy reports accompanied by shrewd observations. Constantly he deplored class structure and predicted social upheaval. While in Britain he wrote: "The majesty of England is after all fragile at the base, the feet of the statue are of clay. Its day will come, sooner or later, whether tomorrow or the next century, no man can foretell."[31]

Dana was back in Paris when Louis Napoleon was elected president of the newly established republic. With supreme disdain he wrote: "I have no faith in the sincerity of Louis Napoleon's adherence to the Republic. His history is marked with examples of falsehood too glaring to allow any confidence to be placed in his protestations even were he a man of sufficient intellect and character to be capable of genuine sincerity. There is no doubt that he would much rather be Emperor than President."[32]

Greeley, printing these words, might have winced at Dana's tone of arrogant superiority. Later, however, he could only admire the other's insight. When Louis eventually overthrew the republic and made himself emperor, it became clear that Dana's dire prediction had been on the mark.

At Harvard, and at Brook Farm, Dana had admired those idealists who sought to improve the world. While hoping for the best, however, he had learned to expect disappointment. This inherent cynicism toward authority and the establishment would color his view of worldly affairs for the rest of his life.

Ulysses Grant, riding up to White Haven in the summer of 1848, was markedly different from the young officer the Dent family had known earlier. He was back from the war, had proven himself in combat, and now moved with quiet confidence. Julia, smiling, laughing, radiant, was more than ready to end the long engagement and set the date for their marriage. Her mother, who had always liked this prospective son-in-law, was in full agreement. Even Julia's father, the Colonel, was reconciled to the match. Moreover, Julia's 12-year-old sister, Emmy, considered the "captain" (people now called him by his brevet rank) as handsome as ever but "sturdier and more reserved."[33]

First, however, Grant had to visit his family in Ohio. Father Jesse, as might be expected, was eager to show off his newly distinguished son. Jesse, the neighbors said, "would stop any time in the rain to talk about Ulysses."[34] As people crowded around to ask the "captain" about the war, Jesse looked on and beamed. Obligingly, Grant would answer their questions and talk knowledgeably, even at length; he was no longer the shy youth people once thought to be "backward." However, of his own personal exploits he'd say very little.

Then it was back to White Haven, where began what Emmy would recall as "happy days for us all."[35] The wedding was scheduled for August 22 and would take place at the Dents' winter home, at Fourth and Cerre Streets in St. Louis. Grant asked his friend Pete Longstreet to serve as best man. The reliable Longstreet—Robert E. Lee would later call him "my old war horse"—was a good man to have around.

The ceremony, called by Emmy "a sweet, old-fashioned wedding," went off on schedule.[36] It was a moment of supreme happiness for Ulysses and Julia, and in the coming years, their marriage would bring great joy and comfort to each of them.

6

"WHO CAN REASON
WITH HIM?"

ULYSSES GRANT and his bride, looking optimistically to a future in which they would "live happily ever after," set off on a leisurely honeymoon, during the day visiting friends and relatives in Kentucky and Ohio, and at night, as innocent newlyweds, discovering the wondrous joys of married love. Wanting to prolong this happiest of times, Grant requested a 2-month extension on his leave. The extension was granted, after which he was ordered to report to his regiment's newly established headquarters in Detroit, Michigan.

According to the papers, the standing army was being reduced to 8,000 men. Making drastic cuts in the military after a successful war was the way it was done in a democracy; whether or not it was prudent was another question, as future Americans would often learn to their dismay. For Grant's regiment, the Fourth Infantry, it meant having too many missions and being scattered to seven different locations along the northern frontier, from western Michigan to upstate New York.

Arriving in Detroit, Grant learned he'd been replaced as regimental quartermaster. Therefore he wouldn't be at headquarters. His new station would be at Madison Barracks, in Sackets Harbor, New York, a cold, bleak village on Lake Ontario.[1] He and Julia arrived there in November 1848. That same month, a presidential election had been held.

On election day, Grant, still on leave, had been visiting relatives in Kentucky. Like many regular army officers, he had not voted. This was deliberate. Despite any personal opinions, officers on active duty, especially West Pointers, generally tried to remain politically neutral.

The election went to the Whig candidate, Mexican War hero Zachary Taylor, who defeated Democrat Lewis Cass and Free-Soiler Martin Van Buren. Except for his military record, people didn't know much about Taylor, and in this case, said Greeley, "his silence was wisdom."[2] In the *Tribune* editor's opinion, Taylor had won votes in both the free and slave states "by reason of his persistent and obstinate silence and reserve on the vexed question of slavery in the Territories."[3]

Greeley, who would have preferred an abolitionist, considered "Old Rough and Ready" too soft on slavery. Earlier, in fact, he'd said: "If we nominate Taylor, we elect him, but we destroy the Whig party."[4] Once the nomination was secured, however, he had given his reluctant support, saying, "The country does not deserve a visitation of that pot-bellied, mutton-headed, cucumber Cass."[5]

The 1848 election also brought an opportunity for Greeley. David Jackson, a New York Democrat found guilty of 1846 election fraud, had finally been expelled from the House. The Whigs needed to nominate someone to fill the remaining months of Jackson's term. The political bosses in Albany offered the opening to Greeley. Although he acted coy initially, he was probably delighted. With something less than candor, he later wrote: "I at first resolved to decline . . . but the nomination was so kindly pressed upon me, with such apparently cogent reasons therefor, that I accepted it."[6]

If elected, he would serve the remaining 3 months of Jackson's term. Another Whig, James Brooks, was nominated to fill the same seat during the next full term. Both men won handily, riding in on Zachary Taylor's coattails. Soon it was evident that Greeley would *not* be a passive short-termer. Always the champion of "Go West," he was presently on the floor introducing a bill "authorizing each landless citizen . . . to occupy and appropriate a small allotment of the National Domain free of charge." When asked why an urban New Yorker busied himself with far-off public lands, Greeley said it was because *he* represented more landless men than anyone else on the floor![7]

Greeley the gadfly next turned his attention to congressional travel expenses. As a congressman, he had access to information "not easily found by outsiders," and he said the current law, allowing mileage payment for commuting over the traditional "usually traveled" routes, was overly generous. He calculated (and printed on the *Tribune*'s front page) what could be saved if those he named were to travel not by the "usual" but by the swiftest and cheapest means. Editorially, Greeley added that "the usually travelled route for a great many Members of the last Congress was an exceedingly crooked one, even for politicians." Although the members had followed standard practice and done nothing illegal, Greeley had managed to embarrass many of his new associates, including a certain Abraham Lincoln of Illinois.[8]

Greeley, personally scrupulous in financial matters, abhorred dishonesty in others. Years later he said that when in Congress he knew of 10 or 12 members who were generally presumed to be "on the make." "I would gladly believe," he added, "that this class has not since increased in numbers or in impudence; but the facts do not justify that presumption."[9]

His political partners, Thurlow Weed and William Seward, sensed that this brief stint in Congress, rather than satisfying Greeley's political ambition, was causing it, along with his self-esteem, to expand with each passing day. In a letter to Weed, Seward (a newly elected senator) said he'd looked in on the lower chamber and seen Greeley in action: "He won't let them adjourn until three o'clock, and martyrizes himself five or six times a day by voting against the whole House. I am sorry, but who can reason with him?"[10] It was not the way to win friends, but Greeley didn't care—he was having a ball! Almost gleefully, he wrote his longtime friend Margaret Fuller that he'd made himself "the most detested man who had ever sat in Congress."[11]

As his abbreviated term came to a close, Greeley said publicly that he wanted nothing from the now-empowered Whigs and that he was happy to be out of politics. Privately, however, he couldn't resist putting out a feeler through Whig politician Schuyler Colfax, saying, "I would just as soon be talked about for Postmaster General as not."[12] And if postmaster general wasn't in the cards, perhaps a diplomatic mission abroad?

The hints fell on deaf ears. When no appointment was forthcoming from the new Whig administration, tension grew between Greeley and his presumed political supporters, the twin dispensers of New York patronage, Thurlow Weed and William Seward.

Greeley left Washington for New York in March 1849. That same month, Charles Dana returned from Europe on the steamship *United States*. The passage had taken 28 days, and for a time it was feared the ship had been lost at sea.[13] People at the *Tribune*, happy to learn the rumors of a ship catastrophe were unfounded, welcomed him back. Soon Greeley and Dana, reunited, were once more working together. Associates noted, however, they were not always working in harmony.

As Julia and Ulysses Grant settled into their cramped quarters at Madison Barracks, they heard about an exciting gold strike in California. Horace Greeley's *Tribune* was proclaiming: "We are on the brink of the age of gold." As the fever spread like wildfire, newspapers said that $15 million in gold pebbles had already been picked up. Every family seemed to be affected, and all over the country men were packing up, fighting for bookings on steamships, or studying maps for the overland journey.[14] More people heading west also resulted in more missions for the army, as it was called on to protect them.

In the spring of 1849, Grant was reinstalled as regimental quartermaster, which meant returning to Detroit, where he said, "two years were spent with but few important incidents."[15] That might have been true professionally, for, as he insisted, "I was no clerk, nor had I any capacity to become one. The only place I ever found in my life to put a paper so as to find it again was either a side coat-pocket or the hands of a clerk . . . more careful than myself."[16]

On the personal side, however, there *was* a big event—the arrival on May 30, 1850, of Frederick Dent Grant, named for Julia's father. At her parents' urging, Julia had returned to White Haven to give birth. Before long there was another move. The Detroit headquarters was being abandoned, and for the Grants, it was back to Sackets Harbor. That was fine by Grant, who said he was "delighted" with Sackets Harbor and hoped they might remain there "for a long time to come."[17]

The Grants settled into a comfortable family routine. Not only did Ulysses accompany Julia to Presbyterian church services, he even gave up alcohol and joined the local chapter of the Sons of Temperance, whose by-laws ordered: "No brother shall make, buy, sell, or use, as a beverage, any spirituous or Malt Liquors, Wine, or Cider."[18]

The following year, the Grants' happy domesticity was brought to an abrupt halt. Julia, now into her second pregnancy, was learning the realities of army life. The Fourth Infantry, including her husband, the regimental quartermaster, was ordered to the Pacific Coast. Because of her condition, she would not be able to accompany them. For who knew how long, she'd be separated from her beloved "Lyss."

Horace Greeley had an eye for journalistic talent, and at the *Tribune*, that talent was allowed to flourish. There was Charles Dana, of course, but there were others as well, including the gifted George Ripley, a former Brook Farm transcendentalist who was now the *Tribune*'s literary editor. Because of Greeley's love of European culture, that was no small thing; on any given day the paper might carry three front-page columns dealing with European art and literature. Horace Greeley's greatest find, however, may have been Henry J. Raymond, a *Tribune* original at age 20. Of

Raymond he'd one day say: "I never found another person, barely of age and just from his studies, who evinced so signal and such versatile ability in journalism as he did. Abler and stronger men I may have met; a cleverer, readier, more efficient journalist I never saw."[19]

In April 1851, with things going well at the paper, Greeley was off to London for the grand opening of Prince Albert's World's Exposition at the Crystal Palace in Hyde Park. Greeley, suitably impressed, exuded superlatives. The Crystal Palace "was one of the noblest, most magnificent, most graceful edifices ever seen." As for the exposition itself, nothing else "so comprehensive, so instructive, has since been or ever will be presented . . ."[20]

From England, Greeley traveled to France and Italy; then it was back to England and home, where a surprise awaited him. His protégé, Raymond, was leaving the *Tribune* to start his own paper, the *New York Times*. Moreover, Raymond had enticed key staff members from other papers to join him, including several from the *Tribune* itself. Soon the *Times* was in head-to-head competition with the *Tribune*, and before long Raymond was even rivaling Greeley for the political favors of Weed and Seward. The outraged Greeley would now describe the estimable Raymond as "that little viper."[21]

Meanwhile, the Whig Party was falling into disarray. Much of the fault lay with the "Know Nothings," a group filled with hate and prejudice and violently opposed to Catholics and foreigners. By this time they had become an important Whig force. Many who disagreed with them were leaving the party in disgust. Did the "Know Nothings" fear losing jobs to "outsiders"? Or was their campaign a clever scheme of pro-slavery people wanting to divide the North while the South remained united in its one great interest, the defense of slavery? Greeley, who urged the Whigs to focus on their anti-slavery principles, thought this might be the case. In any event, the tolerant Greeley despised the bigoted "Know Nothings," as did Dana, who vowed never to mention them in the *Tribune* except "to give 'em a devil of a whale."[22]

Throughout it all, the hyperactive Greeley maintained his never-ending crusades. Added to the cause of anti-slavery was temperance, free land in the West, abolishing the fugitive slave law, cracking down on prostitution, and cleaning up the streets of New York. At one point he also advocated reducing all government salaries, greatly cutting down the navy, and "abolishing the Army, which is an absurd nuisance, unworthy of the Nineteenth Century."[23]

In 1852, the Whigs nominated Gen. Winfield Scott for the presidency. Earlier, Greeley had written Schuyler Colfax to say, "I suppose we must run Scott, and I hate it."[24] Personally, he considered the man "an aristocratic, arbitrary ass."[25] However, despite any personal feelings about Scott or about the military in general, he knew the Whigs had never won except with a military man as their candidate.

That fall, when Scott lost the election to the Democrat, Franklin Pierce, a disgusted Greeley said he was going to abandon politics and take up farming, leaving Dana to take care of the paper. He did—for a week or 2.

Some of the Fourth Infantry would travel to the Pacific Coast by sailing "around the Horn." Most, however, including Grant, would land at Panama, travel overland to the Pacific, and then board a second ship for California.

On July 5, 1852, from Governors Island in New York Harbor, Grant wrote: "Dear Dear Julia, we sail directly for the Isthmus. I never knew how much it was to part from you and Fred until it came to the time for leaving . . ."[26]

For Grant, the crossing of Panama turned into a grueling nightmare. Soon after landing, the regiment, led by crusty Col. Benjamin Bonneville, found itself in the middle of a raging cholera epidemic. A third of the way across the isthmus, Bonneville, hoping to lessen exposure time to the disease, decided to proceed ahead with most of the troops. As he left, he made Grant responsible for bringing forward the sick, the women and children, and all the regimental baggage. Every possible difficulty was encountered. The promised transportation did not appear; new arrangements had to be made. Once under way, tropical rains turned the trails into wallows of oozing mud. Every hour, cholera claimed another victim. Men dropped in place, some to die. When they did, Grant and his party buried them in shallow graves and kept going. With stubborn determination, Grant pressed on, finally arriving at Panama City, on the Pacific, with his groaning, vomiting, muddy band of civilians and soldiers. By the time it was over, more than a hundred men of the Fourth Infantry lay in jungle graves or swayed with the tides on the bottom of Panama Bay.

One of Grant's biographers, Lloyd Lewis, saw the trek across Panama as a critical event in Grant's development: "As long as he would live," Lewis wrote, "he would talk more of Panama than of any of his battles . . . The sick and dying men, the rain and the mud, the burdens thrown upon him by the incompetent Bonneville had, however, lifted him from his own homesickness and had revealed to him his unguessed powers at the business of managing a company of military men."[27]

By the end of September, Grant was at Fort Vancouver, on the Columbia River in Oregon (later Washington) Territory, settling in to a lonely job as post quartermaster. Every waking moment he thought of Julia, of little Fred, and of the baby he'd yet to see, Ulysses Grant Jr., born in Ohio on July 22 as his father was thousands of miles away, slogging along a muddy trail in a steaming Panama jungle.

Grant constantly thought about ways to earn money so Julia and the children could join him. He surely couldn't provide for them on army pay. Although he was called "captain," it was an honorary brevet rank, a reward for Mexican War gallantry. To the paymaster, he was still a lieutenant. And even after his captaincy came through, living costs were so high that the situation wouldn't be much different. "A cook could not be hired for the pay of a captain," Grant would say. "The cook could do better."[28]

Although several money-making schemes were attempted, nothing worked out. Someone said ice was selling at fabulous prices in San Francisco, so Grant and two other officers shipped 100 tons by way of a Pacific Mail sailing schooner. Later they learned that adverse winds had delayed the schooner, and by the time it got to San Francisco, other ships had arrived from Alaska, prices had fallen, and their investment was wiped out.

Next, Grant and his friend, Lt. Henry Wallen, tried shipping cattle and pigs to Frisco, with Wallen going along to do the marketing. "We continued that business," said Wallen, "until both of us lost all the money we had."[29]

Finally, Grant leased a large plot of land and planted what promised to be a highly profitable crop, only to have it decimated by floodwaters. Discouraged and dejected, he wrote Julia, "I have been quite unfortunate lately. The Columbia is now far over its banks and has destroyed all the grain, onions, corn, and about half the potatoes upon which I had expended so much money and labor."[30]

In the fall of 1853, following his promotion to captain, Grant was ordered to Fort Humboldt, California, to become commander of the Fourth Infantry's "F" Company. His friend Wallen, watching Grant head down the Columbia on a schooner bound for California, thought he had never known "a stronger, better, or truer man."[31]

At Fort Humboldt, Grant, no longer busy at quartermaster duties, had an abundance of free time on his hands—too much of it. He began to brood and to drink. "My Dear Wife," he wrote, "You do not know how forsaken I feel here!"[32]

Grant constantly thought about home and family. He was bored, lonely, and to make matters worse, he was now serving under Col. Robert Buchanan, "Old Buch," a martinet with whom he'd had a disagreement years earlier.

Years later, an army contractor who'd been at Humboldt offered a shrewd appraisal of Grant's situation: "The line captain's duties were fewer and less onerous than the quartermaster's had been and the discipline was far more rigid and irksome. No greater misfortune could have happened to him [Grant] than this enforced idleness. He had little work, no family with him, took no pleasure in the amusements of his brother officers . . . the result was a common one—he took to liquor."[33]

For months, Grant had talked of resigning and, like many of his classmates, trying his hand at civilian life. Then, in the spring of 1854, matters came to a head.

In later life, Grant never explained what caused him to make the move at that particular time. One story, as good as any since it came from Rufe Ingalls, a close friend and a former West Point roommate, said that: "Grant, finding himself in dreary surroundings, without his family, and with but little to occupy his attention, fell into dissipated habits, and was found, one day, too much under the influence of liquor to properly perform his duties. For this offense Colonel Buchanan demanded that he should resign or stand trial. Grant's friends at the time urged him to stand trial, and were confident of his acquittal, but, actuated by a noble spirit, he said he would not for all the world have his wife know that he had been tried on such a charge. He resigned his commission and returned to civil life."[34]

Whatever the circumstances, on April 11, 1854, Grant submitted his letter of resignation with a request that it become effective 3½ months later, on July 31. Buchanan forwarded the letter, recommending approval but with no further comment. The resignation began making its way through army channels. Grant, with a 60-day leave in his pocket, left Fort Humboldt and headed for home. Ironically, if any one of his earlier leave or transfer requests had been granted, he would have gone back east, rejoined his family, and probably stayed in the service. Now, however, he was telling friends: "Whoever hears of me in ten years, will hear of a well-to-do old Missouri farmer."[35]

Horace Greeley often disagreed with opinions expressed in the *Tribune* by his managing editor, the strong-willed Charles Dana. At times Greeley even went so far as to tell his readers that a particular point of view was Dana's, not his. Nevertheless, he continued to give Dana his head. He had no objection, for example, when Dana hired a certain wild-eyed Londoner to report on European affairs. Dana's new correspondent was the well-known but impecunious Karl Marx, author of the Communist Manifesto.[36]

For $10 a week, Marx submitted letters on politics, economics, and wars. Frequently the money from Dana was his sole source of income. At times material would be added by Marx's colleague, Friedrich Engels, who once charged that Dana lifted whole sections of their articles and ran them as editorials. It was one more example, Engels said, of "lousy, petty-bourgeois cheating!"[37]

In 1854, Horace Greeley was again getting the political itch. Meeting with Thurlow Weed at the Astor House in New York, Greeley suggested the time had come for him to run for governor. Weed, stalling, said he no longer controlled the state convention, so he doubted he could secure the nomination for Greeley.

"Is there any objection to my running for lieutenant-governor?" Greeley then asked.

Again Weed was negative. He later reported: "After a little more conversation, Mr. Greeley became convinced that a nomination for lieutenant-governor was undesirable, and left me in good spirits."[38]

Then came the final humiliation. Weed's choice for lieutenant-governor turned out to be none other than Greeley's rival, that "little viper" editor of the New York Times, Henry J. Raymond. "No other name could have been put upon the ticket so bitterly humbling," Greeley said.[39]

By 1854, whole groups of disillusioned voters had abandoned the existing political parties. People no longer knew what the Whigs stood for, and the Democrats, at least in the South, seemed to be allied with slaveholders. With men of both parties jumping ship, new coalitions were forming with names such as "Know-Nothing," "Free-Soiler," "Fusion," "Independence," "Temperance," and "Anti-Nebraska," the latter being opponents of the Nebraska Bill, which seemed to tolerate the entrance of slavery into free-soil Nebraska. With so many unattached factions, the time was ripe for a unifying name and a unifying voice.

A rally at a church in Ripon, Wisconsin, came up with the title "Republican." The name began catching on. In Washington, 30 congressmen endorsed it; in Michigan, members of a new party declared: "We will cooperate, and be known as Republicans."[40]

Then, on June 16, 1854, Horace Greeley supplied the voice. In an editorial read throughout the Northeast and the Midwest, he called for a new national party: "We should not care much whether those united were designated Whig, Free Soil Democrats or something else; though we think some simple name like *Republican* would more fitly designate those who had united to restore our Union to its true mission of champion and promulgator of Liberty rather than propagandist of slavery."[41]

At election time, Greeley swallowed his pride long enough to support Seward. However, it was for the last time. A few days later he wrote the senator a long, rambling, bitter letter. "It seems to me a fitting time," he began, "to announce to you the dissolution of the political firm of Seward, Weed, and Greeley, by the withdrawal of the junior partner. . . ."[42] From now on, Greeley and the *Tribune* would go it alone.

"It is bad to see him so unhappy," Seward told Weed.[43] Then, hoping to patch things up, he paid a call on Greeley. It didn't help; maybe it would have been better if Weed had been the caller. Greeley could always understand Weed's sheer joy in devious political manipulation. What annoyed Greeley was Seward's hypocritical assertion of high moral aims while joining in those same manipulations. He ignored the fact that people often accused Greeley himself of such manipulations.

Ulysses Grant's letter of resignation had been wending its way through channels, collecting endorsements that recommended it be approved. From Colonel Buchanan at Fort Humboldt it went to Headquarters, Department of the Pacific. Then it was east to Army Headquarters in New York, and from there to the Army Adjutant General in Washington.

Finally, on June 2, 1854, the letter received a last endorsement:

> Accepted as tendered:
>
> JEFFERSON DAVIS
> Secretary of War[44]

7

HARDSCRABBLE

HIS ARMY CAREER had once looked so promising. Now it was ended, and for the first time in 15 years, Ulysses Grant was a civilian. There were, of course, regrets over his lost career. Also, he feared old army friends were telling each other that Sam Grant had resigned because of an alleged drinking problem. Still, he was now back at White Haven, reunited with his beloved Julia, and that was good. As the distinguished Bruce Catton once wrote: "One hardly ever thinks of this particular couple in that way, but the fact is that they shared one of the great, romantic, beautiful loves of all American history."[1]

For the present, Julia said, they could stay with her parents at White Haven. Later they could live in the house, now empty, that Julia's brother Louis had built nearby. It was called "Wish-ton-wish," Indian for "whippoorwill," and Julia was assured they'd be welcome to use it indefinitely. That was a help. But although Grant appreciated the Dents' hospitality, he feared he and his pro-slavery father-in-law would start arguing about politics if they lived too long in close contact. The sooner he and his family had a place of their own, the better he'd like it.

Julia owned 60 acres on the Dent estate, a gift from her father. On that land, Grant could put in a crop and start building a house. Realistically, however, he knew it wouldn't be that easy. He had no money to buy the seed and farm implements he'd need to get started. Moreover, their third child was due in a few months. At least initially, his only source of income would be from cutting and selling cordwood.

Although Julia owned three slaves, they were former house servants unsuited for farm work. It was a thing neighbors might laugh about—a man owning three slaves yet having to do his own work in the field. Worse than that, in the neighbors' opinion, was Grant's hiring free blacks to help and paying them more than the going wage. One of the freedmen, Uncle Jason, recalled in later years, "Some of the white men cussed about it, but Cap'n he jis' kept right on payin' for the work jis' the same."

Mary Robinson, a house servant at White Haven, said that Grant, in addition to being "the kindest husband and the most indulgent father I ever saw," was "a very kind man to those who worked for him and he always said he wanted to give his wife's slaves their freedom as soon as he was able."[2]

Horace Greeley, although a man of a thousand reforms, had a special abhorrence for slavery and alcohol. He was quick to seize on an incident that demonstrated the wickedness in *both* his favorite hatreds: "On August 2, 1854," wrote Greeley, "a Dr. R. H. Graham, of New Orleans, who had been drinking, roused a New York hotel at five in the morning by ringing all the bells. When another guest, whose wife was an invalid, expostulated, Graham fatally stabbed him with a sword cane." Greeley called the crime "one of those brutal murders which seem peculiarly to belong to the institution of slavery." Since his own New York was notorious for its murders, Greeley had to stretch to make his point.[3]

In December 1854, leaving Dana in charge of the paper, Greeley went to Washington to report on the new session of Congress. "I hate this hole, but am glad to have come," he wrote back. "It does me good to see those who hate the *Tribune* fear it yet more."[4] He proceeded to send voluminous copy from the nation's capital. Often included were instructions about editorial positions the *Tribune* should adopt. Sometimes the wires got crossed, and on one occasion the temperamental Greeley fumed: "DANA: I shall have to quit here or die, unless you stop attacking people without consulting me. . . . Do send someone here and kill me if you cannot stop this, for I can bear it no longer."[5]

Dana, by this time one of the *Tribune*'s stockholders, ran the paper with a businessman's eye, limiting both the size of each edition and the number of extras. By contrast, Greeley believed "a daily newspaper should print everything as fast as it is ready, though this should oblige it to issue two supplements a day."[6] Inevitably there was a clash. By the following spring, Greeley was telling Dana, "I wish you would humor my prejudices a little, and when I send two or more dispatches, not make them into one. . . . I would stay here forever and work like a slave if I could get my letters printed as I send them, but the Tribune is doomed to be a second-rate paper, and I am tired."[7]

Far from being second-rate, the *Tribune* had a nationwide circulation, daily and weekly, of more than 220,000 by the summer of 1856. It clearly had a major impact on public opinion, and as Ralph Waldo Emerson put it: "Greeley does the thinking for the whole West at $2 per year for his paper."[8]

Meanwhile, Charles Dana was gaining influence in his own right. The nation's focus that summer was on "Bleeding Kansas," where pro-slave and free-soil factions were in murderous, violent conflict. When New Yorkers held a mass meeting in support of the Free-Soilers, Dana was one of the speakers. His views were reflected by the next man on the program, Representative Samuel Galloway of Ohio, who said: "The crisis has come. Here are two antagonistic powers about to come into collision—Freedom and Slavery. Which shall be the governing principle of our American institutions?"[9]

Early each morning, Dana might be seen leaving his home at 90 Clinton Place and walking briskly to the *Tribune* offices. The observant Walt Whitman, who saw him frequently, described Dana as: "A straight, trim-built, vigorous man, well-dressed with strong brown hair, beard and mustache, and a quick, watchful eye. He steps alertly by, watching everybody . . . a man of rough, strong intellect, tremendous prejudices fully relied on, and excellent intentions."[10]

Dana might disagree with Greeley on some matters, but in 1856 he joined him in supporting the first-ever Republican to run for president. "I tell you," wrote Dana, "John C. Fremont is the man for us to beat with, and the only one."[11] He and Greeley both considered the Democrat James Buchanan too soft on slavery. The same applied to Millard Fillmore, nominee of the Whigs and "Know-Nothings." In November, however, with Fillmore siphoning off votes from the Republicans, Buchanan won the election despite receiving less than 50% of the popular vote.

To Ulysses Grant, as to many other army officers, John C. Frémont, the famed explorer known as the "Pathfinder," was a shallow, vain adventurer, far too erratic to be entrusted with the presidency.[12] At election time, Grant cast his vote for Buchanan. In later years a well-known epigram had him saying, "I voted for Buchanan because I didn't know him and voted against Fremont because I did know him." In his *Memoirs*, perhaps with postwar hindsight, Grant claimed he voted as he did because of a dread of war and a belief that Buchanan was the only candidate whose election would postpone or prevent secession.[13]

Earlier that year, the Grants had moved into a two-story house he called Hardscrabble. By calling it that, perhaps he was mocking the pretentious names the Dents had given their own places. Grant still lacked capital, and cordwood remained his only source of income. Day after day he drove a wagonload of wood into town. When the wood was sold, he returned home and began gathering another load. Occasionally, as he traveled the streets of St. Louis, officer friends from the past would recognize the weary-looking man in the army overcoat of fading blue. When they stopped to talk, Grant tried hard to ignore the embarrassed looks of sympathy and curiosity.

By the spring of 1857, Grant's situation was desperate. Much as he hated doing it, he wrote his father and asked for help: "Dear Father, Spring is now approaching when farmers require not only to till the soil, but to have the wherewith to till it. For two years I have been compelled to farm without either of these facilities, confining my attention therefore principally to oats and corn: two crops which can never pay . . . I want to vary the crop a little and also to have implements to cultivate with. To this end I am going to make the last appeal to you. I do this because, when I was in Ky. you voluntarily offered to give me a Thousand dollars to commence with and because there is no one els [sic] to whom I could, with the same propriety, apply."

He went on to explain that he would consider this a loan, one he would repay at 10% annual interest, "and with this if I do not go on prosperously I shall ask no more from you."[14]

It is not known how Jesse responded to this "last appeal." In any event, Ulysses went on farming. By late summer, although his wheat crop was a disappointment, he had raised a fair crop of corn and oats. His efforts were in vain. Once again a financial panic had devastated the country. Farmers were unable to sell their crops, businesses were going bankrupt, and money was nowhere to be found.

On December 23, 1857, despite his poverty, Grant decided that his family must have presents on Christmas morning. Above all there must be something for Julia, who was again pregnant. (Six weeks later she would give birth to Jesse Root Grant, their fourth and last child.) In St. Louis, Grant went to the pawnshop of J. S. Freligh. There, for the sum of $22, he surrendered his "gold hunting watch, detached lever and gold chain."[15]

If Grant saw the *Tribune* on Christmas Day, he might have read Horace Greeley's account of observations made during a recent speaking tour. "The West is very poor. I think a larger proportion of the people of Michigan, Indiana, Illinois, Wisconsin and Iowa are under the harrow now than at any former period."[16]

In the spring of 1858, Colonel Dent, now a widower, moved to St. Louis and rented White Haven to Ulysses and Julia. For a time things looked promising for the Grants. That summer, however, cold weather damaged all the crops. Then Ulysses became severely ill and unable to work. He had to face facts; it was time to abandon his sad attempt at farming. Grant helped Colonel Dent sell the White Haven farm equipment and rent out the land. Then, after selling Hardscrabble, he sought work in St. Louis.

As a favor to the Dents, Grant was given a job in the real estate office of Harry Boggs, the Colonel's nephew. The firm was now called Boggs & Grant, but since Grant had no money to put into the business, he was in truth little more than a clerk.[17] At the new office, collecting rents and trying to sell real estate, Grant still found time to read the papers and talk politics. That fall of '58, much attention was being paid to a series of debates between the "Little Giant," Stephen Douglas, and a man they called the "Railsplitter," Abraham Lincoln.

Horace Greeley had been disappointed by the Republicans' failure to win the '56 election. Next time around, he was determined that things would be different. The Whigs were no longer a factor. And the Democrats? If Greeley had his way, they would tear each other apart over the issue of slavery.

To help this along, Greeley would say good things about Stephen Douglas. The "Little Giant" had supported popular sovereignty in Kansas, and pro-slave southerners hated him for it. Gleefully, Greeley wrote Schuyler Colfax: "Douglas has broken the back of the Democratic Party. It will hold him responsible for the loss of Kansas, and will never forgive him—never!"[18] Personally, Greeley considered Douglas to be a "low and dangerous demagogue." Therefore, he didn't hesitate to bestow a partial kiss of death by having the *Tribune* support him. As southerners wrote off Douglas, that same support would keep the "Little Giant" a leading figure among Democrats in the North. Greeley's actions, he told Colfax, had deepened the impression among southerners that Douglas was "a disguised abolitionist and virtual ally of the Black Republicans."[19] Other Republicans, however, failing to comprehend Greeley's devious long-range plan, howled their resentment.

Earlier, Greeley had urged Illinois Republicans to let Douglas run for the Senate unopposed. When they went against his advice and nominated Lincoln, Greeley could not bring himself to support Lincoln wholeheartedly. "Greeley is not doing me right," Lincoln complained.[20]

Thanks in part to the *Tribune*, Douglas won the election. His presence in the Senate, as Greeley had foreseen, widened the rift within his own party. That winter, Greeley was in Bloomington, Illinois, on a lecture tour. Lincoln also happened to be in town. When their paths crossed, Greeley evidently invited Lincoln to call on him at his hotel. Lincoln did not accept the invitation.[21]

By August 1859, Grant knew he was not bringing in enough business to justify his role in the partnership. In fairness to Boggs, he had to quit. Seeking other employment, he applied for the job of county engineer. Rejection brought another bitter disappointment. A letter to his father told what happened: "I have waited for some time to write you the result of the action of the County Commissioners upon the appointment of a County Engineer. The question has at length been settled, and I am sorry to say, adversely to me. The two Democratic Commissioners voted for me, and the freesoilers against me. . . . You may judge from the result . . . that I am strongly identified with the Democratic party! Such is not the case. I never voted an out and out Democratic ticket in my life. I voted for Buch. for President to defeat Fremont but not because he was my first choice."[22]

He had failed in the army, failed as a farmer, failed at everything he'd tried since. Once again he was forced to make a "last appeal" to his father, even if it meant a return to the hated tanning business. In the spring of 1860, at Jesse's suggestion, Grant moved to Galena, Illinois, to work in the family's leather store. In effect, Ulysses would be but a clerk, working for his brother Simpson. Ulysses didn't mind; at least he wasn't being relegated to the god-awful, reeking tanyards.

In the months that followed, the citizens of Galena came to know Grant as a quiet, devoted family man who had rented a little house on High Street and who was a steady if uninspired worker at the leather store. Wasn't it a pity, they thought, that such a good man had never amounted to much? His small circle of friends, however, knew but the surface characteristics of Sam Grant. As one writer said, "It took the most sensitive of observers to penetrate past Grant's exterior to the real man."[23]

On May 16, 1860, Republicans gathered in Chicago at a massive wooden hall known as the Wigwam. Convention atmosphere was one of enthusiastic optimism. As nominating proceedings got under way, the clear favorite was William Seward of New York. For months his canny supporter Thurlow Weed, known as the "Dictator," had been in constant motion. Weed, making deals and trading favors, was doing whatever it took to put his man over the top. That included winning newspaper support, notably that of Henry Raymond's *New York Times*. He had failed, however, to win over Horace Greeley, who had not forgotten past slights. Nor would he.

Nevertheless, Weed was telling delegates: "We think we have in Mr. Seward just the qualities the country will need. He is known by us all as a statesman. . . . We expect to nominate him on the first ballot."[24] Meanwhile, Horace Greeley was busy telling everyone who'd listen that the party could not win with Seward. They must find another candidate, perhaps his own choice, Edward Bates of Missouri. On the floor, Greeley spoke not for New York—Weed had refused to include him—but as a delegate from distant Oregon.

Greeley, a member of the platform committee, worked "long and earnestly," he later said, to exclude any planks "needlessly offensive or irritating" to the South. He hoped to isolate southern slaveholders, who he knew were in the minority, and hold out to non-slaveholders in the South the prospect of national harmony.[25]

A majority, 234 votes, would be needed to nominate Seward. On the first ballot he had 173½, well ahead of favorite sons Lincoln of Illinois and Simon Cameron of Pennsylvania. Salmon P. Chase of New York came next. Greeley's man, Bates, with only 48 votes, was a distant fifth. Greeley, giving up on Bates, switched to Lincoln. He moved from one delegation to another, arguing, cajoling, pleading. A western delegate said, "He looked like a well-to-do farmer fresh from the clover fields. He seemed to find a place in our hearts at once."

The second ballot showed Seward and Lincoln in a virtual tie. Momentum had shifted, and it was all but over. After the third ballot, with one delegation after another switching to Lincoln, the "Railsplitter" was declared the party nominee. "Greeley has slaughtered Seward, but has saved the Republican party," shouted the chairman of the Indiana delegation. The correspondent of *Harpers Weekly* wired home that Greeley's triumph had made the *Tribune* "the great organ and censor" of the Republican Party.[26]

Seward accepted defeat gracefully, writing Weed: "You have my unbounded gratitude . . . I wish that I was sure that your sense of disappointment is as light as my own."[27] That fall, Seward won Greeley's admiration by campaigning vigorously for the Republican ticket. Greeley later described Seward's speeches as "of a remarkably high order, alike in originality, dignity, and perspicuity."[28]

Greeley still hoped to placate the South and avert secession. That was why he'd given his initial support to the moderate Missourian Edward Bates. Dana, however, setting the tone for *Tribune* editorials, was relentless in his attacks on slavery. Writing of the "Land of Legree and the home of the slave," he didn't care about giving offense—as long as the offended were slaveholders. By this time a Texas sedition law had rendered it a felony even to receive the *New York Tribune.*[29]

Then came the election. In Springfield, as Lincoln learned of his victory, his demeanor impressed Greeley's man on the scene: "His bearing is altogether very striking. . . . There is something beyond all art in the frank and generous sunshine of his countenance. It is full of fine expression."[30] Republicans were refusing to acknowledge that Lincoln's election meant secession. Similarly, southern extremists wouldn't admit that secession meant war.

As soon as Lincoln's victory became known, South Carolina called for a secession convention. "The tea has been thrown overboard," said the *Charleston Mercury.* "The revolution of 1860 has been initiated."[31]

Northerners were outraged. "South Carolina is too small for a republic and too big for a lunatic asylum," said one.[32] South Carolina seceded on December 20, followed by Mississippi on January 9, Florida on January 10, Alabama on January 11, Georgia on January 19, Louisiana on January 26, and Texas on February 1. Rumbling war clouds were gaining in intensity, becoming ever blacker, ever more packed with violence. When those clouds unleashed their ghastly storm, every American life would be affected, not only the citizens of 1860 but the sons and daughters of generations to come.

Soon Horace Greeley, Charles Dana, and Ulysses Grant, three good but very different men, would carve out their respective roles. The first two did not know the third, or even know he existed. Their paths would soon cross, however, and in a way that would change the course of American history.

On April 15, 1861, men came running from the telegraph office in Galena, Illinois, shouting that Fort Sumter had fallen. It was stunning news. Until that moment, some had still argued that the seceding states would be allowed to depart in peace and that there would be no war. Since then, "war or peace" arguments had been common. For his part, Sam Grant had suspected all along that it would come to a fight. However, considering the overwhelming assets the North could bring to bear, he was convinced such a war would be over within 90 days.

President Lincoln had issued a call for volunteers, and throughout the North the response was quick and enthusiastic. Men were caught up in the moment. As their brains deliberately ignored the horrors of war, their ears heard only tunes of glory. Volunteers, said the *Chicago Tribune*, would be no problem: "There is now every indication that the whole force of ninety-four regiments called for by the President could be readily furnished by Illinois alone, and that the quota of six regiments assigned to Illinois could be obtained in Chicago almost at the tap of the drum."[33]

In Galena, citizens had a rally, complete with patriotic speeches and a call for volunteers to form a local company. They asked Sam Grant, the only local man with honest-to-goodness military experience, to preside over the meeting. He accepted the chair, and the decision was to prove important. The temporary prominence brought him to the attention of the vigorous Elihu Washburne, the U.S. Congressman from the Galena district.

Galena (or, more precisely, Jo Daviess County, Illinois) formed its company. Grant declined an offer to serve as company commander. Modest though he was, he knew his background fitted him for something higher. However, he offered to train the company and accompany it to its initial encampment. An item in the *Chicago Tribune* read: "Galena, April 25th—The Jo Daviess Guards . . . left here this evening for Springfield. The parting scene at the depot was very affecting."[34] Also saying their farewells at the station were Ulysses and Julia Grant. The departure of the short, plain ex-soldier received no special mention in the press.

The Jo Daviess Guards arrived in Springfield the next day. Grant helped herd them out to Camp Yates, an assembly point named for Governor Richard Yates of Illinois. At the moment, Yates was having his problems. Thousands of volunteers were starting to arrive, creating supply problems and administrative chaos. An interview with the governor was arranged by Congressman Washburne, and Grant was put to work. Undoubtedly he disliked the clerklike duties he was assigned, but evidently he did them well. On May 4, the governor made him an honorary colonel and put him in charge of Camp Yates. As an added duty, Grant began traveling the state to muster in the newly formed regiments. At Mattoon, the raw recruits took a liking to the quiet, dignified, Mexican War veteran and named their camp after him. A reporter cheerfully explained the action to the folks back home:

> Headquarters Camp Grant
> Seventh Congressional District
> May 24, 1861

CHRISTENING OF CAMP

The statement that this camp was christened Grant in honor of Col. Grant, only created the query, doubtless, with many of your readers, as to who Col. Grant is, that he should be so complimented as to have the would-be star regiment of the state christened after him. Col. U.S. Grant is a West Pointer of some military notoriety—I believe, for some time of the regular U.S. Army, now mustering officer for the State of Illinois.[35]

On that same May 24, Grant wrote the adjutant general in Washington, offering his services to the federal government. Years later the letter was discovered in a musty file—unanswered.[36]

In Springfield, meanwhile, Governor Yates was becoming aware that strange and unqualified individuals were assuming positions of great responsibility. A case in point was Silas Goode of Decatur, the man whose regiment Grant had sworn in at Mattoon. Not long after Goode had taken command, one of his officers had complained to Grant that "Goode was impossible, drank too much, quoted Napoleon all the time, and went around at night in a cloak like Bonaparte's telling sentries 'I never sleep.'"[37]

By early June, discipline had vanished entirely in Goode's regiment. The men had no uniforms. They robbed hen roosts for miles around and caroused all night in the saloons of Mattoon. Moreover (and this must have been a compelling reason for executive action), they were becoming known as "Governor Yates' hellions." Yates relieved Goode and offered the regimental command to Grant. His acceptance made him colonel of the 21st Illinois Volunteers.

On June 16, Grant, still in civilian clothes, appeared casually before the regimental adjutant and said he "guessed he'd take command."[38]

8

"TO RICHMOND! TO RICHMOND!"

HORACE GREELEY had played a major role in Abraham Lincoln's winning of the presidency. In Greeley's opinion, this gave him the right—even the duty—to tell Lincoln how to handle things. Two days after the election he editorialized: "If the cotton states shall decide that they can do better out of the Union than in it, we insist on letting them go in peace. . . . And whenever a considerable section of our Union shall deliberately resolve to go out, we shall resist all coercive measures designed to keep her in."[1]

This, of course, was advice Lincoln could never accept. Even so, he had to reckon with Greeley's influence. In 1860, the *Tribune's* circulation, more than 200,000, far exceeded that of its nearest rival, the *Herald*. Many readers thought every word in the *Tribune* was written personally by Greeley. Moreover, they tended to accept his pronouncements as gospel and thought of "Uncle Horace" as a friend. It didn't matter that Greeley was an odd eccentric, erratic and unpredictable, and that even his fiercest views were subject to frequent change. They accepted him—along with his fads, ranging from socialism, to vegetarianism, to prohibitionism. Presently, it was said, he was dabbling in spiritualism, attending séances where his recently deceased child "talked" to him by means of spirit "rappings."[2]

Actually, and *not* generally known, *Tribune* policy was increasingly being shaped by managing editor Dana. While Greeley believed in nearly everything, Charles Dana believed in practically nothing, neither God nor man, only in sound journalism. He had started as an idealist, but having seen the venality of public life, he had become a hardened cynic. When attacking corruption, or what he now perceived as southern treason, he could be ruthless. A managing editor, he said, should be "a being to whom the sentiment of remorse is unknown."[3]

Early on, Greeley had believed that non-slaveholders in the South, clearly in the majority, would have the good sense, as well as the votes, to prevent secession. With secession a fact, he had to admit these had been false hopes. Nevertheless, he still believed the "errant sisters" should be allowed to depart in peace.

Not so for Dana. Soon after Fort Sumter was fired upon, the hawkish Dana began calling for action. Although the raw troops gathering near Washington were far from ready to do battle, the powerful *Tribune* began putting on the pressure.

Throughout June of '61, the *Tribune*'s masthead read:

THE NATION'S WAR CRY
Forward to Richmond! Forward to Richmond!
The Rebel Congress must not be allowed to
meet there on the 20th of July
BY THAT DAY THE
PLACE MUST BE HELD BY THE NATIONAL ARMY!

Shrilly, insistently, the paper screamed: "Mr. President, Lieutenant-General Scott, Messieurs Secretaries, when shall the bayonets flash to the 'Forward' of the Centurion of the conquering line? . . . On to Richmond, then is the voice of the people. . . . Again, we repeat, On to Richmond! . . . Let her still sowing of the wind, have a generous harvest of the whirlwind, and let it be *now*. . . . To Richmond! To Richmond!"[4]

The sentiment was Dana's, although the words were written by Fitz Henry Warren, the paper's Washington correspondent. Understandably, however, the nation attributed the lines to Greeley, who'd given at best only tacit approval. With public pressure mounting (and with many 100-day enlistments about to expire), General-in-chief Winfield Scott reluctantly permitted Gen. Irvin McDowell to set his army in motion. McDowell advanced, and on July 20, 1861, he was soundly defeated by Confederate Gen. P. G. T. Beauregard at Bull Run.

The army had been routed, and Washington was in panic. At the War Department, the weary, 75-year-old Winfield Scott spoke in anguish: "I deserve removal because I did not stand up, when my army was not in condition for fighting, and resist it to the last."

Lincoln, hearing the remark, interrupted to say, "Your conversation seems to imply that I forced you to fight this battle."

That undoubtedly was what Scott believed. Out of consideration for Lincoln, however, he replied evasively: "I have never served a President who has been kinder to me than you have been."[5]

At the *Tribune*, Dana lashed out, looking for someone to blame: "We have fought and been beaten. God forgive our rulers that this is so . . . The 'sacred soil' of Virginia is crimson and wet with the blood of thousands of Northern men, needlessly shed. . . . A decimated and indignant people will demand the immediate retirement of the present Cabinet."[6]

Dana's editorial had made the *Tribune*'s position even worse. Rival papers unanimously claimed that the *Tribune*, by prodding the government into precipitous action, had only itself to blame. The *Philadelphia Press*, for example, after saying "our army has been routed and many of its regiments demoralized," went on to describe "a premature advance on the enemy without sufficient force, which may be attributed to the clamors of politicians and newspapers like the *New York Tribune*."[7] The country tended to agree. Anti-*Tribune* sentiment became widespread; cancellations poured in to the subscription office. Greeley tried to counter, but he wrote, rather than justification, what sounded more like a self-pitying alibi.

Were people holding him responsible for the war cry "Forward to Richmond" and the article demanding a change in the cabinet? If so, they were wrong, said Greeley. "The simple fact that not one of these paragraphs was either written or in any wise suggested or prompted by me suffice for that charge." Then, with the tone of a martyr, he added, "If I am needed for a scapegoat for all the military blunders of the past month, so be it. Individuals must die that the nation may live. If I can serve her best in that capacity, I do not shirk from the ordeal."[8] Reading between the lines, it appeared he was accepting some of the blame for himself but was mainly holding others, notably Dana, responsible for the *Tribune*'s fall from grace.

Years later Greeley changed his mind. With the war won, he had no need to disassociate himself and could write: "The war-cry 'Forward to Richmond!' did not originate with me, but it is just what should have been uttered, and the words should have been translated into deeds."[9]

Now, however, shaken and almost deranged, Greeley went to bed with what the doctors called "brain fever." Then he took pen in hand and wrote directly to the president. By any standard it was a weird letter, and in later years he'd say he was "all but insane" when he wrote it:

> Dear Sir: This is my seventh sleepless night—yours, too, doubtless—yet I think I shall not die, because I have no right to die. I must struggle to live, however bitterly. You are now considered a great man, and I am a hopelessly broken one. . . . if our recent disaster is fatal—do not fear to sacrifice yourself to your country. . . . If the Union is irrevocably gone, an armistice for thirty, sixty, ninety, one hundred and twenty days—better still for a year—ought at once to be proposed with a view to a peaceful adjustment. . . . Yours in the depth of bitterness, HORACE GREELEY.[10]

Again it was advice Lincoln could not accept. A lengthy armistice would provide the South the stature it needed for international recognition. That must not happen. The war must be pursued without letup, and Lincoln knew it. No doubt shaking his head, Lincoln pigeonholed Greeley's letter.

In late July, as the nation tried to digest the calamitous news of Bull Run, journalists knew they could no longer sing of war in terms of romance and glory. Not after the *Tribune* reported, "All was lost to that American army, even its honor."[11] Nor after the *Times* painted scenes that ". . . beggar description. The ground was strewn with the dead, the dying, and the wounded—here lay one man with his leg shot off, there another with a wound in his head, another with an arm shot off, and hundreds wounded in nearly all the various parts of the body."[12]

At that point the 21st Illinois Volunteers were still unblooded. Grant's regiment, stationed at Mexico, Missouri, was deployed on a routine mission, guarding the line of the North Missouri Railroad. One day in early August, the regimental chaplain came hurrying to Grant's tent waving a copy of the *Missouri Democrat*. In the paper, said the chaplain, was an announcement that Grant had been recommended for promotion to brigadier general.

Grant said it was "Congressman Washburne's work," and so it was. Elihu Washburne had been impressed by Grant when they met at that Galena town meeting. When promotions were given out in Washington, the influential Washburne had managed to obtain a brigadier's star for Grant. He presumed Grant was deserving; it had also been sound politics to secure a reward for a man from his district.

There it was, exactly in the middle of the list of new brigadiers, the name "Ulysses Grant of Illinois, graduate West Point, Captain in the Mexican War, and promoted for Colonel of Volunteers." Added to the list was a comment: "Most of the appointments are such as the people will approve on the strength of services rendered; others of them, to say the least, have yet to demonstrate their worthiness for so responsible a trust."[13] It was now up to Sam Grant to show whether or not he was one of the "worthy" ones.

Grant's boss, with headquarters in St. Louis, was the arrogant "Pathfinder," John C. Frémont. (When a premature, ill-advised Frémont order freed the slaves and confiscated the property of disloyal Missourians, people had urged Lincoln to get rid of the man.) For now, Frémont assigned Grant to command the District of Southeast Missouri at Ironton. Grant, the new brigadier general, named two men as aides: William S. Hillyer and Clark Lagow. They were poor choices, and this reliance on friends and acquaintances perhaps foreshadowed problems that would bedevil Grant's presidency. He later admitted: "Neither Hillyer nor Lagow proved to have any particular taste or special qualifications for the duties of a soldier."[14] However, he then made an extremely good selection when he named John A. Rawlins, a young Galena lawyer, his chief of staff. Rawlins, he later wrote, "remained with me as long as he lived . . . was an able man, possessed of great firmness. . . . I became very much attached to him."[15]

Grant arrived at Ironton, as did four regiments of infantry. Until then the place had been held by only a weak detachment of short-term volunteers, ready to go home since their term of enlistment had expired. The Union commander on the scene was Col. B. Gratz Brown, a man who would cross Grant's path again. (During the 1872 political campaign, Brown would run for vice president on the opposing ticket.) In his *Memoirs*, Grant described Brown's situation at Ironton, and not without a touch of humor: "Some of his troops were ninety days' men and their time had expired some time before. . . . General Hardee was . . . some twenty-five miles further south, it was said, with five thousand Confederate troops. Under these circumstances Colonel Brown's command was very much demoralized. . . . Brown himself was gladder to see me on that occasion than he ever has been since."[16]

Within days, Grant was replaced at Ironton by Gen. Benjamin Prentiss. Frémont, their mutual boss, had ordered the change after wrongly assuming that Prentiss was senior to Grant. Then, on August 27, the papers printed a copy of War Department General Order Number 62. It gave official confirmation of the recent general officer promotions; it also listed the new generals in proper order of rank. Significantly, Grant stood 10 names above Prentiss on the list; in army parlance he "ranked Prentiss by ten files."

Accordingly, Frémont ordered Grant to reassume command. The headquarters, meanwhile, had moved from Ironton to Cape Girardeau, on the Mississippi, 65 miles to the southeast. The *Missouri Democrat* ran a story headed SALUTE IN HONOR OF GEN. GRANT. It might have been the first time Grant's name appeared in a headline; the story began like this: "At Cape Girardeau—A salute was fired on Saturday morning [August 31] in honor of Gen. Grant, who had taken possession of quarters proffered him in the St. Charles Hotel."[17]

The boom of the salute gun was not the only sound heard at Cape Girardeau. There was also an extremely loud roar from Benjamin Prentiss. As an amateur soldier, Prentiss understood little and cared less about the niceties of seniority. Believing Grant's arrival and assumption of command to be a direct insult, he refused to turn over command. Grant remained firm; under his mild exterior was solid rock. Prentiss then sputtered and did a number of things all at once: he asked for leave, which was refused; he submitted his resignation; then he placed himself under arrest so as to go to St. Louis and confront Frémont.

Earlier that week, as it happened, Horace Greeley's *Tribune* had become annoyed with Prentiss for passing on false information about the "exploits" of his command: "The fine little story of his marching on Greenville, and taking 850 prisoners at Bloomfield, was of course premature, as he had not visited either of those places."[18] It might have been with a sense of pleasure that they then reported what they called "the exciting events of Sunday afternoon": "Gen. Prentiss having applied to Gen. Grant in vain for leave of absence to visit St. Louis and investigate the matter of relative rank, and ascertain from Fremont how the change came to be made, forwarded his resignation."[19]

By this time Grant seems to have adopted a policy of being frank and open with the press. He would take reporters into his confidence, asking them to tell the truth but not reveal information of value to the enemy. Often such a policy can work, as it did for the most part for American leaders during World War II. However, every war has seen unscrupulous reporters who are willing to hurt the national effort, even betray secrets, for the sake of a story. Grant would encounter a few such men.

Military censorship was a problem that would not be solved to everyone's satisfaction during the Civil War, or in any war since. One thing for sure—it did no good to treat the press as enemies. At Fort

Monroe, for example, Maj. Gen. Ben Butler had issued an order circumscribing reporters while complaining that his plans were getting to the enemy.

This brought a scathing rejoinder from Charles Dana: "Whose fault is this? Is the Major General such an old lady that he cannot hold his tongue? . . . Do reporters, eluding the sentinels, attend his councils of war in feminine disguise? . . . If officers, in violation of military law and personal confidence, are weak enough to tattle, shoot them or hang them, we do not care which; but to suppose that paid men, sent expressly to obtain information, will not use it when obtained, is to exhibit a fatuity unworthy of a Major General."[20]

Meanwhile, Dana's man in Washington, Sam Wilkeson, was currying favor with Secretary of War Simon Cameron. The inept Cameron, who would soon be replaced by Edwin M. Stanton, had received a good bit of well-deserved criticism. Shamelessly, Wilkeson wrote a "puff" piece praising Cameron to the skies, then sent a copy of it to the secretary along with a fawning note: "The satisfaction of doing justice to a wronged statesman, is not equalled by the pleasure with which I sincerely pay a tribute of respect to a maligned good man."

The ploy succeeded, and while other Washington reporters were being subjected to tight censorship, Wilkeson could brag to the home office that he had made a "conquest." Soon a telegram went from the War Department to H. E. Thayer, chief censor: "My Dear Sir—It is my wish that you neither suppress nor alter the telegrams of Mr. Samuel Wilkeson. Please send them as they are written and signed by him. Respectfully, Simon Cameron."[21]

The next stop for Grant was the town of Cairo, Illinois, where the Ohio flowed into the Mississippi. It was a place where reporters already had clustered. It had both a hotel and good access to a telegraph office. In the months to come, the label "Cairo war correspondent" would be affixed to someone who reported the war without leaving the comfort of a hotel room.[22]

On September 4, 1861, as he arrived in Cairo, Grant had been a general less than a month. Nevertheless, he was taking over his third command, and for the third time he was inheriting a crucial situation. This time the problem was Kentucky.

In September 1861, Kentucky was still hoping (rather naively) to sit out the war as a neutral. So far both the Union and the Confederacy had respected that neutrality, lest any overt action cause the state to jump to the other side.

When Grant had been at Cairo but a single day, a scout reported that a Confederate force had moved into Kentucky. Already two towns had been occupied. Next stop seemed to be Paducah, 45 miles up the Ohio from Cairo.[23]

The Union had many commanders who, in a similar situation, would have debated, would have queried higher headquarters, would have hemmed and hawed until it was too late to do anything. Grant was not one of them. By nightfall two regiments were loaded aboard transports on the Cairo waterfront. By the next morning, Paducah was occupied. Reporters made much of the move and of the evident belief in Paducah that Confederates, rather than Federals, were due to arrive: "Cairo—Sept. 6—This morning at eleven o'clock, General Grant . . . took possession of Paducah, Ky. He found secession flags flying in different parts of the city, in expectation of greeting the arrival of a southern army, which was reported 3,000 strong, sixteen miles distant. The loyal citizens tore down the secession flags on the arrival of our troops."[24]

The occupation had gone peacefully. Wanting it to remain that way, Grant issued a proclamation to the citizens of Paducah:

> I have come among you, not as an enemy, but as your fellow citizen. Not to maltreat or annoy you, but to respect and enforce the rights of all loyal citizens.
>
> An enemy in rebellion against our common government has taken possession of and planted its guns on the soil of Kentucky and fired upon you. . . . I am here to defend you against this enemy, to assist the authority and sovereignty of your government.
>
> I have nothing to do with opinions, and shall deal only with armed rebellion and its aiders and abettors. You can pursue your normal avocations without fear. The strong arm of the Government is here to protect its friends, and punish its enemies. Whenever it is manifest that you are able to defend yourselves and maintain the authority of the Government and protect the rights of loyal citizens, I shall withdraw the forces under my command.
>
> N.S. Grant [sic], Brigadier
> General, Commanding[25]

The proclamation demonstrates Grant's growing self-confidence. He was no longer the beaten-down farmer or the melancholy leather goods clerk. Back in his true element, the military, he was acting with calm assurance, issuing a statement both politically and psychologically sound. Shrewdly, he referred to "our" government and to the citizens of Paducah as friends; at the same time he subtly flexed the "strong arm of the Government" and let enemies draw their own conclusions.

Along with other papers, the *New York Tribune* printed the proclamation in full. For the first time, Grant had come to the attention of both Greeley and Dana. He was still, however, decidedly unknown. The erroneous initials "N.S.," which had been a typo in the *Missouri Democrat*, had run the same way in the *Tribune*. Evidently no one in New York knew the difference.

First comments about the move were somewhat guarded. The papers said only: "The action of Gen. Grant in taking Paducah is a matter of vital importance."[26] By the next day, however, it was apparent that all had gone well and that it was safe to say so. The *Chicago Tribune* spoke approvingly of Grant's proclamation; it also liked the way he had sent for leading Paducah citizens (including the mayor) and enlisted their help in maintaining order.

Also praised was Grant's initiative: "The credit of this expedition is due to Gen. Grant, who took the responsibility to make it without waiting for orders from headquarters. It was made on information that the rebels were moving on Paducah; it has been entirely successful and is approved by Gen. Fremont."[27]

Before occupying Paducah, Grant had notified Frémont of his intentions, had also sent a message to the Kentucky legislature informing them that Confederate forces had invaded their state. Frémont had approved the seizure of Paducah, but he resented his subordinate's having communicated directly with a state government. Of more importance to Grant, however, was the vote of approval from Abraham Lincoln. Kentucky Governor Beriah Magoffin (supposedly neutral but definitely leaning southward) had written Lincoln demanding that Federal troops be withdrawn immediately. Lincoln replied with what the papers called a "pointed negative": "I most cordially sympathize with your Excellency in the wish to preserve the peace of my own native state, Kentucky; but it is with regret I search, and cannot find, in your not very short letter, any declaration or intimation that you entertain any desire for the preservation of the Union. Your obedient servant, A. Lincoln."[28]

Frémont sent Gen. C. F. Smith to take over at Paducah, thus removing the city from Grant's area of responsibility. Grant returned to Cairo, looked over the situation, and decided his main job was training the troops under his command.

It was a staggering task: changing a group of citizen soldiers into an army ready to do battle. Training of officers would have first priority. It was not a mere question of teaching military tactics. Officers first had to learn the very essence of a military commission: the sense of duty, honor, and personal conduct that would be expected. With General Order Number 5, issued upon his return to Cairo, Grant began to shake things up:

> It is with regret the General commanding sees and learns that the closest intimacy exists between many of the officers and soldiers of his command; that they visit together the lowest drinking and dancing saloons; quarrel, curse, drink and carouse on the lowest level of equality. . . . Discipline cannot be maintained when the officers do not command respect, and such conduct cannot insure it.
>
> In this military district discipline shall be maintained, even if it is at the expense of the commission of all officers who stand in the way of attaining that end.[29]

One of the Cairo reporters said that Grant's order was "having a capital effect upon the morale of the camps at and about Cairo. . . . Some of the volunteers, and especially the shoulder strap gentry, may chafe under it, but the good sense of the Army will sustain Commanding Generals in enforcing all wholesome discipline."[30]

Literally everything needed to be done at Cairo, and Grant got busy. He set troops to work constructing better living quarters. He secured a competent surgeon and nurses, thereby improving the medical situation. He had new fortifications built and outposts established. Using navy gunboats, he halted the shipments of contraband that had been moving downriver to the Confederates.

Grant's fellow townsman from Galena, Lt. Col. A. C. Chetlain, wrote Congressman Washburne: "Grant is doing wonders in and about Cairo in his quiet way."[31] Civilians were turning into soldiers, and by now were even staging parades and reviews. Early in the war, many officers used reviews as opportunities for speechmaking. Not Grant. He watched the formations, sat his horse quietly, said nothing except to thank the colonel in charge when a review was over.[32]

On the whole, it was a routine, uninspiring period. The special correspondents, who referred to themselves simply as "specials," reported, "All quiet at Paducah. It is duller than ever at Cairo."[33]

Meanwhile, free copies of Mr. Greeley's *Tribune* came to camp. It was a clever public relations gesture, and the *Tribune* man on the scene duly reported it in self-congratulatory fashion: "A liberal supply of THE TRIBUNE arrived on Wednesday, calling forth the gratitude of both officers and soldiers."[34]

In the absence of action, rumors begn to fill the void. This was not surprising; rumors have found fertile ground in every army throughout history. The *New York Tribune* remarked: "We now begin to understand why the scriptures mention 'rumors of wars,' as of such consequence, for these constant reports, dying away only to be revived, vex the brave and frighten the timid."[35]

In the absence of war news, the major story of the day was the status of General Frémont, who seemed to provoke continual controversy. The newspapers took sides, the politicians took sides, and so did most of the men in uniform. It was a wise officer who remained neutral. This was almost axiomatic for Grant, who believed a regular army man should not become involved in politics. Many men never recognized this, and many careers ended abruptly as a result.

For the moment, the war seemed to be on hold. Grant would later write: "From the occupation of Paducah, up to the early part of November, nothing important occurred with the troops under my command."[36]

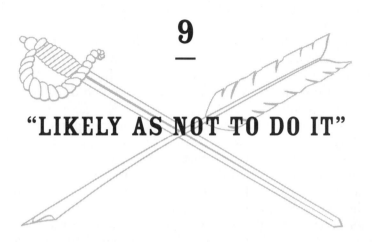

9

"LIKELY AS NOT TO DO IT"

THE TROUBLES in November might in a way be traced to Jeff Thompson, a picturesque, aggressive leader of some 3,000 Missouri state guards. Using his loosely organized force as guerrilla irregulars, Thompson had a wonderful knack for stirring things up. A story in the *New York Tribune*, probably written by Dana's man Albert Richardson, said Thompson, after burning some Missouri bridges, had managed to evade his pursuers.[1] The follow-up story then poked fun at Thompson, saying that he had been "routed in no time" but had saved "nearly his whole force by . . . alacrity and fleetness in flight."[2] Rather than joshing Thompson, Richardson might better have noted that "hit and run" raids were *proper* tactics for a guerrilla leader.

At the beginning of November, the irregulars were reported in the vicinity of Greenville, Missouri. Grant was told to send someone to "help drive Thompson into Arkansas." In compliance, he dispatched Col. Richard Oglesby with four Illinois regiments. Grant even amplified the order a bit. Whereas St. Louis had wanted Thompson "pursued," Grant told Oglesby he wanted Thompson "destroyed."[3]

"The object in taking so small a force," wrote the *Tribune* man accompanying Oglesby, "is that Jeff may not be frightened, and that he may be induced to meet us." The story went on to say that the object of the expedition was to clear out southeastern Missouri, thus establishing a new base of operations against Columbus and Memphis. This was an exaggeration; actually, the purpose was much more limited. The story gave Thompson's strength as some 5,000 to 6,000 men, also an exaggeration.[4]

Soon another order told Grant to conduct a demonstration to his south. Confederate Gen. Leonidas Polk, at Columbus, Kentucky, was said to be sending troops into southwestern Missouri. A "demonstration" would presumably worry Polk and make him think twice before dispatching any more troops.[5]

On November 6, Grant loaded some men on transports, arranged for the gunboats *Tyler* and *Lexington* to act as convoys, and started down the Mississippi. On board the transports were five regiments of infantry and two companies of cavalry, some 3,100 men in all. Early next morning, Grant received a message saying that Confederates from Columbus were streaming across the river into Missouri, apparently moving to intercept Oglesby. It was a logical move for the Southerners, and it increased Grant's desire to hold Polk's main body at Columbus.[6]

Another commander might have fired a few shots and left. In military language, a "demonstration" is an ostentatious movement to attract attention but that avoids serious commitment. Technically, that much had already been accomplished. One historian called this "an hour heavy with destiny," since Grant's decision "would show the kind of general that he was."[7] The decision was to attack.

Grant knew there was a small Confederate camp at Belmont, immediately opposite Columbus. He resolved to land his men on the western shore, break up the camp, then return. His troops were organized into two brigades. One was commanded by Gen. John A. McClernand, a quarrelsome, overly ambitious Illinois politician; the other by Col. Henry Dougherty. Soon the men in blue began to advance and to drive in the Confederate pickets.[8]

Leonidas Polk watched the action from an observation post on the bluffs at Columbus. To oppose McClernand's lead troops, he hurried Gen. Gideon Pillow across the river with four regiments. Nevertheless, as Grant wrote in his official report, the Confederates were "driven foot by foot, from tree to tree, back to their original encampment." Suddenly all resistance ceased. Southerners ran to the river and huddled near the banks for protection. With that, the green Northerners began to celebrate, breaking ranks, cheering, looking for souvenirs in the abandoned camp. Grant knew the battle was far from over. He galloped from point to point, trying to restore order.

From Columbus, artillery batteries began lobbing shells into the Belmont camp. Polk poured more troops across the river, and this time

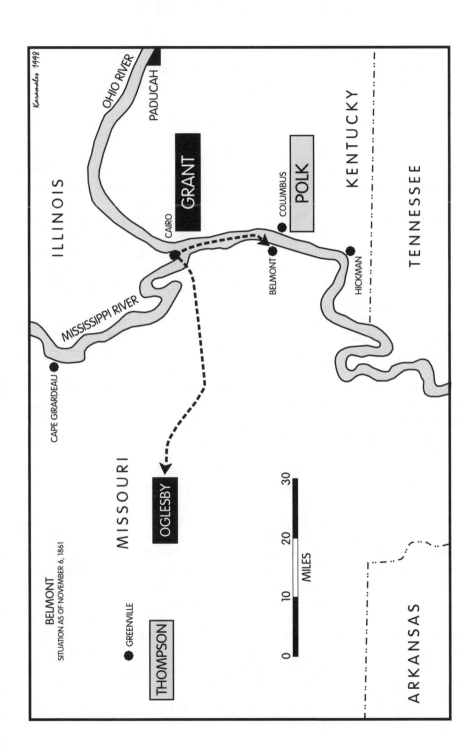

BELMONT
SITUATION AS OF NOVEMBER 6, 1861

81

steamboats put them ashore *behind* Grant, thus cutting off the Union men from their boats. Oddly enough, the first man to discover the encircling movement and report it to Grant was the medical officer, Dr. John Brinton.[9]

All at once jubilation gave way to panic. Some of the officers said they were surrounded—there was nothing to do but surrender! Grant calmly remarked that they had cut their way in; they could just as easily cut their way out. More hard fighting remained, and at one point Grant himself was almost killed or captured. However, the troops managed to force their way back to the transports and climb aboard.

As the last boat cut its lines and backed off, Grant was the only Union man left between the enemy and the transports. The boat captain saw him, stopped the engines, and had a plank run out from the deck to the shore. With a neat bit of horsemanship, Grant slid his horse down the bank, then trotted aboard along the single plank. He was the last Union soldier to leave Belmont.[10]

In some units, the withdrawal to the boats had resembled a rout. Despite this, morale was high. Many laughed and joked as they came aboard. They had become "veterans," had been in a real battle, and somehow felt rather pleased with themselves.[11]

Compared to some of the mighty battles that took place later, Belmont was rather insignificant. Today its main interest comes from having been Grant's first action as an independent commander. In November 1861, however, Belmont was major news. Then, as now, it was hard to evaluate.

A Union solder, writing in his diary, came as close as anyone to estimating the numbers involved: "In this fight at Belmont 1,200 of our men at first completely whipped 2,400 of theirs . . . then the whole of ours, 2,600 ran like the devil before and through 5,600 of theirs. These are the true figures."[12] Personally, Grant always considered the Belmont expedition a success. He wrote in his *Memoirs* that the "objects for which the battle of Belmont was fought were fully accomplished."[13]

In the North, editors were waiting for news of the battle. Newspaper historian J. Cutler Andrews said the reporting was "confused" since "very few Northern reporters actually saw the fight and those who did were comparatively inexperienced journalists."[14] (It may well be, in fact, that *no* reporters accompanied the expedition and that all reports were based on interviews secured after the expedition's return to Cairo.)

The first story in Greeley's *Tribune* said: "We have a meager account of an expedition to Belmont, Mo., under Generals Grant and McClernand with 3,500 men. They routed about 7,000 men after a fight of several hours, their baggage, horses, mules, and cannon taken, with a loss on our side of from 300 to 350 men. The Rebels were finally reenforced from Columbus, and the force from Cairo compelled to retire. No official report of this engagement has been received at the War Office."[15]

Soon, however, Grant's official report *was* received and made public. It reflected optimism, haste, and a desire to put his best foot forward:

> Cairo, Nov. 8—Our loss yesterday was about 250 killed, wounded and missing—about one half killed or mortally wounded.
>
> The victory was complete. We carried from the field all the rebel artillery, but had to leave . . . several guns for want of teams.
>
> One hundred and thirty prisoners were brought to this place. Gen. McClernand and myself had a horse each shot from under us.
>
> Prisoners taken report that a large force were prepared to start to join Price. This move will no doubt prevent it.[16]

Grant received no reaction from Frémont; by this time the "Pathfinder" was no longer on hand. For some time, stories had appeared speculating that Frémont was on his way out. Then, after weeks of suspense, not only for Frémont but also for his supporters such as the *New York Tribune*, the other shoe dropped. In early November it was announced that Frémont had been relieved. His replacement, and therefore Grant's new boss, would be the careful, scholarly, and somewhat pompous Gen. Henry Wager Halleck, a man the regular army called "Old Brains."[17]

Green reporters, with limited information, couldn't decide if Belmont had been a victory or a defeat. Consequently it was reported both ways. The *New York Herald* said that Grant had won a victory "as clear as ever warriors gained." On the same day, the *Missouri Republican* was saying flatly that "we have met the enemy and they are not ours."[18]

For sheer confusion, however, the *Weekly Missouri Democrat* won the prize. A dispatch of November 8 spoke of "the gloom which saddened all our hearts at the news of our defeat at Columbus." However, the very next issue of the same paper, in a story by a different correspondent, said that Belmont was "in every sense, a brilliant engagement and a fruitful victory."[19]

Accounts had been based on fragmentary information and hearsay; confusion was understandable. Grant understood this and accepted it.

He also knew that he himself was fair game for press criticism. That, too, could be accepted. There were, however, two people he needed to reassure. He sat down and wrote an account of the battle, essentially the same letter, to his wife and to his father. Julia read the letter and cherished it. Jesse, however, somewhat true to form, brought the letter to the local newspaper office. On November 11, a story in the *Cincinnati Gazette* began:

> From a private letter of Gen. Grant to his father, hurriedly written on the night of the 8th, we are permitted to extract the following:

> Day before yesterday I left Cairo with about 3,000 men in five steamers convoyed by two gunboats, and proceeded down the river. . . . The next morning the boats were dropped down just out of range of the enemy's batteries, and the troops debarked. During this operation our gunboats exercised the rebels by throwing shells into their camps and batteries.
> When all ready we proceeded about one mile toward Belmont, opposite Columbus, when I formed the troops into line, and ordered two companies from each regiment to deploy as skirmishers, and push on through the woods. . . . They had gone but a little way when they were fired upon, and the ball may be said to have fairly opened.
> The whole command, with the exception of a small reserve, was then deployed in like manner and ordered forward. The order was obeyed with great alacrity, the men all showing great courage. . . . I feel truly proud to command such men. . . . Our men charged through, making the victory complete, giving us possession of their camp and garrison equipage, artillery, and everything else. . . . We burned everything possible and started back, having accomplished all that we went for, and even more. . . . The object of the expedition was to prevent the enemy from sending a force into Missouri to cut off troops I had sent there for a special purpose, and to prevent reinforcing Price. . . . We found the Confederates well armed and brave. . . . There was no hasty retreating or running away. Taking into account the object of the expedition, the victory was most complete. It has given us confidence in the officers and men of this command.[20]

In recent years, Julia and Jesse had seen Ulysses fail again and again. Now he wanted them to see him in a new light. They did. Julia's faith had never wavered. As for Jesse, there is something poignant in the thought of his rushing to publicize the letter. After years of disappointment, he now felt validated. Even the Georgetown scoffers would have to admit he'd been right all along—Ulysses was truly "remarkable."

Nevertheless, the Belmont controversy continued to rage, particularly in Chicago. The *Chicago Tribune*, which later became a staunch supporter of Grant (it once warned Bennett's *New York Herald* to "keep its copperhead slime off our Illinois General"), was at this stage highly critical.[21] On November 9, editor Charles H. Ray roared: "The disastrous termination of the Cairo expedition to Columbus is another severe lesson on the management of this contest with the rebels. Our troops have suffered a bad defeat. Hundreds of men have been killed and wounded, and other hundreds taken prisoner. The loss of the enemy is far lighter than ours. The object of the expedition was not attained."[22]

Within days, Ray was forced to change his tune. His Cairo correspondent wrote that Belmont, rather than a defeat, was a "decided and valuable victory." By November 14, the paper was printing Grant's official report and correctly stating what his objectives had been. Two days later there was also a letter to the editor from an outraged reader, claiming: "We accomplished everything we went for. Belmont is taken, is in ashes, and is now abandoned by the enemy." Adding to Ray's embarrassment was a dispatch from Cairo to the *Louisville Journal* that said Ray's editorials showed "a determination to embarrass and disparage our army."[23]

Since the initial reports in the *Chicago Tribune* were so critical, Grant might have been thankful for one odd bit of misreporting. The first dispatch named each of the Union regimental commanders at Belmont. It also spoke of the men being "formed in line of battle, with Gen. McClernand in command of the Cairo troops." Grant's name was not even mentioned![24]

Back in New York, Greeley and Dana were similarly confused about the command relationship at Belmont. First reports, instead of naming Grant as overall commander, gave the impression that he and McClernand had been equal.[25] The *New York Tribune* was also having difficulty with other details. On November 11, it reported—"though not on the most trustworthy authority,"—that "Gen. Ogilvie [*sic*—Colonel Oglesby] had met Jeff Thompson, killing 300 and losing 50."[26] The actual results of Oglesby's venture were given the next day in the

Missouri Republican. The headline said it all: RETURN OF OGLESBY'S EXPEDITION—THEY ENCOUNTERED NO ENEMY.[27]

The Belmont controversy would eventually reach the floor of Congress. The *Missouri Democrat*, under the heading "Congressional Proceedings," quoted the following exchange:

> MR. FOUKE [D-ILL.]—I was not in the hall when the gentleman from Kansas commenced his speech; but from what I have been told, I wish to ask the gentleman if he stated that the battle of Belmont was a defeat to our army?
>
> MR. CONWAY [R-KANS.]—I did.
>
> MR. FOUKE—Upon what authority did you make it?
>
> MR. CONWAY—On the authority of the newspapers.
>
> MR. FOUKE—It is proper that I should set this matter right. It is but justice to those brave soldiers who fell upon that noble field, which was a victory, that this falsehood should be at once nailed to the counter.[28]

Inevitably, some of the Belmont stories criticized the way Grant and McClernand had performed. Once again Grant sat down to write his father. Theirs was a special relationship, one in which a dutiful son continually sought the approbation of a severe and watchful father. The dismal Hardscrabble years would always cast their shadow, and although he was now doing well, the son still needed to reassure a father who might have doubts. "All who were on the battlefield," he wrote, "know where General McClernand and myself were, and there is no need of resort to the popular press for our vindication."[29]

Ulysses Grant, or at least his name, was now recognized nationally. However, when a sketch in *Leslie's Illustrated* pictured a mounted Grant waving his saber and leading the charge at Belmont, his face was turned away, presumably because the staff artist had no earthly idea of Grant's appearance![30]

Back at Cairo, Grant resumed the training program. It was well he did, for as noted in Greeley's *Tribune*, Henry Halleck, a stickler for military efficiency, arrived in St. Louis on November 18 to assume command of the Department of the West.[31]

By this time, unfortunately, Grant had to deal not only with inefficiency but also with fraud. A ring of unscrupulous civilian contractors and speculators had risen around St. Louis. Using various pressure tactics, they had managed to secure a near monopoly of army business.

Grant simply refused to sign any voucher he considered exorbitant. (The dishonesty was not limited to civilians. Grant also got rid of Capt. R. B. Hatch, an unscrupulous quartermaster. Hatch, in turn, spread rumors to the effect that Grant was drinking again, and to excess. Ample evidence indicates that this was simply not true.)[32]

In time, Grant's firm stand brought him into conflict with several disgruntled businessmen, among them Leonard Swett, a lawyer known to be friendly with Abraham Lincoln. Swett, said Grant, "wrote me one or more letters on the subject, rather offensive in their manner."[33] Swett next threatened to go to Lincoln, whereupon Grant told him to do so if he wished. Meanwhile, Grant would keep buying goods at what he considered fair prices, and if worse came to worst, he might even seize the Illinois Central Railroad (in which Swett had an interest) in order to move those goods. Grant told Swett to leave the Cairo District, even threatening to lock him up or shoot him if he did not. Years later, Swett wrote that he *did* go to Lincoln, who told him he'd better be careful. If this man Grant threatened to shoot him, he was as likely as not to do it.[34]

"Specials" employed by Greeley and Dana were expected to earn their pay not only by digging up stories but also by making them lively. Albert Richardson, their man at Grant's Cairo headquarters, was happy to oblige. And if he was ever stuck for material, he could always rely on Jeff Thompson and his irregulars for a good story. On one occasion he wrote that Thompson had stopped a steamboat near Commerce, Missouri, then:

> . . . took off a few bushels of beans and a keg of whiskey. He made the boat furnish dinner for himself and officers, then she was permitted to proceed . . . to St. Louis.
> Upon hearing the news, General Grant starts off with a regiment or so after Jeff, but of course without taking him. . . . He is not likely to molest us again for some time, and, as Missouri is ruined, it will be well enough to let him subsist upon the people, even though a majority are Union men, for they are such miserable specimens of men that they will do nothing to defend themselves.[35]

If all else failed, a shrewd reporter might just submit something catering to Greeley's prejudices. One such item, for example, soundly criticized most of the officers at Cairo for using profanity. Although this might have found favor with the proper Greeley, one can imagine the reaction from Dana, who could swear round oaths with the best of them.[36]

By the same token, *Tribune* specials sometimes filled space by quoting Scripture. At the end of 1861, as Grant canceled furloughs, bought horses and mules, and built up his supply of ammunition, Richardson used biblical prose to predict action: "The coming events cast their shadows before."[37] This couldn't be carried too far, of course. On one occasion a reporter began a battle dispatch: "To God Almighty be the glory! Mine eyes have seen the work of the Lord and the cause of the righteous hath triumphed." Dana replied with a single sentence: "Hereafter, in sending your reports, please specify the number of the hymn and save telegraph expenses."[38]

The *New York Tribune*, carrying on Greeley's tradition and supplemented by Dana's firm editorial hand, continued to tread on toes without regard to hurt feelings. No one was immune, neither senior officers, members of the administration, nor the president himself. In late December, for example, "Old Brains" Henry Halleck was criticized for straitlaced administrative procedures and what the *Tribune* called "ill-advised orders."[39]

Grant, on the other hand, by this time seemed to be doing rather well with the press. An editorial in the *Louisville Journal* referred to him as "the able and accomplished officer in command at Cairo." Mentioning a rumor that he was to be removed, the editor said if that was the case, "we take it for granted that General Halleck has . . . a more important post for General Grant to fill . . . for certain it is that General Grant, to say nothing of the vigor and success with which he administered the affairs of his division, is the especial dread of the rebels at Columbus and thereabouts, who openly confess their high sense of his ability and prowess. We ourselves have seen this confession in the rebel journals."[40]

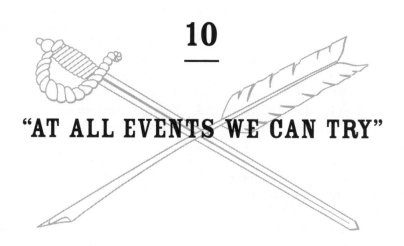

10

"AT ALL EVENTS WE CAN TRY"

EARLY IN 1862, Abraham Lincoln determined to replace Simon Cameron, his inept Secretary of War. Some said Cameron was corrupt, but that might not have been true. Charles Dana, for example, knew him and spoke well of him. Cameron was, however, a complete failure as a manager. He signed bad contracts, made bad appointments, wasted time for himself and others. Although he did the best he could, working in a difficult period at a job beyond his capabilities, the War Department under Cameron had degenerated into an inefficient, chaotic mess.[1]

Cameron was named ambassador to Russia, permitting him to exit with dignity. His surprising replacement was a hard-nosed attorney, Edwin M. Stanton, a lifelong Democrat who in the past had been no friend to Lincoln. Greeley's Washington correspondent called the appointment a "bombshell."[2] In the end, however, it turned out to be one of Lincoln's shrewdest moves; Stanton proved to be the right man for the job. Moreover, the choice was well received by the public, especially after a Dana editorial credited Stanton with "the highest qualities of talent, courage, and uncompromising patriotism."[3]

Dana sent a copy of the editorial to Stanton, who welcomed the personal praise and doubly welcomed support from the powerful *Tribune*. On February 24, hoping to solidify that support, Stanton wrote to Dana, and after thanking him for the editorial, said: "Every man who wishes the country to pass through this trying hour should stand on watch, and aid me. . . . I know the task that is before us—I say *us*, because the Tribune has its mission as plainly as I have mine, and they tend to the same end. . . . But patience for a short while only is all I ask, if you and others like you will rally around me."[4]

Those words resonated with Dana, who was all for a vigorous prosecution of the war. Greeley, more of a pacifist, was still hoping for an early negotiated peace. Meanwhile, *Tribune* circulation continued to fall as its coverage of the war was overshadowed by the colorful, aggressive *New York Herald*. A gloating James Gordon Bennett "bemoaned" the *Tribune's* financial problems and with a mock sigh, wrote: "Alas for Greeley!" Since the *Herald* had not had Greeley's "sad trials in pecuniary matters," Bennett facetiously offered to "give him $1,000 to send him south, if he will only go."[5]

On February 1, Stanton again wrote Dana. He mentioned the many problems he was encountering, including pressure from Congress over appointments. It was, he said, "discouraging in the extreme—it often tempts me to quit the helm in despair." He concluded, however, with words calculated to woo even the cynical Dana: "The only consolation is the confidence and support of good and patriotic men; to their aid I look for strength."[6]

It was the beginning of a long Stanton/Dana relationship, one that served the country well. Each man was a capable, unsentimental pragmatist, demanding of subordinates but equally demanding of himself. Their relative positions, and strong personalities, perhaps kept the relationship from ever ripening into warm friendship. Always, however, there would be sincere mutual respect. Dana would call Stanton "intense," saying that he "was entirely absorbed in his duties, and his energy in prosecuting them was something almost superhuman." The same might have been said of Dana.[7]

For several weeks, Grant, at Cairo, had been pondering the strategic advantages to be gained from controlling the major rivers. Specifically, he had been eyeing two vital waterways to his east and the Confederate forts that guarded them: Fort Henry on the Tennessee River and Fort Donelson on the Cumberland.

Grant believed the forts could be taken. He was supported in this by Commodore Andrew Foote, the crusty and able commander of the Cairo gunboats. Grant went to St. Louis and proposed the move to Halleck. Later he recalled their meeting: "I was received with so little cordiality that I perhaps stated the object of my visit with less clearness than I might have done, and I had not uttered many sentences before I was cut short as if my plan was preposterous. I returned to Cairo very much crestfallen."[8]

Grant and Foote, however, were persistent. On January 28, in separate messages, both men wired Halleck for permission to move against Fort Henry. Halleck gave his consent, and Grant's restless headquarters was jubilant. Excited officers shouted, cheered, and stomped their feet. Grant looked on amused, then suggested they really didn't need to make so much noise that General Polk would hear it down at Columbus.[9]

On February 2 and 3, gunboats and transports got under way. On board the transports were some 23 regiments, around 17,000 men.[10] Grant had done his best to keep the move a secret, and in most cases he had succeeded. Quite a few of the reporters were left behind initially, and "forced to display some agility in overtaking his advance."[11]

A *Chicago Tribune* reporter, however, perhaps with the help of inside information, sensed what was happening. Even before the boats left Cairo, he filed a story:

> Sunday night, Feb. 2
>
> The grand expedition up the Tennessee and Cumberland rivers is about to start. The last of it moves in the morning. It will attack Forts Henry and Donelson. The force to be engaged is fully 22,000 men.
>
> The military authorities will not permit any dispatches relating to the expedition to be sent.[12]

The last sentence is a puzzler. Obviously this was a dispatch "related to the expedition." And if no such messages were to be sent, how had the reporter managed to do so? According to one story, so improbable it might well be true, a Cairo censor thought the story was false. This man, new on the job, operated under the theory that all true information helpful to the enemy should be blue-penciled but that any false information, which might confuse one's opponent, should be passed.[13]

By February 6, Grant was in position near Fort Henry. "About ten o'clock in the morning," reported the *Chicago Tribune*, "the land forces on both sides of the river began to move—McClernand's division on the east side of the river, and those under Generals Smith and Wallace on the west side."[14] The dispatch, while naming three subordinate commanders, failed to mention Grant. The omission was probably intentional. Several reporters, one of whom was annoyed with Grant because he had been excluded from Grant's headquarters, had agreed to omit his name from their accounts.[15]

Foote's gunboats steamed within range and began to exchange shots with Fort Henry. The fort, poorly constructed and situated too close to the swollen Tennessee, was nearly indefensible; some of it was already underwater. Even before the firing began, Confederate Gen. Lloyd Tilghman had evacuated most of his forces and sent them streaming eastward toward Fort Donelson.

As the Union ground forces were moving into position for an assault, they suddenly heard cheering from the gunboats. Fort Henry had raised a white flag; Tilghman was en route to Foote's flagship to surrender. A rather breathless account of the bombardment was written from one of the gunboats. The only reference to Grant was rather disparaging:

> It was magnificent: the whistling shot . . . and the cheering of our men as our shots took evident effect. . . . At precisely 1:40, the enemy struck his flag, and such cheering, such wild excitement as seized the throats and arms and caps of the 400 or 500 sailors of the gunboats. Well, imagine it. . . .
>
> The land forces under command of General Grant did not arrive at the fort till after the rebels had surrendered, and their army escaped.[16]

Following the surrender, several of the reporters tried to interview the defeated General Tilghman. His response showed a somewhat remarkable naïveté about the ways of the press. "Sir," the general was quoted as saying, "I do not desire to have my name appear in this matter in any newspaper connection whatever. If General Grant sees fit to use it in his official dispatches, I have no objection; but, Sir, I do not wish to appear at all in this matter in any newspaper report."[17]

The reporters nodded sympathetically, then made sure to get the correct spelling of the general's name and something of his background. The *New York Tribune*, among others, ran the Tilghman interview in full.[18] As it turned out, the unfortunate Tilghman had little opportunity to learn either the practical or the cynical side of war correspondence. He later returned south in a prisoner exchange, resumed fighting for the Confederacy, and was killed a year later at Baker's Creek, Mississippi.

One of Grant's first acts was to send a report to Halleck in St. Louis: "Fort Henry is ours. The gunboats silenced the batteries before the investment was completed. I think the garrison must have commenced the retreat last night." He then announced, almost as an afterthought, one of the most momentous decisions of the entire war: "I shall take and destroy Fort Donelson on the 8th . . ."[19]

Grant's cavalier thinking about Fort Donelson was also shown in a conversation with Dana's man, Albert Richardson, who was on the point of leaving with the story of Fort Henry's capture. Grant advised him to wait a day or so, saying, "I am going over to attack Fort Donelson tomorrow." Richardson asked if he knew how strong it was, and Grant replied: "Not exactly, but I think we can take it; at all events we can try."[20]

As news of Fort Henry's capture reached New York, the papers took out their largest type. A *Herald* headline hailed THE IMPORTANT VICTORY IN TENNESSEE. Subheads said: "Important Naval Victory—Surrender of Fort Henry to the Union Gunboats—The Union Troops Not in the Fight."[21]

In reporting the victory, the *Chicago Tribune* gave credit to Foote ("it was wholly a navy victory") and to Halleck (". . . planned the whole thing, and although he was in St. Louis, he had a big finger in the pie"). As for Grant, it merely implied that he had failed to get in the rear of the camp in time to cut it off.[22]

Among the generals, the *Chicago Tribune* seemed to favor McClernand, a prominent Illinois politician. When the column on the east bank had been "advancing on the fort," it had been "commanded by McClernand"; when it had failed to seal the escape route, it became "Grant's."

In a strange reversal, some army officers in Washington were in turn criticizing Foote—for not having waited for the land forces to get into position.[23] The situation was a bit awkward, but fortunately Grant and Foote, two professionals, understood and liked one another. With no interservice rivalry on the part of the principals, the situation passed quietly.[24]

Grant was overly optimistic in predicting the fall of Fort Donelson by February 8. For one thing, Fort Henry itself had to be straightened up and its stores and possessions itemized. (One report said the property captured at Fort Henry was "valued at upwards of $200,000.")[25] Also, the Union gunboats, a big factor in Grant's plans, were either off on another mission or under repair back at Cairo. In any event, it was February 12 before Grant's army began slogging the 12 muddy miles to Fort Donelson.

General Halleck promptly sent an official report of Fort Henry's capture. Although some of the newspapers had slighted Grant, and others had made it sound as if he, Smith, and McClernand had been equally in charge, the official telegram of congratulations quite properly mentioned only Grant and Foote. A reply to Halleck from Gen. George McClellan, commander-in-chief of the Union armies, said: "Thank Gen. Grant, Flag Officer Foote, and their commands for me."[26]

On the evening of February 12, the first elements of Grant's forces arrived in Fort Donelson's vicinity. The two lead divisions were deployed in a rough semicircle, pinning the Confederates against the Cumberland River. Smith's division was on the left; McClernand's on the right. By the next morning, the investiture was complete, even though the Confederate force, approximately 18,000, was temporarily larger than the Union group opposing it.

Roughly, Grant's plan was to bottle up Donelson from the land side, then let Foote's gunboats pound the fort into submission. On February 13, a limited attack was made against the Confederate left flank. Grant's major effort, however, would be postponed until the gunboats arrived.

By this time it was evident that Fort Donelson was far sturdier than Fort Henry. Donelson had been well constructed and well sited—overlooking the Cumberland River near the town of Dover. Inside the fort was much accurate artillery. Outside the fort proper, the treacherous sharpened stakes known as abatis reinforced sturdy earthen breastworks.

During the overland march, the weather had been unseasonably mild, and many of Grant's men had casually discarded blankets and overcoats as too cumbersome to carry. That night they regretted it as a freezing rain turned to sleet and snow. Men shivered miserably in the frosty dawn as Foote's gunboats glided down the Cumberland and started shelling. Confederate gunners answered shot for shot. Soon the boats began to falter under Southern marksmanship. The flagship *St. Louis*, for example, suffered 59 hits. The pilothouse was demolished, the pilot was killed, and Foote himself was wounded.

The crippled gunboats stopped engines and drifted downstream, out of range. Inside the fort, Confederates cheered lustily. It was now clear that the tactics that had beaten Fort Henry were never going to overcome Fort Donelson.[27]

That evening, however, despite having defeated the gunboats, the Donelson commanders were pessimistic. Generals John Floyd, Gideon Pillow, and Simon Bolivar Buckner all saw the situation as Grant saw it—Donelson was a potential trap, and their army would be lost if it stayed there. They determined to break out. The plan was for Buckner, with a reduced force, to hold the Confederate right and center. Then, on the left, Pillow would attack and open the road leading south. Once the penetration was made, Buckner would act as flank guard while the withdrawal proceeded.

Initially, Pillow's attack met with stunning success. The assault was directed against McClernand's division, which was driven back in dis-

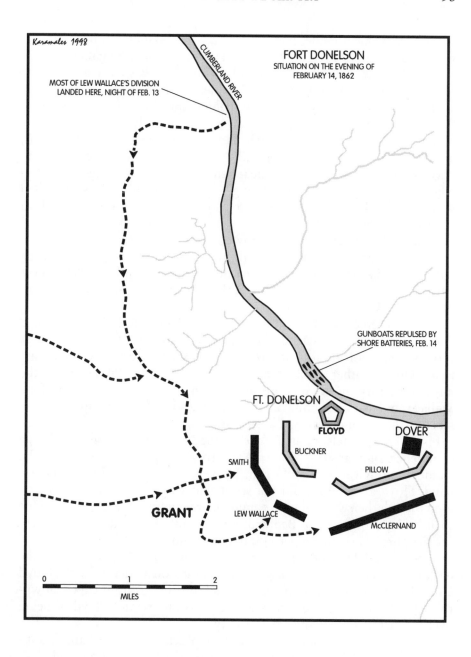

Karamales 1998

CUMBERLAND RIVER

FORT DONELSON
SITUATION ON THE EVENING OF
FEBRUARY 14, 1862

MOST OF LEW WALLACE'S DIVISION
LANDED HERE, NIGHT OF FEB. 13

GUNBOATS REPULSED BY
SHORE BATTERIES, FEB. 14

FT. DONELSON

FLOYD

DOVER

SMITH

BUCKNER

PILLOW

GRANT

LEW WALLACE

McCLERNAND

0   1   2
MILES

order. Grant, meanwhile, had gone to the gunboats to confer with the wounded Commodore Foote. Grant heard the firing; he galloped back to find that McClernand's line had broken. This was truly a "moment of truth." McClernand had lost 1,500 men, and survivors of his demoralized division were trying to rally behind the thin lines of Gen. Lew Wallace. Smith, on the left, was too far away to help.

The Confederate attack, which had done so well up to this point, began to lose momentum. Logically, Grant sensed that such a strong effort by the Confederate left meant their line was stretched thin elsewhere. He had also noticed, among the enemy dead, knapsacks filled with rations. These were men, he reasoned, who had not planned on returning to the fort.[28]

As described later in a biography co-authored by Dana, Grant "saw at once that the rebels had been fighting for a road to the open country. Fully appreciating the situation, he said to those about him: 'Whichever party makes the first attack will win the day, and the rebels will have to be very quick if they beat me!'"[29]

Grant ordered Smith to attack from the Union left. He also asked Foote and Wallace to lend the attack all possible support. Smith's prompt and vigorous assault seized the breastworks on the Confederate right. On the other flank, the incompetent Gideon Pillow made the mistake of turning his men around and marching back into the fort. Wallace and McClernand, on the center and right, thereupon retook most of the ground that had been lost.[30]

Inside Fort Donelson, as darkness ended the day's fighting, a strange conference of war took place. A narrow escape route, close to the Cumberland River, was still open. However, the two senior officers on hand, Floyd and Pillow, did not see it that way. They felt all was lost, even though their subordinate commanders might argue otherwise. One such leader, Col. Nathan Bedford Forrest, stated, "I did not come here for the purpose of surrendering my command." The disgusted Forrest, leading some 1,500 men, found an open route and slipped away in the darkness. Then a Southern brigade was loaded on available boats, Floyd and Pillow climbed aboard themselves, and the group escaped downriver. (Later, Confederate prisoners accused Pillow and Floyd of being overly concerned with their own safety.)

Back at Fort Donelson, Simon Bolivar Buckner, one of Sam Grant's close friends at West Point and in Mexico, was now in command.[31]

During the night, Grant was regrouping his forces and planning to attack at first light. At about 3:00 A.M., a flag of truce came through the lines. With it was a message from Buckner suggesting a temporary armistice so that "commissioners" could be appointed "to agree upon terms of capitulation."

In his own hand, Grant then wrote out what would become one of the most famous messages in American military history:

> HEADQUARTERS ARMY IN
> THE FIELD,
> Camp near Donelson,
> February 16, 1862
>
> General S.B. Buckner
> Confederate Army
>
> Sir,
> Yours of this date, proposing armistice and appointment of Commissioners to settle terms of capitulation, is just received. No terms except an unconditional and immediate surrender can be accepted. I propose to move immediately upon your works.
>
> I am, sir, very respectfully,
> Your ob't. sevt.,
> U. S. GRANT
> Brig. Gen.[32]

Thanks to Floyd, Pillow, and the Union army, Buckner was hardly in the best of humors. He and Grant had been close friends. Moreover, he had once befriended Grant when Grant needed a friend very much.[33] Perhaps he felt that Grant should be remembering such things. In any case, Grant's unyielding note caused Buckner to respond rather peevishly:

> The distribution of the forces under my command incident to an unexpected change of commanders and the overwhelming force under your command compel me, notwithstanding the brilliant success of the Confederate arms yesterday, to accept the ungenerous and unchivalrous terms which you propose.
>
> I am, sir,
> Your very obt. svt.,
> S. B. BUCKNER
> Brig. Gen. C.S.A.

That was that. In a few hours, Grant was accepting the surrender of nearly 15,000 men, including Generals Buckner and Bushrod Johnson. In addition, he had captured large quantities of arms and ammunition, artillery, horses, and commissary stores.[34]

For the first time, the North had a major victory to celebrate. In Chicago, it was reported, the town "was on the rampage . . . was crazy with delight and insane with jubilation upon the receipt of the glorious news from Fort Donelson."[35] In New York, where the celebration was equally enthusiastic, Donelson was called "the most important victory yet achieved by the armies of the government," one that would "probably prove to be the most disastrous defeat which the rebel cause has yet suffered."[36]

Although some of the first newspaper accounts had barely mentioned Grant, his was the predominant role, one that could not be ignored. Besides, his actions during the battle, plus his forceful note to Buckner, made wonderful copy! Follow-up stories not only featured Grant but tried to give him "color." The New York Herald, for example, painted an image of ferocity as it described his planning "a simultaneous assault from every point" and giving orders "to take the enemy at the point of the bayonet."[37] The New York Tribune, not to be outdone, even gave the public a physical description of Grant: "About 45 years of age, sandy complexion, reddish beard, medium height, pleasant, twinkling eyes and weighs 170 pounds. He smokes continually."[38] If the reporter had checked, he would have found that Grant was still 2 months shy of his 40th birthday.

This was truly Grant's hour. Dana wrote: "The news of this splendid victory spread like lightning. The name of Grant was hailed with joy, while the deeds of his gallant army were read with eager delight by every loyal citizen and trusted soldier throughout the land."[39]

Perhaps the best personal news for Grant was a prompt recommendation by President Abraham Lincoln that he be promoted. The papers reported: "Gen. Ulysses S. Grant, the hero of Fort Donelson, has just been unanimously confirmed by the Senate as Major General, an honor conferred in testimony of his gallant conduct in battle."[40]

Some say the American Civil War marked the end of chivalry. If so, undoubtedly the end was hastened when the New York Times jeered at Buckner for his reference to "ungenerous and unchivalrous terms," calling his sentence "one of the silliest ever written." The Times went on to say: "Let the insurgents understand that we are not sacrificing our brothers by thousands and our money by millions for the sake of having knightly passages at arms with them."[41]

Grant's demand for "unconditional surrender," coinciding precisely with his initials and composed, though unconsciously, as if by a public relations artist, had captured the public imagination. One witty editor referred to ". . . the signature, which he gives to all his official papers—thus, U. S. GRANT. The puzzle is with a great many, what is shadowed forth by U. S. One suggests that it means United States GRANT; another, that it represents Union Saver GRANT; while a third, deriving some countenance from his answer to Gen. Buckner, insists that the letters stand for Unconditional Surrender GRANT. This ought to be satisfactory, inasmuch as it has passed into history."[42]

In the flush of victory, however, a misunderstanding arose between Grant and Halleck. Much of it was due to faulty communications. Certain administrative reports had not been received at Halleck's headquarters, and for Halleck, a devout worshiper of paper, this was a mortal sin. (Later, one of the telegraph operators was discovered to be a Southern sympathizer; several critical messages had never been delivered.) Reading the correspondence, moreover, it appears that Halleck was almost embarrassed by Grant's rapid movements. Grant, not he, had taken the initiative. Also, for some time Halleck had considered replacing Grant with someone more "experienced." He now realized the play had been taken away from him.

Grant's first indication of something wrong came in a harsh telegram from Halleck: "You will place . . . Smith in command of expedition and remain yourself at Fort Henry. Why do you not obey my orders to report strength and positions of your command?" On top of this, Halleck also complained about Grant to Washington. At one point he wired McClellan: "It is hard to censure a successful general immediately after a victory, but I think he richly deserves it. I can get no returns, no reports, no information of any kind from him. . . . I am worn out and tired with his neglect and inefficiency."[43]

In Washington, McClellan and Stanton, feeling it was, after all, Halleck's department, said he had their backing if he found it necessary to relieve Grant from command. Further messages flashed between Grant and Halleck. At one point Grant himself asked to be relieved, thinking that Halleck's unreasonable complaints had destroyed his [Grant's] usefulness. Halleck kept referring to "Washington," and Grant did not learn until after the war that Halleck himself had been the source of the problem.[44]

In any event, by mid-March the situation was more or less laid to rest. Halleck had been given complete command in the West (which undoubtedly put him in better humor), and he wrote Grant: "Instead of relieving you I wish you as soon as your new army is in the field to assume the immediate command and lead it on to new victories."[45]

That was exactly what Grant intended. Not one to rest on his laurels, he knew the victories at Fort Henry and Fort Donelson had created new opportunities. While Halleck was busy in St. Louis tidying up paperwork, Grant was looking south and contemplating his next offensive.

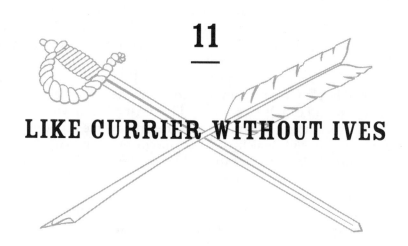

11

LIKE CURRIER WITHOUT IVES

GREELEY AND DANA had assembled a fine group of wartime reporters, men such as Albert Richardson, Junius Browne, Sam Wilkeson, Henry Villard, and Howard Gay. Nevertheless, the *Herald*, with its lively style and its aggressiveness, kept gaining circulation at the *Tribune*'s expense.

In the first 6 months of the war, the weekly edition of the *Tribune*, which provided Greeley most of his profits, had lost 30,000 subscribers. Part of the decline was his own fault: He always wanted space to air pet projects. When his longtime friend John Frémont was being criticized, for example, Greeley ran 30 columns of documents in Frémont's defense.[1]

Despite all this, there was no denying the *Tribune*'s, and Greeley's, preeminence. Everyone knew of Greeley the eccentric crusader; the author of witty, profound editorials; the man determined to provide the nation with moral, political, artistic, and intellectual leadership. He had, in truth, become an almost mythical figure. "His entrance into a tavern, much more into a lecture hall, raises gratulating shouts," Ralph Waldo Emerson wrote, "and I could scarcely keep the people quiet to hear my abstractions, they were so furious to shout Greeley! Greeley! Greeley! Catch me carrying Greeley into my lecture again! . . . I had as lief travel with . . . Barnum."[2]

Abraham Lincoln was well aware of Greeley's influence. In December 1861, even before Stanton was writing Dana to win *Tribune* support, Lincoln was indirectly doing the same with Greeley. In a letter to former

Kansas governor Robert J. Walker (but intended for Greeley's eyes), Lincoln implied that the *Tribune* would be provided inside information, then wrote: "I have the highest confidence in Mr. Greeley. He is a great power. Having him firmly behind me will be as helpful to me as an army of 100,000 men." Having assured the recipient that he wanted Greeley to see the letter, Lincoln poured on the syrup: "If he ever objects to my policy, I shall be glad to have him state to me his views frankly and fully. I shall adopt his if I can. If I cannot, I will at least tell him why. He and I should stand together, and let no minor differences come between us, for we both seek one end, which is the saving of our country. . . . Now, Governor, this is a longer letter than I have written in a month—longer than I would have written for any other man than Horace Greeley."

When an intermediary brought the letter to Greeley, his eyes lit up and he exclaimed of Lincoln, "He is a wonderful man—wonderful. . . . You must let me keep this letter . . . I want to look at it when I am down-hearted."[3]

Before long, however, Greeley had resumed his criticism of the administration and was saying that no inside information had been forthcoming. As a good journalist, Greeley was forever skeptical toward those in authority, whether they were politicians or generals. Months earlier, he had said as much in a letter addressed to young men seeking to enter politics: "The moral I would inculcate is a trite one, but none the less important. It is summed up in the Scriptural injunction, 'Put not your trust in princes.' Men, even the best, are frail and mutable, while principle is sure and eternal."[4] That was Greeley's creed. If he did not always live by it himself, at least he always preached it to others.

Early in 1862, Greeley and Dana, like Secretary Stanton, were critical of George McClellan, the posturing, arrogant general who, in Lincoln's words, had "the slows." "If General McClellan isn't going to use the army," Lincoln once said, "I wish he would let me borrow it for a while."

The *Tribune* continued to hammer McClellan. Reporter Edmund Stedman of the *World* wrote his editor: "The Tribune and its ten million adherents are howling against the General." Stedman went on to say, "The soldiers in the camp idolize McClellan . . . and are enraged at the attacks made on him. The rank and file have stopped buying the *Tribune,* so the army newsmen tell me."[5] Although the army and the other major papers were solidly behind McClellan, he was widely regarded as the underdog—clear evidence of the *Tribune*'s power.[6]

In contrast to the flamboyant *Herald,* the *Tribune* had long seemed a bit stodgy. However, when news of Fort Donelson was received, a jubilant Dana put out an extra with a screaming headline: FREEDOM!

FORT DONELSON TAKEN![7] He placed the story prominently on page one, beneath a cut of the American flag. Curiously, the news had not come from either the War Department or reporters on the scene. One of his reporters, at Fort Monroe on Chesapeake Bay, had learned of Fort Donelson's capture from exchanged prisoners just out of Richmond.[8]

Dana would always remember that moment. "The effect was electrical," he would write. "It was the first significant victory over the rebellion, and filled the country as well as the army which gained it with confidence and enthusiasm; yet the Government and its military chiefs were amazed. They could hardly understand that this unknown man and undisciplined army had gained such an advantage over the public enemy, while the Army of the Potomac [McClellan's], with its perfect equipment and organization, its large number of trained officers and its enormous preponderance of force, had not yet begun its forward movement."[9]

Dana, continuing his courtship of Stanton, gave much of the credit for Donelson to the spirit Stanton had instilled in the army. The politically astute Stanton, knowing that such praise might be misconstrued, promptly wired the Tribune: "I can not suffer undue merit to be ascribed to my official action. The glory of our recent victories belongs to the gallant officers and soldiers that fought the battles. No share of it belongs to me."[10]

Perhaps the Tribune—that is, Dana—had gone too far. Dana asked his man in Washington to see if Mr. Stanton meant to "repudiate" the Tribune. Stanton's answer to Dana was friendly and reassuring: "It occurred to me that your kind notice of myself might be perverted into a disparagement of the Western officers and soldiers to whom the merit of the recent victories justly belongs, and that it might create an antagonism between them and the head of the War Department."

Stanton said no repudiation was intended. He'd let Dana decide whether his letter disclaiming credit should be published, adding, "On this, as on any future occasion, I defer to your judgment. We have one heart and one mind in this great cause, and upon many essential points you have a wider range of observation and clearer sight than myself; I am therefore willing to be guided by your wisdom."[11]

This was heady praise indeed. Dana might well have shown the letter to Greeley. If so, it would only have inflamed the resentment that had been building in Greeley over the past several months, an animosity that probably went back to Bull Run and earlier. Whatever their differences, however, Dana and Greeley fully agreed with each other, and with Stanton, about the deficiencies of George McClellan.

When the capture of Fort Donelson was announced, McClellan's friends claimed that he had directed it from his headquarters in Washington. This, of course, was absurd. Then an Associated Press reporter, describing a speech by Stanton, wrote: "Secretary Stanton in the course of his address paid a high compliment to the young and gallant friend at his side, Major-General McClellan, in whom he had the utmost confidence, and the results of whose military schemes, gigantic and well matured, were now exhibited to a rejoicing country."

This sounded fishy to Dana, who wired Stanton to ask if he had really said such things. Stanton answered Dana privately: "The paragraph to which you called my attention was a ridiculous and impudently impertinent effort to puff the general by a false publication of words I never uttered. . . . P.S. Was it not a funny sight to see a certain military hero in the telegraph office at Washington last Sunday . . . capturing Fort Donelson *six hours after* Grant and Smith had taken it sword in hand and had victorious possession! It would be a picture worthy of Punch."[12]

Dana's power at the *Tribune* continued to grow, as did his differences with Greeley and his reputation in Washington. Greeley saw what was happening and became more and more convinced that he had delegated too much to his managing editor. "No one man can manage a newspaper for another in such a crisis as this," Greeley told Sam Wilkeson, "and I am peculiarly unfortunate in this respect."[13] To exacerbate the problem, Greeley was forced to admit that the Tribune was losing money. He told Wilkeson, "I do not see how we are going to live through the War as times go."[14]

Financial problems, of course, were nothing new for Greeley. For years, more through necessity than choice, he had supplemented his income by speechmaking, traveling widely for months at a time while Dana took care of the *Tribune*. He once wrote his friend, Schuyler Colfax, "I am so horrid poor that I am going off lecturing tomorrow and shall be away half this winter."[15]

The speechmaking, often with a political theme, was causing Greeley to be spread extremely thin. John Russell Young, a future *Tribune* managing editor, would say: "Mr. Greeley would be the greatest journalist in America if he did not aim to be one of the leading politicians in America."[16]

Oddly enough, Greeley's financial problems began in years when the paper was generating huge profits. So why was he always strapped for funds? For one thing, he was inherently generous, a man whose skepticism did not extend to acquaintances. He would always listen to a hard-luck story and was forever lending money with little hope of repayment. (One such deadbeat borrower was the wild-eyed, impoverished poet Edgar Allan Poe.) Then there were the speculative investments. Another future editor, Whitelaw Reid, said those investments included "wild lands destined never to be anything else, copper mining shares, dessicated egg companies, patent looms, photolithograph companies . . ."[17]

Over the years, Greeley had given away or sold much of his *Tribune* stock. This included magnanimous distributions to employees. After once owning 50 of the 100 *Tribune* shares, Greeley was down to 15. Dana owned 20.

Other shareholders and the board of managers realized the Greeley/Dana situation was coming to a head. There are many versions of what happened next. However, it appears that Greeley met with the board and put it bluntly. Either he or Dana had to go. In the public mind, Greeley and the *Tribune* were one and the same. If that perception were to change, who knew what might happen? The board couldn't take that chance.

Dana confided to a friend about what happened: "On Thursday, March 27, I was notified that Mr. Greeley had given the stockholders notice that I must leave or he would, and that he wanted me to leave accordingly. No cause of dissatisfaction being alleged . . . I sent a friend to ascertain if it was true. My friend came and reported that it was true. . . . On Friday, March 28, I resigned. . . . On Saturday . . . Greeley called another meeting, said . . . that it was a damned lie . . . and finally sent me a verbal message . . . to remain as a writer of editorials, but has never been near me since to meet the damned lie in person."[18]

Dana cleaned out his desk, left the building, and sold his *Tribune* stock. He never looked back. Too smart not to have anticipated something like this, he might even have felt relieved to have the break made final. The news, however, came as a shock to New York journalism. Every paper in town, and many out of town, covered the story. Dana, after all, had been the first man ever to hold the title of "managing editor," and as one writer phrased it: "After fifteen years, the *Tribune* without Dana seemed as incongruous as Currier without Ives."[19]

In Washington, Dana gave an oversimplified reason for the split, saying that "Greeley was for peace, and I was for war, and as long as I stayed on the Tribune there was a spirit there which was not his spirit." This wasn't quite true, nor was it fair to Greeley. By this time he *did* support the war, although only on limited terms and mainly as a moralistic crusade to end slavery.[20]

On March 28, the *Tribune*'s trustees, although accepting Dana's resignation, passed a resolution assuring him of "their keen sense of his many noble and endearing qualities [and] that he still holds the highest place in their esteem and affection."[21]

Some years later, Dana received what amounted to an apology from Oliver Johnson, one of the *Tribune*'s board members. Johnson said he had been "reflecting upon the part I took in terminating your connection with the *Tribune*. If I had felt then as I did not long afterwards, I should not have done it. In other words, if I had known then what I know now as to Mr. Greeley's state of mind in relation to war, I would sooner have let him go off, as he threatened to do, than sought your removal to retain him."[22]

Gen. Henry Wager Halleck was an able administrator and a conscientious soldier. As a judge of men, however, he was wretched. In the summer of 1862, for example, he would write: "It is the strangest thing in the world to me that this war has developed so little talent in our generals. There is not a single one in the west fit for a great command."[23] As he wrote, his department included, among others, Ulysses S. Grant, William Tecumseh Sherman, George H. Thomas, and Philip H. Sheridan.

Despite the triumph at Fort Donelson, Halleck seemed to believe that Grant had merely "muddled through" to victory. Accordingly, when it was decided in March 1862 to send an expedition deeper into Tennessee, Halleck placed it under the venerable C. F. Smith and told Grant to remain at Fort Henry. Smith was to proceed up the Tennessee River to the vicinity of Savannah, Tennessee. Grant, who was Smith's immediate superior, dutifully relayed the instructions.

Halleck had decided to concentrate at Savannah. Once his forces were assembled, he would take the field himself and lead a stately advance. As part of the plan, he ordered Gen. Don Carlos Buell (now part of Halleck's command) to march overland from Nashville to Savannah.[24]

Smith and five Union divisions arrived in the Savannah vicinity in mid-March. Part of the force, under General Sherman, went 9 miles farther south to the vicinity of Pittsburg Landing. Smith kept the headquarters at Savannah. Later, when a sixth division arrived, nearly all the Union troops were pushed across the river to the Pittsburg area.

A few days later, Grant was freed from the restraints imposed by Halleck. At Halleck's suggestion, he traveled upriver and assumed command of Smith's expedition.

At about this time, Smith suffered what appeared to be a minor injury—raking the shin and calf of one leg as he jumped into a small boat. The doctors had ordered him to bed, however, and it was well that Grant was on hand to take charge. Tragically, the leg became infected. Nineteenth-century medicine being what it was, the doctors were unable to check the spreading poison. A month later, Smith died, a gallant "soldier's soldier," admired and respected by all who knew him.[25] A most fervent admirer had been Grant himself. Smith, a handsome man of erect martial bearing, had been commandant at West Point during Grant's cadet days. At the time, Grant regarded the then-Captain Smith and Gen. Winfield Scott as "the two men most to be envied in the nation."[26]

Just as Halleck wanted to mass at Savannah, the Confederates were planning a similar concentration some 30 miles to the southwest. At Corinth, just over the border into Mississippi, Gen. Albert Sidney Johnston was assembling a mighty army. By the end of March, he had nearly 45,000 soldiers under his control. Leading them were some of the South's finest officers, including P. G. T. Beauregard, Leonidas Polk, William Hardee, and Braxton Bragg. Johnston himself, of course, was as formidable an opponent as could have been found. Grant's Mexican War role model, Zachary Taylor, once called Johnston "the best soldier I ever commanded."[27]

Grant and Smith, realizing the Confederate force was growing, favored an immediate offensive. Halleck, waiting for Buell, told them to avoid serious engagement. Reporters smelled a major battle and a major story. "It is difficult to see," wrote one, "how the two adverse armies at Savannah and Corinth can be long kept apart."[28]

Accurately, the *Chicago Times* analyzed the Northern intentions: "A battle . . . appears probable. . . . An attack will hardly be ventured upon by Gen. Grant until he is joined by Buell's army."[29]

Grant spent most of his time at Pittsburg Landing visiting troop units and talking to division commanders. However, he maintained his headquarters at Savannah, which would be the point of contact with Buell upon the latter's arrival.

Interestingly, little mention had been made of Grant's problems with Halleck. Certainly rumors of the quarrel were rampant, and the *New York Tribune* even made the mistake of saying that Buell had arrived and assumed command.[30] The *Chicago Tribune*, however, although wrong as to place, got it right as to command: "The supposition that Gen. Buell is to command the army at Corinth [*sic*] is ill-founded. Gen. Grant is his superior in rank, and the charges against him being now withdrawn, he is at the head of his old army, prepared for a victory."[31]

Days passed, and Buell's arrival was expected momentarily. Grant, meanwhile, was weakened by intestinal trouble, the malady known to millions of World War II soldiers as the "GIs" but in Grant's army more colorfully called the "Tennessee Quick-Step." By April 2, however, it was reported that he was "entirely recovered from his illness."[32]

Grant realized a Confederate attack was possible, but somehow neither he nor any other top Union commander really expected such a thing. Oddly enough, the newspapers *did.* On April 2, there appeared a prescient editorial in the *New York Tribune,* possibly written by Howard Gay, who had replaced Dana a few days earlier. Paying attention to rumors, and perhaps having read Southern journals, the writer headed his piece THE EXPECTED BLOW. After saying that no eastern action seemed likely, he wrote: "On the other hand, we see much that indicates a determination on the part of the Secession chiefs to strike a sudden and heavy blow in the Southwest. They are evidently concentrating their forces at Corinth or some other point near the south line of Tennessee, with intent to hurl the great mass of them suddenly on an exposed detachment of ours . . ."[33]

If the newspapers could see this, why didn't Grant? By the same token, why didn't his superiors, Generals Halleck and McClellan, see the danger? All in all, there was enough blame to go around. And even if no attack seemed likely, there still should have been fortifications. However, Smith and Sherman, the two men who had selected the Pittsburg position, didn't believe much in entrenchments. Like most professional officers of the day, they believed "an army which dug itself in would lose the aggressive touch."[34] Consequently, neither they nor Grant had ordered any field fortifications to be constructed. This was a critical mistake that would not have been made later in the war.

On the whole, however, the Pittsburg position was a good one. Five divisions (Sherman, Prentiss, W. H. L. Wallace, Hurlbut, and McClernand) were arranged to allow some measure of all-around protection, plus a certain amount of defense in depth. Union troops held the high ground; their flanks were secured by Owl Creek on the west and Lick Creek on the east. If the Confederates attacked, they would have to come head-on in a frontal assault. To the north, the sixth division, under Lew Wallace, provided a reserve and guarded against an enveloping move against Crump's Landing.

On April 5, signs pointed to Confederate activity close to the Union lines. Both Grant and Sherman, however, believed it was only another reconnaissance. Grant wired Halleck: "I have scarcely the faintest idea of an attack (General one) being made upon us, but will be prepared should such a thing take place."[35]

What he didn't know was that Johnston's army was on the move, coming ever closer. As dawn broke on April 6, Johnston was telling his officers, "Tonight we will water our horses in the Tennessee River." Nearby was a log Methodist meetinghouse known as Shiloh Church.

12

"ALL HEARTS WERE STILLED"

IT WAS a quarter of a century since Lt. Jake Ammen had come home to Georgetown on vacation and led the drill of the militia company. That was when he talked to Jesse Grant about the possibility of young Ulysses attending the Military Academy. Since then, after leaving the army, Ammen had been both a professor of mathematics and a civil engineer.[1] Now, however, Ammen was back in uniform, a colonel leading a brigade under General Don Carlos Buell. At the moment, Buell's army, including Ammen's brigade, was marching to link up with that same Ulysses Grant.

Although Buell had been ordered to join forces with Grant, no one, neither Halleck nor Grant, had told him to hurry. Consequently, he took his time, even allowing a burned bridge over the Duck River to delay him for 10 days while he methodically built another. Ammen's division commander, Gen. William Nelson, had grown impatient with Buell's dawdling. When he found the Duck to be fordable, he secured Buell's permission to go on ahead. Nelson told Ammen to move his men out at daybreak.

"I inquired if the bridge would be done," Ammen wrote in his diary. "No; but the river is falling," Nelson had answered, "and damn you, get over, for we must have the advance and get the glory." Even so, neither Ammen nor any other part of Buell's army had reached Grant by the fateful morning of April 6.[2]

Despite his belief that no attack was imminent, Grant had decided to move his headquarters from Savannah to Pittsburg Landing. At about 6:00 A.M. or Sunday, April 6, as he and his staff were having coffee, cannon fire could be heard to the south. Grant set down his cup and said, "Gentlemen, the ball is in motion. Let's be off." Within 15 minutes, general, staff, clerks, orderlies, and horses were aboard the steamer *Tigress* and headed upstream.[3]

This time, as Grant would learn, he was not facing a Floyd or a Pillow, someone who'd let him take the initiative. Wisely, Johnston had decided not to wait for Grant and Buell to join forces. Instead, as he told his staff, he would first "hammer" Grant, then turn on Buell when he arrived. He was cutting it close; by this time Buell was almost at hand. The day before, in fact, Ammen and the rest of Nelson's division had arrived at Savannah.

Early Sunday morning, a three-company Union force, prowling in front of Prentiss's division, came upon the first Confederate units as they massed for the attack. (An oddity of Shiloh was that it began with defending Northerners initiating the action.) Prentiss's units withdrew, Southern leaders gave the order, and thousands of Confederates surged forward. Johnston's three corps were formed in line, one behind the other. Firing broke out all across the front as contact was made. Pickets fell back, and Union officers hastily formed their units.

Cheering Southerners came on with a rush. The first regiments they struck were raw ones. Many Northerners, officers as well as privates, fled in panic. Later it would be said that most had been surprised while asleep, even bayoneted in their cots, but this simply wasn't true. And although some ran, many more stood and fought. Confederate casualties early in the day attest to the ferocity of the daybreak struggle.

Johnston's formation, with successive units attacking along the same axis, caused troops to be intermingled almost immediately. However, it also massed 30,000 attackers on a narrow frontage against one third their number. The leading Northern divisions (Sherman and Prentiss) retreated toward the river.[4]

The *Tigress*, meanwhile, was setting Grant ashore at Pittsburg Landing. Before leaving Savannah, he had written hasty notes to Buell and Nelson asking them to "move up the river to Pittsburg."[5] En route, he had also paused at Crump's Landing long enough to tell Lew Wallace to get ready to come forward. (Shiloh, a mixed-up battle from the start, was confused even more by the presence of two division commanders named "Wallace.") While Grant shouted instructions to Wallace from

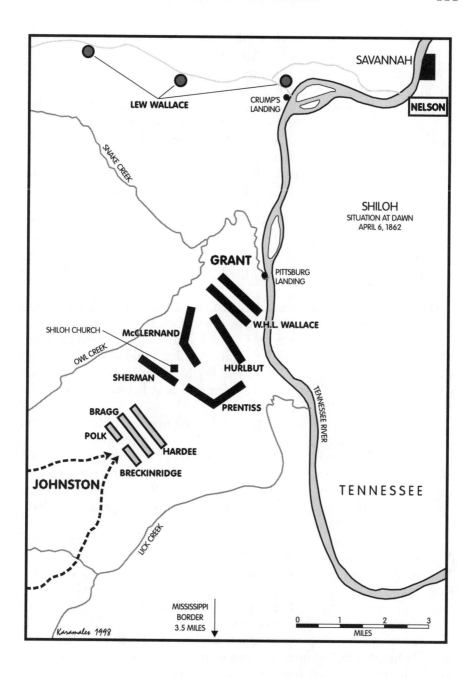

the steamboat's deck, Whitelaw Reid, an enterprising correspondent, leaped aboard the *Tigress* as a hitchhiker.[6]

As Grant arrived at the landing, things were not going well for the Union. Horace Greeley later wrote of this moment with dry understatement: "Gen. Grant had arrived on the battlefield about 8 A.M.; but early as was the hour, his army was already beaten. As this, however, is a circumstance of which he is not easily convinced, it did not seem to make as vivid an impression on him as on others."[7] Grant quickly galloped to each division area. He told the commanders to hold as long as possible, arranged for ammunition resupply, and directed the employment of his reserves.

Prentiss, the man who had once disputed Grant's seniority, seemed to be catching the worst of it. Grant sent what reinforcements he could find, most of them from Stephen Hurlbut's division, and told Prentiss to hold his ground. Similarly, on the Union right, he had McClernand reinforce Sherman.[8]

The bloody fight continued. By noon, the Confederate divisions had lost all cohesion and were fighting a series of small unit actions. Bragg, Hardee, and Polk were moving along the line at will, each man directing whatever forces happened to be in his vicinity.[9] Johnston, the overall Southern commander, was hit in the leg by a bullet that severed an artery. The gallant Johnston bled to death almost before he realized he had been wounded.[10]

On the Union side, confused and frightened men continued to stream to the rear. By early afternoon, they were being reformed and sent forward again to patch the line. Frequently they were placed in position by Grant himself. One military analyst cited 18 separate movements and actions that Grant carried out in a space of 9 hours and concluded that "during the turmoil, his activity and generalship appear . . . to have been quite wonderful."[11]

By late afternoon, however, a vast crowd of Union stragglers and deserters were huddled under the sheltering bluffs of Pittsburg Landing. Their number has been estimated as ranging from 5,000 to 15,000.[12] Shaken and demoralized, most of them ignored the officers who begged them to return to battle. Every Civil War fight had its stragglers, but Shiloh put them on display most clearly. The creeks flanking the field funneled them back to the landing, and there the river halted their flow.[13] On other fields, men who ran were scattered for miles and miles. At Shiloh, they huddled together in a cowering mass.

Nelson's division, arriving late Sunday afternoon, was appalled by the sight of the many Union refugees. Significantly, this was also the scene first viewed by most of the arriving correspondents; it was also the place where most of them collected interviews and formed impressions.[14]

On the Union right, Sherman's division, now intermingled with McClernand's, continued to fall back. It had long since abandoned the vicinity of the little Shiloh meetinghouse that would lend its name to history. On the Union left, the battered divisions of Prentiss and W. H. L. Wallace combined forces and held gamely. Confederate dead were heaped in front of Prentiss's position, a site they named the "Hornet's Nest." At about 5:00 P.M., however, with his division shattered and encircled, Benjamin Prentiss raised the white flag. Most of W. H. L. Wallace's men broke out to the rear. Their able commander, however, had been mortally wounded.

Prentiss's surrender brought a momentary lull. Some of the Southerners even took time to search the Union camp for souvenirs. It was reminiscent of Belmont, but this time the disorganized victors wore gray uniforms rather than blue.

For the moment, firing slackened. Grant's staff officer, Col. J. D. Webster, used the respite to gather together every available piece of artillery. Eventually he had more than 50 guns blazing away. Their fire was supplemented by the Union gunboats, since by this time the fighting was close enough to the Tennessee River to put the boats within range.

About this time, Nelson's fresh division was crossing the Tennessee and heading for Pittsburg Landing. One of the first ashore was Jake Ammen, leading his brigade and pushing his way through the huge crowd of listless soldiers. Nearby, a chaplain was exhorting the men in a loud, frantic voice: "Rally, men, rally and we may yet be saved! O rally, for God and your country's sake, rally . . ." The excited Ammen, fearing the effect this might have on new arrivals, shouted: "Shut up, you Goddamned old fool, or I'll break your head. Get out of the way."[15] Soon Ammen's brigade, plus other units of Nelson's division, were in position guarding Webster's guns.

The Confederates were now being led by P. G. T. Beauregard, replacement for the fallen Johnston. Beauregard had inherited a disorganized situation. His units were hopelessly intermingled and his lead elements were being punished dreadfully by Webster's batteries. Try as he might, Beauregard was unable to mount another sustained effort. The crisis for the Union troops had passed.

Grant, meanwhile, had been riding constantly along the Union line. All who saw him that day remembered his composure. As the news of Prentiss's surrender spread, someone found the nerve to ask Grant if the day was lost. "Oh no," he said. "They can't break our lines tonight—it is too late. Tomorrow we shall attack them with fresh troops and drive them, of course."

Reporter Whitelaw Reid, close enough to hear this, said years later that "from that moment I never doubted Grant would be recognized not only as a great soldier but a great man."[16]

Although Nelson's men were now on hand, Lew Wallace's troops did not arrive until after dark. After initially taking a wrong road, the weary and frustrated division had marched and countermarched for hours. Had they arrived in time, the issue might have been decided then and there. Wallace, an ambitious man, would have had his day of glory, and Grant's use of a reserve to turn the tide would have been cheered. As it turned out, Lew Wallace's fame would come from the pen, not the sword—history knows him best for his classic novel *Ben Hur.*

Darkness fell, bringing with it a cold and penetrating rain. Huddling under a tree, Grant was no more successful in obtaining rest than were the soldiers.[17] A staff officer asked whether, in view of the army's demoralized state, they should make preparations for retreat. Grant growled: "Retreat? No, I propose to attack at daylight and whip them."[18]

At dawn, Grant sent his army forward. Even considering the addition of fresh troops, it is remarkable that an army hurt so badly on Sunday could still attack on Monday. Stubborn Confederates held on until midday. At last the Southern line began to waver. Sensing the moment of decision, Grant led two regiments to a decisive point and sent them charging forward. The line buckled, and Beauregard decided to retire.[19]

As the Southerners withdrew, Federal troops reclaimed their original positions. They seemed content to stay there. It was an ideal time for relentless pursuit, but Grant's army simply didn't have the strength. Grant sent a note suggesting that Buell might be able to press home the advantage. (The note, in the form of a "recommendation," indicated his uncertainty about the command situation.) Buell did not press on, however, and the chance was lost.

With hindsight, it is easy to speak of lost opportunities. At the moment, however, it must have seemed that pursuit was physically impossible. The Union army had lost more than 13,000 killed, wounded, or missing. Confederate casualties were more than 10,000.[20]

Shiloh, the mightiest battle America had ever seen, was finished. The newspapermen now hastened to write the story.

First paper to receive the news was the *New York Herald*, which carried what was perhaps the war's most dramatic "beat." Credit went to the unscrupulous but artful Frank Chapman, who went to Fort Henry and obtained access to the army's telegraph by pretending he was a member of Grant's staff.[21] As a consequence, Chapman's story reached the East even before the official reports. On April 9, a *Herald* extra carried Chapman's story. It began in the melodramatic fashion of Civil War journalism and went on to report an unqualified Union triumph. Among its many inaccuracies was a gross exaggeration of the casualties:

> One of the greatest and bloodiest battles of modern days has just closed, resulting in the complete rout of the enemy who attacked us at daybreak Sunday morning. . . .
>
> The slaughter on both sides is immense. We have lost in killed and wounded and missing some eighteen to twenty thousand, that of the enemy is estimated at from thirty-five to forty thousand.[22]

Chapman mentioned that no reinforcements had arrived the first day and that Lew Wallace had taken the wrong road. Then he went on to praise Grant lavishly. Whether or not praise was warranted, it was a common *Herald* practice to laud senior officers quite indiscriminately in hopes that the *Herald* would thereby get news more readily.[23] In any case, Chapman went all out as he told of Grant's "recklessly riding along the lines during the entire [first] day, amid the unceasing storm of bullets, grape, and shell." He also described the second day's action, when Grant (perhaps having better judgment than Johnston about the proper role of an army commander) had led two regiments to the front but had not actually joined the charge. In the Chapman version, however: "Gen. Grant rode to the left, where the fresh regiments had been ordered, and finding the rebels wavering . . . ordered a charge across the field, himself leading, as he brandished his sword and waved them on to the crowning victory, while cannon balls were falling like hail around him."[24]

Soon after the *Herald* dispatch reached Washington, it was read aloud to the U.S. Senate. Congressman Schuyler Colfax then asked permission to read it in the House. According to the *Herald*, "all hearts were stilled and the very breathing almost suppressed till the last word of the dispatch was read." Accompanying the story in the *Herald* was a message from the White House: "I congratulate you on your success in the description of the Beauregard battle. It is now being read by the President. I congratulate the nation on the grand Union victory."[25]

Today it seems unreal to picture Lincoln gaining his first information of Shiloh from a newspaper. At the time, however, it was understandable. Lincoln had come to rely on the correspondents for their insights as well as their speed. Once he invited a group to the White House and said: "I am always seeking information. You newspapermen are so often behind the scenes at the front I am frequently able to get ideas from you which no one else will give."[26]

To supplement the Chapman story, the *Herald* ran biographical sketches of Halleck, Grant, Buell, and other leading generals.[27] Grant's sketch included both inaccuracy and "puffery." It told of his graduating from West Point "with honors" and also said he had been "engaged as a colonel . . . in several of the contests in southeastern Missouri."[28] He had, of course, finished in the middle of his class at West Point. As a colonel, he had *not* served in southeastern Missouri. His assignment to that section was concurrent with his promotion to brigadier general.

The sketch went on to say that Grant's "action in every instance has been applauded both by his superior officers and the people." This was contradicted a few sentences later when reference was made to Grant's trouble with Halleck. The writer predicted, however, that "the manner in which he has conducted the present action will remove from him all the remains of his former discomfiture. General Grant is a noble, brave and efficient soldier, as his actions have plainly proved."[29]

Although the Chapman story has gone down in journalism history as a clear first, or "beat," actually the *Herald* had received an even earlier dispatch. The first report came from W. C. Carroll, a correspondent serving (in a not-uncommon Civil War practice) as a volunteer aide on Grant's staff. Carroll said later that he had raced to send the "true story since he feared that Buell and others might try to bring Grant into disrepute by a series of false and slanderous reports."[30] He did, in fact, get there first, but no one seems to have paid him much attention. In its regular edition of April 9 (before the Chapman extra), and buried on page seven, the *Herald* carried a "private dispatch . . . from one of General Grant's staff," saying, "we have fought and won the hardest battle ever fought on this continent."

That day the *Herald* noted editorially: "The appetite for news has been satisfied today with the intelligence of the surrender of Island No. 10 and the splendid victory of General Buell and General Grant near Pittsburg Landing."[31]

News of the battle spread. In St. Louis, Halleck said there had been "terrible loss on both sides" but added: "We have gained a complete victory, and driven the enemy back within his fortifications."[32]

Horace Greeley's *Tribune*, among others, also ran the Chapman story. While the *Herald* had a definite "beat," the *Tribune*'s extra appeared the same day, April 9. (Under Associated Press rules, the account was available to those willing to share the telegraph tolls once the initial recipient was on the streets with the story.)[33]

The next day, Greeley reported a presidential proclamation asking all clergy to lead their congregations in prayers of thanksgiving. He also described the "profound sensation" created in Boston by news of the victory and said that in Poughkeepsie, "All the bells of the city were rung and cannon fired."[34]

Wilbur Storey's *Chicago Times*, a paper that normally had little enthusiasm for the Northern cause, was for the moment both ardent and inaccurate as it said: "The decisive blow was given by Gen. Grant, who headed a charge of six regiments in person . . . on the enemy's center with such force that they broke and ran."

The paper seemed to be following Storey's famous directive: "I want news, and when there is no news, send rumors!" In reporting on General Johnston, who had been hit by a bullet and bled to death, Storey's paper had its own fanciful version: "Apparently fearless of danger, he rode along the entire front, waving his sword, shouting . . . when . . . a cannon ball struck him, crushing his skull, killing him instantly."[35]

Of course, errors were just as common in the New York papers. The *Herald* reported that Grant had been slightly wounded in the ankle and that C. F. Smith had been "severely wounded."[36] The truth was that Grant had injured his ankle in a riding accident two days before the battle; Smith, ill on his deathbed, had, of course, never left Savannah.

Southern papers, it must be noted, were just as bad about false reports. On April 7, for example, the *New Orleans Picayune* said that General Buell and his staff had been captured; on April 10, the *New Orleans Daily Delta* reported the death of William Tecumseh Sherman.

Alongside the distortions and falsehoods, however, were some vivid, emotional stories composed with sincerity and depth. Case in point was a memorable description of a Union field hospital written by Ned Spencer of the *Cincinnati Times*: ". . . the dead and wounded are all around me. The knife of the Surgeon is busy at work, and amputated legs and arms lie scattered in every direction. The cries of the suffering victim, and the groans of those who patiently wait for medical attendance, are most distressing to any one who has sympathy for his fellow man. . . . I hope my eyes may never again look on such sights."[37]

The North had been rejoicing and offering prayers of thanksgiving, but suddenly the pattern shifted. In the words of historian William Woodward: "For a few days the Northern press was aflame with exultation—then, as the details and gossip came in, comment, analysis and vituperation began."[38] Almost overnight, Ulysses Grant the hero would be converted into a favorite press target.

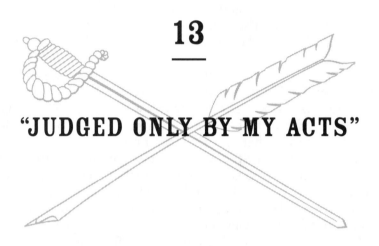

13

"JUDGED ONLY BY MY ACTS"

IRONICALLY, most of the stories of Shiloh were written by men who never saw the battle. This was resented by soldiers such as Shiloh veteran Teddy Chase, who overheard two reporters talking outside his tent well after the fighting had ended. One asked the other where he'd been, saying, "There has been a lively scrimmage going on."

"Yes, I judged so," said the other, "but I kept well out of the way of those bullets and shells till late in the afternoon when the stragglers came along, and I've got enough for more stuff than I can send in two days."

"By George," said the first man, "you're mighty lucky. I haven't a line and I must send something." According to Chase, the two then agreed to write multiple stories based on what the first chap had been told by stragglers.[1]

As Grant would point out: "The distant rear of an army engaged in battle is not the best place from which to judge correctly what is going on in front."[2] Nevertheless, "eye-witness" accounts began to appear, many based on self-justifying stories from those who had fled in panic.

Then, as papers began printing the staggering casualty lists, the country decided there must have been serious blunders. A search began for people to blame. The *Chicago Times*, among others, said the army had been completely surprised. So did the *Chicago Tribune*, which described an attack while Prentiss's men were at breakfast and told of refugees at Pittsburg Landing who "utterly refused to fight."[3]

Understandably, the Illinois papers focused their criticism on units from other states. The 50th Ohio, said the *Chicago Tribune*, was "ordered to the rear in disgrace for refusing to fight."[4] In response, a cashiered Ohio colonel—who had cried "Retreat! Save yourselves!" at first sight of the enemy—began spreading tales back home at Grant's expense, saying he was an incompetent, lazy drunkard.

Next, Ohio Governor David Tod went on the offensive, saying Ohio men were not cowards; they had been done in by the "criminal negligence" of the high command. Ohio's lieutenant-governor chimed in, saying that most of the soldiers felt "Grant and Prentiss ought to be courtmartialed or shot."[5]

In a way, Ohio citizens were more ego-involved with Ohio troops than with the overall Union effort. This is better understood if one remembers the violent state pride of the 19th century, one of the war's major precipitants. Exacerbating the Ohio situation was a story in the *Cincinnati Gazette* written by Whitelaw Reid, the man who hitchhiked to Shiloh on Grant's boat. Reid claimed he had no desire to "defend" Ohio; he merely wanted to explain the battle. After talking to innumerable officers and men, Reid described all phases of Shiloh. His account was a masterpiece of reconstruction, particularly when one considers the absence of a centralized battle plan.

He began with the florid prose typical of the day: "Fresh from the field of the great battle, with its pounding and roaring of artillery, and its keener voiced rattle of musketry still sounding in my wearied ears; with all its visions of horror still seeming seared upon my eyeballs, while scenes of panic-stricken rout and brilliant charges . . . are burned . . . indelibly upon the brain, I essay to write what I know of the battle of Pittsburg Landing."[6]

The brilliant Reid had done the best job of any Shiloh reporter. Nevertheless, he had piled error upon error, all of them reflecting badly upon Grant and Prentiss. For example, Reid said Prentiss and his division had been captured by 10:00 Sunday morning, yet these men had held out until 5:00 P.M. and had probably saved the day with their heroic stand. As Grant pointed out: "If it had been true, as currently reported at the time and yet believed by thousands of people, that Prentiss and his division had been captured in their beds, there would not have been an all-day struggle with thousands killed and wounded on the Confederate side."[7]

As for Grant, Reid said there "was no appearance of his making any preparation." Indeed, he wrote: "General Grant did not arrive on the field until after nearly all the disasters had crowded upon us." However, since Reid had arrived on the same boat, he must have known that Grant had arrived on the scene promptly and had gone immediately to the front. Reid further chastised Grant by saying that Lew Wallace's division, which might have "turned the tide . . . was not ordered up till noon."[8]

The truth was that Grant had sent orders to Wallace as soon as he arrived at the battlefield and had repeated them, with much urgency, several times thereafter.

Buried deep in the story was a pious phrase disclaiming any intention to malign: "It is idle to criticize arrangements now—it is so easy to be wise after a matter is over." Still, whatever Reid's intentions might have been, he had managed to write one of the most devastating criticisms in the history of wartime reporting.

Other papers, like wolves sensing blood, began pressing the attack. Finally, the *New York Herald* was moved to say: "There is no mistaking the universality of the sentiment that General Grant was accountable for the reverse of Sunday . . . a word in his defense is scarcely to be heard in any quarter. . . . If he be not amenable to the charges . . . he is the best abused man in the country."[9]

Up to this point, the *New York Tribune* had been generous in its treatment of Grant. Now it turned on him. Horace Greeley not only joined the howling, he became a vicious leader of the pack. Soon he reprinted Reid's story from the *Cincinnati Gazette* and demanded to know who was responsible for "the pushing forward of a mere fragment of our forces . . . with the Tennessee River in their rear, and no support immediately available, but whoever is, has much to answer for."[10] Greeley also noted the discrepancy between Union and Confederate accounts of the battle, saying, "There surely is stupendous lying on one side or the other. We trust it is not on ours."[11]

Grant's refusal to be beaten, and his counterattack on the second day, had resulted in a Union victory. Nevertheless, the *Tribune* insisted that Southern generals had proven superior. "The generalship on the part of the Confederates was consummate—far exceeding ours," Greeley wrote, after which he referred to the "utter inefficiency and incompetency, if not downright treachery, of some of our higher officers."[12]

He said all that on April 16. Two days later, he repeated Reid's error as he told of Prentiss's division being "demolished without loss to the enemy." By this time, Grant's official report had been published. The *Tribune* dismissed it scathingly: "Gen. Grant's lame dispatch is as foggy as are most others. . . . The Rebel generalship of Sunday was the best and ours of that day all but the worst ever seen on this continent."[13]

By April 21, Greeley was warming to his task, writing freely of "mismanagement and criminal weakness" and asserting that "the field was lost on Sunday by the incapacity and criminal negligence of the Generals and regained on Monday by the unequalled pluck and splendid fighting of the soldiers."[14] Now that he had Grant in his sights, Greeley was relentless. A few days later he was saying: "There was no more preparation by General Grant for an attack than if he had been on a Fourth of July frolic."[15]

It was an unequal struggle. Greeley could hurl charge after charge. No one, certainly not one of the *Tribune*'s reporters, was about to dispute him. Grant's only recorded reaction was a remark to the *Tribune*'s Albert D. Richardson: "Your paper is very unjust to me, but time will make it all right. I want to be judged only by my acts."[16]

Nevertheless, Grant was deeply hurt by the press attacks. He was a man of compassion and sensitivity, yet he was being pictured as a "clumsy butcher."[17] The Ohio papers were especially abusive. Although Grant had grown up in Ohio, he had moved out of state, which made him fair game. Later he would develop a rather thick skin for this sort of thing. At the time, however, the frustrations of the prewar years were still too close for him to be impassive. He must have wondered what his friends and relatives were thinking. Did he fear people back home would again think him a failure?

It was difficult for this quiet man to speak out in his own defense. Finally, however, he wrote an awkward letter to the *Cincinnati Commercial*. He said he would continue to do his best to bring the war to a speedy close and that personally he was "not an aspirant for anything at the close of the war." As for the charges against him, ". . . those who showed the white feather will do all in their power to attract attention from themselves. I had perhaps a dozen officers arrested for cowardice in the first day's fight. These men are necessarily my enemies. As to the talk about a surprise here, nothing could be more false."[18] That last sentence was disputable; nevertheless, for the rest of their lives both Grant and Sherman would deny being surprised at Shiloh.

For the historian, Shiloh is the hardest Civil War battle to analyze, the hardest from which to glean the truth, the hardest one for fixing blame. It is easy to understand the confusion. Generals on both sides defended their actions stoutly. In the North, supporters of Grant and Buell each claimed the victory belonged only to their man. In the South, Beauregard's adherents blamed Johnston for the defeat; supporters of Johnston returned the compliment. (Beauregard himself, meanwhile, kept insisting that Shiloh was a Confederate triumph!) And to complicate matters, papers both north and south had based most of their stories on the testimony of stragglers and deserters.

As the attacks continued, Congressman Washburne rose on the floor of Congress and, with political hyperbole, spoke out in Grant's defense: "There is no more temperate man in the army than General Grant. He never indulges in the use of intoxicating liquors at all. He is an example of courage, honor, fortitude, activity, temperance, and modesty, for he is as brave as he is modest and incorruptible. . . . It has been well said that 'Falsehood will travel from Maine to Georgia while Truth is putting on its boots.'"[19]

In reward, Washburne received a gentle note from Julia Grant thanking him for his "noble and generous remarks . . . bearing as they do the impress of truth . . . in regard to a matter in which I feel so great a personal interest."[20]

Later, Grant himself wrote to Washburne: "To say that I have not been distressed at these attacks would be false, for I have a father, mother, wife & children who read them and are distressed by them and I necessarily share with them in it. Then too all subject to my orders read these charges and it is calculated to weaken their confidence in me and weaken my ability to render efficient service in our present cause. . . . Notoriety has no charms for me and could I render the same services . . . without being known in the matter, it would be infinately prefferable to me."[21]

Washburne was being loyal to Grant, the man he had helped to elevate. Still, he was an Illinois politician, and he must have had second thoughts when he received a letter from the powerful Joseph Medill, editor of the *Chicago Tribune*. Medill told Washburne he was wasting his time with Grant: "Want of foresight, circumspection, prudence and generalship are all charged upon the wretched man. But we need not dispute about it. I admire your pertinacity and steadfastness in behalf of your friend, but I fear he is played out. The soldiers are down on him."[22]

Medill, however, was assuming too much. The army had won a victory, and the men felt pride in themselves. By some intangible process, raw Western recruits had become veterans. They had been blooded, had prevailed in battle, and they identified with Grant as their leader. Private Charles Wills of the Eighth Illinois Infantry read the newspaper slurs on Grant and wrote home: "Damn the New York *Tribune*. . . . If those *Tribunes*, big and little, were where any regiment in this army could get at them they wouldn't stand fifteen minutes."[23]

While Medill was confidently asserting that the soldiers were "down" on Grant, Charles Wills was writing: "That Pittsburg battle was one awful affair, but it don't hurt us any. Grant will whip them the next time completely."[24]

The soldiers might be supporting Grant; the newspapers might be condemning him. His fate, however, would ultimately rest with just one man. When a prominent Pennsylvania Republican went to the White House and repeated the charges against Grant, the president heard the man out. Then Abraham Lincoln gave his measured reply: "I can't spare this man; he fights."[25]

A few days after resigning from the *Tribune*, Charles Dana wrote his longtime friend and college classmate William Henry Huntington. He described the circumstances of his leaving the paper, then said: "What I shall do, I don't know. I have had several propositions, but none that exactly suits. First of all, I am going to have a rest. . . . Then I shall naturally gravitate back into journalism somewhere and somehow."[26]

He was wrong on two counts. For someone as energetic as Dana, there would never be much of a "rest." Also, that "gravitating" to journalism would take far longer than he ever imagined. There was no urgency in deciding what to do next, for by this time Dana was financially secure, having sold his *Tribune* stock and having also made several wise investments. So what should he do? Obviously, as a fervent Union man well-known to members of the administration, he would not lack for opportunities.

Dana went to Washington, where he was welcomed cordially by various cabinet officers. Evidently he was also taken to see the Bull Run battlefield. On April 18, after he no doubt read the *Tribune* and saw Greeley's continued bashing of Grant, Dana wrote a friend: "I have no idea that I shall ever go back to the *Tribune* in any manner. . . . Tomorrow I expect to go out to Manassas on horseback with a small escort and one or two generals."[27]

Soon it was intimated that Dana could have a diplomatic position, but he wasn't interested. Feeling strongly about the war, he wanted somehow to serve in a more direct capacity. One offer came from Treasury Secretary Salmon P. Chase, who was concerned about the crisis in English textile mills brought on by a lack of raw cotton. Perhaps the English, already tilting toward the Confederacy, could be placated if Dana found and purchased cotton on their behalf in areas controlled by the Union. In addition to cotton bought for overseas shipment, the North also needed cotton for its own mills. Dana said he was interested, but first he wanted to perform a task assigned him by Secretary of War Edwin Stanton.[28]

The job Stanton had in mind would call for hard-nosed integrity. He asked Dana to go to Cairo, Illinois, a major military depot furnishing supplies and munitions to Union forces in Missouri, Kentucky, and along the Mississippi. "The quartermaster's department at Cairo had been organized hastily," Dana later explained, "and the demands on it had increased rapidly. Much of the business had been done by green volunteer officers who did not understand the technical duties of making out military requisitions and returns. The result was that the accounts were in great confusion, and hysterical newspapers were charging the department with fraud and corruption."[29] So far, not much cash had been disbursed; it would be up to Dana to examine the accounts, correct overcharges, and straighten out the chaos. After taking care of a few personal matters, he would be on his way.

Soon after Shiloh, Henry Halleck left St. Louis to take personal command of Grant's Army of the Tennessee, Buell's Army of the Ohio, and John Pope's Army of the Mississippi. Halleck now had over 100,000 men under his control, enough to warrant a lightning thrust against Beauregard's weakened Confederates down at Corinth.

Rapid movement, however, was not in Halleck's nature. "Old Brains" first had to tidy things up administratively. He divided the army into three corps—left, center, and right—under George Thomas, Don Carlos Buell, and John Pope. John McClernand was given command of the reserve. Where did that leave Grant, who was senior to each of the four? Orders came appointing him as the army's second-in-command. In truth, it was a "nothing" job, and everyone knew it as such. Evidently Halleck still didn't trust him.[30] Grant protested, and in writing: ". . . As I believe it is generally understood through this army that my position differs but little from that of one in arrest and as this opinion may be much strengthened from the fact that orders to the Right Wing and Reserve, both nominally under my command, are transmitted direct from headquarters without going through me, I deem it due myself to ask either full restoration to duty, according to rank, or to be relieved entirely from further duty with this Department."[31]

That was laying it on the line—openly challenging Halleck to either relieve him or give him proper responsibilities. Halleck did neither. He asserted his right to issue orders directly to subordinate units if he thought it necessary. Then he assured Grant that he had the position to which his rank entitled him, adding somewhat hypocritically: "For the last three months I have done everything in my power to ward off the attacks which were made upon you. If you believe me your friend you will not require explanations; if not, explanations on my part would be of little avail."[32] Whether or not Halleck was being frank, for the moment his answer would have to suffice.

After 3 weeks, slowly, ponderously, the army began to advance. True to form, Halleck was being cautious. His goal, rather than winning, seemed to be not to lose. Each day the army made a sluggish advance, then it would halt and start digging. The Union offensive became merely a moving ripple of entrenchments, and men in blue, marching, sweating, digging, day after day, became rather disgusted with the whole thing.

"The National armies were thoroughly intrenched all the way from the Tennessee River to Corinth," Grant wrote. "For myself I was little more than an observer." Personally, he was "satisfied Corinth could have been captured in a two days' campaign commenced promptly on the arrival of reinforcements after the battle of Shiloh."[33]

Finally, Corinth was occupied, but by this time Beauregard had vacated the place. A series of trains had come to Corinth and hauled everything away—all the men, all the equipment, all the supplies. When empty railcars had arrived, however, Confederates had been told to cheer as though hailing the coming of reinforcements. The ruse was eminently successful. Halleck, fearing a heavily occupied fortress, moved cautiously. When he finally captured Corinth, he had gained only a badly smashed Mississippi railroad crossing—nothing more.

Since Beauregard was falling back, would Halleck pursue? No, he said. "There is no object in bringing on a battle if this object can be obtained without one. I think by showing a bold front for a day or two the enemy will continue his retreat, which is all that I desire."[34] Halleck was satisfied. In his opinion he had gained a victory, and he so reported it.

Grant did not agree. Although other generals might think in terms of *places*—Corinth, Richmond, or wherever—Grant knew that they were wrong. The object of war was to defeat the enemy's army. If you do that, the fruits of victory follow automatically. If you capture only towns and cities, leaving enemy forces intact, the war goes on. Grant understood this. Abraham Lincoln, appreciating Grant because "he fights," was beginning to understand it also.

Shortly after the fall of Corinth, redheaded William Tecumseh Sherman heard that Grant, evidently depressed, had applied for a 30-day leave to begin the next morning. Sherman determined to stop him. He rode over to Grant's headquarters and asked his friend why he was leaving. "Sherman, you know I am in the way here," Grant said. "I have stood it as long as I can and no longer."

Where was he going? "St. Louis," Grant said. Did he have any business there? "Not a bit," Grant said. At this point, "Cump" Sherman proceeded to give Grant what he needed—a frank, unvarnished talking-to. Look at his own case, Sherman argued. Early in the war people had called him "crazy," but he had hung on, and after Shiloh he'd been given new life. By the same token, Grant should also hang on. If he left, regardless of what happened, he'd be out of things. On the other hand, if he stayed, some "happy accident might restore him to favor and his true place."

Grant reconsidered. A week later he sent Sherman a note saying he'd decided to stay. Sherman said he was glad to hear it, "for you could not be quiet at home for a week when armies were moving."[35]

Halleck had no immediate offensive plans, so he proceeded to scatter his forces. For the next few months, he would be content to occupy strategic points and leave well enough alone. For Grant, one happy result of this was being restored to command of the Army of the Tennessee, which included the divisions of Sherman and McClernand. Having received permission to establish his headquarters at Memphis, he set out for there on June 21.

Dana had arrived at Cairo in mid-June. An order signed by Stanton had made Dana a member of a commission "to examine and report upon all unsettled claims against the War Department at Cairo, Ill., that may have originated prior to the first day of April, 1862."[36] Dana and two fellow commissioners reviewed the claims, examined the evidence, and paid claimants as they saw fit. It was a major task. Nearly 1,700 claims were reviewed, of which a quarter, amounting to some $150,000, were rejected. Some were turned down because of inadequate documentation. Others, said Dana, "were rejected on proof of disloyalty. The commission regarded complicity in the rebellion as barring all claims against the United States."[37]

During his free time, Dana relaxed by taking horseback rides along the river or to nearby military installations. "My longest and most interesting trip," he wrote, "was on the Fourth of July, when I went down the Mississippi to attend a big celebration at Memphis." It was on this trip that he first met Ulysses Grant. Officers had given a dinner, and Dana was seated between Grant and his chief-of-staff, John Rawlins.

Throughout his adult life, Dana had met many prominent men: business leaders, politicians, senior generals, even heads of state. On the whole, they had caused him to become a true cynic, ever alert for signs of egotism, arrogance, insincerity. His dinner companion, he found, was a welcome change. Dana later wrote: "I remember distinctly the pleasant impression Grant made—that of a man of simple manners, straightforward, cordial, and unpretending."[38]

Dana's biographer, James Harrison Wilson, noted the significance of that meeting, saying, "the acquaintance which began casually at Memphis developed into a cordial friendship [and] finally became the principal influence which secured the administration's, and especially Stanton's, cordial and unhesitating support for General Grant till the close of the war, and without which his extraordinary career must have come to an untimely end."[39] Strong words—that without Dana, Grant would not have survived. And without Grant, who could say what would have happened with the war or the nation?

When Sherman convinced Grant to hang on, he had suggested that some "happy accident" might revitalize Grant's career. A week after that first meeting between Grant and Dana, the "happy accident" came to pass. Henry Halleck was summoned to Washington to become general-in-chief. Grant, by seniority, would assume the lion's share of what Halleck left behind. Specifically, Grant would head the department embracing northern Mississippi, western Tennessee, and Kentucky west of the Cumberland River. More important, he would now have command of two armies, some 80,000 men.[40] Henceforth, plain, quiet Sam Grant was a man to be reckoned with.

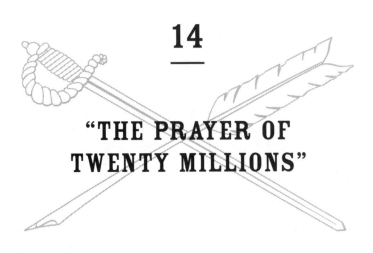

14

"THE PRAYER OF
TWENTY MILLIONS"

FOR MANY YEARS, Horace Greeley had urged the government to provide free land to those who followed his advice to "Go West." Finally, when the Homestead Act was passed into law, in May 1862, even Speaker of the House Galusha Grow saw the act as a personal triumph for Greeley. "Its friends," Grow told him, "are more indebted for success to the unwavering support given it by the New York *Tribune* than to aught else."[1]

Soon Greeley was writing: "Young men! Poor men! Widows! Resolve to have a home of your own! If you are able to buy and pay for one in the East, very well; if not, make one in the broad and fertile West!"[2]

Greeley's other great cause was abolition. Believing slavery to be profoundly evil, he had railed against it fervently and consistently. And although he considered slavery the root cause of a tragic civil war, he saw that same war creating an opportunity to end the practice once and for all. "We do not see how the Union and Slavery can both be upheld," he wrote.[3] Freeing the slaves, he maintained, was not only morally right, it was also a practical step toward victory: "Do you ask how to put down the rebellion? Destroy Slavery. Do you ask how to prevent European intervention? Destroy Slavery."[4] Again and again, an impatient Greeley called on the president to take action—and at once.

"He thought the world might be reformed in a day—in his day," wrote Beman Brockway in 1891 of his old friend Greeley. "When a thing is to be done, his idea was that it should be done now—this very day and hour."[5] Lincoln also detested slavery, but as a practical politician, he was forced to live in the realm of the possible. If he acted prematurely, emancipation might be seen as the desperate act of a weakened government. Lincoln knew he had to wait for the proper moment.

Earlier in the year, Greeley had lectured at the Smithsonian to a crowd packed with abolitionists. According to a *Tribune* correspondent, someone had asked Lincoln if he planned to attend. "I will," he said. "I never heard Greeley, but I want to hear him. . . . I want to hear what he has to say about us."

At the lecture, Lincoln was on the platform as Greeley proclaimed that the destruction of slavery was the "one sole purpose of the war." As he said this, he looked directly at Lincoln. The audience cheered at what appeared to be a direct challenge to the president. Lincoln sat impassively. Later, Lincoln asked Homer Byington, a *Tribune* correspondent in Washington, "What in the world is the matter with Uncle Horace? Why can't he restrain himself and wait a little while?"[6]

Greeley, the self-ordained presidential adviser, was not willing to wait. He pleaded with Lincoln to take action, writing in July 1862: "We do not fear that the right thing will not ultimately be done, but that it will be done too late."[7]

On August 19, Greeley's plea turned into a demand. A shrill, lengthy editorial was titled "The Prayer of Twenty Millions." It was composed, Greeley said, "only to set succinctly and unmistakably before you what we require, what we think we have a right to expect, and of what we complain . . ." In column after column, he cited the nation's reasons for the *immediate* abolition of slavery.[8]

As always, Greeley believed that his opinions were everyone else's and that he had almost an obligation to set Lincoln straight. In his mind, theirs was a special relationship, one well analyzed by the remarkable blind scholar James Trietsch, who wrote: "Fundamentally a pacifist, Horace Greeley was mentally overcome by the internal conflict, by the length of it and by the bloody cost of it. He endeavored to guide Lincoln into what he believed was a pathway to peace. But his advice was as erratic as his mind was unstable; his influence upon Lincoln, who soon fathomed Greeley's unreliability, was therefore negligible."[9]

Lincoln's reply to the so-called prayer, appearing in the *Tribune* a few days later, was one of deliberate moderation: "I have just read yours of the 19th, addressed to myself through the New York Tribune. . . . If there be perceptible [*sic*] in it an impatient and dictatorial tone, I waive it in deference to an old friend, whose heart I have always supposed to be right; as to the policy 'I seem to be pursuing' as you say, I have not meant to leave any one in doubt; I would save the Union. I would save it the shortest way under the Constitution. The sooner the national authority can be restored, the nearer the Union will be 'the Union as it was.' . . . If I could save the Union without freeing any slave I would do it, and if I could save it by freeing all the slaves I would do it, and if I could save it by freeing some and leaving others alone I would also do that. . . . I have here stated my purpose according to my view of my official duty; and I intend no modification of my oft-expressed personal wish that all men everywhere could be free. Yours, A. Lincoln."[10]

The *New York Times*, among others, approved of the way Lincoln had handled the situation. It also used the opportunity to take a slap at Greeley. Of Lincoln's reply, the *Times* said, "It is in infinitely better taste, too, than the rude epistle to which it is an answer. . . . The President not yet seeing the propriety of abdicating in behalf of our neighbor, consoles him with a letter that assures the country of abundant sanity in the White House."[11]

That summer of '62, according to Grant, was his "most anxious period of the war." Halleck's once-mighty army, he wrote, "had now become so scattered that I was put entirely on the defensive in a territory whose population was hostile to the Union." Until he was reinforced, Grant had to bide his time. Meanwhile, he had to safeguard a number of points, any one of which might be hit by the Confederates, who now had the initiative.[12]

Back east, with Robert E. Lee again on the move, little attention was given to Grant and the West. On July 3, for example, a *New York Tribune* reporter, writing from Grant's Memphis headquarters, had as his main point only that the city was "intensely hot, and the citizens apparently suffer under it quite as much as the Northerners."[13]

Thirsty for news from the West, true or not, the *Tribune* next reported (a full year ahead of time) the fall of Vicksburg. Next day a headline admitted it was all a mistake: VICKSBURG NOT YET TAKEN. In truth, despite some shelling by a navy gunboat, the city was not even under siege. The same issue wrote disparagingly: "Gen. Halleck's magnificent army is widely scattered, one division here, another there, and Buell's force gone to North Alabama."[14]

At the moment, Grant was having a problem with reporter Warren Isham, one of the true rascals of Civil War journalism. Isham's paper, the *Chicago Times*, was a leading supporter of the disloyal, antiwar

Northerners known as "Copperheads." Isham, despite having been cautioned earlier by Grant, was keeping the wires busy with fabrications. Always they were stories calculated to hurt Union morale. The last straw came on August 8, when an Isham story in the *Chicago Times* described the arrival at Mobile of 10 impregnable English-built gunboats, giving the South a fleet superior to anything the Union possessed. Grant sent a clipping of the story to Sherman, saying it was "both false in fact and mischievous in character." He told Sherman to have the man arrested and sent to prison "for confinement until the close of the war." Sherman, who hated the press as much as anyone, was more than happy to oblige. The rival *Chicago Tribune*, saying Isham's story had been made out of whole cloth, applauded Grant's action. Three months later, with the point having been made, Grant let the man off.[15]

Back east, at the end of August, Union forces under General John Pope were at Manassas, about to fight the battle of Second Bull Run. Horace Greeley, professing modesty in military science, nevertheless stood ready to advise. On September 2, 1862, he urged editorially that all available forces be concentrated under Pope: "It seems to us evident that the Union cause has suffered already from the multiplicity of independent commands. . . . But as we disclaim all acquaintance with strategy, our judgment in the premises is of no account. But Napoleon has taught people as ignorant as we are that the first rule in war is to *be strongest on the decisive point, no matter how weak everywhere else.*" In this, said Greeley, the North should follow the example of rebels Lee and Stonewall Jackson.[16] By the next day, it appeared that Pope was retreating. Greeley wrote: "The American Republic is now grappled in a life-and-death struggle with a gigantic and fiendish Rebellion."[17] On September 5, as it became clear that the North had suffered a crushing defeat, the headline read: GEN. POPE AND MCDOWELL SEVERELY DENOUNCED. The story began: "Slowly and sullenly the two armies of the Republic, outgeneraled and defeated, have fallen back from the battlefield to Centreville, from Centreville to Fairfax, from Fairfax to the Potomac."[18]

By mid-month, with Lee and Jackson now near Sharpsburg, Maryland, Greeley was writing almost in panic: "The Rebels are upon us; the life or death of the Union is a question not of months, but of days."[19] Then, on September 17, the battle of Antietam saw the greatest bloodbath in American history, with 17,000 wounded and nearly 6,000 dead. In a single day, more than twice as many Americans had been killed as in the War of 1812, the Mexican War, and the Spanish-American War *combined.*[20]

Lee was forced to pull back, to patch up his army and ponder his next move. Basically, Antietam had been a draw. The North, however, claimed it as a victory, which gave Abraham Lincoln the moment he'd been waiting for. Now, following Antietam, he had a position of relative strength. On September 23, it was proclaimed: "That on the first day of January in the year of our Lord, one thousand eight hundred and sixty-three, all persons held as slaves within any State, or designated part of a State, the people whereof shall then be in rebellion against the United States, shall be then, thenceforward, and forever free."[21] It was a pivotal moment in the American saga.

Two days after Antietam, things began heating up in the West. Confederates under General Sterling Price had seized the Union post at Iuka, Mississippi, some 20 miles east of Corinth. Grant saw it not as a problem but as an opportunity. "It looked to me," he would write, "that if Price would remain in Iuka until we got there, his annihilation was inevitable."[22] Grant sent forces under Generals E. O. C. Ord and William S. Rosecrans to hit Iuka from two directions. Unfortunately for Grant, the fighting was inconclusive. Rosecrans had failed to block one of the roads leading out of Iuka, and Price managed to get away to the South.[23] The *New York Tribune*, however, hailed Iuka as "A Gallant and Brilliant Victory," one that again showed the "superiority of Western Troops."[24]

The next action took place at Corinth, by then a Union strongpoint held by Rosecrans. Confederates led by General Earl Van Dorn launched a well-planned, violent attack. In Grant's words, Van Dorn "came near success, some of his troops penetrating the Union lines at least once, but the works that were built after Halleck's departure enabled Rosecrans to hold his position until the troops of both McPherson and Hurlbut approached toward the rebel front and rear. The enemy was finally driven back with great slaughter; all their charges, made with great gallantry, were repulsed. The loss on our side was heavy, but nothing to compare to Van Dorn's."[25]

Greeley's *Tribune* carried an enthusiastic account of the Corinth battle accompanied by a large front-page map showing "The Seat of War in the South-West." Headlines proclaimed a GREAT VICTORY BY ROSECRANS.

"The principal facts," said the story, "are corroborated by Gen. Grant's latest dispatches to the War Department." (Six months earlier, his dispatch from Shiloh had been called "lame" and "foggy." The *Tribune* had now made him a valid authenticator.) Included in the story was a Rosecrans message to Grant—"The enemy are thoroughly routed"—and one from Grant to Halleck saying Grant had directed Rosecrans "to urge on the good work."[26]

Although Rosecrans was being praised for the victory, Grant was disappointed in him for not having pursued Van Dorn more vigorously. Later he'd write: "Two or three hours pursuit on the day of the battle . . . would have been worth more than any pursuit commenced the next day could possibly have been."[27] Nevertheless, Rosecrans, man of the hour, was promoted to major general. Soon the sluggish Buell, in eastern Tennessee, was relieved and Rosecrans was sent to replace him. That was fine by Grant. In his *Memoirs*, he said he'd found Rosecrans to be reluctant to follow orders, and ironically, he'd been about to relieve him on the very day the promotion was announced.[28]

Julia Grant, describing the incident, said she had just joined Ulysses at his headquarters, a "straggling old country house" in Jackson, Tennessee. They had been discussing his problems with Rosecrans, which had become serious, even though Grant said, "Rosy is a fine fellow." Later, she said, Ulysses came out of his office holding up a slip of paper and smiling. "There is good news, good news. Rosecrans is promoted and ordered to take command of the Army of the Cumberland. I feel so happy. It is a great compliment, and he leaves us feeling friendly in place of the other way, which I fear would have come, as he was going wrong and I would have had to relieve him. His promotion is a real pleasure to me."[29]

Rosecrans was being praised by all, and a willingness to relieve him, albeit reluctantly, shows a growing self-assurance on Grant's part. Also significant by this time is the ability of this inherently quiet man to verbalize his feelings about the war and slavery. Not surprisingly, they paralleled those of Lincoln. A few weeks earlier Grant had written his father: "I am sure that I have but one desire in this war, and that is to put down the rebellion. I have no hobby of my own with regard to the Negro, either to effect his freedom or to continue his bondage. If Congress pass any law and the President approves, I am willing to execute it."[30]

In the meantime, however, Grant was doing a great deal to speed the emancipation process. In a letter to his sister, Grant wrote that whenever the army occupied new territory, former slaves "follow in the wake of the army and come into camp. I am using them as teamsters, hospital attendants, company cooks, and so forth, thus saving soldiers to carry the musket."[31] Also, unlike most commanders, Grant was looking out for the welfare of the former slaves. He ordered John Eaton, chaplain of an Ohio regiment, to set up an agency to put them to work, collect payment on their behalf, and use the funds to feed, clothe, and shelter them. It was a daunting task, and Eaton, who didn't want the job, protested directly to Grant. The chaplain said he was happy where he was. Also, since he had little military rank, he was sure to run into major problems. Since Eaton would be reporting directly to him, Grant said, "I will take care of you." Eaton soon saw that Grant had given a great deal of thought to the future of the black man. If he could show his worth as an independent laborer, Grant explained, he could later shoulder a musket and eventually become a citizen. "Never before," wrote Eaton, "had I heard the problem of the future of the Negro attacked so vigorously and with such humanity combined with practical good sense."[32]

In mid-October, Grant's district was elevated to a full military department with Grant as its commander. It would include Cairo, Forts Henry and Donelson, western Kentucky and Tennessee, and as much of northern Mississippi as he could get.[33] For Grant, this meant a new measure of independence, allowing him once more to think in terms of offense rather than defense. In his mind, a plan began to develop: cutting loose from all these occupied points, assembling his army, and attacking south along the Mississippi Valley. He notified Halleck that he was beginning to mass his troops at Grand Junction, halfway between Memphis and Corinth. He planned to move from Grand Junction to Holly Springs, Mississippi, and from there farther south. Halleck said he approved of the plan and promised to send reinforcements.

"Reinforcements continued to come from the north," Grant would write, "and by the 2d of November I was prepared to take the initiative. This was a great relief after the two and a half months of continued defense over a large district of country, and where nearly every citizen was an enemy ready to give information of our every move."[34]

That same month, Charles Dana was back in New York, having completed his work auditing claims for the War Department. Around mid-November, he received a telegram asking him to return to Washington for another special assignment. Upon arrival, he went to see Secretary Stanton, who was evidently pleased with the work he'd done at Cairo. Stanton then made a rather flattering offer, saying he'd like to appoint Dana as an Assistant Secretary of War. Dana said he'd accept.

"All right," said Stanton, "consider it settled." Moments later, as Dana left the War Department, he ran into a fellow New Yorker, Maj. Charles Halpine, and mentioned his new job as Stanton's assistant. Halpine immediately repeated the story to some newspaper people; the next morning it was reported in all the New York papers.

The hot-tempered Stanton, offended by the premature "leak," withdrew the appointment. Dana regretted what had happened, even though he'd had no idea that Halpine was going to repeat the story, and in any case he failed to see the harm. However, the deed was done, and at least for the moment, Dana was free to seek other opportunities.[35]

Before accepting that earlier assignment, Dana had talked to Treasury Secretary Salmon P. Chase about the nation's need for cotton, both for its own mills and for shipment to England. Since he was no longer committed to Stanton, Dana undertook a private venture. He formed a partnership with two business acquaintances, Roscoe Conkling and George W. Chadwick, to buy cotton. Although Stanton had been annoyed with him, he hoped it was temporary. In any case, he told his partners he'd see Stanton again and ask for a letter commending their venture to the appropriate military authorities.

As Grant was planning his offensive, he was unaware of events taking place in Washington that affected him directly. Suddenly he began to hear disturbing rumors about Gen. John McClernand's having "a separate and independent command within mine, to operate against Vicksburg by way of the Mississippi River."[36] Grant didn't know the half of it. For months, the energetic, overly ambitious McClernand had been scheming to become the leading military figure in the West. To accomplish this, he was counting on the support of a fellow Illinois politician, the president of the United States.

Northwestern states, McClernand told Lincoln, were tiring of the war, and a serious political crisis was building in the great farm belt north of the Ohio River. These were states that depended on the Mississippi for exporting their grain. Unless the river was opened, the economic problems would soon inflame the anti-war sentiments that were already brewing. So who could solve the problem? According to McClernand, none other than himself. He proposed raising a mighty midwestern volunteer army, which he would use to capture Vicksburg and free the Mississippi. Moreover, McClernand told Lincoln, those West Point generals were all like McClellan—afraid to take action. Therefore, Lincoln should "let one volunteer officer try his abilities." (Horace Greeley, it might be noted, had much the same opinion of West Pointers. He once made the fantastic suggestion that Treasury Secretary Chase be placed at the head of the Army of the Potomac.)

Raising an army was fine, but both Halleck and Stanton hesitated to give an independent command to an amateur soldier swayed by political motives. Nevertheless, McClernand's offer was accepted, and Lincoln himself endorsed a top secret order approving the expedition. The order, carefully worded, said: ". . . a sufficient force not required by the operations of General Grant's command shall be raised, an expedition may be organized under General McClernand's command against Vicksburg, and to clear the Mississippi river and open navigation to New Orleans." A final paragraph said that "the forces so organized will remain subject to the designation of the general-in-chief [Halleck], and be employed according to such exigencies as the service in his judgment may require."[37]

There was a loophole in the order, presumably deliberate. Lincoln and Stanton, each an attorney capable of wording something in an ironclad manner, had not done so. What they'd said, in other words, was that McClernand was to have his independent command *if* Grant didn't need his men and *if* Halleck finally approved.

The rumors persisted, always indicating a separate effort being launched from Memphis. This confused Grant, who'd heard nothing of this officially. Pointedly, he asked Halleck what was going on: "Am I to understand that I lie still here while an expedition is fitted out from Memphis, or do you want me to push as far south as possible?"[38]

Halleck was constrained politically from being completely frank. Nevertheless, despite his failings as a field soldier, "Old Brains" could play political games with the best of them. As fast as McClernand raised new regiments, Halleck sent them to Grant. Shrewdly, he hoped Grant could get his campaign well enough under way to take precedence over anything McClernand might come up with. His reply to Grant's query, although somewhat cryptic, gave Grant what he needed: "You have command of all troops sent to your department and have permission to fight the enemy where you please."[39]

That was enough for Grant. Rapidly, he organized his army into a left, center, and right wing under Generals C. S. Hamilton, William Tecumseh Sherman, and J. B. McPherson, respectively. Then he got under way. Sherman, moving out of Memphis, took with him the troops McClernand thought were his.

On December 18, by order of the president, Grant was told to divide his force into four corps, one of them to be under McClernand. With a straight face, Grant wired McClernand, who was still in Springfield: "I hope you will find all the preliminary preparations completed on your arrival and the expedition ready to move."[40]

McClernand arrived in Memphis on December 28, by which time his "private army" had already moved out. He had to hurry to catch up, now having discovered that instead of operating independently, he would be but one of four commanders under Grant. He'd been had. Halleck, acting quite legally (and presumably with the knowledge of Stanton and Lincoln), had outfoxed him. So had Grant, and for this McClernand would never forgive him. In his *Memoirs*, Grant summed it up rather neatly: "I doubted McClernand's fitness; and I had good reason to believe that in forestalling him I was by no means giving offence to those whose authority to command was above both him and me."[41]

On December 20, Grant suffered a setback when Earl Van Dorn seized the Union depot at Holly Springs and destroyed everything in sight. A Richmond paper exulted: "The scene was wild, exciting, tumultuous; Yankees running; tents burning; torches flaming; Confederates shouting; guns popping; sabers clanking; Abolitionists begging for mercy; women . . . clapping their hands, frantic with joy . . ."[42] Grant had advanced as far as Oxford, Mississippi. Now, having lost his base of supply, he was forced to withdraw to Grand Junction.[43]

As 1863 began, Rosecrans was locked in a fierce struggle at Stones River against Confederate Gen. Braxton Bragg. Charles Dana was en route to Memphis to buy cotton. Horace Greeley was hailing the signing of the Emancipation Proclamation, saying, "it is the beginning of the end of the rebellion. . . . GOD BLESS ABRAHAM LINCOLN!"[44] Privately, however, he was grumbling that the order didn't go far enough, since it failed to include slaves in the border states. Ulysses Grant was in northern Mississippi, commanding the Army of the Tennessee and about to embark on the long, tortuous road to Vicksburg. The very outcome of the war might depend on whether or not he was successful.

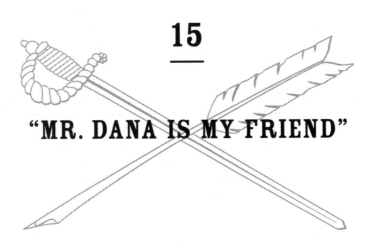

15

"MR. DANA IS MY FRIEND"

GRANT'S PLAN, initially suggested by Sherman, had been set in motion in December. It involved two separate armies, the first commanded by Sherman, accompanied by the gunboats of Adm. David Porter. They would steam down the Mississippi to the mouth of the Yazoo, proceed up the Yazoo, make a landing, and then go after Vicksburg. Grant, meanwhile, with the second force, would hold the attention of Confederate Gen. John Pemberton by advancing south along the line of the Mississippi Central Railroad.[1]

It had not worked out. Grant's supply base at Holly Springs had been lost, forcing him to pull back. At about the same time, raiders led by Nathan Bedford Forrest had slashed all Union communications, leaving Sherman in the dark about Grant's failure to contain Pemberton.

On December 29, well-entrenched Confederates at Chickasaw Bluffs, with help from Pemberton, gave Sherman a bloody setback. Alert Southerners, as well as geography, had now made it clear that approaching Vicksburg from the north was just not feasible. The Yazoo delta ran for 200 miles and was cut by countless rivers, creeks, and bayous. A Union army encumbered by supplies, ammunition, and artillery pieces would find it impossible to cross. Also certain was that Vicksburg, high on a fortified bluff bristling with weaponry, could not be taken from the river.

What remained, then, was somehow getting the army east of Vicksburg so as to launch an assault from solid ground. There appeared to be various ways to accomplish this—none of them easy. Before he was through, Grant would try them all.[2] He might, for example, get beyond Vicksburg by swinging south through Louisiana and staying west of the river. Even if he did, however, without navy transports he couldn't get his army across the mighty "Father of Waters." Those transports, unfortunately, would be unavailable as long as the guns of Vicksburg blocked their passage south.

On January 2, McClernand, accompanied by his new bride, arrived to take over from Sherman and assume command of what he proudly named the Army of the Mississippi. Doubtless he was just as happy to have missed the disaster of Chickasaw Bluffs. Ahead, he saw only Vicksburg and glory. And would not the road from Vicksburg lead to higher places, at least to the Senate, perhaps even the White House? Porter's reaction was typical. He wrote a newsy letter to his friend and fellow admiral Andrew Foote: "McClernand has arrived and will take command. Sherman, though, will have all the brains."[3]

While they waited for Grant, Sherman suggested a move up the Arkansas River to capture Fort Hindman, which posed a threat to any Vicksburg expedition. McClernand agreed, especially after Admiral Porter said he'd support the effort with his gunboats.[4] The fort, near the town of Arkansas Post, surrendered to the joint expedition on January 11. The pompous McClernand, bragging that "his star was in the ascendant," continued to irritate his fellow officers. Once, when Porter spoke sharply to the Illinois politician, Sherman cautioned him, "My God, Porter, you'll ruin yourself if you talk that way to McClernand; he is very intimate with the President and has powerful influence." Porter, angry over a perceived insult to Sherman, said, "I don't care who or what he is, he shall not be rude to you in my cabin."[5]

Grant didn't think much of the Arkansas venture. He ordered a return to the Mississippi and wired Halleck that McClernand had been "off on a wild goose chase." Because of an inherent dislike of the scheming McClernand, who was an easy man to dislike, Grant was being both hasty and unfair. However, it worked both ways. On January 16, McClernand wrote Lincoln from Arkansas Post: "I believe my success here is gall and wormwood to the clique of West Pointers who have been persecuting me for months. How can you expect success when men controlling the military destinies of the country are more chagrined at the success of your volunteer officers than the very enemy beaten by the latter in battle?"[6]

Grant changed his tune after learning that taking Fort Hindman had been Sherman's idea, not McClernand's. Meanwhile, Grant said he would combine forces and take personal charge of the river expedition. McClernand's scheme was foiled; he would *not* have his own independent army.

Evidently, Secretary of War Stanton and Charles Dana were back on good terms. In January 1863, Dana arrived in Memphis armed with gracious letters of introduction from Stanton to appropriate Union generals. One was to Grant, saying in effect: "Mr. Dana is my friend; you can rely upon what he says, and if you can be kind to him in any way you will oblige me."

Soon Dana saw that a flourishing cotton trade was still providing the South with both goods and gold. He wrote Stanton that it was hurting the war effort: "The mania for sudden fortunes made in cotton," he explained, ". . . has to an alarming extent corrupted and demoralized the army. Every colonel, captain, or quartermaster is in secret partnership with some operator in cotton; every soldier dreams of adding a bale of cotton to his monthly pay. I had no conception of the extent of this evil until I came and saw for myself." Dana suggested that the government buy cotton at fixed rates, then put it up for public auction. His point was reinforced by the fact that he was arguing against his own pocketbook. "My pecuniary interest," he noted, "is in the continuance of the present state of things, for while it lasts there are occasional opportunities of profit to be made by a daring operator; but I should be false to my duty did I, on that account, fail to implore you to put an end to an evil so enormous, so insidious, and so full of peril to the country."

Before mailing the letter, Dana showed it to Grant, which resulted in a postscript: "P.S.—Since writing the above I have seen General Grant, who fully agrees with all my statements and suggestions, except that imputing corruption to every officer, which of course I did not intend to be taken literally."[7]

When Dana returned to Washington, his suggestions were discussed personally with Stanton and Lincoln. Before long they were put into effect.

Horace Greeley continued to hope for a negotiated end to the fighting. "It is impossible to make a good War or a bad Peace," he would write.. Shaken by the defeat at Chickasaw Bluffs, which came on the heels of incredible Union losses at Fredericksburg, he told his readers: "If three more months of earnest fighting shall not serve to make a serious impression on the rebels; if the end of that term shall find us no further advanced than its beginning; if some malignant Fate has decreed that the blood and treasure of the Nation shall ever be squandered in fruitless efforts—let us bow to our destiny, and make the best attainable peace."[8]

Greeley was but one of many who preferred a permanent Confederacy to a continued war. Nathaniel Hawthorne, for example, Dana's one-time Brook Farm associate, was saying, "It would be too great an absurdity to spend all our Northern strength for the next generation in holding on to people who insist on being let loose."[9]

The *Tribune* editor, however, seemed to be taking the lead in such matters. He entered into correspondence with the infamous Copperhead Clement L. Vallandingham, a self-styled "apostle of peace." Vallandingham, deemed by many a traitor, urged Greeley to join him in urging Confederate recognition. Greeley also met privately with Henri Mercier, emissary of Napoleon III, to discuss possible mediation by the French. Napoleon, of course, would have liked a permanently divided America so as to give France a free hand in Mexico. Despite Greeley's good intentions, when his machinations became known he was compromised before the nation.[10]

Although Ulysses Grant had assumed overall command of the Vicksburg expedition, with the influential McClernand on hand, he sensed there might be trouble ahead. Indeed, as his fellow officers became ever more disgusted with McClernand, Grant was getting an earful. On January 20, he wrote frankly to Halleck: "I regard it as my duty to state that I found there was not sufficient confidence in General McClernand as a commander, either by the Army or Navy, to insure him success. Of course, all would co-operate to the best of their ability, but still with a distrust. This is a matter I made no inquiries about, but it was forced upon me."[11]

For Grant, the first order of business was finding a way to bypass Vicksburg. Across from the city, the Louisiana shore formed a long, narrow peninsula. If the river could be diverted so as to cut through the peninsula's narrow base, Vicksburg would be left high and dry. Earlier, Union soldiers had started cutting a canal to do just that, and Halleck said the president himself favored such an undertaking. Accordingly, Grant set soldiers to work digging an ambitious ditch. Even if it didn't work out, it would give many thousands of immobilized soldiers something to do.[12]

Unfortunately, the mighty Mississippi was not to be tamed so easily. Union engineers had built a shoulder to shield the new canal until the moment came to divert the river. Long before that moment, floodwaters wiped out the shoulder and made the ditch worthless. Horace Greeley, describing that moment in the campaign, would write: "And now, after some days of hesitating effort, it was decided that the canal was an abortion—The Father of Waters having paralyzed it by his veto; while the batteries of Vicksburg frowned grimly, defiantly as ever."[13] With stubborn determination, Grant said they'd just have to try other means of getting around those batteries.

Some 50 miles to the northwest lay Lake Providence, which by a system of waterways flowed into the Mississippi well below Vicksburg. Perhaps those meandering creeks and rivers could be made navigable and provide a safe, bloodless route. As always, Grant respected the opinions of Sherman, who said of the Lake Providence alternative: "It is admirable and most worthy of a determined prosecution. . . . This little affair of ours here on Vicksburg Point is labor lost."[14]

In the East, where McClellan had been dismissed for a second time, the Army of the Potomac appeared to be in the worst condition yet. After his disastrous performance at Fredericksburg, Gen. Ambrose E. Burnside had led the army on what was called the "Mud March." Bad roads and ghastly weather had forced him into an embarrassing U-turn and a humiliating return to camp. The army was sullen, desertions were increasing, and Burnside, yet another failed Union general, was replaced by the glory-seeking Joe Hooker. As this was happening, disaffection with the war was on the rise, particularly in the northwest. In Lincoln's words, "the bottom was out of the tub."

Horace Greeley now believed the best Union general was William Rosecrans. The *Tribune* had praised "Old Rosy" for his performance at Corinth. It had also reported the fierce, inconclusive battle of Stones River, where Rosecrans faced off against Braxton Bragg, as being a Union victory. Accordingly, Greeley had an idea, a "king-maker" scheme both devious and unrealistic. He sent his friend James R. Gilmore to talk to Rosecrans and see if the latter was "sound" on the slavery question. If so, would he like to run for president? If he would, Greeley boasted, he would force Lincoln to resign, put Vice President Hannibal Hamlin in his place, and give Rosecrans command of the whole Union army. Thus the war would be finished promptly and Rosecrans would become the natural Republican candidate for the presidency in November 1864.

Although Greeley had tremendous influence, it's hard to believe that anyone, even Greeley, could have taken such a plot seriously. In any case, the honorable Rosecrans emphatically declined, saying, "My place is here. The country gave me my education and has a right to my military services." A few months later, when Rosecrans performed poorly at Chickamauga, leaving his subordinate George Thomas to save the day, Greeley no doubt was just as happy that his offer had been rejected.[15]

By March, the once-promising Lake Providence route had to be abandoned. Rising waters had made it impossible to force a way through the tree roots, swampland, and maze of overhanging branches. Undeterred, Grant turned his attention to yet another possibility, this one to the northeast at Yazoo Pass and Haynes Bluff. If nothing else, he was being persistent. However, would it be enough to satisfy Lincoln?

The New York Times was saying that Grant was "stuck in the mud of northern Mississippi, his army of no use to him or anyone else."[16] In a similar vein, the New York World asserted, "the confidence of the army is greatly shaken in Gen. Grant, who hitherto undoubtedly depended more upon good fortune than upon military ability for success."[17]

Lincoln, needing results, had shown a willingness to relieve men who failed. Already there were enough dismissed generals for a fair-sized infantry squad, men named McDowell, Frémont, McClellan, Buell, and Burnside. With public dissaffection on the rise, particularly in the northwest, would it not make sense to replace Grant with a northwestern figure, the well-known McClernand?

Grant's career was hanging in the balance. Before taking action, however, Lincoln and Stanton, neither of whom had ever met the man, wanted to know more. They needed, in effect, a firsthand report from a trusted agent, a man with no personal ax to grind—a man like Charles Dana.

Stanton wired Dana in New York, asked him to return to Washington. When he arrived, Stanton told him they needed someone to evaluate Grant. People had doubts about this western general, and the complaints were piling up. Frankly, he and Lincoln needed "to settle their minds" about Grant. Dana would be furnished a cover story, but actually he would be Stanton's personal emissary, reporting directly to the secretary on Grant and Grant's army. This underhanded role was not the happiest of missions, especially for someone who liked plain talk and honest dealing. Obviously Dana was under no obligation to accept.

"Will you go?" Stanton asked him.

"Yes."

"Very well. The ostensible function I shall give you will be that of special commissioner of the War Department to investigate the pay service of the Western armies, but your real duty will be to report to me every day what you see."

On March 12, 1863, Dana received orders that masked his true role. On paper, he was to be only a special commissioner "to investigate and report upon the condition of the pay service in the Western armies." He set out at once for Memphis.[18] With the benefit of historical hindsight, we now know he was embarking on one of the war's most crucial missions. His reports would determine the fate of Grant, the future of the Vicksburg expedition, and perhaps even the outcome of the entire war.

Dana arrived in Memphis on March 23 and began sending reports back to Halleck. The information, however, was basically secondhand, and as he said, his sources were "few and uncertain."[19] He suggested to Stanton that he could do a better job by being at Grant's headquarters. Stanton, who agreed, gave him remarkable carte blanche, saying: "You will consider your movements to be governed by your own discretion, without any restriction." By the end of the week, Dana was on his way to Grant.[20]

While Dana was traveling south from Memphis, Grant was moving in the opposite direction. On April 1, along with Admiral Porter and the trusted "Cump" Sherman, Grant was taking a look at the Yazoo Pass/Haynes Bluff expedition. He didn't like what he saw, and he wired Halleck: "With present high water the extent of ground upon which troops could land . . . is so limited that the place is impregnable."[21] The next day he wrote Porter: "After the reconnaissance of yesterday, I am satisfied that an attack upon Haynes Bluff would be attended with immense sacrifice of life, if not with defeat." He ended the note with a significant suggestion: "I would, Admiral, therefore renew my request to prepare for running the blockade at as early a day as possible."[22]

On April 6, as Dana arrived at Grant's headquarters, the Vicksburg campaign was at a crucial point. Grant had decided to abandon all the previous ditch-digging and bypass efforts. Instead, he would ask the navy to run as many boats as possible past the Vicksburg batteries. Then he would move the army south, both by marching and by water, staying west of the Mississippi. He would cross the river below Vicksburg, perhaps at Grand Gulf, and approach Vicksburg from the south. This meant separating himself from his base of supplies and living off the land. It was a brave decision, one of great moral courage, and it was his alone—even the loyal Sherman was skeptical.

It is worth taking a look at both men as they were when Dana met with Grant. Dana was 43 years old; Grant was 41. Dana had left the idealistic serenity of Brook Farm some 17 years earlier, and nearly everything since had turned him away from that youthful idealism. Both in Europe and at home, he had observed people of influence: heads of state, politicians, journalists, business leaders. He had seen corruption, greed, naked ambition, and double-dealing. He had, in short, become a confirmed cynic.

And what of the man Dana had been sent to observe? Frankly, he was a puzzle. It was hard to believe that this was a commander of over 100,000 men, for as one officer said, he seemed as "plain as an old shoe." He wore a common soldier's blouse, a battered felt hat, cavalry trousers stuffed into muddy boots; only the stars on his epaulets indicated anything out of the ordinary. Previously Dana had seen generals riding the lines accompanied by cavalry escorts and showy staffs. Grant, however, rode alone or with an orderly or two on hand to carry any necessary messages. Also, while other generals seemed to enjoy staging impressive parades and reviews, Grant, who even as a cadet had disliked parades, was more thoughtful of the foot soldier: "I do not wish the troops to pass in review but merely to be drawn up in line so that I can ride by them and see the men."[23]

A private soldier, describing Grant, said, "The soldiers seem to look upon him as a friendly partner of theirs, not as an arbitrary commander. As he passes by, the private soldiers feel as free to greet him as they would to address one of their neighbors when meeting him at home. 'Good morning, General,' 'Pleasant day, General,' and like expressions are the greetings he meets everywhere. The soldiers when meeting him are never embarrassed by the thought that they are talking to a great general." In the Army of the Potomac, when George McClellan rode by, men would greet him with loud cheers or by throwing their hats in the air. For Grant, wrote the soldier, "a pleasant salute to, and a good-natured nod from him in return, seems more appropriate."[24]

One can but imagine the effect this had on Dana. The erstwhile cynic was apparently stunned by the contrast between Grant and others he'd seen. Here was, he said, "the most modest, the most disinterested, and the most honest man I ever knew, with a temper that nothing could disturb, and a judgment that was judicial in its comprehensiveness and wisdom. Not a great man, except morally; not an original or brilliant man, but sincere, thoughtful, deep, and gifted with courage that never faltered."[25] For Dana, that was more than enough to ensure both his friendship and his unswerving support.

Soon after their first conversation, Dana told Grant of his true mission. The payroll investigation cover story had fooled no one, nor

Ulysses S. Grant as a brevet second lieutenant of the 4th Infantry. As a young officer, Grant served with distinction in the Mexican War. Like Horace Greeley, however, he considered it an "unholy" cause waged for political purposes. *(USMA Library, Special Collections Division)*

Lt. Gen. Ulysses S. Grant at Cold Harbor in 1864. Already, said Congressman Elihu Washburne, he had "fought more battles, and won more victories, than any man living." Nevertheless, said one of Grant's men, "The private soldiers feel as free to greet him as they would to address one of their neighbors upon meeting him at home." *(National Archives)*

Horace Greeley, editor of the *New York Tribune*, was one of the nation's most influential figures, both in politics and in shaping public opinion. He and his managing editor, Charles Dana, made their paper a leading voice in the crusade against slavery. *(National Archives)*

Newspaperman Charles A. Dana as assistant secretary of war. *(Massachusetts Commandery, Military Order of the Loyal Legion and the U.S. Army Military History Institute)*

From Vicksburg to Appomattox, Dana was a member of Grant's inner circle. Here he
sits with Grant's council of war at Massaponax Church, Virginia, on May 21, 1864.
Grant is directly in front of the trees; Dana is on his left. On Dana's left, reading a
newspaper, is Grant's chief of staff, John A. Rawlins. *(Massachusetts Commandery,
Military Order of the Loyal Legion and the U.S. Army Military History Institute)*

From an illustration by Thomas Nast depicting Lee's surrender to Grant at Appomattox.
Acknowledging the power of the wartime press, Grant said that Nast "did as much as
any man to preserve the Union and bring the war to an end." *(Harper's Weekly)*

Nast and other Grant admirers saw Grant's 1868 nomination for the presidency as a fitting reward for the hero of the Union.
(*Harper's Weekly*)

Diogenes Has Found the Honest Man.—
(Which Is Diogenes, and Which Is the Honest Man?)

August 3, 1872

Increasingly critical of Grant's presidency, Greeley ran against him in 1872 as a candidate of both the Democrats and the Liberal Republicans. Grant's supporters took great delight in portraying the supposedly upright Greeley as an ally of the notorious William "Boss" Tweed, head of New York's corrupt Democratic political machine.
(*Harper's Weekly*)

A Burden He Has To Shoulder.

October 24, 1874

This Nast cartoon highlights some of the reasons Grant would later say, "I was never as happy in my life as the day I left the White House. I felt like a boy getting out of school." *(Harper's Weekly)*

Grant as president. As he prepared to leave office in 1877, he told Congress he had "acted in every instance from a conscientious desire to do what was right. . . . Failures have been errors of judgment, not of intent." *(National Archives)*

did it seem Dana ever intended it to. Plain and simple, he was Edwin Stanton's paid informer, sending coded messages directly to the secretary. With a different cast of characters, it could have been an inflammatory situation. Some officers were uneasy about it, and one even grumbled that they ought to throw this Washington spy into the river. Grant, however, recognized Dana for what he was—an honest reporter. He welcomed him into the headquarters inner circle. Significantly, so did John Rawlins, Grant's chief of staff, who was almost an alter ego. No doubt with a smile, Grant told Dana to write what he pleased; the more reports Dana sent to Washington, the fewer would be Grant's obligations!

"I think Grant was always glad to have me with his army," Dana would write. "He did not like letter writing, and my daily dispatches to Mr. Stanton relieved him from the necessity of describing every day what was going on in the army. From the first neither he nor any of his staff or corps commanders evinced any unwillingness to show me the inside of things. In this first interview at Milliken's Bend, for instance, Grant explained to me so fully his new plan of campaign—for there was now but one—that by three o'clock I was able to send an outline of it to Mr. Stanton."[26]

As Dana was writing Stanton, Grant likewise was telling Halleck what he had in mind: "In about three nights from this time Admiral Porter will run the Vicksburg batteries with such of his fleet as he desires to take below and I will send four steamers, the machinery protected from shot by hay bales & sand bags, to be used in transporting troops and in towing barges. . . . The embarrassments I have had to contend against on account of extreme high water cannot be appreciated by anyone not present to witness it." Then, in an apparent reference to Dana, he added: "I think however you will receive favorable reports of the condition and feeling of the Army from every impartial judge, and from all who have been sent from Washington to look after its welfare."[27]

Grant's plan called for the army to cross the river below Vicksburg and attack Grand Gulf, with McClernand's corps taking the lead. This didn't sit well with the other commanders. Both Sherman and Porter protested; so did Dana, who brashly offered his own opinion of McClernand. Grant, however, stood firm. McClernand's corps was in the best position to make the assault; he was a friend of the president; and besides, as the highest ranking officer next to Grant, he deserved the opportunity. Dana reported the conversation to Stanton, adding, "I have remonstrated so far as I could properly do so against intrusting so momentous an operation to McClernand."

This resulted in a slap on the wrist from Stanton, who promptly reminded Dana that he was there only as an observer. If he tried offering advice, it might "lead to misunderstanding and troublesome complications." A chastened Dana got the message. After that, he said, "I scrupulously followed his directions."[28]

On the night of April 19, Porter sent seven gunboats, three steamboats, and several barges on a run past the Vicksburg batteries. From a headquarters boat anchored a bit north along the far shore, Grant watched them softly glide away in the darkness. Dana, alongside Grant, saw the fleet as a "mass of black things . . . floating darkly and silently." Then as the fleet came opposite Vicksburg, he saw flashes of light and heard a roar of cannons. Dana counted some 525 discharges. In the end, however, although nearly every craft had been hit, only one steamboat had been lost, and not a single man.[29]

Six days later, on April 22, another six steamboats, along with 12 barges, ran the Vicksburg gauntlet. One steamboat was sunk, one disabled, and one badly damaged. Again, however, not a man was lost.

Grant, moving his army swiftly south through the creeks and bayous, arrived at a place called Hard Times, across the river from Grand Gulf. He urged McClernand to move swiftly, before Grand Gulf could be reinforced. A disgusted Dana wrote of McClernand: "I was astonished to find, now that he was ordered to move across the Mississippi, that he was planning to carry his bride, with her servants, and baggage along with him, although Grant had ordered that officers should leave behind everything that could impede the march."

On April 26, Dana wrote, "Grant sent for McClernand, ordering him to embark his men without losing a moment. In spite of this order, that night at dark, when a thunderstorm set in, not a single cannon or man had been moved. Instead, McClernand held a review of a brigade of Illinois troops . . . about four o'clock in the afternoon."[30]

Grant wrote an angry note to McClernand, but for the moment held on to it. On April 29, after Porter's gunboats had engaged in a lengthy gun duel with the Grand Gulf batteries, it was seen that the place was far stronger than anticipated. Accordingly, it was decided to make the landing 10 miles farther south, at Bruinsburg.

To confuse Pemberton as to the main effort, Grant asked Sherman, who was still north of Vicksburg, to make a diversionary attack. His order made it clear, however, that he knew he was giving Sherman a tricky assignment. Would the troops understand that this was only a secondary effort? And when it was over, would it be perceived as yet another failure, with newspapers having a field day at Sherman's expense? This brought a growl from Sherman: "Does General Grant think I care what the newspapers say?"

Sherman said he'd make "as strong a demonstration as possible," regardless of what might be reported. Unlike Grant, Sherman could never accept the role of a free press. In the past, reporters had urged that he be relieved, had called him crazy, and had casually revealed information of value to the enemy. By this time his resentment had evolved into outright hatred, and in his note to Grant, he minced no words: "The men have sense and will trust us. As to the reports in newspapers, we must scorn them, else they will ruin us and our country. They are as much enemies to good government as the secesh, and between the two I like the secesh best, because they are a brave, open enemy and not a set of sneaking scoundrels."[31]

No doubt with a smile, Grant read Sherman's note and probably decided this was one message he would *not* share with Dana, his new friend from the world of journalism. Personally, though, Grant could sympathize with Sherman. In his *Memoirs*, he would recall that period and a press that "pronounced me idle, incompetent, and unfit to command men in an emergency, and clamored for my removal." Worrying how this might affect his father, he'd written him that the "howlings" of the press were "painful," but had insisted that "there is no one less disturbed than myself." Then, knowing Jesse's tendency to sound off, he'd added: "I beg that you will destroy this letter. At least do not show it."[32]

For the moment, the press was the least of Grant's worries. He got to work pushing his men across the river. In the early morning of April 30, one division of McClernand's, and the entire corps of James McPherson, were on the far shore. It was a moment to remember and to savor. "When this was effected," he wrote, "I felt a degree of relief scarcely ever equalled since. Vicksburg was not yet taken it is true, nor were its defenders demoralized by any of our previous moves. I was now in the enemy's country, with a vast river and the stronghold of Vicksburg between me and my base of supplies. But I was on dry ground on the same side of the river with the enemy. All the campaigns, labors, hardships and exposures from the month of December previous to this time that had been made and endured, were for the accomplishment of this one object."[33]

16

"YOU WERE RIGHT,
AND I WAS WRONG"

NORTH OF VICKSBURG, Sherman made his "demonstration." Enthusiastic troops put on a good show, marching and countermarching until it seemed far more men were on hand than was actually the case. Pemberton took the bait, concluding that the landing south of Grand Gulf must be only a feint. Consequently, after receiving a panicky message about a force "such as has never before been seen at Vicksburg," he recalled some 3,000 troops who had been sent to challenge Grant. This was a comfort to Dana, who had fretted when the *true* plan was published in Northern papers. Ironically, however, Dana said that the Confederates probably thought those accurate reports were merely a blind.[1] In any case, Grant for the moment had the advantage of surprise; it was up to him to make use of it. Above all, he must move quickly.

As fast as troops were landed, they were set on the road to Port Gibson, marching throughout the evening and into the night. Early on May 1, leading elements ran into Confederate outposts west of town and sharp skirmishing began. Grant seemed to be everywhere. One soldier recalled seeing him as they went into action, repeatedly urging men forward, telling them to "push right along—close up fast."[2]

What began as skirmishing developed into a full-fledged battle. The outnumbered Southerners gave a good account of themselves but were finally forced to withdraw. At sundown, Confederate Gen. John Bowen sent word to Pemberton that "he would have to retire under cover of night to the other side of Bayou Pierre and await reinforcements."[3]

That evening Grant wrote Admiral Porter: "Our day's work has been very creditable . . . Our forces are on the move, and will lie very close to Port Gibson tonight—ready for early action tomorrow."[4]

Another message went to McClernand. It typified the sense of urgency that would set the tone for the campaign: "Push the enemy with skirmishers well thrown out, till it gets too dark to see him. Then place your command on eligible ground where night finds you. Park your Artillery so as to command the surrounding country and renew the attack at early dawn and if possible push the enemy from the field or capture him."[5]

Pemberton, who now sensed that Grant was the main threat, wired Jefferson Davis: "Am hurrying all re-enforcements I possibly can to Bowen. Enemy's success in passing our batteries has completely changed character of defense."[6]

When word got back to New York, Greeley's *Tribune* proudly proclaimed: "Glorious Victory at Port Gibson."[7]

As the Confederates withdrew, they left burned bridges in their wake. However, engineers spurred on by Grant's staff officer, James Harrison Wilson, rebuilt them and erected pontoon rafts to sustain the momentum. Always the emphasis was on speed, and Grant's orders were filled with phrases such as "Do this with all expedition. . . . Time is of immense importance."[8]

For the first time in 3 weeks, Charles Dana was not alongside Grant. As "non-essentials," he and 13-year-old Fred Grant had been left behind at Bruinsburg when fighting became imminent. Earlier, Grant's wife, Julia, had returned north with the younger Grant children, leaving Fred behind. One suspects that Julia thought this oldest son might have bad memories of the family's lean years. Perhaps she now wanted to ensure that he appreciated fully his father's new status.[9]

Young Fred and Dana set out on foot separately to catch up with the army. Along the way they met up. Dana wrote: "We tramped and foraged together until the next morning, when some officers who had captured two old horses gave us each one."[10]

Later that day, Grant got a chuckle from seeing his proud young son and the urbane special commissioner arriving like beggars on what he described as "two enormous horses, grown white from age, each equipped with dilapidated saddles and bridles."[11]

Dana was happy to exchange mounts a few days later. A Confederate officer, after being questioned by Grant, pointed out that his horse was personal property. "Of course while I am a prisoner," the officer said, "I do not expect to be allowed to ride the horse, but I hope you will regard him as my property, and finally restore him to me."

"Well," said Grant, "I have got four or five first-rate horses wandering somewhere about the Southern Confederacy. They have been captured from me in battle or by spies. I will authorize you, whenever you find one of them, to take possession of him. I cheerfully give him to you; but as for this horse, I think he is just about the horse Mr. Dana needs." After that, said Dana, whenever he and Grant rode together, Grant "always had some question to ask about that horse."[12]

The army was moving rapidly, heading for Jackson by way of Raymond. A jubilant Grant wrote Halleck: "This army is in the finest health and spirits. Since leaving Millikins Bend they have marched as much by night as by day, through mud and rain, without tents or much other baggage, and on irregular rations, without a complaint and with less straggling than I have ever before witnessed."[13]

Perhaps for the first time, the administration learned the boldness of Grant's plan. Dana wrote Stanton that Grant "will disregard his base and depend on the country for meat and even for bread. Beef cattle and corn are both abundant everywhere."[14]

Meanwhile, Grant told Sherman to hurry forward, explaining that as he advanced he intended to live off the land. "All we want now are men, ammunition and hard bread—we can subsist our horses on the country, and obtain considerable supplies for our troops."[15] Later, Sherman would abandon his own base without hesitation as he marched through the South. For now, though, he failed to comprehend Grant's idea. He cautioned that there was only a single road to bring supplies forward from Grand Gulf, and it would soon be jammed.

Grant set him straight: "I do not calculate upon the possibility of supplying the army with full rations from Grand Gulf. I know it will be impossible without constructing additional roads. What I do expect, however, is to get up what rations of hard bread, coffee and salt we can and make the country furnish the balance." Many considered Sherman the brightest of the Union generals; Dana, for instance, called him "a man of genius and of the widest intellectual acquisitions." With this message, however, Grant showed he was well capable of furthering Sherman's military education.[16]

McPherson's corps took Raymond after a brief fight and was sent racing for the railhead of Jackson. Sherman, on parallel roads, headed the same way. So far Grant had been guarding the crossings of the Big Black, not wanting Pemberton to get in his rear and cut the road to

Grand Gulf. Now he forgot about having an enemy in his rear—this army *had* no rear, only a front! "As I shall communicate with Grand Gulf no more," he wired Halleck, ". . . you may not hear from me for several days."[17]

Joe Johnston, who had been named overall Southern commander for Mississippi, was at Jackson with a small force of only 6,000 men. He was hoping soon to receive reinforcements from the East, hoping also to combine his troops with those of Pemberton so as to give Grant a real fight. However, Grant wasn't about to wait for Johnston's army to grow; he sent Sherman and McPherson on into Jackson. The badly outnumbered Confederates could do little more than fight a delaying action. After a few hours, they fell back, leaving the Mississippi capital to the Union army—and to Grant. That night, it was said, Grant slept in the very hotel room Johnston had occupied the night before.[18]

Dana had been doing the country, and Grant, a great service. Thanks to his reports, people in Washington had finally seen the merits of Grant and the problems being created by McClernand. Now, while they were at Jackson, a courier brought Dana a wire. He passed it to Grant; it was one of the best presents Grant ever received.

> General Grant has full and absolute authority to enforce his own commands and to remove any person who by ignorance in action or any cause interferes with or delays his operations. He has the full confidence of the Government, is expected to enforce his authority, and will be firmly and heartily supported, but he will be responsible for any failure to exert his powers. You may communicate this to him.
>
> E. M. Stanton,
> Secretary of War[19]

In other words, if Grant found it necessary to relieve McClernand, which seemed more and more likely, he would have the administration's backing.

So far, so good. However, the campaign still hung in the balance. An astute Richmond editor wrote a good analysis: "Affairs have become very critical in the Southwest. Grant's army have taken possession of the capital of Mississippi, the City of Jackson. This, besides being of itself a painful and disastrous event, places the enemy in the rear of Vicksburg, and cuts off supplies from that place. A battle or an evacuation and retreat must definitely ensue. Grant, by coming so far inland, loses all support from the navy, and exposes his communications to intercep-

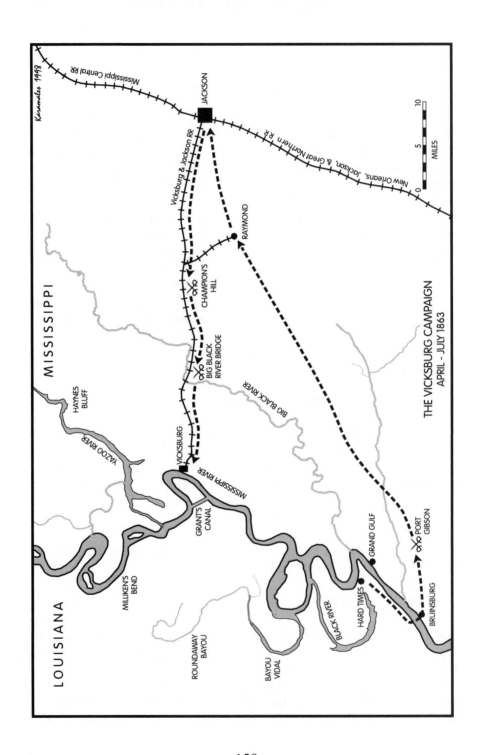

THE VICKSBURG CAMPAIGN
APRIL - JULY 1863

tion. The move is a bold one, and must be made to cost him dearly, or it will cost us dearly."[20]

At the beginning of May, Robert E. Lee and Stonewall Jackson, maneuvering brilliantly, had soundly trounced Union Gen. Joe Hooker at Chancellorsville. Hence the good news from the West was doubly welcome. Horace Greeley's headlines told the story: RAPID MARCHES AND CONTINUOUS VICTORIES—THE REBELS DRIVEN TO THE WALL—NO REST FOR THEM THERE EVEN—PORTER CO-OPERATING WITH GRANT—HE AT-TACKS AT NIGHT AND GRANT FIGHTS IN THE DAY TIME—THE REBELS ROASTED BETWEEN TWO FIRES. At Jackson, it was said, "Gen. Grant personally directed the movements, and was under fire. He rode into the city at the head of the column."[21]

When word came that Pemberton was trying to link up with Johnston, Grant began moving westward to head him off. Midway between Jackson and Vicksburg, the Union advance encountered Pemberton, drawn up in a good defensive position on Champion's Hill. Alvin Hovey's division, from McClernand's corps, attacked with gusto, and sharp fighting ensued. Then, from McPherson's corps, John Logan —a political general, but a good one—came in on Pemberton's northern flank. McClernand was ordered to hit the southern flank, but was sluggish in doing so. Fighting continued, and casualties were heavy on both sides. Finally, after 4 hours of heavy fighting, the Southerners fell back. In Grant's opinion, it was McClernand's fault the victory was not complete. "Had McClernand come up with reasonable promptness," he later wrote, ". . . I cannot see how Pemberton could have escaped with any organized force."[22]

Nevertheless, it *was* a victory, and in the East it was so reported. "Grant on the High Road to Vicksburg," said the *New York Tribune*. On the front page, a large map portrayed "The Battle Fields of Baker's Creek and Black River Bridge."[23] Grant's report referred to the battle as that of "Baker's Creek," and back east it was called that initially. Reporter Sylvanus Cadwallader of the *Chicago Times*, however, had headed his story "Champion's Hill." "Millions of people," he bragged to Grant, "would read of it by that name in my dispatches, while your official report naming it Baker's Creek was growing mouldy in the pigeon-holes of the War Department." Grant laughed and said that might be true—and it was.[24]

That night, Grant later recalled, "found McPherson's command bivou-acked from two to six miles west of the battle-field, along the line of the road to Vicksburg." Grant himself took shelter on the porch of a house serving as a Southern hospital, "filled with wounded and dying who had been brought from the battle-field we had just left." He was filled with compassion. During the fighting, he could see the enemy mowed down and not be too affected by it. Once the battle was over, however, Grant said he was "naturally disposed to do as much to alleviate the suffering of an enemy as a friend."[25]

The next day, at crossings of the Big Black River, a Confederate rear guard was swept aside, and the advance continued through a country broken by countless creeks and streams. Soldiers improvised bridges out of cotton bales, old logs, and lumber gained by tearing down any nearby buildings. By May 18, they were on the outskirts of Vicksburg. The siege had begun.

As the noose tightened around the city, Sherman was at Grant's side, impulsively blurting out an apology: "Until this moment, I never thought your expedition a success. I never could see the end clearly, until now. But this is a campaign; this is a success if we never take the town."[26]

"On the 19th," Grant wrote, "there was constant skirmishing with the enemy while we were getting into better position. The enemy had been much demoralized by his defeats at Champion's Hill and the Big Black, and I believed he would not make much effort to hold Vicksburg. Accordingly, at two o'clock, I ordered an assault."[27] This time Grant was wrong; the Confederates, now behind well-prepared fortifications, beat off the attack.

The men in blue were still confident, however, and Grant wanted to capitalize on that enthusiasm. On May 22, after a heavy preliminary bombardment, he ordered an attack all along the line. With Sherman on the right, McPherson in the center, and McClernand on the left, the three army corps jumped off against the Confederate works. Initially there were a few limited successes. In general, however, whenever a penetration was made the enemy was able to counterattack and restore the line.

Just as the attack seemed to have stalled, McClernand sent word that his men were in the trenches and could keep going if the rest of the army supported them. Although Grant was skeptical, he nevertheless sent reinforcements to McClernand and told Sherman and McPherson to resume their attacks. However, McClernand's optimism had been misplaced. The new attacks, while causing more casualties, accomplished nothing.[28] In his report to Stanton, Dana said: "At 2 p.m. McClernand reported that he was in possession of two forts of the rebel line, was hard pressed, and in great need of re-enforcements. . . . McClernand's report was false, as he held not a single fort, and the result was disastrous." For good measure, Dana added, "My own judgment is that McClernand has not the qualities necessary for a good commander, even of a regiment."[29]

Grant's report to Halleck was similar: "Gen. McClernand's dispatches misled me as to the real state of facts . . . He is entirely unfit for the position of Corps Commander both on the march and on the battle field. Looking after his Corps gives me more labor, and infinitely more uneasiness, than all the remainder of my Dept."[30]

The following day, Dana reported that Grant had determined to relieve McClernand. However, since it was obvious that Vicksburg was doomed, he would wait until the city surrendered, at which time he'd persuade McClernand to request a leave of absence.[31]

Greeley's *Tribune*, which to this point had been lavishing praise on the campaign, now became critical. Under the heading "The Rebels Making A Firm Resistance," a grim reporter wrote "of the carnage near Vicksburg on the 22d," calling it, "nothing more than a single charge of the enemy's works, which should have been simultaneous, but was not. It was unsuccessful and disastrous, whether from bad management or disobedience of orders on the part of those to whom high commands were intrusted, or from the dreadful character of the work to be performed, I will not attempt to decide. There appears to have been a want of cooperation between subordinate and superior officers and commands. . . . A second attempt to take Vicksburg by assault will not be made, I think. The place can be reduced in a short time, and at a very small sacrifice of life, by regular approaches, and that plan will probably be adopted by Gen. Grant."[32]

Grant's chief-of-staff, John Rawlins, was a self-appointed guardian of Grant's reputation and morals. In Dana's words, Rawlins watched over Grant "day and night, and whenever he commits the folly of tasting liquor hastens to remind him that at the beginning of the war he gave him [Rawlins] his word of honor not to touch a drop as long as it lasted."[33]

On June 6, Rawlins handed Grant a note that began: "The great solicitude which I feel for the safety of this army leads me to mention, what I had hoped never again to do, the subject of your drinking." Rawlins then said he might possibly be "doing you an injustice by unfounded suspicion." Still, he had heard that the general recently had a glass of wine at Sherman's headquarters, and he had seen a box of wine in Grant's tent; the wine was supposedly being saved to celebrate the capture of Vicksburg. And now, Rawlins wrote, "I find you where the wine bottle has just been emptied, in company with those who drink and urge you to do likewise. . . . If my suspicions are unfounded, let my friendship for you and my zeal for my country be my excuse for this letter."[34]

That same day, Grant decided to go up the Yazoo as far as Satartia to see how operations there were coming on. At breakfast, he asked Dana if he'd like to go along. Dana said he would, and together they rode to Haynes Bluff, where they boarded a small steamer reserved for Grant's use. According to Dana, "Grant was ill and went to bed soon after we started." Then, before they reached Satartia, Dana learned that enemy guerrillas had occupied the place and it would be unsafe to proceed. Dana went to Grant's cabin and gave him the news. Should they proceed? Grant, said Dana, was "too sick to decide." He left the decision to Dana, who gave the order to turn back.

Next morning, said Dana, "Grant came out to breakfast fresh as a rose, clean shirt and all, quite himself. 'Well, Mr. Dana,' he said, 'I suppose we are at Satartia now.'" No, Dana explained, they were back at Haynes Bluff.

Now comes the story that gives this incident special interest. According to a book later written by reporter Sylvanus Cadwallader, Grant went on a fearful binge during that trip, riding wildly cross-country while roaring drunk, falling off his horse, and finally being led to safety (and saved from disgrace) by Cadwallader, the hero of the tale. Cadwallader wrote all this when he was an old man, and his book remained unpublished until 1955. Nevertheless, Grant on a wild, drunken escapade makes a good story, and many people have swallowed it wholesale. However, those who studied it closely, scholars such as Kenneth P. Williams and John Simon, were able to poke large holes in it. Dana himself, when asked about it, said flatly that "Cadwallader was never along on the trip." Perhaps Bruce Catton summed it up best: "It is extremely hard to see how the Cadwallader story can be classed as anything but one more in the dreary Grant-was-drunk garland of myths."[35]

Despite all this, it appears that *something* happened on that trip. Evidently, using Rawlins's note as a reference, Grant had one or more drinks the evening before. If he continued drinking, and heavily, Dana's word, "sick," might have been a euphemism for "intoxicated." However, Dana's reports to Stanton said nothing about drinking. If they had, it could have been the end of Grant's career; this silence—if indeed silence was necessary—was yet another way in which Dana rescued that career. In any case, nothing that occurred on that trip caused a single casualty or delayed the capture of Vicksburg by a single minute.

In mid-June, newspapers (with help from McClernand's staff) printed an order in which McClernand congratulated his corps at the expense of Sherman and McPherson. A furious Sherman sent the clipping to Grant and pointed out that a War Department order forbade such publication without prior clearance. "It perverts the truth to the ends of flattery and self-glorification," Sherman wrote, "and contains many untruths, among which is one of monstrous falsehood." McClernand, when questioned, not only said he was responsible for the order but also said he'd stand by what was written. That did it. On June 18, Grant published an order relieving McClernand and replacing him with Gen. E. O. C. Ord. As expected, McClernand wrote directly to Lincoln to protest. By this time, however, thanks to Dana, Lincoln knew the facts. Grant had the president's support.[36]

On the northern flank of Grant's army, Sherman had disposed his troops so as to intercept Johnston should he try coming to Pemberton's aid. It was also agreed that Sherman would go after Johnston full force once Vicksburg surrendered.

Meanwhile, more trenches were dug, with the siege line drawing ever closer to Vicksburg. A *Tribune* headline read: THE ANACONDA TIGHTENING HIS COILS.[37]

By the end of the month, it was clear that the city was slowly starving. In Vicksburg, a hungry soldier wrote Pemberton: ". . . If you can't feed us, you had better surrender us . . . I tell you plainly, men are not going to lie here and perish . . . This army is now ripe for mutiny, unless it can be fed."[38]

Although surrender seemed imminent, Grant was taking no chances. A massive assault was scheduled for July 6. However, at 10:00 on the morning of July 3, white flags appeared on the Confederate works. (Back east at the same hour, 3 days of bloody fighting were reaching a climax at a small Pennsylvania town called Gettysburg.)

Two horsemen rode forward carrying a note for Grant: Pemberton proposed an armistice and the appointment of commissioners to discuss terms of surrender. In the note, Pemberton maintained he was capable of holding out for a long time. However, he wanted to avoid "the further effusion of blood," which could be "shed to a frightful extent if the siege continued." The bearer of the note, General Bowen, who had known Grant in Missouri before the war, said he'd like to talk to Grant.

Grant liked and respected Bowen. However, he'd be friendly after the surrender—not before. He refused to see Bowen but indicated he'd be willing to meet with Pemberton. His return message said: ". . . the useless effusion of blood you propose stopping by this course can be ended at any time you may choose, by the unconditional surrender of the city and garrison. Men who have shown so much endurance and courage as those now in Vicksburg will always challenge the respect of an adversary, and I can assure you will be treated with all the respect due to prisoners of war. . . . I have no other terms other than those indicated above."[39]

That afternoon, Pemberton and two of his officers rode out to meet with Grant. Grant was accompanied by McPherson and A. J. Smith. The little group drew off to one side, near a stunted oak tree. In later years, with a touch of humor, Grant would write of that tree: "It was but a short time before the last vestige of its body, root and limb had disappeared, the fragments taken as trophies. Since then the same tree has furnished as many cords of wood, in the shape of trophies, as 'The True Cross.'"[40]

Dana, sitting on the ground nearby, noted that Pemberton seemed "excited and impatient." After some discussion, it was agreed that Grant would prepare a letter giving final terms. He did so, proposing that the Confederates would stack arms in front of their lines, wait in place for paroles to be signed, and then be released. Some felt that paroling, rather than insisting on unconditional surrender as prisoners, was too generous. However, Dana, in favor of parole, said: "It would at once not only tend to the demoralization of the enemy, but also release Grant's whole army for offensive operations . . ." Just after daylight on July 4, Pemberton's note was received: "The terms proposed by you are accepted." At 10:00 A.M. the surrender was completed. At 11:00 A.M., Grant rode into the city. At his side was Dana.[41]

News was first flashed to the East by Admiral Porter. "And This On Our Ever Glorious Fourth of July," rhapsodized the *New York Tribune*. Greeley, now an ardent admirer of Grant, editorialized: "Admiral Porter's official dispatch announces the surrender of Vicksburg to 'the United States Forces'—under Gen. Grant, he might more gracefully have added."[42]

Meanwhile, one of Greeley's reporters was describing the scene: "The long agony is over. After a siege unparalleled in ancient or modern warfare, on account of certain peculiarities incident to the characters of the combatants as well as the field of operation, Vicksburg has at last fallen into the hands of Gen. Grant's army . . . At this hour of triumph, it is impossible to restrain commiserating thoughts concerning the late and now surviving defenders of the not inaptly called heroic city. Their hopes, their pride, their property are buried in graves deeper and gloomier than those in which rest their dead companions in arms."[43]

Grant received a memorable note from Sherman, saying in part: "Did I not know the honesty, modesty and purity of your nature, I would be tempted to follow the example of my standard enemies of the press in indulging in wanton flattery; but as a man and soldier and ardent friend of yours, I warn you against the incense of flattery that will fill our land from one extreme to the other. Be natural and yourself, and this glittering flattery will be as the passing breeze of the sea on a warm summer day. To me the delicacy with which you have treated a brave and deluded enemy is more eloquent than the most gorgeous oratory . . ."[44]

It was good advice, for soon accolades began pouring in. Most were accepted, appreciated, and forgotten. However, Grant would always cherish one particular letter:

> MY DEAR GENERAL: I do not remember that you and I ever met personally. I write this now as a grateful acknowledgment for the almost inestimable service you have done the country. I wish to say a word further. When you first reached the vicinity of Vicksburg, I thought you should do, what you finally did—march the troops across the neck, run the batteries with the transports, and thus go below; and I never had any faith, except a general hope that you knew better than I, that the Yazoo Pass expedition, and the like, could succeed. When you got below and took Port Gibson, Grand Gulf and vicinity, I thought you should go down river and join Gen. Banks; and when you turned Northward East of the Big Black, I feared it was a mistake. I now wish to make the personal acknowledgment that you were right, and I was wrong.
> Yours very truly,
> A. Lincoln[45]

17

"WET, DIRTY AND WELL"

AFTER THE disastrous Fredericksburg campaign, Horace Greeley declared that Ambrose Burnside's "usefulness as commander of the Army of the Potomac was at an end."[1] Lincoln agreed, and Burnside was shunted off to the Army of the Ohio. There, in June 1863, Burnside blundered again, issuing an order against disloyal statements, suppressing the *Chicago Times*, and banning circulation of the *New York World* in his department. Greeley, a fierce defender of press freedom, chaired a meeting of newspaper representatives and issued a heated protest to the administration. Under pressure from Greeley and others, Lincoln agreed to have Burnside's ill-advised order withdrawn.[2]

Later that same month, however, Greeley came to the president's support. Lee was on the move, bringing his army north into Pennsylvania, and on the eve of battle, the arrogant "Fighting Joe" Hooker, a man whose talent did not match his ambition, was replaced by Gen. George Meade. Greeley wrote: "We believe that every decided failure by a commander should be promptly followed by his displacement. . . . In judging the President harshly, people forget the truth that the human race has in all history produced but a few really great generals. Mr. Lincoln has been required to make brick, straw or no straw."[3]

On July 3, as guns roared at Gettysburg, Greeley was writing: "These are the times that try men's souls! The peril of our country's overthrow is great and imminent."[4] Fortunately for the Union, and the nervous Greeley's state of mind, the North was victorious both at Gettysburg and at Vicksburg. Grant's Vicksburg campaign, according to Greeley, was unequaled "in brilliancy of conception and . . . execution."[5] Not long before he had favored Rosecrans; perhaps he now saw Grant as that "really great general" the country needed.

Greeley was often erratic, but he had never wavered in his hatred of slavery. In early June he'd written: "The day of compromises and concessions has gone by. The Rebellion has made every honest and thinking American an Abolitionist."[6] Not everyone agreed. Former slaves were drifting north and competing for low-paid jobs; laborers in New York, many of them recent immigrants, saw blacks as the cause of their problems. They cursed emancipation, cursed the new conscription law, and went on to curse Greeley for supporting both blacks *and* the draft.

On July 13, violent anti-draft rioting broke out in New York City. A mob stormed the enrollment office, smashed the lottery machinery, and set fire to the building. Soldiers trying to stem the tide were met with a fusillade of bricks and stones. Two of them were beaten to death with their own muskets. Thousands joined the rioting, burning buildings, clubbing policemen to death, chasing and killing blacks.

Rioters shouted that Greeley was "the nigger's friend—lynch him!" Someone heard a mob singing "We'll hang old Greeley from a sour apple tree!" That night scores of men broke into the *Tribune* offices, smashing desks and burning papers before a swarm of policemen drove them off. The next night they were back again. A supply of muskets had arrived from Governors Island, and printers and editors, fully armed, went on doing their job. The peace-loving Greeley protested the presence of guns: "Take 'em away! I don't want to kill anybody, and besides they're a lot more likely to go off and kill us."

As rioters outside the building shouted and threatened, Greeley was advised to slip out the back way. He refused, and when it was time for his dinner, he left by the main entrance and walked through the mob. Not a hand was laid on him.

By the time it was over, the riots had claimed hundreds of lives and whole city blocks were in ruins. Remarkably, the *Tribune* managed to come out on schedule. Greeley wrote: "Relentless and cruel and cowardly as all mobs are, the actions of this at least are equal to any that have yet earned a record in history. . . . Resistance to the Draft was merely the occasion of the outbreak; absolute disloyalty and hatred to the negro were the moving cause."

As for the *Tribune*, Greeley said, ". . . . the mob appeared in front of our office . . . Reenforced at dark by ruffians from the upper part of the city, they made their assault upon this building, completely sacking its publication office. By the timely, energetic and brave efforts of a company of policemen under Capt. Thorne, the whole structure was barely saved from destruction."[7]

Vicksburg was secured, and Grant was eager to get moving again. Dana wrote Stanton: "General Grant, being himself intensely occupied, desires me to say that he would like to receive from General Halleck as soon as practicable either general or specific instructions as to the future conduct of the war in his department."[8]

In the meantime, Grant sent Sherman to drive Joe Johnston out of Mississippi. By July 17, Johnston had retreated, evacuating Jackson, the Mississippi capital, and "destroying the roads as he passed." He had such a head start, Grant said, that "pursuit was useless."[9]

Dana wrote his final reports and headed home. Those reports contained, among other things, candid evaluations of key officers, with special praise for Grant and Sherman. Perceptively, however, he also identified a major Grant flaw, the same one that would later bedevil Grant's presidency. After writing of a certain officer's incompetence, Dana said: "General Grant knows, of course, that he is not the right person; but it is one of his weaknesses that he is unwilling to hurt the feelings of a friend, and so keeps him on."[10]

Stanton, a man not known for compliments, had told Dana his reports were "looked for with deep interest," adding, "I can not thank you as much as I feel for the service you are now rendering."[11]

Back in the nation's capital, Dana found that Grant was the man of the hour, especially since Meade, the hero of Gettysburg, had become something of a disappointment. From Washington, Dana wrote his friend Colonel Wilson: "I got here very safely, and I find everybody in distress because Meade failed to capture Lee. There can be no question that a vigorous attack, seasonably made, must have resulted in the surrender of his entire army."[12]

Lincoln and Stanton, still looking for that "really great general," began to think of Grant as a replacement for Meade. Dana, who doubted that Grant would want the job, was asked to sound him out.

In early August, Grant wrote Dana: "General Halleck and yourself were both very right in supposing that it would cause me more sadness than satisfaction to be ordered to the command of the Army of the

Potomac. Here I know the officers and men and what each general is capable of as a separate commander. There I would have all to learn. Here I know the geography of the country and its resources. There it would be a new study. Besides, more or less dissatisfaction would necessarily be produced by importing a general to command an army already well supplied with those who have grown up with it. . . . I feel very grateful for your timely intercession in saving me from going to the Army of the Potomac. While I would disobey no order, I would beg very hard to be excused before accepting that command."[13]

A few days earlier, John Rawlins had arrived in Washington, sent there by Grant, who was becoming less of a political innocent. If there was any more fallout from the McClernand situation, Rawlins could help Dana explain things. Grant also gave Rawlins a letter for Lincoln. The final paragraph must have delighted the president: "I would be pleased if you could grant Colonel Rawlins an interview, and I know in asking this you will feel relieved when I tell you he has not a favor to ask for himself or any other living being. Even in my position it is a great luxury to meet a gentleman who has no ax to grind, and I can appreciate that it is infinitely more so in yours."[14]

At about this time there were ominous stirrings south of the border. French Emperor Napoleon III, taking advantage of America's preoccupation with its own war, was trying to establish a French presence in Mexico. A French army had occupied Mexico City and was prepared to install Austrian Archduke Maximilian as emperor of Mexico. Lincoln wrote Grant that, "in view of recent events in Mexico, I am greatly impressed with the importance of reestablishing the national authority in western Texas as soon as possible."[15] This was a job for Gen. Nathaniel Banks, whose headquarters was in New Orleans. Accordingly, Grant was asked to send an army corps to Banks for operations west of the Mississippi.

Grant went to New Orleans to coordinate the move. While he was there, hundreds of curious citizens turned out to see the famed hero of Vicksburg. There was a reception in his honor, followed the next day by an impressive military review involving two full army corps. Grant, as reviewing officer, trooped the line mounted on a borrowed horse. He later described the accident that followed: "The horse I rode was vicious and but little used, and on my return to New Orleans ran away and, shying at a locomotive in the street, fell. . . . My leg was swollen from the knee to the thigh, and the swelling, almost to the point of bursting, extended along the body up to the arm-pit. The pain was almost beyond endurance."[16] A week or so later, Grant was carried on a litter to a waiting steamboat for the return to Vicksburg.

Back in Washington, Stanton had another mission for Dana, this time he was to observe Rosecrans's Army of the Cumberland. (Actually, he was supposed to have visited Burnside's army first, but this had proved unfeasible.) Ever since the battle of Stones River, fought at the beginning of '63, Rosecrans had been in eastern Tennessee, giving various reasons for his lack of activity. Dana, catching up with him at Chattanooga, had a letter from Stanton saying the bearer was "one of my assistants, who visits your command for the purpose of conferring with you upon any subject which you may desire to have brought to the notice of the department."[17] Before long, Dana was sending copious reports. These, after being initally favorable to Rosecrans, grew increasingly critical.

Then came the battle of Chickamauga. On September 19, a telegrapher at his side, Dana sent no less than 11 dispatches—almost a play-by-play account of the fighting. A sampling of those first-day reports shows an excess of optimism:

> 10:30 A.M.: "Rosecrans has everything ready to grind up Bragg's flank."
>
> 2:30 P.M.: "The fight continues to rage . . . Decisive victory seems assured to us."
>
> 4:30 P.M.: "I do not dare to say our victory is complete, but it seems certain. Enemy silenced on nearly whole line."
>
> 7:30 P.M.: "Rosecrans will renew the fight at daylight. His dispositions are now being made."[18]

That night Dana attended Rosecrans's council of war, and the next morning he was with him on the Union right when screaming Confederates broke through the line. He looked over at Rosecrans, known as a devout Catholic, and saw him make a hasty sign of the cross. With that, Dana figured they must be in real trouble. As he later recalled: "I saw our lines break and melt away like leaves before the wind. . . . The whole right of our army had apparently been routed."[19] Dana turned his horse and returned to Chattanooga, some 12 miles away. There he found Rosecrans, seemingly unaware that the battle still raged. On the Union left, steady George Thomas was holding firm and earning the sobriquet "Rock of Chickamauga." Thomas's star was definitely rising.

And Rosecrans, the man Greeley once wanted to sponsor, would never again be a major figure.

Dana's message to Stanton made a bad situation look even worse than it was: "My report to-day is of deplorable importance. Chickamauga is as fatal a name in our history as Bull Run."[20] Later, when Thomas's stand became known, things looked a bit brighter. Also, since Confederate leader Braxton Bragg did not follow up on his victory, Union troops were able to dig in and hunker down around Chattanooga. Nevertheless, they were now hemmed in.

As for Dana, his opinion of Rosecrans went into freefall. "While few persons exhibited more estimable social qualities," he would say, "I have never seen a public man possessing talent with less administrative power, less clearness and steadiness in difficulty, and greater incapacity than General Rosecrans. . . . with great love of command, he was a feeble commander."[21]

Since it was clear that the Army of the Cumberland had lost confidence in Rosecrans, Dana suggested to Stanton that someone from the West, notably Grant, might be the man to take over. He did not know that Grant had already been summoned.

Grant, although still sore, was able to get out of bed and hobble about on crutches by this time. The partial mobility came none too soon. In early October there was a message from the War Department: "It is the wish of the Secretary of War that as soon as General Grant is able he will come to Cairo and report by telegraph."[22]

At Cairo, there was another message, telling him to proceed immediately to the Galt House in Louisville, Kentucky, where a War Department representative would meet him with instructions. He should take with him his whole headquarters staff. Evidently a new assignment was in the works.

When Grant got as far as Indianapolis, he learned that a special train had just arrived carrying the War Department personage he was to meet. It was none other than the gruff, somewhat intimidating, Secretary of War himself. The black-bearded Edwin Stanton, wheezing from asthma and nursing a cold, came aboard Grant's train. Despite his condition, Stanton advanced briskly, seized the hand of Grant's bearded medical director, Dr. E. D. Kittoe, and began pumping it vigorously. "General Grant," said Stanton, "I recognized you at once from your pictures!"

When the real Grant stepped forward, the embarrassed Stanton might have been disappointed to find the conqueror of Vicksburg so short and plain; all his life Grant was never one to stand out in a crowd. However, the embarrassment was short-lived, and soon the pair got down to business. Stanton dismissed his own train, and aboard Grant's, as it chugged on to Louisville, the secretary explained that he and Lincoln were solving the command problem in the West once and for all. The three armies of the Ohio, the Cumberland, and the Tennessee were being combined into a newly created Military Division of the Mississippi. Grant would be named to command it.

Stanton showed Grant two sets of orders. One left army commands unchanged, the other had George Thomas replacing Rosecrans. Without hesitation Grant chose Thomas.[23]

It's impossible to know exactly how much Grant owed his promotion to Dana, the man Lincoln called "the eyes of the government at the front."[24] Obviously, however, he'd been a factor. Each Dana dispatch, after being read at the War Department, had been sent promptly to the White House. In those dispatches, Dana had given Grant a glowing report card, and it surely hadn't hurt.

Dana, still in Chattanooga, received a message from Washington asking him to meet Stanton at the Galt House in Louisville. He set out in bad weather along muddy, narrow roads jammed with wagons. Incoming drivers, with half-starved horses, and with roads growing progressively worse, were forced to throw overboard much of their cargo in order to lighten their loads. Meanwhile, they blocked wagons making a return trip. It had become a frustrating gridlock. At one point 500 teams were halted between the mountain and the Tennessee River, unable to move and with no forage for the dying animals.

After threading his way through a sickening mass of carcasses, Dana finally reached a railhead and boarded a train. At Nashville, however, well short of Louisville, an officer came aboard his train. "General Grant wants to see you," the officer said.

The startled Dana hadn't seen Grant since Vicksburg and had no idea he was in Tennessee. When Dana entered the general's compartment, Grant said, "I am going to interfere with your journey, Mr. Dana. I have got the Secretary's permission to take you back with me to Chattanooga. I want you to dismiss your train and get in mine; we will give you comfortable quarters."

"General," Dana said, "did you ask the Secretary to let me go back with you?"

"I did. I wanted to have you."[25]

Despite Grant's assurances, most of the journey was on horseback and far from "comfortable." Rawlins later described the route, saying "valleys were the muddiest and the mountain road the roughest and steepest of ascent and descent ever crossed by army wagons and mules. . . . one riding over it, if he did not see it with his own eyes . . . would not believe it possible for him to do so."[26] Once Grant's horse slipped in the glutinous mud and fell, aggravating the general's injured leg. Finally, after 2 weary days, and amid a chilling rain, Grant and his party reached Thomas's headquarters in Chattanooga.

That night young Capt. Horace Porter, meeting Grant for the first time, saw, "a general officer, slight in figure and of medium stature, whose face bore an expression of weariness. He was carelessly dressed, and his uniform coat was unbuttoned and thrown back from his chest. He held a lighted cigar in his mouth, and sat in a stooping posture, with his head bent slightly forward. His clothes were wet, and his trousers and top-boots were spattered with mud." Next morning Dana's dispatch began: "Grant arrived last night, wet, dirty and well."[27]

The hungry army in Chattanooga, Grant realized, was in effect blockaded. All supplies had to be brought from Nashville, but the government controlled rail lines only as far as Bridgeport, on the Tennessee River. As Grant later explained: "Bragg, holding Lookout and Raccoon mountains west of Chattanooga, commanded the railroad, the river, and the shortest and best wagon-roads, both south and north of the Tennessee, between Chattanooga and Bridgeport."[28] By rail, Bridgeport was only 26 miles away. The Union army, however, was forced to use the narrow, treacherous, 60-mile mountain route. Fortunately, Thomas and his able engineer, W. F. "Baldy" Smith, had a plan for breaking the siege.

Next morning, despite the pain in his injured leg, Grant rode out with Thomas and Smith to see what they had in mind. Smith outlined a plan that relied on both daring and stealth. Grant liked what he heard and gave orders to set the plan in motion.

At 3:00 A.M. on October 27, in pitch darkness, a Union brigade climbed into 60 crude pontoon boats and began drifting downriver. Silently, using oars only for steering, they floated past unaware Southern pickets. Then, when they reached a point known as Brown's Ferry, they stormed ashore and quickly overran a Confederate outpost. As men in blue dug in on their tiny beachhead, a second brigade came along the north shore carrying guns and lumber. The pontoons, no longer needed for transportation, went into a hastily erected bridge. By 10:00 the next morning, the bridge was in place and men were crossing to the far shore, enlarging and fortifying the beachhead.

The plan also involved Joe Hooker's army at Bridgeport. Grant had Hooker cross to the south shore of the Tennessee and begin marching east. Before long he was within a mile of the beachhead, ready to link up. Bragg finally realized what was happening. That night he sent James Longstreet, Grant's friend from the old army, to attack the division of Gen. John Geary, thereby cutting off Hooker. After brisk fighting, Longstreet was repulsed. At one point some Union mules, terrified by the shooting, broke loose from their traces and stampeded in the direction of the enemy. In the darkness, the wild galloping sounded like a cavalry charge, causing a Southern detachment to break and run. Afterward, a witty quartermaster, wanting to recognize such "distinguished" service, asked that the mules, because of their gallantry, "have conferred upon them the brevet rank of horses."

By the evening of October 28, with the river line secured, Grant was able to wire Halleck: "General Thomas' plan for securing the river and south side road hence to Bridgeport has proven eminently successful. The question of supplies may now be regarded as settled."

Although the plan had been conceived and implemented by Thomas and Smith, it came so soon after Grant's arrival that soldiers tended to give him much of the credit for opening what they called "the cracker line." With obvious pride, Grant would write: "In five days from my arrival in Chattanooga the way was open to Bridgeport and with the aid of steamers and Hooker's teams, in a week the troops were receiving full rations. It is hard for any one not an eye-witness to realize the relief this brought."[29]

Near the end of October, Grant rode out to inspect the lines. He came to a point where pickets on either side of a stream had on their own established an informal truce. A Union soldier, recognizing him, shouted, "Turn out the guard for the commanding general!"

"Never mind the guard," Grant said. Taking only a bugler with him, he rode forward cautiously, only to hear a Confederate sing out, "Turn out the guard for the commanding general—General Grant!" Good-natured Confederates promptly formed in line and rendered a salute. Grant lifted his hat to return the salute, then rode on. The British military historian J. F. C. Fuller, telling of the incident, said dryly, "It was truly a picturesque war."[30]

Sherman and his army were coming east, and with their help, Grant planned to force Bragg from Missionary Ridge and begin driving south. First, however, he was faced with new concerns. He learned that Longstreet had withdrawn from the Chattanooga area and was threatening Ambrose Burnside's army, around Knoxville in eastern Tennessee. Once again, Grant showed his confidence in Dana, sending him to Burnside to evaluate the situation.

On November 9, Dana started for Burnside's headquarters along with Colonel Wilson and an assigned cavalry escort. At Knoxville, meeting Burnside for the first time, Dana was not impressed. Perhaps he had been influenced by Burnside's past problems with the press plus his abysmal performance at Fredericksburg. In any case, Dana said current plans seemed to fluctuate by the hour. First there was talk of retreat, then of holding in place until relief came from Grant, then of sending out a spoiling force to delay the enemy. All in all, Dana and Wilson concluded that no action was imminent. They returned to Chattanooga, arriving there on November 17.[31]

The following day, November 18, 1863, some 600 miles to the north, Abraham Lincoln was in Gettysburg, Pennsylvania, to help dedicate a cemetery. His brief remarks began "Four score and seven years ago" and concluded with a stirring resolve "that these dead shall not have died in vain; that this nation, under God, shall have a new birth of freedom, and that government of the people, by the people, for the people, shall not perish from the earth."

Generations of future schoolchildren would learn and recite Lincoln's memorable Gettysburg Address. The next day, however, the anti-Lincoln *Chicago Times* would say: "The cheek of every American must tingle with shame as he reads the silly, flat and dishwatery utterances of the man who has to be pointed out to intelligent foreigners as the President of the United States."[32]

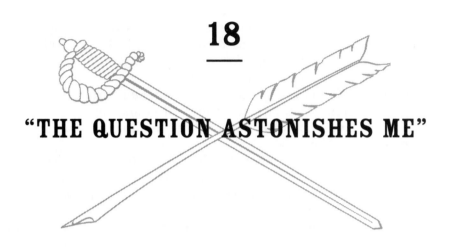

18

"THE QUESTION ASTONISHES ME"

DANA REPORTED his return to Chattanooga, which brought a friendly message from Stanton: "Your dispatches of yesterday are received. I am rejoiced that you have got safely back. My anxiety about you for several days has been very great."[1] Stay where you are, Dana was told, and keep sending those valuable dispatches. He did, and soon was able to report that Grant had a plan for breaking out of Bragg's encirclement.

Meanwhile, Longstreet's attack on Knoxville had gotten under way, and Grant was being urged to go to Burnside's aid. Like any skilled fighter, however, he knew a good offense was the best defense. "Reinforcements could not help Burnside," he would write, "because he had neither supplies nor ammunition sufficient for them; hardly, indeed, bread and meat for the men he had. There was no relief possible for him except by expelling the enemy from Missionary Ridge and Chattanooga."[2]

As for holding off Longstreet, Grant wasn't about to second-guess the man on the spot. He gave Burnside a vote of confidence. "Being there," he told him, "you can tell better how to resist Longstreet's attack than I can direct."

All the same, people in Washington were in what Grant termed an "agony of suspense." "My suspense was also great," he admitted, "but more endurable, because I was where I could soon do something to relieve the situation."[3]

Earlier, Sherman had come forward to meet with Grant and Thomas. On November 15 they had made their plans, then Sherman had returned to hurry his men forward. Under the plan, Sherman would march his army, under cover of the hills, to a point opposite Bragg's right flank, the north end of Missionary Ridge. That night "Baldy" Smith would lay a pontoon bridge so Sherman could cross the river. Then, at dawn and supported by the corps of Oliver Howard, Sherman would hit Bragg's right flank. On the far flank, Hooker would attack the Confederates on Lookout Mountain. Thomas, in the center, would cooperate as circumstances required. Ideally, it would be a double envelopment, with both Sherman and Hooker aiming for the enemy's rear. Grant wanted to smash Bragg entirely, not just force him to withdraw. However, as Dana pointed out, "It is almost never possible to execute a campaign as laid out, especially when it requires so many concerted movements as this one."[4]

Thomas began the action on November 23, rolling his men forward against Bragg's intermediate outposts on the hills fronting Missionary Ridge, the highest of which was called Orchard Knob. That night, with Dana on hand to observe, Sherman prepared to cross the Tennessee. A Union captain remembered filing silently to the river's edge and being handed a spade for later entrenching. He and his men climbed into waiting pontoon boats, and Sherman himself was on hand, saying softly, "Be prompt as you can, boys, there's room for thirty in a boat."

Pickets on the far shore were soon overpowered, and at daybreak, said the captain, his men were "digging in like beavers." Presently, he said, "an old Quaker farmer came down to expostulate with us for ruining his farm by such digging. The scene was ludicrous, and the boys gave a derisive little cheer for 'Broad-brim.'"[5]

During the night, engineers had managed to complete a bridge. "It was marvelous," said Dana, "with what vigor the work went on. Sherman told me he had never seen anything done so quietly and so well . . . he did not believe the history of war could show a bridge of that length—about thirteen hundred and fifty feet—laid down so noiselessly in so short a time."

That same evening, on the Union right, Hooker's men were climbing the slopes of Lookout Mountain. Everything seemed to be in place, and Dana wired Stanton: "Grant has given orders for a vigorous attack at daybreak by Sherman on the left, and Granger [commanding a corps of Thomas's army] in the centre, and if Bragg does not withdraw the remainder of his troops, we shall have a decisive battle."[6]

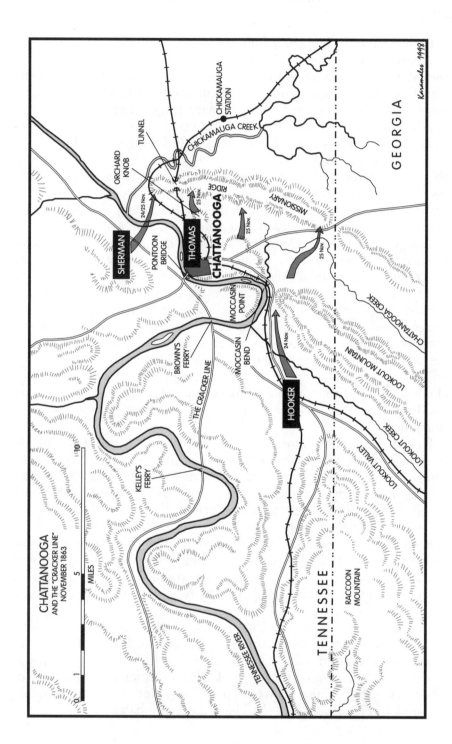

CHATTANOOGA
AND THE 'CRACKER LINE'
NOVEMBER 1863

MILES
0 1 5 10

Kenneder 1998

GEORGIA

CHICKAMAUGA
STATION

CHICKAMAUGA CREEK

TUNNEL

ORCHARD
KNOB

24/25 Nov.

25 Nov.

MISSIONARY RIDGE

25 Nov.

SHERMAN

PONTOON
BRIDGE

THOMAS

CHATTANOOGA

25 Nov.

MOCCASIN
POINT

CHATTANOOGA CREEK

BROWN'S
FERRY

THE CRACKER LINE

MOCCASIN
BEND

24 Nov.

LOOKOUT MOUNTAIN

HOOKER

KELLEY'S
FERRY

LOOKOUT CREEK

LOOKOUT VALLEY

TENNESSEE

TENNESSEE RIVER

RACCOON
MOUNTAIN

178

On November 24, Sherman moved forward and seized high ground. Ahead was an eminence known as Tunnel Hill, which he believed was the north end of Missionary Ridge. He told Grant he'd be in position to attack the ridge at dawn. However, he was seriously mistaken about his location. Between Sherman and Missionary Ridge lay another deep valley with steep sides. Moreover, now facing him was Gen. Pat Cleburne with one of the South's finest divisions.[7]

The next day, Grant was on Orchard Knob with the ubiquitous Dana, watching a battle spread out in a mighty panorama. In a rare Civil War event, an army commander could observe his entire force in action simultaneously. Sherman was attacking on the left; Hooker on the right. In the center, Thomas stood ready to help.[8]

Soon it became clear that Sherman's force was bogged down. Hooker's men, however, were more fortunate as they scaled a peak once thought impregnable. It would later be known as the "Battle Above the Clouds," but in truth it wasn't that much of a battle. By this time most Confederates had been withdrawn from Lookout Mountain in order to reinforce the line elsewhere. Grant told Hooker to keep going and to try getting behind Bragg's left flank. Hooker's lead elements, however, were stalled for hours by a destroyed bridge and the swollen waters of Chattanooga Creek.

With action now on both flanks, it was time to relieve the pressure by striking the center. Thomas was ordered to "carry the rifle pits at the foot of Missionary Ridge and when carried to reform his lines on the rifle pits with a view to carrying the ridge."[9]

Thomas sent four divisions forward, some 20,000 men, more than Pickett had had at Gettysburg. In Dana's words: "It was a bright, sunny afternoon, and as the forces marched across the valley in front of us as regularly as if on parade, it was a great spectacle."[10]

The blue ranks surged forward, bayonets bristling and all flags flying. As they approached the base of Missionary Ridge, men broke into a run. In an amazingly short time, they swarmed over the defenders and carried the first line of rifle pits. Many Confederates surrendered; others began racing upward to the presumed safety of the next line. Union officers saw what was happening and urged their men to keep going. As Grant watched, startled by this new turn of events, inspired soldiers charged upward, sweeping everything before them, past the middle line of rifle pits and all the way to the summit. Bragg's army was on its way back to Georgia.

According to legend, the charge up Missionary Ridge was made by enthusiastic, impulsive troops acting on their own initiative. It made a good story, to which Dana contributed greatly by writing, "The storming of the ridge by our troops was one of the greatest miracles in military history. . . . Neither Grant nor Thomas intended it. Their orders were to carry the rifle pits along the base of the Ridge and capture their occupants, but when this was accomplished, the unaccountable spirit of the troops bore them bodily up those impracticable steeps . . ."[11]

British analyst J. F. C. Fuller said Dana was wrong when he called it a "miracle." "It was nothing of the sort," Fuller said. "It was an act of common sense. . . . The attacking troops, seeing their enemy run, instinctively ran after him; thus they carried the ridge in one bound instead of two."[12]

Officers at all levels realized they would be exposed to plunging fire from above if they stayed where they were. Therefore, when the enemy began running, they urged their men to follow. For example, Philip Sheridan, a division commander in Thomas's army, was yelling at the top of his voice, "Forward, boys, forward! We can go to the top!"

While neither Grant nor Thomas had given an order to keep going, it was always their intention to press the attack after regrouping. Nevertheless, the story persisted that the soldiers had done it on their own. A colonel in Sheridan's division would cite four of his officers "for the gallant manner in which they encouraged their men up the side of the mountain." Another report from that division, this by a brigadier general, began: "I ordered the command to storm the ridge . . ." In truth, men went up Missionary Ridge for a traditional military reason—their officers told them to.[13]

In any case, Chattanooga was secure. Grant could now turn his attention to Burnside's predicament at Knoxville. First, though, he had to consider Bragg. Was he really heading south? Or might he regather his forces and move toward a linkup with Longstreet? On November 27, Grant rode forward and saw that the retreat was very real indeed. He later wrote: "The enemy had been throwing away guns, caissons, and small-arms, abandoning provisions, and, altogether, seemed to be moving like a disorganized mob, with the exception of Cleburne's division, which was acting as rear-guard to cover the retreat."[14]

As always, success had to be shared with his beloved Julia. Three days later, his satisfaction showing, he wrote her about "the utter rout and demoralization of the enemy."[15]

Next, Grant designated the corps of Gen. Gordon Granger to go to Burnside's relief. However, when Granger didn't move quickly enough, Grant gave the job to Sherman. He also sent Colonel Wilson to tell Burnside that help was on the way. Dana, as always wanting to be near the action, volunteered to go along.[16]

It turned out that Longstreet had attacked Burnside on November 29 and been repulsed. Then, learning both of Bragg's defeat and Sherman's approach, Longstreet left the area heading northeast. Greeley's *Tribune* was ecstatic: "Decisive news at last from East Tennessee—news more glorious and infinitely more important than if we had heard of a battle and a victory almost anywhere else. The siege of Knoxville is at an end. The Rebel effort to regain East Tennessee is abandoned forever."[17]

With Burnside now in good shape, Dana was free to return to Chattanooga, where Grant was ready with another request. Clearly, the war was over for the winter in eastern Tennessee and northern Georgia. There was no need for Dana to remain, and presumably he would be returning to Washington. In that case, he could help by presenting Grant's future plans to Stanton and Lincoln. Face-to-face, he could amplify what had earlier been put in writing. Basically, rather than going into winter quarters, Grant wanted to mount another offensive—all the way to Mobile, Alabama.[18]

While Dana was talking to Stanton, Grant would write Halleck of his proposal. For the moment, going to Atlanta was not in the cards. Too many mountains to cross; too many bad roads; too few provisions available for an invading army. Going toward Mobile, however, would be of major strategic advantage. "It seems to me," Grant wrote Halleck, "this move would secure the entire states of Alabama and Mississippi and a part of Georgia, or force Lee to abandon Virginia and North Carolina. Without this course the enemy have not got army enough to resist the army I can take."[19]

Finally a Union general was looking at the "big picture" and seeing the war as a whole. So far, men had talked separately of "war in the west" or "war in the east." Now Grant was saying that the North's overwhelming assets should be coordinated, used without letup, and used to win not just battles but a complete and final victory. The implications of the proposal, and of the man making the proposal, were not lost on Lincoln. For the moment, however, or at least until Longstreet was safely out of Tennessee, the Mobile operation would have to be put on hold.

On December 8, the president wrote Grant: "Understanding that your lodgment at Knoxville and at Chattanooga is now secure, I wish to tender you, and all under your command, my more than thanks, my profoundest gratitude for the skill, courage, and perseverance with which you and they, over so great difficulties, have effected that important object. God bless you all."[20]

Congratulations came not only from Lincoln. Predictably, the Chattanooga triumph was cheered long and loud by the Northern press. A

Tribune headline, THE GREAT VICTORY, was followed by words that thrilled people hungry for a Northern success: "The victory at Chattanooga is decisive. The Rebels were beaten at all points . . . and were driven yesterday in full retreat toward Dalton, burning bridges and destroying stores as they fled. Fifty-two cannon, from five to ten thousand prisoners, large quantities of small arms, camp and garrison equipage, and ten flags, are trophies of the fight."

In the same issue, Greeley went out of his way to praise Grant personally: "The victorious army of Gen. Grant is irresistible by any force the enemy can oppose to him. . . . Gen. Grant is master of the whole field—and of himself. To his genius and energy, and to the noble army which he commands, the nation may trust its destiny without fear and without impatience."[21]

The *New York Herald*, not to be outdone, proclaimed: "Gen. Grant is one of the great soldiers of the age . . . without an equal in the list of generals now alive." The *New York World* joined the chorus, saying: "General Grant . . . has evolved a victory for our arms the importance of which it is yet impossible to estimate." It was especially noteworthy, said the *World*, because it was "not coupled with news of a great and terrible slaughter." This was true. For the size of the victory, casualties had been surprisingly light.[22]

With matters quiet for the moment, Grant decided to move his headquarters to Nashville, leaving Thomas in command at Chattanooga. Although his nature was to be a "hands-on" commander, in a position to see the action and, if necessary, to influence it, his responsibilities now extended over a wide geographic area. Nashville, he said, was "the most central point from which to communicate with my entire military division, and also with the authorities at Washington."[23]

Hundreds of miles away, meanwhile, events in Washington were starting to shape Grant's future. In Congress, Grant's supporter Elihu Washburne introduced a bill to revive the grade of lieutenant general. It was obvious, of course, that if a third star became legal, it would be intended for Grant.

Grant might have been flattered, but he didn't think a promotion was warranted. After thanking Washburne for his interest, he said: "But recollect that I have been highly honored already by the government and do not ask or feel that I deserve anything more in the shape of honors or promotion. A success over the enemy is what I crave above everything else . . ."[24]

When the promotion bill became known, Bennett's *New York Herald* hinted that the whole thing was a political ploy of Lincoln's. A cynical editorial said, ". . . the rank is to be revived that it may be conferred on General Grant, in the hope no doubt that such a high military position will switch him off the Presidential track . . . If the politicians think they are going to beat General Grant, General McClellan or any other general out of the Presidency by any humbug of this sort they will find themselves woefully mistaken."[25]

Soon the *Herald* began beating the drums in earnest. The people were sick of politicians, said Bennett. Grant, whose "opinions on parties and party questions" were completely unknown, would be a welcome change. "Let the independent masses of the people, who have cut themselves loose from the machinery of the corrupt and dismantled political parties of the day, take this Presidential business into their own hands and bring General Grant at once into the field. A few town and country meetings . . . will put the ball in motion, and once fairly in motion it cannot be arrested."[26]

Horace Greeley was also cynical—but mostly about James Gordon Bennett. *Herald* "crusades," Greeley suggested, were only devices to boost circulation. Bennett's support, in fact, was a kiss of death. "This vivacious journal," wrote Greeley, "now seeks a new sensation in the person of Gen. Grant. The furor with which it lays hold of its fresh victim indicates that its passion will not last long . . . We have the highest appreciation of Gen. Grant. We believe there can be scarcely any limit set to his powers of endurance. And, having as much confidence in the sincerity of our contemporary as we ever had, we beg leave to assure it that there are some things which even Ulysses S. Grant cannot survive, viz. six articles per day in its columns in favor of his nomination and election to the Presidency."[27]

Now that a Grant candidacy had been mentioned, politicians swung into action. A Democratic functionary from Ohio wrote Grant to ask if he could present Grant's name as a candidate for the presidency. Grant's reply was uncharacteristically abrupt: "The question astonishes me. I do not know of anything I have ever done or said which would indicate that I could be a candidate for any office whatever . . . Nothing likely to happen would pain me so much as to see my name used in connection with a political office. I am not a candidate for any office nor for favors from any party. . . ."

In addition, Grant wisely asked that even his reply be kept secret. "I wish to avoid notoriety as far as possible, and above all things desire to be spared the pain of seeing my name mixed with politics. Do not therefore publish this letter, but wherever and by whatever party you hear my name mentioned in connection with the candidacy for any office say that you know from me direct that I am not 'in the field' and cannot allow my name to be used before any convention."[28]

Others were hearing the "Grant for President" rumors, and those who knew Grant best were quick to squelch them. In January 1864, unpolished David Porter, Grant's navy counterpart during the Vicksburg campaign, told Assistant Secretary of the Navy Gustavus Fox: "Grant could not be kicked into the Presidency . . . he dont like anything but fighting and smokin, and hates politics as the devel does holy water—he dont even want to be a Lieut. General until the war is over."[29]

Lincoln, hearing the rumblings about a Grant candidacy, might have wondered if a third star would give Grant a leg up on a presidential run. All in all, it made him uneasy, and he asked people what they thought. Washburne, his fellow Illinois politician, assured Lincoln that Grant had no such ambitions. Then, at Washburne's suggestion, a man who knew Grant well, J. Russell Jones of Galena, was invited to visit Lincoln to talk about Grant's political leanings. Coincidentally, on the very day Jones left home, he had received a letter from Grant on that very subject. "I am receiving a great deal of that kind of literature," Grant had written, "but it soon finds its way into the waste basket. I already have a pretty big job on my hands, and my only ambition is to see this rebellion suppressed. Nothing could induce me to think of being a presidential candidate, particularly so long as there is a possibility of having Mr. Lincoln re-elected."[30]

At the White House, Jones took out the letter and showed it to the president. "My son," Lincoln said, "you will never know how gratifying that is to me. No man knows, when that Presidential grub gets to gnawing at him, just how deep it will get until he has tried it; and I didn't know but what there was one gnawing at Grant." According to Jones, that incident "established a perfect understanding" between the president and the general.[31]

Washburne and Jones, however, were obviously biased in Grant's favor. For Lincoln, a better source was Charles Dana, who was more likely to be a disinterested party. Dana had done many things for Ulysses Grant. He had supported him against McClernand; he had helped quell a variety of malicious rumors; finally, he had sent in evaluations that greatly influenced Grant's selection for high command. Now it seemed another favor was in order—perhaps the biggest one yet. Dana, when he met with Lincoln, said emphatically that Grant's only ambition was to put down the rebellion. Also, he said, Grant was "not only not a candidate for the Presidency, but was in favor of Lincoln's re-election to that great office when the time came around."[32]

That seemed to put the matter to rest as far as Lincoln was concerned. Washburne's bill to authorize a lieutenant generalcy, however, was another matter. Many were still skeptical about Grant. That included congressmen, cabinet members, even army officers. Didn't he drink too much? And hadn't he just been lucky? After all, they said, in winning those victories, he'd never had to come up against the likes of Robert E. Lee!

Washburne and Dana worked hard to convince the doubters. Dana, known to have spent much time with Grant, was especially persuasive. Earlier, he had written Washburne: "I tell everybody that he is the most modest, the most disinterested, and the most honest man I have ever known. To the question they all ask, 'Doesn't he drink?' I have been able from my own knowledge to give a decided negative."[33]

It took a while, but finally the Washington establishment came to agree with the press and the public at large. They accepted Grant for what he was: their best hope for a Union victory. Congress passed Washburne's bill in late February 1864. First, however, members used the occasion to demonstrate their finest oratory for the benefit of the folks back home. This, of course, included Washburne, who told his fellow congressmen: "Look at what this man has done for his country, for humanity and civilization—this modest and unpretending general. He has fought more battles, and won more victories, than any man living. He has captured more prisoners, and taken more guns, than any general of modern times. When his blue legions crowned the crest of Vicksburg, and the hosts of Rebeldom laid their arms at the feet of this great conqueror, the rebel Confederacy was cut in twain, and the backbone of the Rebellion was broken."[34]

The bill was promptly signed by the president, and on March 3, Grant received a wire from Halleck directing him to report in person to the War Department "as early as practicable." A second wire explained things: "The Secretary of War directs me to say to you that your commission as lieutenant-general is signed and will be delivered to you on your arrival at the War Department. I sincerely congratulate you on this recognition of your distinguished and meritorious service."[35]

19

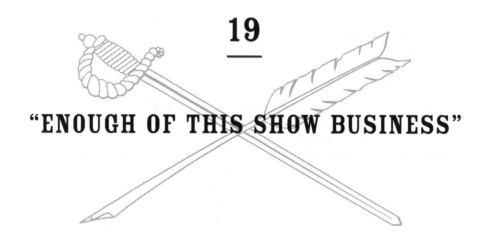

"ENOUGH OF THIS SHOW BUSINESS"

WITH GRANT en route to Washington, Horace Greeley weighed in on the new development: "It has pleased Congress to decree the appointment of a Lieutenant-General, and the President, with the entire assent of both Houses, has selected ULYSSES S. GRANT for the most responsible position.

"We had nothing to say, pro or con, while this matter was in progress; we neither urged the creation of a Lieutenant-Generalship, nor recommended Gen. Grant for the position. But now that the work is done, we most respectfully suggest that the conduct of the War, under the President, be committed absolutely to the Lieutenant-General, and that we all—Congress, Cabinet, and the Press—Republicans and Democrats, Conservatives and Radicals, take hold and strengthen his hands for the immense responsibility devolved upon him."

Greeley the editor might have stopped right there. Greeley the politician, however, needed to hedge his bets. He continued: "Let him not be impeded nor embarrassed in his work either by speeches or articles, advice or criticism, until we shall have given him a fair trial. If he proves a do-nothing, a hang-back, a mistake, let us in due time unite to get rid of him; but first let him have a fair chance to prove that he is the man for his work. Let him not be condemned for one miscarriage, if there shall be one, but generously trusted and sustained until he shall have decisively shown that he can or cannot put down the Rebellion. Then let us act as the good of the Nation shall dictate; but *until* then, let us remember in his behalf Stonewall Jackson's message to his superior: 'Send me more men and fewer orders.'"[1]

It was true that Greeley had been silent about the lieutenant generalcy. He had, however, toyed with the idea of Grant as a possible Republican nominee. Ever since Chickamauga and the fall from grace of his one-time favorite Rosecrans, Greeley the would-be kingmaker had been casting about for someone to sponsor. Was Lincoln so able a president, he asked, "that all consideration of the merits, abilities and services of others should be postponed or forborne in favor of his reelection? . . . We answer . . . in the negative. Heartily agreeing that Mr. Lincoln has done well, we do not regard it as at all demonstrated that Governor Chase, General Fremont, General Butler or General Grant cannot do as well."[2]

Greeley's ideal candidate, of course, would be firmly anti-slavery. More than that, Greeley's man should also want to help former slaves enter mainstream America. Greeley suspected Grant might be the man. As early as December Greeley had begun laying the groundwork with his readers. First he printed an extract of a letter from Grant to Elihu Washburne: "Slavery is already dead and cannot be resurrected. . . . it became patent to my mind early in the Rebellion that the North and South could never live at peace with each other except as one nation, and that without Slavery."[3]

Two days later Greeley followed with: "Gen. Grant practices what he preaches on the Slavery question. Gen. Wadsworth . . . found his praise in the mouths of those who were trying to improve the condition of the freedmen. They united . . . in saying that he heartily cooperated in the matter of enlistments, of the cultivation of abandoned plantations, and of other plans for smoothing the path from Slavery to Freedom."[4]

Nevertheless, and despite Greeley's overtures, Grant kept saying a man in uniform had no right to discuss politics. But after the war? Well, he said with a smile, maybe he'd run for mayor of Galena, "so that if elected he might have the sidewalk put in order between his house and the railroad station."[5]

Washburne conveyed all this to Lincoln, who was relieved to hear it. As for himself, said Lincoln: "A second term would be a great honor and a great labor, which together, perhaps, I would not decline if tendered."[6]

Charles Dana was now working directly under Stanton, having been officially confirmed in January as an Assistant Secretary of War. Personally, he was disappointed that Grant's Mobile plan hadn't been acted upon; he was convinced that Grant, if given his head, could have cleaned up Alabama in 3 months.[7] That was not to be, however, and the industrious Dana soon had other things to worry about.

Stanton asked Dana to straighten out the chaos and corruption in the cavalry bureau. This meant dealing with all aspects of mounted troops—their organization, supply (to include remounts), and their general well-being. Dana managed to have his friend James Harrison Wilson released from Grant's staff and brought to Washington as his assistant.[8]

In his new role, Dana was better able to gather impressions, not only of Stanton but of all the members of Lincoln's cabinet. He gave the highest marks to Stanton, Seward, and Chase. He found Stanton to be "intense," "eloquent," and of the "quickest intelligence." Seward, the secretary of state, had "the most cultivated and comprehensive intellect in the administration." Chase, at Treasury, was an "able, noble, spotless statesman." Highest praise of all was reserved for the president: "Even in his freest moments one always felt the presence of a will and of an intellectual power which maintained the ascendancy of his position. He never posed, or put on airs, or attempted to make any particular impression; but he was always conscious of his own ideas and purposes, even in his most unreserved moments."[9]

Before long, the approachable Dana was the "man to see" at the War Department, especially since he contrasted so sharply with the brusque, imperious Stanton. (Horace Porter, describing an initial meeting with Stanton, said, "I received a very cold bath at his hands, and to this day I never see the impress of his unrelenting features upon a one-dollar Treasury note without feeling a chill run down my back.") There is evidence that Dana eventually came to consider himself at least as qualified as Stanton for the secretary's job.[10]

Before he left Nashville, Grant sent written thanks to Sherman and McPherson, "the men to whom, above all others, I feel indebted for whatever I have had of success."

In turn, Sherman sent Grant enthusiastic congratulations along with heartfelt praise. Then, speaking as a true friend, he added some shrewd advice: ". . . continue, as heretofore, to be yourself—simple, honest, and unpretending . . . Your reputation as a general is now far above that of any man living, and partisans will maneuver for your influence. Preserve a plain military character and let others maneuver as they will." And finally: "Don't stay in Washington. Halleck is better qualified than you to stand the buffets of intrigue and policy." With the latter, Grant was in full agreement. He belonged in the field, not behind a desk.[11]

Arriving in Washington on March 8, Grant registered at the Willard Hotel as simply "U. S. Grant and son, Galena, Ill." A clerk told the short, unassuming stranger that there might be a room available on the top floor. Grant said that would be all right. Then the clerk, seeing the name in the book, quickly switched from boredom to enthusiastic animation, "discovering" much better accommodations on the second floor and insisting on personally carrying the general's bag upstairs.

That evening Grant attended a White House reception, where he soon became the center of attention. "Why, here is General Grant!" said Lincoln, rushing forward to greet him. As the two met for the first time, those on hand noted the sharp physical contrast. At 6 feet, 4 inches, the president towered over Grant by a full 8 inches. "This is a great pleasure, I assure you," said Lincoln as he pumped Grant's hand vigorously. After a short conversation, Lincoln turned Grant over to Secretary of State Seward, who introduced him to the first lady. Seward then brought Grant to the East Room, where most of the crowd had gathered. Cheering citizens pushed and shoved in their effort to catch a glimpse of the western hero. Finally, at Seward's urging, Grant stood on a sofa so everyone could see him and come forward to shake his hand.

Next day, at a White House ceremony, Lincoln formally made Grant a lieutenant general. In attendance was the full cabinet, various staff officers, and a proud young teenager—Grant's son Fred.[12] Later that day, when Grant met with Halleck and Stanton, he asked the former to remain where he was, handling administration, while he himself took the field.

Greeley's *Tribune* applauded the news: "Gen. Grant had a conference today, three hours long, with the Secretary of War and General Halleck upon the military situation in every one of our fighting departments . . . Gen. Grant will go to the Army of the Potomac tomorrow to see its condition, and to find out what it wants. He has hardly slept from his long journey here, and yet is hard at work. It is mentioned with joy among Senators that he is not going to hire a house here, nor make war ridiculous by attempting to maneuver armies and battles in distant States from an armchair in a Washington parlor." The last bit, about maneuvering armies from a Washington parlor, was an obvious slap at McClellan and Halleck, who had tried doing just that.[13]

On March 10, Grant visited General Meade's headquarters at Brandy Station. Staff officers were wary, wondering how Grant and Meade would react to each other. Soon they saw that the pair hit it off quite well. Though the two generals never because close friends, they would develop a sincere mutual respect in the months that followed. It began at this first meeting, when Meade unselfishly volunteered to step down if Grant wanted to replace him with someone such as Sherman. Grant later wrote: "He urged that the work before us was of such vast importance to the whole nation that the feeling or wishes of no one person should stand in the way of selecting the right men for all positions. For himself, he would serve to the best of his ability wherever placed." These were words Grant could appreciate; he'd already had his fill of pompous self-promoters. He later wrote: "This incident gave me even a more favorable opinion of Meade than did his great victory at Gettysburg the July before."[14]

Grant assured Meade that he had no intention of making a change. Moreover, when it was learned that Horace Greeley was in Washington, urging that Meade be replaced, Grant responded by saying: "If I saw Greeley, I would tell him that when I wanted the advice of a political editor in selecting generals I would call on him."[15]

Back at the Capitol, Grant informed Lincoln and Stanton he was returning to Nashville to meet Sherman and turn over command of the western armies. The social activity of the previous 3 days, he told Lincoln, "were rather the warmest campaign I have witnessed during the war."

He couldn't go just yet, said Lincoln. Mrs. Lincoln was planning a dinner party in his honor, and without Grant, Lincoln said, the dinner would be like *Hamlet* with Hamlet left out. Grant bravely stuck to his guns. "I appreciate the honor Mrs. Lincoln would do me," he said, "but time is very important now. And really, Mr. Lincoln, I have had enough of this show business."[16]

At Nashville, Grant and Sherman made their plans. Again Grant stressed coordination, utilizing the North's manpower advantage by hitting the Confederates simultaneously from every point. For the major offensives, it would be Sherman in the West attacking Joe Johnston, Grant in the East going after Robert E. Lee. At the same time, General Nathaniel Banks would conclude his Red River campaign, gather all available forces at New Orleans, and mount an offensive in the direction of Mobile.[17]

Then there was Gen. Benjamin Butler, commanding the Department of Virginia and North Carolina, with headquarters at Fort Monroe. When Butler, a former Massachusetts politician, was military governor of Louisiana, he issued a proclamation aimed at stopping the open abuse of Union soldiers by the women of New Orleans. The order said in part that a female insulting a Union soldier would be regarded as "a woman of the town plying her avocation"—in other words, a prostitute. Ever since, outraged Southerners had despised the man they called "Beast" Butler.

Grant met with Butler at Old Point Comfort, and it was agreed that Butler's army, which until then had been rather immobile, would head down the peninsula to threaten Richmond.

Grant himself would be with Meade, although purists might question the need for *two* commanders at the same site. Grant finessed this by what Dana called a "sort of fiction," whereby Burnside's corps was "held to be a distinct army." The "two" armies, said Dana, "were the excuse for Grant's personal presence, without actually superseding Meade." In theory, Meade would be giving the orders. Everyone sensed, however, that it was to be Grant's show.[18]

Grant set May 4 as the date to launch the spring offensive on all fronts. As he later wrote: "The armies were now all ready to move for the accomplishment of a single object. They were acting as a unit so far as such a thing was possible over such a vast field."[19]

The papers were not making it any easier for Grant to be accepted. Many eastern officers, for example, resented the *Army and Navy Journal*'s saying that "no General arose capable of bringing victory out of the Army of the Potomac" and asserting that western victories had "covered up for a time the humiliation of our failures in Virginia."[20]

During April, nevertheless, Grant and the Army of the Potomac became better acquainted. Reviews were of a different sort than the army had known before. There wasn't the wild cheering such as used to greet McClellan. Instead, Grant trooped the line, looked into men's faces, and men looked back. One soldier summed it up well: "He looks as if he meant it." Similarly, one of Meade's officers said, "Grant wears an expression as if he had determined to drive his head through a brick wall and was about to do it."[21]

A last-minute message from Lincoln said he was well pleased with what had happened to date, that he didn't know the particulars of Grant's plans, nor did he need to. Lastly, he told Grant, "If there is anything wanting which is in my power to give, do not fail to let me know it. And now, with a brave army, and a just cause, may God sustain you."[22]

Grant thanked Lincoln for the expressed confidence and said, "everything asked for has been yielded, without even an explanation being asked. Should my success be less than I desire and expect, the least I can say is, the fault is not with you."[23] Then things got under way.

Meade had been told, "Lee's army will be your objective point. Wherever Lee goes, there you will go also."[24] Grant had been gaining confidence in both Meade and the Army of the Potomac. He'd now see if they were ready for the task ahead. On May 4 the army swung into action, crossing the Rapidan and entering a region known as the "Wilderness." Greeley aptly described it as "a tangled labyrinth."[25] It was there, a year earlier almost to the day, that the Union army had suffered a crushing defeat at the battle of Chancellorsville. This time, if they were lucky, they might slip clear of the Wilderness before the Confederates could react.

In Lee's army there was an air of confidence. They told each other that this man Grant, just like his predecessors, would soon be reeling back in disorder. However, James Longstreet, who knew Grant well, told his fellow officers not to underrate him, "for that man will fight us every day and every hour till the end of this war."[26]

For the men in blue, spirits were also high. On the first day of the campaign, Private August Seiser of the 140th New York Volunteers wrote in his diary: "It is the most beautiful weather and the troops enjoy the lovely spring day, which pleasure is not spoiled by sight of a single Rebel."[27]

Seiser and his comrades soon lost their cheerful optimism. Robert E. Lee had reacted quickly, sending his Army of Northern Virginia crashing against the Union flank. Meade's divisions, one after another, were ordered into action. However, because of the confusing terrain and limited visibility, cohesion was lost almost as soon as a unit was committed.

For 2 ghastly days, the armies struggled and bled. Men fought as squads or as individuals, fought with bayonets, with clubbed rifles, even with fists. "Oftentimes we found the woods so thick in our front that we could not see the enemy," wrote an officer in Seiser's regiment. "Often the burning powder from the discharged rifles in the hands of the enemy would drop at the feet of our men, who would instantly thrust their rifle bayonets through the brush and vines and kill or wound those in their front."[28]

Casualties mounted, more Union than Confederate. (Of the 529 men in Seiser's regiment, only 261 were "present with the colors" after the second day; the other 268 had either been killed, wounded, or captured.)[29] To magnify the horror, sparks set the parched underbrush on fire. Many of the wounded, unable to crawl to safety, burned to death where they lay.

At one point an excited general told Grant they were in a crisis situation. Lee, he said, would likely cut them off by throwing his whole army between them and the Rapidan. Grant's aide Horace Porter said

Grant replied "with a degree of animation which he seldom manifested: 'Oh, I am heartily tired of hearing what Lee is going to do. Some of you always seem to think he is suddenly going to turn a double somersault, and land in our rear and on both of our flanks at the same time. Go back to your command, and try to think what we are going to do ourselves, instead of what Lee is going to do.'"[30]

At the end of the second day, as two exhausted armies lay facing each other, Lincoln was anxiously waiting for news. He sent for Dana, who had been at a reception. Still in evening clothes, Dana hurried to the War Department, where Lincoln was talking to Stanton.

"Dana," said Lincoln, "you know we have been in the dark for two days since Grant moved. We are very much troubled, and have concluded to send you down there. How soon can you start?"

"In half an hour," Dana replied. Before he could get away, however, Lincoln sent for him again, saying he'd had a change of heart. "It's a considerable risk," Lincoln said, "and I don't like to expose you to it."

Dana said he'd be traveling with a cavalry guard and riding a strong horse. If they were attacked, they could probably fight, and if it came to the worst, they could always run. He really wanted to go. "In that case," Lincoln said, "I rather wish you would. Good night, and God bless you."[31]

By the morning of May 7, Dana was at Grant's headquarters, learning of the fierce battle that had been fought on May 5 and 6. Grant had been up early, writing an order for Meade that began: "Make all preparations during the day for a night march to take position at Spotsylvania Court House . . ."[32]

During the day, artillery began moving back so as to avoid jamming the roads that night. Men said it looked like "another skedaddle." It was Chancellorsville all over again—cross the river, get whipped by Lee, head back north with their tails between their legs. Their suspicions were justified; by all normal measures Grant had been beaten. Union losses—killed, wounded, and captured—exceeded 17,000. The Confederates, by contrast, had lost only 7,000. It surely seemed Grant had been whipped. Grant himself didn't feel that way, however, which, as Shelby Foote put it, "was only a way of saying that he had not been whipped at all."[33]

The night move began with weary, discouraged men in blue plodding along, convinced it had been yet another disastrous campaign. Then they came to a fork in the road. A turn to the left would bring them to Ely's Ford and a recrossing of the Rapidan. But suddenly they were turning to the right, toward Spotsylvania Courthouse—going not north but south, toward the enemy. The word spread, some cheering broke out, and there was a new bounce to every step. As one soldier remembered it, "Our spirits rose. We marched free. The men began to sing. . . . That night we were happy." In later years, some called this their personal high point of the war. When Grant said there'd be "no turning back," he had meant it.[34]

Grant had wanted to reach the crossroads of Spotsylvania Courthouse first to threaten Lee's line of communications and cause the other to retreat. Lee, however, had anticipated Grant's move. When Grant arrived at Spotsylvania, he again was faced by Confederate fortifications.

Later, Grant wrote, "More desperate fighting had not been witnessed on this continent than that of the 5th and 6th of May."[35] Nevertheless, although it seemed impossible, the fighting at Spotsylvania was even *more* fierce and intense. At one nightmarish location, forever known as the "Bloody Angle," bodies were stacked eight or ten deep. Fighting was unbelievably savage as men thrust bayonets through chinks in a log parapet or rose to fire point-blank into men huddling behind corpses serving as shields.

As the soldiers did their job, Dana did his. Porter said: "His daily, and sometimes hourly, despatches to the War Department, giving the events occurring in the field constituted a correspondence which is a rare example of perspicuity, accuracy, and vividness of description."[36]

On May 11, Congressman Washburne, who had been accompanying Grant's army, prepared to return to Washington. Did Grant have any message for the president? Grant said he didn't want to write anything that might raise false hopes. Also, he normally communicated through General Halleck. However, if Washburne would wait a moment, he would write something for Halleck that Washburne could show Mr. Lincoln.

Washburne was right about the president's desire for news. Shortly before, when a congressman asked him what Grant was doing, Lincoln had said, "Well, I can't tell much about it. You see, Grant has gone to the Wilderness, crawled in, drawn up the ladder, and pulled in the hole after him, and I guess we'll have to wait till he comes out before we know just what he's up to."[37]

In Washington, people heard that Grant, after the Wilderness, had kept moving south. This was encouraging, especially since they hadn't yet seen the casualty lists. The news, in fact, was enough to bring a celebrating crowd to the White House lawn. They cheered when the president stepped out on the portico, cheered again when he said he supposed their appearance was due to "the good news received today from the army."

Lincoln reminded the crowd that much work remained to be done. However, he said, he'd just seen a message from Grant, and it appeared he had "not been jostled in his purposes." Then Lincoln quoted a line from Grant's dispatch. It brought the greatest cheer yet: "I . . . propose to fight it out on this line if it takes all summer."[38]

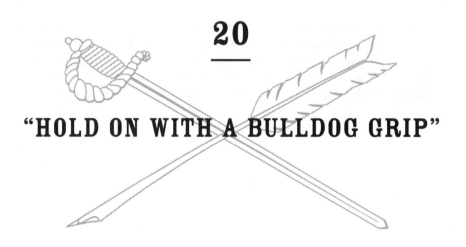

20

"HOLD ON WITH A BULLDOG GRIP"

HORACE GREELEY once tried analyzing Ulysses Grant. What was it, he asked himself, that made Grant a good overall commander? He finally seized on a single point "wherein his fitness for chief command was decided if not preeminent; and that was an utter disbelief in the efficacy of any rosewater treatment of the Rebellion. . . . No love-taps, in his view, would ever persuade the Rebel chiefs to return to loyalty, so long as their military power should remain essentially unbroken; and he had no conception of any mode of breaking that power save by strong armies in bloody battles."[1] A Civil War soldier, whether he wore blue or gray, would have agreed. Grant was above all a realist who fought hard, fought to win, and fought without letup.

After the Wilderness, when the army kept moving south, the national mood was one of elation. "There is no longer any doubt," said the *Tribune* on May 10, "Gen. Grant has won a great victory. The President invokes thanksgiving and prayer . . . Who shall gather into a sentence the religious joy of the nation? No man has the right—or no man, but Ulysses S. Grant."[2]

The next day, however, as monstrous casualty lists began to appear, elation was tempered by cold reality. The *New York Herald* told of "terrible losses," including the much esteemed Gen. John Sedgwick, "killed by a rifle shot from a sharpshooter while standing with some officers of his staff on the outer works." Glumly, the *Herald* predicted,

"... if the enemy gives our forces so much trouble in the future as they have done up to this time, there is much difficulty before them."[3] It was an obviously safe prediction.

Safe, too, was Grant's oracular response to an incredibly dumb query. "General Grant," asked a reporter, "about how long will it take you to get to Richmond?"

Grant replied at once: "I will agree to be there in about four days—that is, if General Lee becomes a party to the agreement; but if he objects, the trip will undoubtedly be prolonged."[4]

On May 12, headlines in Greeley's *Tribune* read: THE FIERCEST FIGHTING IN MODERN TIMES—LEE BEWILDERED AT GRANT'S PERTINACITY—GEN. GRANT AT HIM AGAIN ON WEDNESDAY.

"In so horrible a strife," said the accompanying story, "it must not be supposed that we escape the severest punishment. . . . Roads, fields, and woods are literally swarming with these suffering heroes, who have defied wounds and death that the nation might survive."[5]

Greeley, thinking of the coming election, feared the public would blame Lincoln for the blood-soaked fields. The Republican convention was only a month away, and on May 13 he wrote: "It is advisable for the Union party to nominate for President some other among its able and true men than Mr. Lincoln."[6]

That same day, elections were far from Ulysses Grant's mind. On May 13 he wrote Julia: "The world has never seen so bloody or so protracted a battle as the one being fought and I hope never will again." Lee's men, he said, as bad as their cause, "have fought for it with gallantry worthy of a better."[7]

Meanwhile, both armies had become mud-bound. On May 16, Grant wrote Halleck: "We have had five days almost constant rain without any prospect yet of it clearing up." Then he asked Halleck to "assure the President and Secretary of War that the elements alone have suspended hostilities, and that it is in no manner due to weakness or exhaustion on our part."[8]

After the losses of the previous few days, it would have been foolhardy to keep attacking dug-in Confederates. Grant said, "My chief anxiety now is to draw Lee out of his works and fight him in the open field, instead of assaulting him behind his intrenchments."[9] Lee, however, refused to oblige. Grant would write: "On the 20th, Lee showing no signs of coming out of his lines, orders were renewed for a left-flank movement, to commence at night."[10]

The *Tribune* was cautious as it reported the maneuver: "On Friday evening, Gen. Grant commenced a movement for the purpose of compelling Lee to abandon his position at Spotsylvania (the details of which, for obvious reasons, should not be made public)."[11]

Union losses had been severe, far exceeding those of the Confederates. Nevertheless, each move, not only sideways but *forward*, was causing Lee to yield ground. Greeley's *Tribune* observed: "It is remarkable that whereas formerly the object of all strategy on our side has been to keep the Army of the Potomac interposed between the enemy and Washington, and to cover our capital from attack, it is now Lee who is driven to protect Richmond, and whose movements are made to depend on the menace of his advancing and victorious enemy."[12]

After some sharp but inconclusive fighting, Grant again sidled to the left. The astute Robert E. Lee saw what was happening and realized he couldn't pull back indefinitely. He told his corps commander Jubal Early: "We must destroy this army of Grant's before he gets to the James River. If he gets there, it will be a mere question of time."[13]

Charles Dana was of the same mind. Enemy prisoners now seemed dispirited, and in a burst of misguided optimism he told Stanton: "Rely upon it, the end is near as well as sure."[14]

Grant kept hoping to slip behind Lee, cut his supply line, and thus force his retreat. However, when Union elements arrived at Cold Harbor, they found that Lee had anticipated Grant's move. Confederates were already there and digging in. The graybacks, by now old hands at field fortifications, used those hard-earned skills to establish an almost impregnable position.

The Northern ranks knew what was coming—another assault against foes who were more than ready. On the eve of battle, Horace Porter saw soldiers "calmly writing their names and home addresses on slips of paper, and pinning them on the backs of their coats, so that their dead bodies might be recognized upon the field, and their fate known to their families at home."[15]

June 3 was perhaps Grant's worst day as a commander. Waves of blue-clad soldiers were mowed down in massive frontal assaults with little chance of success. As one Southern veteran remembered it, "the dead and the dying lay in front of the Confederate line in triangles, of which the apexes were the bravest men who came nearest to the breastworks under that withering, deadly fire."[16]

Dana, looking back years later, tried to rationalize: "This was the battle of Cold Harbor, which has been exaggerated into one of the bloodiest disasters of history, a reckless, useless waste of human life. It was nothing of the kind." Less than a year later, he said, Grant attacked even stronger entrenchments at Five Forks. There the attack succeeded, and Lee fled to Appomattox. If Cold Harbor had resulted in a break-through, Lee would have been defeated then and there, and "who would have thought of the losses?"[17]

Nevertheless, Grant would say, "I have always regretted that the last assault at Cold Harbor was ever made."[18]

Now began what would be the final chapter in the Grant/Lee chess game. Grant again sidled to the left, this time to cross the James River, link up with Butler, and establish a new supply base. He would threaten Richmond, not directly, but from the "back door," the city of Peters-burg. The purpose of the move, said Dana, "was, of course, to deceive Lee as to the ultimate direction of the army. The design succeeded far beyond Grant's most sanguine hopes."[19]

On June 21, Abraham Lincoln visited Grant, who was now estab-lished at City Point, on the James. At Lincoln's request, they then toured the Union lines facing Petersburg. Dana, who was with them, said: "As we came back we passed through the division of colored troops which had so greatly distinguished itself . . . on the 15th. They were drawn up in double lines on each side of the road, and they welcomed the President with hearty shouts. It was a memorable thing to behold him . . . passing bareheaded through the enthusiastic ranks of those negroes armed to defend the integrity of the nation."[20]

Meanwhile, Robert E. Lee had tried to relieve the pressure on Rich-mond by threatening the opposing capital. As Grant was crossing the James, Lee sent Jubal Early down the Shenandoah Valley toward Wash-ington. By early July, Early had crossed the Potomac into Maryland, swept past Lew Wallace at the Monocacy, and was endangering the capital. On July 9, Dana returned to Washington, as he said, to "keep Grant advised of developments." He found the city in a state of excite-ment, almost terror. Both Washington and Baltimore were swarming with refugees who had fled before Early's advance. Smoke was rising from outlying factories and towns, and in the capital, hundreds of nerv-ous government clerks had been armed and sent to man the ramparts.[21]

In Grant's opinion, Early posed no real threat to the capital. To the contrary, he believed Early's exposed position made him vulnerable and provided the Union army with a fine opportunity. Grant sent nearly two divisions north, and after assuring Halleck that help was on the way, he tried injecting the other with some of his own aggressive spirit: "We now want to crush out and destroy any force the enemy have sent north. Force enough can be spared from here to do it."

Grant seemed to have little patience with the "nervous Nellies" in Washington. "Boldness," he told Dana, "is all that is needed [to drive] the enemy out of Maryland."[22]

As it happened, though, Dana was one of the nervous ones. Unknown to Grant, his alleged friend Dana was writing an emotional letter to Rawlins condemning Grant for stripping Washington's defenses and accusing Grant of "poltroonery and stupidity . . . its probable consequences are likely to be the defeat of Mr. Lincoln and the election of Gen. McClellan to the Presidency . . ." The generals, he added—and the term seemed to include Grant—"were mental dwarfs and moral cowards." In a postscript, he said Rawlins should feel free to show the letter to Wilson. A perceptive historian, Geoffrey Perret, said: "Among them— Dana, Rawlins, and Wilson—there wasn't enough understanding of Grant or commitment to him to make a single genuine friend."[23]

Ironically, as Dana composed that revealing letter, Early was pulling back. He had managed to destroy some property and create a lot of excitement, but through no fault of his own he had failed in the main purpose of his mission. Refusing to take the bait, Grant had not significantly weakened his Petersburg line in order to soothe the people in Washington.

The very next day, Greeley's headlines told the story: The Great Rebel Raid—They are Recrossing the Potomac with their Plunder.[24] With that, Dana prepared to return to Grant. Stanton, however, asked him to remain at the War Department to assume other duties.[25]

At Petersburg, with both sides digging in, there was a momentary lull in the fighting. On July 27, a *Tribune* dispatch said: "The situation here now can only be expressed, and can be fully expressed, by the old stereotype phrase, 'All is quiet along the lines.' Whether this is the calm that precedes a storm remains to be seen."[26]

In June, despite Greeley's misgivings, Republicans had met in Baltimore and made Lincoln their candidate for the coming election. They had ignored Greeley's advice, which he didn't appreciate. Nevertheless, he was soon given another opportunity to influence national events—a chance to be the nation's peacemaker. He received a letter from Niagara Falls written by a William Jewett. Jewett, a man previously known to Greeley, said he was in touch with "two ambassadors of Davis & Co." They were in Canada, wrote Jewett, "with full and complete powers for a peace," and they wished to talk personally with Horace Greeley. The editor could come to the Canadian border to meet them, or alternatively, he could secure from Lincoln a safe conduct pass so they could come to him. The whole matter, Jewett said, "can be consummated by me, you, them, and President Lincoln."[27]

It seemed odd that such men would want to meet with Greeley rather than the Secretary of State. Nevertheless, the self-confident Greeley felt up to the challenge. Moreover, he considered himself every bit as able as William Seward, a man he no longer called "friend."

Greeley wrote Lincoln at once. Any terms, he knew, would have to include a return to the Union and the abolishment of slavery. With that in mind, he wrote: "I entreat you . . . to submit overtures for pacification to the southern insurgents, which the impartial must pronounce frank and generous . . ." Even if the talks were to fail, he suggested, they should at least be initiated, if only to place on the South the onus of rejecting what was offered. Lincoln saw it differently. First, of course, he doubted that the "ambassadors" were authentic. Second, at this low point in the war, he knew any discussion of peace terms would be perceived as Northern weakness.

Lincoln compromised—and shrewdly. He suggested that Greeley proceed on his own. Then, if things broke down and the matter became public, only Greeley's fingerprints would appear. Greeley, sensing a trap, wrote Lincoln: "Whether there be persons at Niagara (or elsewhere) who are empowered to commit the rebels by negotiation, is a question; but if there be such, there is no question at all that they would decline to exhibit their credentials to me, much more to . . . give me their best terms. Green as I may be, I am not quite so verdant as to imagine anything of the sort . . ." Greeley insisted that he be accompanied by someone from the administration.

The reply was delivered personally by Lincoln's secretary, John Hay. "I am disappointed," Lincoln wrote, "that you have not already reached here with those commissioners. . . . I not only intend a sincere effort for peace, but I intend that you shall be a personal witness that it is made."

When he arrived at Niagara Falls, the still-skeptical Greeley informed the "commissioners" that he had a safe conduct pass enabling them to come to Washington. Their reply was deflating. They weren't *really* empowered to discuss peace, they said; in fact, they would have to refer the whole matter to their superiors in Richmond.

Greeley wired the White House for instructions. In reply, John Hay brought a "To whom it may concern" letter from Lincoln couched in terms the "commissioners" were bound to reject. Greeley was furious. He had hoped to bring these men to Washington without mentioning terms, and might even have suggested that no preconditions existed.

Trying to play shrewd by putting the South in the wrong, Greeley had been outfoxed, both by Lincoln and by the Confederates. The latter cleverly addressed their reply to Greeley rather than Lincoln, gave a copy of it to the press, and made it appear that the North, not the South, had made the initial overtures.

The note ended by thanking Greeley for "the solicitude you have manifested to inaugurate a movement which contemplates results the most noble and humane . . ." It was a kiss of death. As Greeley fumed, rival editors learned what had transpired and did their best to humiliate him. William Cullen Bryant, the poet-editor of the *Evening Post*, said the whole affair was "sickening." Greeley's arch rival, James Gordon Bennett, was even more vicious.

Bennett's *Herald* accused Greeley of "cuddling with traitors." Not only was he guilty of "bungling" and "meddling," Bennett said, Greeley had even been willing to compromise the nation's integrity.[28] He then demanded that Greeley "tell the country, explicity, whether his cooperation in the late peace movement is an effort toward disunion."

Greeley's response, although disingenuous, was nonetheless emphatic: "NO SIR!—Is that plain? We were first impelled to make an effort to bring about a conference between authorized representatives of the respective belligerents by learning, through various channels, that certain distinguished Confederates, then and now in Canada, were holding out to the leading Democrats, who flocked over the river to confer with them, that Peace might be had on a basis, not of Disunion, but of *Union*. . . ."

"We cannot be bullied nor slandered into approval or rejection of hypothetical terms of conciliation. The business of negotiation is devolved by the Constitution on the President and Senate of the United States, and to them we leave it."[29]

Greeley was not one to forgive or forget how Lincoln had used him. In August, as the controversial George McClellan became the Democrats' presidential candidate, Greeley joined a group of Radical Republicans seeking a replacement for Lincoln. In a letter to his friend George Opdyke, Greeley wrote: "Mr. Lincoln is already beaten. . . . And we must have another ticket to save us. . . . If we had such a ticket as could be made by naming Grant, Butler, or Sherman for President . . . we could make a fight yet."[30]

Despite this, Greeley mysteriously leaped on the Lincoln bandwagon the following month. One explanation, which may or may not be authentic, would explain the switch. According to George G. Hoskins, a leading New York State Republican, Lincoln was so disturbed by

Greeley's lack of support that he tried to arrange a face-to-face meeting. Almost humbly he wrote: "DEAR MR. GREELEY: I have been wanting to see you for several weeks, and if I could spare the time I should call upon you in New York. Perhaps you may be able to visit me. I shall be very glad to see you. A. Lincoln."

Greeley showed the note to Hoskins and said he had no intention of answering it. He said, however, that it was all right if Hoskins wanted to see Lincoln on his behalf. Hoskins said he then called on the president, who praised Greeley to the skies, saying he was not only a great admirer of Greeley but also a lifelong reader of the *Tribune*. Hoskins quoted Lincoln as saying that Greeley was the ablest editor in the United States, if not in the world—the most influential man in the country, not excepting the president—the equal, if not the superior, of the country's first postmaster general, Benjamin Franklin.

According to Hoskins, Lincoln then said he was determined, if reelected and reinaugurated, to appoint Greeley to that same office of postmaster general. "He is worthy of it, and my mind is made up," Lincoln supposedly said. Moreover, he hoped Hoskins would tell this to Greeley. When he did, Greeley asked if Hoskins really believed such a lie. As for himself, he did not.

The next morning, nevertheless, the *Tribune* came out foursquare for Lincoln. A two-column editorial proclaimed: "Henceforth, we fly the banner of ABRAHAM LINCOLN for the next President. . . . The work is in his hands. We MUST re-elect him, and, God helping us, we will."[31] Whether or not Hoskins's story is true, it remains a fact that Greeley gave Lincoln his full support throughout the remainder of the campaign.

In front of Petersburg, an ingenious plan had been set in motion. Lt. Col. Henry Pleasants, leader of a unit of Pennsylvania miners, had suggested tunneling under the enemy's line. Kegs of black powder, hundreds of them, would then be placed in underground chambers so as to fashion an enormous mine. When it was set off, the resulting blast would create both enemy casualties and a huge gap in the Confederate works. The Army of the Potomac would have the breakthrough it had sought for weeks.

The mine was exploded early on July 30. A gigantic tower of dirt, flames, and mangled bodies rose into the air. When it settled, a huge crater existed where once there had been a Confederate fort. Unfortunately for the Union, however, those in charge of the operation had made no plans for getting men promptly out of their trenches and through their own obstacles. After the initial delay, when soldiers finally got moving, they milled around in the crater itself, giving the Confederates time to react. "The effort was a stupendous failure," Grant admitted. "It was all due," he believed, "to inefficiency on the part of the corps commander [Ambrose Burnside] and the incompetency of the division commander [James Ledlie] who was sent to lead the assault."[32]

Reporting the event, the *Tribune* said: "To its projector, Lieut. Col. Pleasants . . . all praise for the ingenuity of the conception. . . . That we failed from some cause to avail ourselves . . . for the achievement of a grand and signal victory, cannot be attributed to the mine . . . which did its work. An investigation . . . will determine who is culpable."[33]

Despite the mine setback, Grant continued to poke away at Lee's line. In mid-August he sent Gouverneur Warren's corps around Lee's right flank to seize a portion of the rail line leading into Petersburg. The following month, in a coordinated attack by Ord and Hancock—one north of the James River, the other south—several key positions were seized. Lee was trying to hold too long a line with too small an army, and Grant knew that each attack was making that line stretch farther and farther. Eventually it would crack.

Elsewhere that fall the war was going more or less according to Grant's design. In the Shenandoah Valley, Phil Sheridan, now an army commander, had won decisively at Cedar Creek. In Georgia, the state capital had been abandoned by John Bell Hood after his catastrophic defeat at Peachtree Creek. From a city devastated by flame and bombardment, Sherman had wired, "So Atlanta is ours, and fairly won."

Earlier, Grant had summed up the situation in a letter to Congressman Washburne: "The rebels have now in their ranks their last man. . . . A man lost by them cannot be replaced. They have robbed the Cradle and the grave equally to get their present force. . . . the end is visible if we will be true to ourselves. . . . With the draft quietly enforced the enemy would become despondent and would make but little resistance."[34]

It was clear, Grant told Washburne, that the South was just trying to hold on until the November election. "They hope for a counter revolution. They hope for a peace candidate. In fact, like McCawber, [a reference to the Dickens character Micawber from *David Copperfield*] they hope *something* will turn up."[35]

Even so, the North was so war-weary that many still wanted peace at any price. When states were called on to draft still more men, Northern governors feared such an action would result in widespread rioting. The governors suggested that Grant should be made to furnish troops either to quell or forestall the anticipated disturbances. Showing obvious concern, Halleck wired Grant: "Pretty strong evidence is accumulating that there is a combination formed, or forming, to make a forcible resistance to the draft. . . . To enforce it may require the withdrawal of a very considerable number of troops from the field. . . . Are not the appearances such that we ought to take in sail and prepare the ship for a storm?"

Grant answered in no uncertain terms: "If we are to draw troops from the field to keep the loyal states in harness it will prove difficult to suppress the rebellion in the disloyal states." If necessary, call out the state militias, he said. Whatever the case, let the states solve their own problems and let the army keep pressuring Lee.

One person who liked Grant's response was Abraham Lincoln, by this time a kindred soul. He wired Grant: "I have seen your despatch expressing your unwillingness to break your hold where you are. Neither am I willing. Hold on with a bulldog grip, and chew and choke as much as possible."

Amid the grimness of war, the naturally quiet Grant seldom permitted himself more than an occasional chuckle. Staff officers were therefore startled the day they heard him begin laughing out loud. He read them Lincoln's message, then said with a grin, "It seems the President has more nerve than any of his advisors."[36]

At the White House on November 8, as election returns were being received, Lincoln called Dana to his side. "Dana," he said, "have you ever read any of the writings of Petroleum V. Nasby?"

"No sir," Dana said. "I have only looked at some of them, and they seemed quite funny." Lincoln then proceeded to read a few lines for Dana's benefit. He paused to read one of the election telegrams, then went back to reading more of Nasby's humor.

Nearby, Stanton was fuming. Going into the next room, he motioned Dana to follow. Dana later wrote: "I shall never forget the fire of his indignation at what seemed to him to be mere nonsense. The idea that when the safety of the republic was thus at issue . . . the man most deeply concerned . . . could turn aside to read such balderdash and to laugh at such frivolous jests was, to his mind, repugnant, even damnable. He could not understand, apparently, that it was by the relief these jests afforded to the strain of mind under which Lincoln had so long been living . . . that the safety and sanity of his intelligence were maintained and preserved."[37]

Despite Republican fears once voiced by Greeley and others, the final returns showed that the country had voted overwhelmingly for Lincoln.

The soldier vote in his favor was particularly strong. Democrats had assumed that men fighting the war would surely reject the party that was waging it. Instead, men in the ranks sensed victory and weren't about to abandon the cause for which they had fought so long and hard. Indeed, like Lincoln, they had firmly resolved that the "honored dead shall not have died in vain."

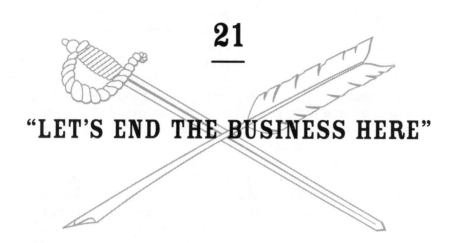

21

"LET'S END THE BUSINESS HERE"

AS 1864 ENTERED its final days, many Northerners remained luke-
warm in their support of the war. Horace Greeley, well aware of
this, wrote, "There is yet much work before us, and we are in great
danger of being betrayed by divisions."[1]

Below the Mason-Dixon line, conversely, belief in the Southern cause
remained an article of faith. Jefferson Davis told the Confederate Congress that, regardless of setbacks, the South would remain "as erect and
defiant as ever."[2] Southern journals echoed Davis's bravado. Upon
Lincoln's reelection, one paper said, "But, perhaps, this also is for good.
It deepens and widens the gulf between us, and renders our success more
certain by rendering failure more dreadful and intolerable."[3]

At City Point, a restless Grant, forced to keep many balls in the air
at once, maintained steady correspondence with each of his scattered
commanders. Horace Porter noted a day when the general wrote 42
separate dispatches with his own hand.[4] Happily for Grant, however,
Julia was there to ease the tension. Porter said the pair "would seek a
quiet corner of his quarters of an evening, and sit with her hand in his,
manifesting the most ardent devotion; and if a staff officer came acci-
dentally upon them, they would look as bashful as two young lovers
spied upon in the scenes of their courtship."[5]

Grant was keeping the pressure on Lee, whose line by this time stretched for nearly 40 miles, from north of Richmond to well beyond Petersburg. Lee's stubborn defense of the Confederate capital, requiring every ragged man, meant that he couldn't send help to the Southern armies opposing Sherman, Thomas, and Sheridan. The plan, it appears, was for Grant to press Lee's Army of Northern Virginia but not to incur needless casualties by attacking their fortifications. Richmond, of course, was not the main objective, and Grant would later write that "the mere occupation of places" couldn't "close the war while large and effective rebel armies existed."[6]

The second week in December, wrote Porter, was "the most anxious period of Grant's entire military career."[7] Sherman, like Grant in the Vicksburg campaign, had abandoned his line of supplies and struck out cross-country; for the most part he and Grant were out of contact. The deliberate Thomas, despite Grant's orders to take the offensive, remained under siege in Nashville. Benjamin Butler, the inept political general, was preparing an attack on Fort Fisher, the strongpoint guarding Wilmington, North Carolina; Grant gave the operation little chance of success. And in Grant's own sector, Meade was preparing to hunker down in winter quarters.

Then Grant's clouds began to lift. Sherman continued his steady march through Georgia, living off the land and leaving in his wake a corridor of Southern grief. Grant wrote him that "information gleaned from the Southern press" indicated "no great obstacle to your progress. . . . Not liking to rejoice before the victory is assured, I abstain from congratulating you and those under your command, until bottom has been struck. I have never had a fear, however, for the result. Since you left Atlanta, no very great progress has been made here. The enemy has been closely watched though, and prevented from detaching against you."[8]

In Tennessee, George Thomas kept trying Grant's patience. Earlier, Confederate John Bell Hood had been repulsed by Union Gen. John Schofield at the battle of Franklin. Thomas, in Grant's opinion, "made no effort to reinforce Schofield at Franklin, as it seemed to me at the time he should have done, and fight out the battle there. . . . Hood was allowed to move upon Nashville and to invest that place almost without interference." To Grant, this was "unacceptable." He wrote Thomas several times, insisting he attack at once.[9]

Finally the methodical Thomas was ready to move. He launched his long-delayed attack on December 15 and sent Hood reeling. Perhaps unfairly, Grant had been within hours of relieving the able "Rock of Chickamauga." He now applauded Thomas's success.

Then, on December 22, following closely on the heels of the Nashville victory, it became clear that Sherman's march to the sea had been a master stroke. An exulting Sherman wired the White House: "To his Excellency President Lincoln: I beg to present you, as a Christmas gift, the city of Savannah, with 150 guns and plenty of ammunition, and also about 35,000 bales of cotton."

Sherman's ability to cut a swath through the South, almost unopposed, validated Grant's strategy of coordinated attacks. As he'd been saying all along, the Confederacy didn't have enough men to compete simultaneously on every front. Earlier, many in Washington had opposed Sherman's expedition, and even Rawlins had urged Secretary Stanton to quash it. Grant, however, had defended it, and now that the march was a proven success, it was widely hailed. Grant had approved the move and would have been blamed for any failure. Nevertheless he gave all credit to Sherman, saying, "the question of who devised the plan of march from Atlanta to Savannah is easily answered: it was clearly Sherman, and to him also belongs the credit of its brilliant execution."[10]

Ben Butler's Wilmington expedition was another matter. The joint army-navy attack on Fort Fisher, Grant told Lincoln, had become a "gross and culpable failure." That did it as far as Butler was concerned. It was noted that if anything happened to Grant, Butler, as next senior man, would become the overall Union commander. Upon Grant's recommendation, Lincoln formally ended Butler's military career. Before the election, removing the politically powerful Butler would have been almost unthinkable. With the election over, Lincoln sent Butler on his way without hesitating. Grant wrote his old friend, Jake Ammen's brother, Capt. Dan Ammen of the navy: "You have no doubt seen by the papers that the very thing you so strongly hoped had already taken place. I mean, Butler had been removed at my request. The failure at Fort Fisher was not without important and valuable results."

After the army withdrew from Fort Fisher, Grant had asked the navy commander on the scene, Adm. David Porter, to stay in position. Another expedition, he said, would be launched, and with a different general. On January 15, troops led by Gen. Alfred H. Terry and supported by Porter stormed and took Fort Fisher.[11]

By March 1865, it was obvious to any thinking person that the end of the war was in sight. The Confederacy was no longer a solid entity. Having been subdivided and sliced by streams of advancing bluecoats, it had become a mere collection of separate islands. On the East Coast, with Joe Johnston offering only feeble resistance, Sherman had advanced relentlessly. After capturing first Columbia, then Wilmington, he was now at Goldsboro, North Carolina, meeting up with the army of John Schofield. In Tennessee, George Thomas's Army of the Cumberland was becoming active, and Phil Sheridan, having eliminated opposition in the Shenandoah Valley, was on his way to join up with Grant. Farther south, meanwhile, Gen. E. R. S. Canby, having left New Orleans, was driving on to Mobile.

Having been under constant pressure himself, Ulysses Grant could empathize with the president. On March 20, he wired Lincoln: "Can you not visit City Point for a day or two? I would like very much to see you, and I think the rest would do you good." Lincoln was only too happy to accept the invitation. Three days later, he and his party were on their way up the James aboard the *River Queen*. The meeting at City Point, between two men who believed in each other, was especially warm and cordial.[12]

Despite his army's weakened condition, the remarkable Lee was still dangerous. Grant told his commanders to prepare for a Confederate spoiling attack designed to create confusion so Confederates could withdraw from their present position in good order.[13] The anticipated attack, led gallantly by John B. Gordon, was made on March 25. It was later described by Horace Greeley.

"Gen. Lee," Greeley wrote, "foreseeing clearly the speedy downfall of the Confederate cause unless averted by a prompt concentration of its remaining forces and a telling blow delivered thereby on some one of our encircling armies . . . resolved to anticipate Grant's initiative by an attack on his lines before Petersburg and Richmond. . . . Gordon charged at daybreak; his men rushing instantly across the narrow space that here separated the confronting lines, and pouring into Fort Steedman [overcame men] who were completely surprised and overwhelmed. . . . Here their triumph ended. . . . their initial success had only isolated them, a comparative handful in the midst of an army of foes. In short, it was the Mine explosion repeated with parts reversed."[14]

In most minds, Robert E. Lee and the Confederacy were one and the same. The war would continue, people sensed, as long as Lee's Army of Northern Virginia was viable. And now the moment had come for Grant to deliver a final, decisive blow. Before striking that blow, however, he would confer with both Sherman and Lincoln.

Sherman arrived on March 27 to talk end-game strategy. "I mean to end the business here," Grant said. Those words excited Phil Sheridan, who by then was also at City Point. "That's what I like to hear you say," said Sheridan. "Let's end the business here!"[15]

Then came a conference with Lincoln aboard the *River Queen*. On hand were Grant, Sherman, and Admiral Porter. Lincoln, the one man who had a right to know everything, never asked what Grant and Sherman proposed to do—he merely wanted to know that they were confident of success. They were. Later in the talk, they discussed the inevitable Confederate surrender and terms that might be offered. Both Grant and Sherman had the impression that Lincoln wanted above all a generous peace that would help reunite the country.

On the morning of March 29, after saying good-bye to Lincoln, who was remaining at City Point to await developments, Grant left for his headquarters, far to the west. The stage was set.

"It is not the intention to attack the enemy in his entrenched position," Grant told Sheridan, "but to force him out if possible." A later dispatch amplified this: "I feel now like ending the matter, if it is possible to do so . . . push around the enemy, if you can, and get on to his right rear."[16]

The aggressive Sheridan was the right man for the job. As his attack gained momentum, Grant added weight to it by placing Gouverneur Warren's Fifth Corps under Sheridan's control. When the methodical Warren moved too slowly to suit him, Sheridan relieved him and put crusty Charles Griffin in his place. One Union soldier said Sheridan was "a tiger, up with the front line always, and in the heat of battle. . . ."[17] By nightfall, the Union had won a decisive battle at a place called Five Forks, behind Lee's right flank. This in turn threatened the Confederate front, and Grant ordered a general attack all along the line.

On Sunday morning, April 2, Jefferson Davis was at church when he received a message from Lee: "My lines are broken in three places. Richmond must be evacuated this evening." Horace Greeley later painted the scene with understated poignance, saying Davis "went quietly, soberly out—never to return as President of the Confederacy. No word was spoken; but the whole assemblage *felt* that the missive he had so hastily perused bore words of doom."[18]

For a few horrifying minutes, the general attack had looked like a failure. Union veterans had learned, at Cold Harbor and elsewhere, that it was foolhardy to go against fortifications. Now they were attacking positions that had been established and improved over a matter of months. In some sectors, as hundreds of men were cut down by massed rifle fire, the grim lesson was repeated.

Suddenly there was a breakthrough. Grant had been right: Sheridan's assault, and the need to oppose it, had forced Lee to weaken his line in several places. Men under Gen. Horatio Wright, finding places that were now thinly held, pierced the line, swarmed over the entrenchments, and drove into open country. It was too much for the weary graybacks; courage and sacrifice could do but so much. Whole divisions had to choose between putting up their hands or fleeing in disorder. Both Petersburg and Richmond now belonged to the Union.[19]

Lincoln first went to Petersburg, meeting briefly with Grant. He then visited Richmond, the former Rebel capital, where he was hailed by swarms of newly freed blacks shouting, "Glory to God! Glory! Glory!" When Lincoln returned to Washington, said Greeley's *Tribune*, he was much stronger "in body and soul" than when he had left.[20]

In Washington, Stanton sent for Dana, told him Richmond had fallen, and said he wanted Dana to go there and report on the condition of affairs. By April 6, Dana was in Richmond, writing Stanton, "The malignity of the thorough rebel here is humbled and silenced, but only seems the more intense on that account. . . . there is a great throng of people after victuals. Confederate money is useless and they have no other."[21]

Farther west, Lee's situation had become desperate. His army was coming apart, and among the casualties was one of his best generals—the legendary A. P. Hill had been killed near Petersburg. Lee's only hope, a faint one, was to cross the Appomattox River, destroy the bridges behind him, and move west to where he'd find rations for his half-starved men. He was being pressed so hard, meanwhile, that he could not take time to reconstitute the shattered army. Moreover, a Union column, finding an old wagon bridge, had crossed the Appomattox River and stood blocking his path to the West.

Confederates had been surrendering in large numbers, and among the prisoners was one of the army's senior generals, the distinguished Richard Ewell. Grant would later tell of a conversation with a man who'd spoken to Ewell. Allegedly, Ewell had said the cause was lost once Grant crossed the James River. The South, he had added, should then have asked for terms using what little leverage it still retained. Now it was too late to ask for anything. The South was beaten, and for any man killed after this, someone was responsible, and it would be little better than murder.[22]

That conversation, Grant said, was a factor in his decision to send a message to Lee. At 5:00 P.M., April 7, he wrote: "The results of the last week must convince you of the hopelessness of further resistance. . . . I feel that it is so, and regard it as my duty to shift from myself the responsibility of any further effusion of blood, by asking of you the surrender of that portion of the Confederate States army known as the Army of Northern Virginia."

Lee answered, saying he didn't agree the situation was hopeless, but he nevertheless asked what terms were being proposed. Grant replied, ". . . peace being my great desire, there is but one condition I would insist upon, namely: that the men and officers surrendered shall be disqualified for taking up arms against the Government of the United States until properly exchanged."[23]

Lee's next note said he hadn't intended to propose surrender, ". . . but as the restoration of peace should be the sole object of all, I desired to know whether your proposals would lead to that end." Grant had to be cautious; he wasn't authorized to hold a general discussion of "peace," which might even imply recognition of the Confederacy. He said such a discussion "could lead to no good." He added, however, ". . . I am equally anxious for peace with yourself, and the whole North entertains the same feeling. The terms upon which peace can be had are well understood. By the South laying down their arms they will hasten that most desirable event, save thousands of human lives, and hundreds of millions of property not yet destroyed. . . ."[24]

This was far different from the "unconditional surrender" demand sent 3 years earlier to Simon Bolivar Buckner at Fort Donelson. Both Grant and Lee now recognized that the South had lost; there was no need to emphasize it. Grant would be as generous as possible to a respected and gallant opponent.

For more than a day, Grant had been suffering from an almost crippling headache. Then, on the morning of April 9, an officer arrived with a message: Robert E. Lee was asking for an interview to discuss terms of surrender. "When the officer reached me," Grant wrote, "I was still suffering with the sick headache; but the instant I saw the contents of the note I was cured."[25] He sent Col. Orville Babcock galloping off to meet Lee and escort him to whatever meeting place Lee selected.

After Babcock met up with Lee, Babcock, Lee, and Col. Charles Marshall of Lee's staff rode into Appomattox Courthouse and entered the home of a Wilmer McLean. Grant arrived a bit later, accompanied by several officers. The others waited outside as Grant entered the McLean parlor. There he and Lee met face-to-face.

In Greeley's words, "The interview was brief; the business in hand frankly discussed, as became soldiers."[26] It is a scene well known to history: Lee in a splendid new uniform, complete with sash and jeweled sword; Grant in muddy boots, wearing the blouse of a private soldier, with only shoulder straps to give evidence of rank. Grant apologized for his appearance, not that he wanted to put on a show, but because he feared Lee might think him discourteous. In both words and actions, he'd do his best to minimize Lee's discomfort.[27]

Terms of surrender were written out by Grant and copied by his secretary, Ely Parker, a full-blooded Seneca Indian from western New York State. As Parker later recalled it, Grant then asked: "General, is that satisfactory?" Lee replied, "Yes, I am bound to be satisfied with anything you offer. It is more than I expected."

Lee asked if the terms could be modified to allow private soldiers to retain any horses or mules they claimed to own. Grant, who'd once worked the land himself, knew the value of a farm animal. He readily agreed, causing Lee to say, "This will have the best possible effect on the men. It will be very gratifying and will do much toward conciliating our people."[28]

Word spread rapidly through the ranks. Veterans of too many battles, men who had seen their comrades fall and die, suddenly realized, almost in wonder, that they themselves had survived. They shouted, cheered, threw their hats in the air, and a few artillerymen even began to fire off salutes. Grant sent word to stop the shooting. The Confederates were once again fellow countrymen, and he did "not want to exult over their downfall."[29]

Historian Kenneth P. Williams said it well: "The military career that Grant ended on that day is inspiring, not only because of his great genius as a soldier, but because of his never-failing courtesy and consideration for others, which at Appomattox were by no means confined to the scene in the McLean parlor. If the kindness that Grant habitually displayed during four hard years of war is not a precious part of the American heritage, we have lost all sense of values."[30]

It was done—the labors of 4 long years had not been in vain. As Lee prepared to leave, Grant followed him out and saluted by raising his hat. Lee raised his own hat in return, then trotted away to break the news to his army. In a moving farewell message, he would tell them: "You will take with you the satisfaction that proceeds from the consciousness of duty faithfully performed; and I earnestly pray that a merciful God will extend to you his blessing and protection."[31]

As Grant was returning to camp, he was reminded that he hadn't yet sent word to Washington. He dismounted, sat down on a large stone, called for pencil and paper, and wrote a message to Secretary Stanton: "General Lee surrendered the Army of Northern Virginia this afternoon on terms proposed by myself."[32]

The following day, Stanton sent Dana to Grant's headquarters to furnish "such details as might be of interest."[33] Dana found that Grant would not be staying to watch the surrender ceremonies. Rather than savoring his triumph, he wanted to get back to where he could start winding things down. This was the man whose only Mexican War boast involved the profits made by his regimental bakery. The war was costing nearly $4 million a day, and Grant, never at heart a warrior, *did* consider himself a cost-conscious man of business!

Julia urged him to first visit Richmond instead of returning directly to Washington. "Hush, Julia," she remembered his saying. "Do not say another word on this subject. I would not distress these people. They are feeling their defeat very bitterly, and you would not add to it by witnessing their despair, would you?"[34]

Lincoln's hope for an easy peace, echoed by Grant at Appomattox, was also the hope of Horace Greeley, who wrote editorially: "We entreat the President promptly to do and dare in the cause of magnanimity! The Southern mind is now open to kindness, and may be majestically affected by generosity."[35]

Dana accompanied Grant as he returned to the capital. They arrived on April 13, and the next morning Grant attended a cabinet meeting. The president insisted, before they got down to business, that Grant, the man of the hour, tell everyone about Lee's surrender. When the meeting broke up, Lincoln pulled Grant aside. Mrs. Lincoln, he said, had arranged a theater party for that evening, with General and Mrs. Grant as honored guests.

Grant demurred, saying that if he and Mrs. Grant were in town they'd be delighted to accompany the President and Mrs. Lincoln. As it was, however, Mrs. Grant was very anxious to get away in order to visit their children, who had been staying in Burlington, New Jersey.[36]

Later that day, the Grants took a train for Burlington, going by way of Philadelphia. As Julia remembered it, their carriage was on its way to the depot when a "dark, pale man rode past us at a sweeping gallop . . ." Then the stranger "rode twenty yards ahead of us, wheeled and returned, and as he passed us both going and returning, he thrust his face quite near the General and glared in a disagreeable manner." The Grants later decided that the wild-eyed horseman must have been the noted actor, John Wilkes Booth.[37]

That evening, in one of America's darkest hours, Abraham Lincoln went to Ford's Theater, where he was shot by that same John Wilkes Booth. The course of history might have been far different had the Grants accompanied the Lincolns that night. The papers had said Grant would be at the theater, and allegedly Booth hoped to kill the general as well as the president. Could Grant have seen Booth in time to forestall him? Might Grant have taken the bullet intended for the president? Or worst of all, might both men have fallen? One can only speculate.

Late that evening, Charles Dana was awakened by a messenger sent by Edwin Stanton. The president had been shot, and Secretary of State Seward had been attacked in his home and critically wounded. Stanton wanted Dana to come at once to the house on Tenth Street where Lincoln lay dying. The secretary, remarkably composed, but also fearing an overall Southern conspiracy, began to dictate orders and messages putting the country on alert.

The Grants had just arrived in Philadelphia when a telegram came saying the President had been assassinated. Grant was urged to return at once to Washington. "It would be impossible for me to describe the feeling that overcame me," Grant would write. "I knew his goodness of heart, his generosity . . . and above all his desire to see all the people of the United States enter again upon the full privileges of citizenship with equality among all."

Then came a further message, this one from Dana: "PERMIT ME TO SUGGEST TO YOU TO KEEP CLOSE WATCH ON ALL PERSONS WHO COME NEAR YOU IN THE CARS OR OTHERWISE; ALSO, THAT AN ENGINE BE SENT IN FRONT OF THE TRAIN AGAINST ANYTHING BEING ON THE TRACK."

In the moment of crisis, Dana had thought instinctively of Grant's safety. The country now needed him more than ever.[38]

22

"LET US HAVE PEACE"

GRANT RETURNED to a capital whose mood had changed overnight. The jubilation had vanished, as had all talk of magnanimity toward the South. Many believed the assassination was part of a Southern conspiracy organized, or at least sanctioned, by Confederate authorities. Among the voices howling for vengeance were those of Stanton, Dana, and the new president, Andrew Johnson.

On the night of April 14, Horace Greeley had penned a scathing anti-Lincoln editorial. Sydney Gay, the *Tribune*'s managing editor, managed to intercept and squash it. By this time Greeley knew Lincoln was dead. Nevertheless, instead of thanking Gay, he began reprimanding him: "They tell me you ordered my leader out of this morning's paper. Is it your paper or mine? I should like to know if I cannot print what I choose in my own paper."

Gay's reply was quick and direct: "The paper is yours, Mr. Greeley. The article is in type upstairs and you can use it when you choose, *but if you run that editorial, there will not be one brick left standing in the* Tribune *building*."[1]

Even Ulysses Grant feared a widespread plot. He told one of his commanders: "Extreme rigor will have to be observed whilst assassination remains the order of the day with the rebels."[2] However, Grant soon decided that Booth and his fellow conspirators had worked alone. Helping his change of heart was a letter from Confederate Richard

Ewell denouncing the assassination. General Ewell, now imprisoned at Fort Warren, in Boston Harbor, expressed feelings of "unqualified abhorrence and indignation." He was shocked, Ewell said, "by the occurrence of this appalling crime, and by the seeming tendency in the public mind to connect the South and Southern men with it."[3]

Lincoln's funeral was held on April 19. Members of the cabinet and other dignitaries were seated at the foot of the catafalque. At its head stood Grant, alone. One observer, correspondent Noah Brooks, said the general "was often moved to tears," consoled only by remembering that Lincoln had spent most of his final days in Grant's company. "He was incontestably the greatest man I have ever known," Grant said.[4]

In his editorial that day, Greeley refused to join those who heaped "extravagant and preposterous laudations on our dead President as the wisest and greatest man who ever lived." Nevertheless, he continued, there were "few graves which will be more extensively, persistently visited, or bedewed with the tears of a people's prouder, fonder affection, than that of Abraham Lincoln."[5]

At dawn on April 21, Lincoln's funeral train, swathed in black, began its slow, mournful journey to Springfield. Later that same day, Grant received a telegram from Sherman announcing the surrender of Joe Johnston's army. As soon as he read the message, Grant realized that Sherman had overstepped his military bounds. His generous terms said that state governments, if the agreement were approved, would take oaths of allegiance and then be readmitted to the Union. Also, Johnston's men would disband only after marching to their respective state capitals and depositing their weapons in state arsenals. The proposal seemed to recognize Confederate legitimacy, and in the wake of the assassination, the timing could not have been worse. President Johnson and his cabinet members, especially Stanton, were quick to reject the agreement and denounce Sherman for signing it.

Grant left immediately to set things straight, traveling inconspicuously so as to save his friend embarrassment. By this time Sherman had learned of the assassination and knew the document was likely to be repudiated. At Grant's request, Sherman and Johnston agreed on new surrender terms, identical with those given to Lee at Appomattox.

It might have blown over, and in his *Memoirs* Grant emphasized that the initial agreement had been only *conditional*. A hysterical Stanton, however, gave a statement to the papers that condemned Sherman and brought forth a torrent of abuse. Some papers even accused him of treason, with one hinting he'd been involved in the assassination plot and had deliberately permitted Jefferson Davis to escape with Confederate gold.[6]

Navy Secretary Gideon Welles wrote in his diary: "We were all imposed upon by Stanton for a purpose. He and the Radicals were opposed to the mild policy of President Lincoln on which Sherman acted, and which Stanton opposed and was determined to defeat."[7]

When people came to their senses, Sherman was restored to his rightful place of national esteem. The rift between Sherman and Stanton, however, would never be healed. When the armies staged their Grand Review in Washington on May 23 and 24, Sherman made a point of refusing to shake Stanton's hand.[8]

In May, wealthy Philadelphia citizens presented the Grants with a handsome house on Chestnut Street. Grant's duties were in Washington, however, and Philadelphia would never be called home. Moreover, it was time for a well-deserved vacation. Grant left on an extended trip, visiting several major cities as well as his former hometowns, Georgetown and Galena. It became a triumphal tour. At each stop, cheering crowds gathered to see the hero of Appomattox. There were numerous events held in his honor, and at a dinner in Albany, the speaker lionizing Grant was none other than his one-time critic Horace Greeley.[9]

Then and later, Greeley spoke of the "honor and esteem" he felt for Grant, pointing out, for example, that although many reproached him for the heavy losses he incurred while taking Richmond, they forgot that his predecessors had lost yet more men in *not* taking it.[10]

Meanwhile, Jefferson Davis had been captured near Irwinsville, Georgia, by one of James Harrison Wilson's cavalry units. After Davis was imprisoned at Fort Monroe, Virginia, Stanton sent for Dana. "I want you to go to Fortress Monroe," Stanton said, "and caution General Miles [the Monroe commander] against leaving Davis any possible method of suicide; tell him to put him in fetters, if necessary. Davis must be brought to trial."

At Fort Monroe, Dana wrote an order authorizing the use of manacles and fetters "whenever advisable." Then he hurried back to Washington, where he was on the reviewing stand during the Grand Review of May 23 and 24.

That more or less wrapped up Dana's official duties. On July 1, he resigned his government post to become editor of the new *Chicago Republican*. With peace at hand, a War Department job promised very little by way of either political or financial opportunity. Dana knew many men, including his old boss Horace Greeley, for whom an editor's desk had been a stepping-stone. That included the Speaker of the House, Greeley's friend Schuyler Colfax, who had once been the editor of a small Indiana newspaper.[11]

Andrew Johnson, spouting the politically correct hard line toward the Rebels, declared, "Treason is a crime and must be made odious." Many of those who had done the fighting, however, were far less vindictive. The soldiers, Grant said, were "in favor of a speedy reconstruction on terms that would be the least humiliating . . . They believed, I have no doubt, as I did, that besides being the mildest, it was also the wisest, policy."[12]

Dissenting voices nevertheless claimed that Grant's leniency at Appomattox was a mistake. The *New York Times*, for one, called on the government to try Robert E. Lee as a traitor. Ben Butler chimed in, perhaps wanting to repay Grant for having relieved him. Butler assured the president that Grant "had no authority to grant amnesty or pardon." In Norfolk, a federal grand jury then indicted Lee and other Confederate leaders for treason.

At Grant's suggestion, Lee petitioned for a pardon, both to protect himself and to establish a precedent for others. Andrew Johnson leaned toward prosecution, but Grant insisted that the Appomattox terms be upheld. The nation's honor was at stake, he said, and when Attorney General James Speed questioned the scope of the Appomattox terms, Grant snapped: "I will be drawn and quartered before they will be violated."[13]

The exasperated general played his trump card. If Johnson didn't relent, Grant said, he'd resign his commission in protest. Knowing his administration would be in serious trouble without Grant, the president backed down.[14]

Many, including Alexander Stephens, Vice President of the Confederacy, had sensed Grant's potential. "He is one of the most remarkable men I have ever met," Stephens told Horace Porter. "He does not seem to be aware of his powers, but in the future he will undoubtedly exert a controlling influence in shaping the destinies of the country."[15] Grant himself was beginning to sense those powers. It remained to be seen how he would use them.

By November, Andrew Johnson was beginning to agree with Grant, Greeley, and others who favored the magnanimous peace Lincoln had wanted. On the other hand, the hard-line Radical Republicans, including Senator Carl Schurz, believed most Southern whites still harbored deep resentment toward the North. A report written by Schurz maintained that countless blacks were victims of ongoing violence. Angry letters from Schurz arguing for continued stern measures toward the South frequently appeared in Northern papers, including Greeley's *Tribune*.

Johnson, hoping to counter Schurz and the Radicals, sent Grant on a fact-finding trip to test the pulse of the South. He was probably the wrong man for the job. Optimistically, Grant heard what he wanted to hear, that war-weary Southern whites were embracing peace and willing to live in harmony with their former slaves. He considered atypical the reports of anti-black violence, and only later would he realize that such behavior reflected deep-seated and durable white racism. In his report, Grant said, "The mass of thinking men of the South accept the present state of affairs in good faith." The people, he wrote, were "disposed to acquiesce and become good citizens."

Gideon Welles said Grant's opinions reflected "practical common sense." Some people claimed he overlooked too many problems in order to support the administration, but Grant tried to submit a balanced report. He acknowledged, for example, that serious problems existed for former slaves, and said that "in some form the Freedmen's Bureau is an absolute necessity until civil law is established and enforced, securing to the freedmen their rights and full protection."[16]

Had all people, North and South, worked together in a spirit of goodwill, Reconstruction might have proceeded smoothly. It was not to be. Even some of Grant's friends thought he was being naive and, as the *Tribune* said, "throwing himself into the arms of the secessionists." After reading Schurz's report, Grant, too, became more concerned about Southern violence. He ordered military commanders in the South to report "all known outrages . . . committed by White people against the blacks, and the reverse."[17]

It is almost impossible to track the twists and turns of Andrew Johnson's Reconstruction policies. Initially, his programs were supported by almost universal goodwill, and of the major Northern papers, only Greeley's *Tribune* was critical at the beginning of 1866. (At one point Greeley even called the president "illiterate." Johnson, in turn, couldn't stand Greeley, saying he was "all heart and no head . . . a sublime old child.")[18]

Johnson blundered from crisis to crisis, and the more people got to know him, the less they liked him. At first, said Grant, Johnson's "denunciations of treason" drove many Southerners "to a point almost beyond endurance." Later, however, Grant said: "Mr. Johnson, after a complete revolution of sentiment, seemed to regard the South not only as an oppressed people, but as the people best entitled to consideration of any of our citizens. . . . Thus Mr. Johnson, fighting Congress on the one hand, and receiving the support of the South on the other, drove Congress, which was overwhelmingly republican, to the passing of first one measure and then another to restrict his power."[19]

Dana's *Chicago Republican*, as the name implied, was strictly partisan, as was nearly every other contemporary newspaper. If truth be told, editors of that era generally saw their job as more the shaping of opinion than the providing of news. And if they had to stretch the truth to get results? Well, that came with the territory. "From the hour I first occupied the position of editor to the present time," a retiring journalist confessed, "I have been solicited to lie on every given subject, and can't remember ever having told a wholesome truth without diminishing the subscription list or making an enemy. . . . Having a thorough contempt for myself, I retire in order to recruit my moral constitution."[20]

Except for subscribers to large metropolitan dailies, Americans interested in politics got their news from the partisan press, and that press depended on party coffers and official funding. Editors acquired tremendous power, and far too often politicians awarded contracts and patronage because of that power. They also listened if an editor recommended someone for office, especially when that someone was the editor himself.

At first Dana had been a loyal supporter of Andrew Johnson. Then, on March 12, 1866, an item in his paper declared: "The scheme to buy up the present managers of the *Chicago Republican* by the government collectorships is very smart, but it won't win." It sounded as though the administration had tried to buy Dana's friendship. Actually, it was the other way around. Dana had asked Johnson to make him collector of the Port of New York, the country's fattest patronage post. Andrew Johnson had turned him down, and from then on, Dana was Johnson's enemy.[21]

Before long, Dana was writing his friend James Harrison Wilson that Johnson was "an obstinate, stupid man, governed by preconceived ideas, by whiskey, and by women. He means one thing today and another tomorrow, but the glorification of Andrew Johnson all the time."[22]

Meanwhile, the Grant/Dana relationship was cooling. The instigator might have been Dana's confidant Wilson, who was something of a busybody. Wilson wrote Dana that he'd discovered a "change in feeling" toward Dana at Grant's headquarters. He thought it began when Dana opposed Washburne's bill to award Grant a fourth star. Dana had called the bill a "dreadful mistake," indicating a desire for rank and money that "detracted from the general's greatness." Whether or not

Grant accepted a promotion was obviously none of Dana's business, so a worry about "greatness" probably reflected a concern for Grant's presidential chances. Perhaps Dana was thinking of the country, or perhaps of things a president might do for his friends. There was evidently little thought about what was best for the general. Although Grant's friend Sherman strongly advised him against entering politics, Dana fully endorsed such a move. Self-righteously, Dana even claimed that Grant had no choice in the matter; it was a question of duty. Although Grant had done much for the country, Dana said, the country had done much for Grant in return and was "entitled to his further sacrifices and services."[23]

Dana said it was "absurd" to think him unfriendly toward Grant. However, if the general resented anything he'd said, he was "sorry to lose his friendship, but yet more sorry that he could withdraw it for such a cause. I think that under such circumstances his misfortune would be greater than mine." From that last sentence, it would appear that Dana the editor was having no problems with self-esteem. In any case, according to Wilson, Dana and Grant remained on friendly if not intimate terms until some time after Grant became president.[24]

By the spring of 1867, Jefferson Davis had been imprisoned for nearly 2 full years. No one had the slightest intention of trying him, and in Horace Greeley's opinion, he should have been released as a token of reunion and goodwill. The opportunity came when the U.S. Circuit Court in Richmond agreed to release Davis if a group of reliable citizens would go bail for him. Friends warned Greeley against getting involved, to which he replied: "I know about all the things that may happen to me, but what I am to do is right and I'll do it."

When Greeley's name appeared on Davis's bail bond, there were nationwide cries of outrage. Abusive letters poured in to the *Tribune*, and thousands of people canceled their subscriptions. Members of the Union League Club of New York, to which Greeley belonged, demanded that he appear before them and face charges of disloyalty. He refused to do so, saying, "I do not recognize you as capable of judging, or even fully apprehending me. You evidently regard me as a weak sentimentalist, misled by a maudlin philosophy. I arraign you as narrowminded blockheads . . ."[25]

Later, in his *Recollections of a Busy Life*, he explained, and with dignity, that it was a matter of principle. "To all who have civilly accosted me on the subject," he wrote, "I trust I have given civil, if not satisfactory, answers; while most of those who have seen fit to assail me respecting it, I have chosen to treat with silent scorn."[26]

The backers of Dana's *Chicago Republican* had never been able to put the paper on a sound financial basis. Eventually, Dana was forced to give up on it. In December 1867, he and a group of prominent Republicans purchased the *New York Sun*. Dana, the new editor, set to work, and as he did, he hung a picture of Horace Greeley on his office wall. Perhaps it was a gesture of respect, or maybe it was just to remind himself of the caliber of the competition.

On January 27, 1868, in his first issue, Dana announced: "In changing its proprietorship, the *Sun* will not in any respect change its principles or general line of conduct. It will continue to be an independent newspaper, wearing the livery of no party, and discussing public questions and the acts of public men on their merits alone." The *Sun*, he added, "will support General Grant as its candidate for the Presidency."[27]

Two months later, in March 1868, Dana agreed to co-author, with James Harrison Wilson, a one-volume life of Grant. "It was issued in ample time," Wilson wrote, "to assist in the election of General Grant to his first term as president."[28]

Grant had been walking a political tightrope. For a time he and Andrew Johnson had worked in harmony. This was fine by Grant, whose whole career had been based on loyal duty to his superiors. His only problem came when Johnson tried to "use" him politically, even bringing him along on a tour of northern cities, a political junket that became known as the "Swing Around the Circle." Johnson tried to give the impression that Grant endorsed administration policies, while Grant tried hard to disassociate himself. In Chicago, he told a reporter that his presence on the train did not imply his support of Johnson; he objected to the use of the army as a "party machine," and he did not "consider the Army a place for a politician." Believing strongly in the subordination of military to civilian authority, however, he did his best not to insult Johnson.[29]

When Johnson's and Grant's paths began to diverge, another kind of duty came into play, duty to justice and to the nation. Grant now knew he'd been wrong in assuming that racism and recalcitrance would be short-lived. Racial violence was widespread; there had been bloody riots in Memphis and New Orleans, where scores of blacks were murdered while civilian police looked on. Clearly, civil authorities could not, or would not, provide justice for the freedmen. It was up to Grant and the military governors to step in.

Johnson, however, overtly favoring Southern whites at the expense of the freedmen, issued a proclamation ending the "insurrection" and saying "peace, order, tranquility and civil authority" existed throughout the nation. Military tribunals were thereby deprived of jurisdiction. From Tennessee, George Thomas told Grant: "The people of the States lately in rebellion are each day growing more and more insolent and threatening in their demeanor, as they find themselves relieved from punishment by military authorities."[30]

Johnson's problems with both Congress and certain cabinet members reached the breaking point, and he decided to take action by removing Edwin Stanton, one of his principal critics. Although Stanton refused to resign, Johnson nevertheless named Grant to replace him on an interim basis.

Grant reluctantly accepted the position. Refusing it, he said, might mean "some objectionable man would be appointed." He explained to Julia that he thought it "most important that someone should be there who cannot be used."[31]

Under the Tenure of Office Act, Johnson's removal of Stanton was illegal. The outraged Senate began drawing up a motion to impeach. By January 1868, Grant discovered that by helping keep Stanton out of office, he himself might be subject to prosecution. Grant told Johnson he'd changed his mind about taking Stanton's job and suggested that someone else be appointed, someone the Senate might find acceptable.

When the Senate voted to reinstate Stanton, Grant informed the president that the Senate's action effectively ended his term as interim secretary. Stanton promptly reclaimed the office, and an irate Johnson claimed that Grant had promised to stay there until a replacement was named. He was outraged, he said, by Grant's "duplicity," and he did his best to embarrass and shame Grant in front of the whole cabinet.

Grant went to Johnson and tried to set matters straight, suggesting that Stanton's mere occupation of a particular room didn't change anything. Why not, he said, issue an order telling the army not to obey anything coming from Stanton? Johnson, however, had no intention of working with Grant. Someone, presumably Johnson, then leaked information to the press disputing Grant's truthfulness. With that, Grant realized that all attempts at reconciliation had failed; it was time for a clean break.

With help from Rawlins, Grant wrote a letter explaining his position. He had accepted the appointment, he said, only to keep the department out of hostile hands and not to help Johnson in his maneuvers against Stanton and Congress. Moreover, he had never promised to retain the office in the face of the Senate's action. "And now, Mr. President," Grant wrote in closing, "when my honor as a soldier and as a man have been so violently assailed, pardon me for saying that I can regard this whole matter, from the beginning to the end, as an attempt to involve me in the resistance of law, for which you have hesitated to assume the responsibility in orders, and thus to destroy my character before the country."

Grant's letter became public, and as historian Adam Badeau later stated, it "made the rupture with Johnson personal, and reconciliation impossible. It was a stroke of political genius, for it also made any candidate other than Grant impossible to the Republicans."[32]

One Republican was not so sure. Earlier, Horace Greeley had said the Republicans could do better than Grant. Perhaps not understanding a military man's unwillingness to speak out on political matters, he roundly criticized Grant's silence. The party's candidate, Greeley said, "must represent and embody Republican principles, and be neither afraid nor ashamed to avow his faith in them and his willingness to stand or fall by them." Indeed, he said, "the American people are not in the mood for any grab-bag experiments."[33]

On February 21, 1868, Johnson defied Congress and named Lorenzo Thomas as interim Secretary of War. Stanton, with Grant's support, refused to give up the office. Three days later, the House of Representatives voted to impeach.[34] Grant agreed with their action—mainly, as he told one senator, because Johnson was "such an infernal liar." However, on May 16, the Senate, acting as a court of impeachment, acquitted Johnson by a single vote.[35]

Less than a week later, Republicans gathered in Chicago and nominated Ulysses Grant for president. As his running mate, they chose Speaker of the House Schuyler Colfax. In a letter accepting the nomination, Grant called for an end to partisan bickering and disharmony. "Let us have peace," he wrote. That was what the nation wanted to hear.[36]

To oppose Grant, the Democrats nominated Horatio Seymour. However, the election was almost a foregone conclusion. It mattered little to the electorate that Grant was no campaign orator and was, in fact, silent on most issues of the day. Grant was the man they trusted and wanted.

Day after day, Dana and the *New York Sun* beat the drums for Grant. Typical was a letter from Thurlow Weed: "We heard last night of the Democratic nomination for President. . . . If I had a thousand votes to cast, they should all be pronounced and deposited for Grant, and against Seymour."[37]

By his silence, Grant gave his opponents little to attack, except perhaps his war record. Thus, when a Democratic paper said Grant defeated Lee only because of overwhelming numbers, Dana promptly countered, saying the "falsehoods invented by the writer in the *World* will prove his want of common sense, as well as his utter disregard of the truth."[38]

The *Sun* was even happy to publicize Grant rallies:

ATTENTION, BOYS IN BLUE!
ONE MORE CHARGE AND
THE EMPIRE STATE IS OURS!

All Boys in Blue Clubs will rally in front of the COOPER INSTITUTE on Friday Evening, October 30th, at 7½ O'Clock. . . . This meeting will cooperate with the meeting of the Republican Clubs inside of the Institute. . . . .[39]

On November 4, a *Sun* headline shouted the results:

GRANT AND COLFAX
Twenty-five States for Grant—
Nine for Seymour—
208 Electoral Votes for Grant—
88 for Seymour

Charles Dana, not without reason, suspected it would never have happened without him. In any case, his editorial proudly noted Grant's rise to prominence: "The election of Gen. GRANT is the finale of an eight years' struggle, which has teamed with events without a parallel in the annals of this or any other nation. . . . Starting in obscurity, and advancing by slow and sure steps, he has reached an eminence where he challenges the respect and the confidence of his countrymen and has made his name a household word throughout the nation. . . . no candid person will for a moment doubt that the interests, the honor, and the glory of the Republic are secure in his hands."[40]

Grant, at Washburne's house to hear the returns, took everything calmly, almost resignedly. One observer said he'd seen him more excited over a game of cards. Early the next morning Grant strolled home, and when he saw Julia, all he could say was, "I am afraid I am elected."[41]

23

"A FOOL NOT TO GIVE IT"

CHARLES DANA, John Rawlns, and James "Harry" Wilson, by this time a rather solid triumvirate, had never wavered in wanting Grant to become president. Friends such as Sherman, Porter, and Babcock, however, had always seen the downside, and even before Grant was nominated, Orville Babcock was telling Elihu Washburne: "I am one of those who hope Genl Grant will not become President. I look upon it as a great misfortune to him."[1]

Whether or not they saw the presidency as a personal "misfortune," everyone knew the general was a political neophyte. Grant didn't seem too concerned about that. He believed the people had called on him to serve, and as he once told Andrew Johnson, "This is a republic where the will of the people is the law of the land."[2] The people, in other words, not the fortunes of a particular political party, were what counted. It was a noble credo; it was also hopelessly naive.

When a group of Pennsylvania Republicans called on him to urge the appointment of a Pennsylvania cabinet member, Grant said that although Republicans had voted for him, he didn't consider himself a "representative" of any political party. That was probably a mistake, but he meant what he said.[3] In the military, he had always despised self-promoters, believing an officer should advance by merit, not by politicking. What he failed to recognize was that he was now in a new arena, where seeking favors, and distributing them, was the name of the game.

Even Horace Greeley—no, *especially* Horace Greeley—knew Grant couldn't do business that way. Nevertheless, Uncle Horace seemed to appreciate the independent attitude; the *Tribune* applauded when some 500 written job applications were received by Grant's secretaries and consigned to the wastebasket.[4]

Meanwhile, Grant supporters were still in the dark as to which wing of the party he favored. When he was first nominated, Dana had reported: "Even now he does not carry the banner of the Republicans in any distinctive sense, but they rather follow his lead because they trust in his patriotism, confide in his wisdom, and believe the prestige of his great renown can secure victory."[5] On the eve of election, they still weren't sure. Was he a Conservative like Andrew Johnson, lenient toward Southern states, believing in their goodwill, and ready for them to reassume a proper role in national affairs? Or was he a Radical like Carl Schurz, condemning the outrages against the freedmen and, like the Democrats, willing to support harsh retaliatory measures? Greeley's *Tribune* said that out of 20 papers, nine had declared Grant was a Radical, nine had denied any such thing, and two had said he was nonpartisan.[6]

In the run-up to the inauguration, party leaders were dumbfounded as Grant drew up a cabinet list without asking their advice. It would have been prudent, for example, to consult the self-important Charles Sumner, head of the Senate Foreign Relations Committee, about potential Secretaries of State. Sumner, who might have wanted the job himself, never forgave the slight.[7]

On March 4, 1869, Ulysses S. Grant was sworn in as the 18th president of the United States. At age 46, he would be the youngest man to hold that office until 1901, when William McKinley's assassination catapulted 41-year-old Theodore Roosevelt into the job. Grant's inaugural speech repeated the epigram of the acceptance letter, words that would one day be on his tomb: "Let Us Have Peace." A central theme, however, concerned reducing the national debt, which had swollen 20-fold because of the war. Just as after Appomattox, when he'd hurried to Washington to stop—or at least slow—war expenditures, he again wanted to show his financial prudence. Perhaps his own sorry financial history still cast a shadow; the son of Jesse Grant needed to prove he could balance the books.

Greeley's friend Schuyler Colfax, recently Speaker of the House, was the new vice president. Often called the "Smiler," the amiable Colfax was a man they said "never lost a friend and never made an enemy."[8]

Even before Grant took office, his friends were waiting expectantly for their respective appointments. Elihu Washburne wanted to be Secretary of State, but Grant didn't think he was up to the job. To give him "prestige," he'd give him the State posting for a week, then send him off as ambassador to France.

John Rawlins, although dying from tuberculosis, also expected an appointment. Grant thought a position in the Southwest might be good for his health. To Grant's surprise, Rawlins said he didn't want that; what he *really* wanted was to be Secretary of War. Rawlins, a profane, ill-tempered paper pusher, the self-appointed guardian of Grant's morals, by now assumed far too much credit for the general's success. Grant appreciated the man's loyalty, however, and he believed loyalty should work both ways. Rawlins became Secretary of War. Six months later he was dead, having spent most of that time in a sickbed.

Then there was Charles Dana, who might also have expected a cabinet position. When Grant's choices were announced, Dana just *knew* he was more capable than someone like Adolph Borie, a little-known Pennsylvanian proposed as Secretary of the Navy. (The Pennsylvanians had their appointment, but Borie was *not* someone they knew.) Actually, Borie didn't want the job. He accepted it reluctantly, resigned 3 months later, and was replaced by George Robeson, a capable young lawyer from New Jersey.[9]

Wilson, who had Rawlin's ear, urged that Dana be given the lucrative job of New York Customs Collector, the same job he'd sought earlier from Andrew Johnson. Rawlins said it would be done. Assuming that Rawlins had cleared it with Grant, Wilson (no doubt taking some of the credit for himself) happily relayed the news to Dana, who thought it was the least Grant could do.[10]

Just as Greeley had considered himself responsible for Lincoln's becoming president, Dana felt justified in feeling the same way about Grant. Wilson's opinion, which surely echoed Dana's, was that his friend Dana, "in becoming the eyes of Grant, as well as the government, had . . . played an important, if not a determining, part in connection with the fortunes of both Grant and the country. It can scarcely be denied that had Dana, during the Vicksburg campaign, taken a different course, and instead of doing all in his power to strengthen Grant's hands, had reached the conclusion . . . that Grant was not only unfit to be trusted with such great responsibilities, but ought to be relieved, the career of that general might very well have come to a premature end."[11]

In other words, Grant owed Dana—immensely. Surprisingly, the collector position went to naval officer Moses Grinnell, derided by Wilson as "a gentleman of much less consideration." Perhaps it was an example of Grant's resenting someone's "politicking" for a job. In any case, Dana undoubtedly felt angry, even humiliated. Almost overnight he went from supportive admirer to vicious critic. A month later he was offered a lesser post, that of Custom House Appraiser, as consolation. He turned it down, and although he might easily have done the work while still editing the *Sun*, his letter of refusal said rather haughtily: "I already hold an office of responsibility as the conductor of an independent newspaper, and I am persuaded that to abandon or neglect it for the functions you offer me would be to leave a superior duty for one of much less importance."[12]

When rival papers said he was "bearing a grudge," Dana laughed it off: "If Grant could have had the *Sun*'s support by giving an office to its editor, he was a fool not to give it." Although he claimed his attacks weren't personal, his argument weakened when he continued to emphasize his many services for Grant for which he'd received nothing in return.[13]

Dana's opinion of editorial status, high to begin with, would continue to grow and swell. A few years later he said that A. K. McClure, editor of the *Philadelphia Times*, would make a "brilliant" Secretary of State, but: "What a descent it would be! The truth is that, except in some immense and unusual patriotic emergency, such as the late civil war afforded, no capable editor can properly accept any public office except that of President."[14] With that incredible statement, Dana showed a complete abandonment of his youthful idealism. Evidently, he came to consider the power of an editor second only to the power held by a president, and in his later-life value system, power was what counted.

For Treasury Secretary, Grant named Alexander Stewart, a wealthy New York merchant. Congressmen, still bristling over Grant's failure to consult them, resurrected a 1789 law saying no one engaged in trade could hold the Treasury post. Grant asked to have the law repealed, and Stewart even offered to put his assets in a blind trust (a practice a later age would adopt), but Sumner managed to block the move. The battle lines were drawn. To replace Stewart, Radical senators suggested George S. Boutwell. Accepting the inevitable, Grant withdrew Stewart's name and submitted that of Boutwell, who proved to be a good choice.[15]

Rockwood Hoar, a distinguished Massachusetts congressman, became Attorney General. Gen. Jacob Cox, a war hero, was nominated for Secretary of the Interior; Marylander J. A. J. Creswell for Postmaster General. Grant's best appointee might have been Hamilton Fish, a former senator and New York State governor, who was named Secretary of State.

Stewart, Hoar, Cox, Creswell, Rawlins—all were Republicans but none had held national office, and it shocked the party leaders. Elsewhere reactions were mixed. Greeley's *Tribune* seemed to applaud, saying, "The new Cabinet means business emphatically."[16]

Dana, however, took a different tone. On the very day the *Tribune* praised the nominees, a *Sun* article began: "Who is Borie? That is the main inquiry. The Republicans seemed unable to answer the question. Everybody seemed at sea on this point. . . . The politicians can scarcely contain their disappointment and chagrin."[17]

Hoping to avoid partisan pressures, Grant had made his choices secretly, and had done so clumsily. Fish and Borie, for example, learned of their nominations through the newspapers and had to be cajoled into accepting. To make things worse, some of the appointees had contributed to the purchase of houses for the Grants. Grant evidently saw these gifts only as expressions of gratitude to a war hero, and to the honest Grant, who'd perhaps been overly impressed by the successful businessmen he was meeting, there was no quid pro quo. However, appearances were bad, and Dana went on the offensive.

The previous year, while Grant was receiving those gifts, Dana was saying of him: "In the midst of wide-spread venality and corruption, no man has ever doubted his honesty."[18] Now, a mere month after the inauguration, he was referring to Grant's "frightful blunderings and flounderings" and attacking him for giving office to men "chiefly distinguished for having conferred on him costly and valuable benefactions."[19]

Although Grant normally kept his feelings to himself, he admitted to Hamilton Fish that "he was much hurt when Dana began to assail him in the *Sun*."[20] All the same, as he continued to appoint friends and relatives, he left himself wide open. His father, Jesse, for example, was made the Galena postmaster, and one critic suggested that "civil service examinations would soon have two questions: 'Were you a contributor to either of Grant's three houses, in Philadelphia, Washington, or Galena?' and another, 'Are you a member of the Dent family, or otherwise connected by marriage with General Grant?'"[21]

An opposing wing of the Republican Party in Mississippi, believing such things, nominated for governor "Judge" Lewis Dent, Julia's brother. Lewis badly misjudged his brother-in-law, who promptly told him his election would not be "for the best interest of the State and country." Grant threw his support to Dent's opponent, who won by a two-to-one margin.[22]

Bit by bit, however, with Grant and the cabinet steadily learning the ways of Washington, things began to improve. One observer told Washburne that "matters have settled down very quietly, and the Administration is getting into good working trim. It . . . is true to the principles of the Republican party, and the mistakes it made in appointments are spots on the sun—they do not seriously affect its brightness. I think the Administration will prove a success. The party is full of soreheads, but they alone will never destroy the party."[23]

One such success was that of Treasury Secretary Boutwell, whose prudent measures, including the redemption of government bonds, were beginning to reduce the national debt. This was in accord with Grant's stated wishes. Nevertheless, Dana insisted that any economy and retrenchment of the administration was due "very much to Mr. Boutwell and not at all to General Grant."[24]

Even Horace Greeley seemed pleased with the situation, although by then, having hired the capable Whitelaw Reid as managing editor, Greeley devoted much less time to the *Tribune*. He was frequently away on lecture tours ranging as far as Texas, and was otherwise involved with whatever crusade occupied him at the moment. Prolific as ever, he was also writing his memoir, *Recollections of a Busy Life*, and editing volume two of *The American Conflict*.[25]

That summer both the *Sun* and the *Herald* (sounding like Hearst papers of a later day) screamed for U.S. action against Spain in support of Cuban rebels. It was America's "duty," Dana wrote, "at once to interfere in Cuba . . . But this is a duty which we cannot hope to see performed by an Administration so barren of great ideas and so deficient in character."[26]

At this point an unscrupulous duo, Jay Gould and Jim Fisk Jr., concocted a scheme to corner the gold market, drive up the price, and make a sensational killing. Joining the plot was Grant's new brother-in-law, Abel Corbin, an elderly financier who may well have wooed Grant's sister Jenny as much for political as romantic reasons. The scheme relied heavily on the timing of government gold sales. If the Treasury held off selling, the price would continue to rise.

Fisk and Gould tried using Corbin to influence Grant. They also tried buying influence from Grant's White House secretary, young Horace Porter, placing an order for $500,000 in gold in Porter's name. When Porter learned of it, he immediately rejected the transaction.[27]

In September 1869, John Rawlins died. On the way to Connecticut for the funeral, Grant stayed in New York City with the Corbins. There he got wind of the scheme, which by that time had caused the price of gold to soar astronomically. An outraged Grant asked Boutwell how much gold he was preparing to sell. "Enough to break the market," Boutwell said, "perhaps three million dollars."

"Better make it five," said Grant. Boutwell did just that, and on September 24, 1869, afterward known as "Black Friday," the market broke. Fisk, Gould, and speculators following their lead were wiped out. Seeking revenge, they implied that the Grants had been involved in the scheme. A congressional investigation led by James A. Garfield, no friend of Grant, exonerated all members of the Grant family except the greedy Corbin.[28] At first Dana accepted this. By the following year, however, he was saying: "President Grant has denied that he had anything to do with the gold conspiracy, except to break it down, the facts proved in the case do not bear out his denial . . . he still stands before the tribunal of the people with the guilt of this unparalleled conspiracy upon him."[29]

The *Tribune*, meanwhile, had also begun to criticize the administration. Knowing Greeley's longtime political ambition, Grant tried to appease him by offering an appointment to the Court of St. James. Greeley told Vice President Colfax he wanted none of it. Then, following Lincoln's example, Grant tried flattery. He wrote John Russell Young, a former *Tribune* managing editor, a letter intended for Greeley's eyes: "Mr. Greeley is an honest, firm, untiring supporter of the Republican party. He means its welfare at all times. But he is a free thinker; jumps at conclusions; does not get the views of others who are just as sincere as himself . . . I have long desired a free, full talk with Mr. Greeley, because I have confidence of his intentions. I have thought at times of inviting him to Washington for that purpose; but I have been afraid that the object might be misinterpreted."

Greeley didn't answer, and when a friend was invited to see Grant, Greeley said, "I advise you to let him severely alone . . . At all events, I shall."[30]

Meanwhile, Dana was pestering Greeley with tongue-in-cheek homage. With mock solemnity, the *Sun* proclaimed Greeley's fitness for political office, recommending him at various times for Secretary of State, Postmaster General, Minister to England, Minister to China, Minister to Spain, United States Senator from Virginia, Congressman in New York State, Governor of New York State, City Comptroller, or even State Prison Inspector. When Dana proposed Greeley for governor, he also suggested that the Democrats nominate the notorious William "Boss" Tweed as his opponent. Was it malice, or was it just Dana enjoying a good joke at Greeley's expense?[31]

In his common-sense, decent way, Grant tried to do what was best for the country. Even his soundest, most farsighted ideas, however, were often thwarted by hostile members of his own party. In his very first message to Congress, perhaps remembering his own ghastly trek across the Isthmus of Panama, he recommended building a canal connecting the Caribbean and the Pacific. He sent surveying parties to select the best route seven different times, but the project received little support.

In 1870, Grant sent the Senate a treaty providing for the annexation of Santo Domingo, the present Dominican Republic. Under the treaty's terms, the islanders would hold a plebiscite to determine if they wanted to become part of the United States. Indications were that the Santo Domingans would vote for it overwhelmingly. Grant believed this would give the United States a valuable toehold in the Caribbean. It would also provide an outlet for persecuted former slaves wishing to resettle.

Most of the press, with the exception of Dana's *Sun*, favored the treaty. However, under the influence of Charles Sumner and Carl Schurz, the Senate voted it down. Schurz, for example, said the island blacks were "indigestible, unassimilable," and "could not be trusted with a share in governing our country." It seemed the Radical champion of the freedmen was an inherent racist.

Ironically, only a few years after Grant's death, the United States would use a shooting war with Spain to acquire, among other things, Puerto Rico and a naval base in Cuba. Grant would not have approved. "I would not fire a gun to annex territory," he said. "I consider it too great a privilege to belong to the United States for us to go around gunning for new territories."[32]

A frequent Washington visitor was Grant's father, Jesse, basking in the glow of his son's success. When he came to town, however, he didn't stay at the White House. Julia's father, the unreconstructed former slave owner, now lived there, and the two men despised each other.[33]

Meanwhile, the newspaper attacks continued—not only on Grant but on nearly every other member of his administration. Only Schuyler Colfax seemed immune. But finally even the "Smiler" fell into disfavor, especially after he addressed a Correspondents' Club dinner and rebuked the scandalmongers among them. Colfax, a former editor himself, should have known better. The press would always have the last word.[34]

When Horace Greeley criticized Grant, he tried to be supportive. The inexperienced president, he said, might well be "expected to make mistakes on details," but he was solid on the things that mattered. After all, Greeley asked, "on what great question has General Grant disappointed the just hopes of the people?"[35]

By 1872, however, having become increasingly critical of the administration, Greeley decided that he could no longer support Grant for a second term. As the year began, the 60-year-old Greeley was again on the road, driving himself mercilessly. In February he wrote a friend: "I rode all night from a lecture in Maine, arriving late on a broken down train in a blistering snowstorm. I worked all day, and then stood up four hours shaking hands."[36]

Greeley had a new managing editor, Whitelaw Reid, the man who'd written the vitriolic Shiloh article that had done so much to damage Grant's early reputation. Reid, with what he called "an instinctive dislike of men of General Grant's calibre and character," helped Greeley attack Grant on an almost-daily basis. Among other things, they blamed Grant for the misrule of carpetbag regimes in the conquered South, criticized Reconstruction policies that failed to reconstruct, and demanded that Southern whites get back their voting rights.[37]

With the '72 election coming up, the mainstream Republican Party was sticking with Grant. After all, asked the *New York Times*, "was anyone ready to trust the Democrats with power?" Other papers joined in, with one saying Grant's policy had been "eminently judicious and patriotic. The Republican Party demands his renomination because he has been its truest and best servant and minister."[38]

Across the country, state and local conventions were endorsing Grant for a second term. The California message was typical: "If Grant is the nominee we will carry the state by a hard fight. With any other we lose." Adding his "amen" was the Reverend Henry Ward Beecher, who told a Brooklyn audience there "had never been a President more sensitive to the wants of the people."[39]

Grant was finding that politics made for strange bedfellows. Among his congressional supporters, known as the "Stalwarts," were a dour former antagonist, the physically unattractive Ben Butler, and the friendly, handsome Roscoe Conkling, a power broker from upstate New York. Each man was a dedicated practitioner of the spoils system. Unfortunately, if he wanted to get anything done, Grant had to put up with the cynical way in which Colfax, Butler, and the other Stalwarts dispensed patronage.

Schurz and Sumner led the opposing, anti-Grant wing of the party. They didn't believe Grant deserved a second term or, perhaps more important, that he could win one. The strategy of these men, the so-called Liberal Republicans, was to set up a new party and find an alternate candidate. Accordingly, a Liberal Convention was set for Cincinnati in early May. They knew a third party, by itself, had little chance of success; what they needed was a candidate who'd appeal to Democrats as well as to all categories of anti-Grant Republicans. Early on, the movement leaders sought the support of Horace Greeley, a leading Liberal voice.

Forming a new party, chancy as it might be, held a certain fascination for Greeley. After all, he'd been at the birthing, had even been something of a midwife, when the new Republican Party got *its* start. His old political itch, never far below the surface, began to take over. And if a new candidate were needed, what better man than himself?

Carl Schurz, together with three powerful editors, "Marse Henry" Watterson of the *Louisville Courier-Journal*, Samuel Bowles of the *Springfield-Republican*, and Horace White of the *Chicago Tribune*, maneuvered to control the Cincinnati convention. Their choice was Charles Francis Adams, a man of "faultless background, political distinction, and civic virtue." It seemed a done deal, but Schurz and the others hadn't reckoned with Whitelaw Reid, who arrived in town and insisted on joining their inner circle. Since he represented the powerful *New York Tribune*, they couldn't ignore him. Immediately, Reid began pushing for Greeley.

On the first ballot, Adams had a clear lead, with 205 votes to Greeley's 147. As the voting continued, the lesser candidates began dropping out. With Reid persuading, arm-twisting, cajoling, they began throwing their support to Greeley. Five hours later, on the sixth ballot, Greeley was nominated. The delegates then selected ex-senator B. Gratz Brown of Missouri as his running mate. Reid dashed out and sent a one-word telegram to the *Tribune* office. "Nominated. W.R."[40]

The conspirators had been outmaneuvered. That evening a smiling Reid hosted them at what he called a "victory dinner." Except for the man from the *Tribune*, they were not happy campers. "Frostier conviviality I have never sat down to," wrote Watterson. "Horace White looked more than ever like an iceberg, Sam Bowles diplomatic but ineffusive, Schurz was as a death's head at the board . . . We separated early and sadly, reformers hoist by their own petard."[41]

When the news reached New York, a cannon salute was fired in City Hall Park in Greeley's honor. Before long thousands of people had gathered in the square outside the *Tribune* building. They began to cheer: "Yee-ay, Horace! Go it, Uncle Horace!" The white-haired editor, specs drooping, shuffled to his window, stared at the crowd, and waved.[42]

24

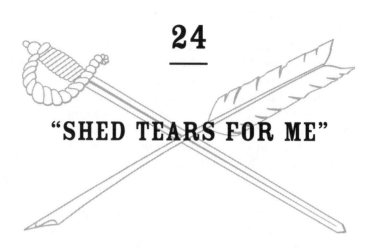

"SHED TEARS FOR ME"

THE COUNTRY was shocked beyond belief. What were the Liberal Republicans thinking of? Did those fools in Cincinnati seriously think Uncle Horace should be *president*? Greeley was fun to read, was even a pretty good philosopher, but wasn't he, well, peculiar? Wasn't he known for changing his position, constantly complaining about one thing or another, or forever carrying on about some wild crusade? Even those who loved the amiable eccentric saw Greeley the candidate as a figure of ridicule.

"We suppose," wrote Edwin Godkin in the *Nation*, "that a greater degree of incredulity and disappointment . . . has not been felt . . . since the news of the first battle of Bull Run." Fellow editor William Cullen Bryant was equally appalled, calling Greeley's nomination "sheer insanity."[1]

That was also the opinion of Thurlow Weed, who said he didn't think any body of men "outside a lunatic asylum" could have nominated Greeley. But they had. In sum, wrote Hamilton Fish, "it would be difficult to find any American of high intelligence and honesty who was worse equipped than Greeley. . . . Erratic, uncertain, violent in his temper and unwise in his judgment, a bad judge of men and open to the influence of the grossest flattery and personal adulation, with an ambition and craving for office."[2]

Carl Schurz, who with Sumner had launched the third party, couldn't believe what had happened. In spite of his well-laid plans, Reid and Greeley had somehow moved in and taken over the Liberal Republican movement. Sitting down, Schurz wrote Greeley an abusive, 11-page letter in which he threatened to withdraw his support. In his opinion, "the first fruit of the great reform movement, so hopefully begun, was a successful piece of political huckstering . . . the whole movement . . . captured by politicians of the old stamp."[3]

Schurz, however, had nowhere else to go. For that matter, neither did the Democrats, who were in a box. Despite the mud hurled by Dana and others, the people still liked Grant. The only chance of defeating him was by uniting behind a single candidate—and that meant Greeley. The Democrats met in Baltimore, made him their nominee, and even adopted his entire platform. It was a bitter pill; among other things, the free-trade Democrats had to embrace Greeley's protectionism. He grew "dizzy," Greeley said, at the thought of being endorsed by the party he had assaulted for so long.[4]

Initially, Dana's reaction to candidate Greeley was tolerant amusement. He began referring to him as "Doctor" Greeley, made note of the neat blue suit that had replaced the floppy linen duster, and treated the whole thing as a joke. When Greeley first met with the Democrats, for example, the *Sun* described the event like a scene from a comic opera: "At noon yesterday, Dr. Greeley was sitting at his buffet writing desk in the rear extension room of the Lincoln Club House, engaged in deep and apparently earnest consultation with the Hon. Samuel Sinclair and Whitelaw Reid, Esq., of the *Tribune*. At that hour the door of the club house opened, and a procession of nearly one hundred gentlemen in white hats entered. . . . The procession filed through the deep parlors of the club house, and halted at the door leading into the temporary sanctum of the ex-editor."

"Finally a gentleman stepped forward, and touching Mr. Sinclair on the shoulder, intimated to him that some gentlemen desired to speak to Mr. Greeley. Mr. Sinclair jumped up as if he had been shot. Mr. Whitelaw Reid also jumped up as if he had been shot. Dr. Greeley, observing the gentlemen in waiting, looked up blandly, bowed politely, and smiled. . . . Dr. Greeley reached out his honest, hard-fisted right hand, and cordially grasped the proferred member of the Democratic leader. Thus was the meeting of Liberal Republicanism and Orthodox Democracy consummated and the lion and the lamb brought into hearty union."[5]

In past elections, nominees had stayed home looking "presidential" while others did the campaigning. Grant was happy to continue the practice; admittedly, he was no orator. On the other hand, Greeley went full speed ahead. For years he had traveled widely; he'd do so again. Turning the *Tribune* over to Reid, he set out barnstorming the country. The first stop was New England, where he spoke 15 or 20 times a day. Next he headed west, to Pennsylvania and on into Ohio, maintaining an almost-frantic pace. In small Ohio towns, just after harvest time, thousands of curious farmers came in their buggies to hear the famed Uncle Horace. Seeing him was, of course, not the same as giving him their vote.

As always, when it came to phrasemaking, Greeley was the master. Henry Watterson, initially skeptical of Greeley's candidacy, found himself being impressed. "He was in a state of querulous excitement," Watterson wrote, but "before the vast and noisy audiences which he faced he stood apparently pleased and composed, delivering his words as he might have dictated them to a stenographer." According to Watterson, the talks "were marvels of impromptu oratory, mostly homely and touching appeals . . . convincing in their simplicity and integrity; unanswerable from any standpoint of sagacious statesmanship or true patriotism if the North had been in any mood to listen and to reason."[6]

Despite Greeley's sincerity, the New York press was being mercilessly cruel. Now that Greeley was allied with the Democrats, cartoonist Thomas Nast pictured him as a bumbling crony of the infamous Boss Tweed. Equally damaging was a collection of *Tribune* editorial statements, many self-contradictory, that appeared under the title *What I Know About Politics*, the intent being to show that he knew nothing. "If anyone could send a great nation to the dogs," concluded the *New York Times*, "the man is Greeley."[7]

While Greeley's candidacy was mostly treated with laughter, Grant's was met with venom. Most vitriolic was the *New York Sun*. In his attacks, Dana abandoned all sense of propriety or decency. He knew firsthand the kind of man Grant was, and he'd written often of Grant's unimpeachable character. Nevertheless, during the campaign and in the months preceding, he labeled Grant a drunkard with a passion for liquor and a despot hoping to build a family dynasty.[8] Furthermore, he alleged Grant was anti-Catholic, anti-Negro, and anti-Semitic.[9] On various days the *Sun* charged Grant with a tendency toward kidnapping, a sympathy with bigamists, and with being a heathen.[10] On top of all this, wrote Dana, the man was a boor without humanity, intellect, or courtesy.[11]

Sometimes the *Sun* combined clumsy humor with its attacks—for example, as an imaginary conversation between Grant and presidential aide Fred Dent. In it, Dent tries to discuss national affairs, but Grant only talks about horses. Again and again Dent brings up business, but Grant ignores him and seems concerned only about a sick colt.[12] And so it went, even to printing a poem from "A Greeley Voter," with verses such as:

> There's that wonderful paper, the Sun, which sheds light on
>   every one.
> It goes strong for Greeley, and condemns Useless freely,
>   In all which we agree with the Sun.

> The late leather dealer called Hiram, in days not long past did
>   buy rum,
> But now, as you see, things different be,
>   He don't buy, but "receives"—the sly chum.[13]

The first duty of an editor, Dana once wrote a friend, was "to stir up the animals."[14] He was doing his best, and in September 1872, with its greatest bombshell yet, the *Sun* revealed widespread corruption involving the new Union Pacific Railroad.

In July, it seemed, Congress had awarded Union Pacific vast grants of public land, a loan of $27 million in government bonds, and certain privileges in regard to issuing securities. At some point Congressman Oakes Ames had organized a construction company called the Credit Mobilier with stockholders almost identical to those of the Union Pacific company. Then, needing additional legislation, Ames distributed Credit Mobilier stock to leading congressmen and members of the administration.

The result was a major scandal (not involving Grant, though the *Sun* implied it did), and it came just weeks before the election. Nevertheless, the Credit Mobilier affair had little effect on the voters, who had already decided how they would cast their ballots.[15] Seemingly they ignored the dirty tactics practiced by both parties on the state and local level, which they evidently saw as "business as usual." (In Pennsylvania, for example, blacks from Maryland and Virginia were imported to "work for Massa Cameron and vote for Massa Grant.")[16] In short, the voters knew Grant to be honest, and he was their man.

That was surely the opinion of the upright Secretary of State, Hamilton Fish, and when a Southerner asked about Grant's alleged drunkenness, Fish seized the opportunity to put the matter to rest: "I have known General Grant very intimately since the close of the war. I have been with him at all hours of the day and night—have traveled with him days and nights together—have been with him on social and festive occasions as well as in hourly intercourse of close official relations. I have never seen him in the most remote degree under any excitement from wine or drink of any kind."

"I have never known exhaustion and fatigue of travel, or of continual anxious labor, to lead him to any undue indulgence in any stimulant of drink. The very close personal association which I have had with him for many years justifies me in saying that the imputation of drunkenness is utterly and wantonly false, and that his use of wine is as moderate and proper as that of a gentleman need be."[17]

Fish's letter has the ring of truth, as do similar wartime letters written by Rawlins, Dana, and others. However, since Dana was a major player in perpetuating the tales of Grant's drinking, it's worth digressing to look at the overall picture. Despite the accusations of Dana and the *New York Sun*, there is not a single reliable witness to Grant's ever overindulging while president.[18] With the exception of the highly dubious Cadwallader memoir, the same is true of Grant during the war.

Perhaps it all began in the gossipy, intimate circles of the prewar regular army, where rumors circulated freely when Grant resigned his commission. In 1862, for example, when Henry Halleck maliciously wrote George McClellan that he feared Grant had resumed "his former bad habits," McClellan obviously knew what he meant.

As was discussed in chapter 6, alcohol was at least part of the problem when Grant left the army in 1854. After that, however, even though he sometimes took a drink (and at times might even have had too much), his drinking was under control. The evidence is conclusive on this point, just as it is clear that nearly *everyone* knew of the problem. Any veteran knows how a rumor can spread, especially if it involves a general. The authorities in Washington had heard of Grant's drinking, his fellow officers knew of it, and so, presumably, did nearly every soldier in the ranks.

Throughout the war, understandably, men with reason to hate Grant, including cashiered officers and fraudulent contractors, spread stories about Grant's drinking. Obviously, the reporters also heard the rumors, but unlike Dana in the postwar period, they refrained from printing them. On one occasion, in fact, when Joseph McCullagh of the *Cincinnati Gazette* submitted a story along those lines, he was told that his paper would not publish such a charge.[19]

Even today, people hearing Grant's name tend to nod knowingly and say, "Oh, yes. He drank." The truth is that if Grant had a serious problem, which itself is doubtful, it was a problem he had under control for his entire public life. Nevertheless, Dana and a few others managed to perpetuate the image of an out-of-control, alcoholic Grant. Unfortunately, most historians have failed to challenge this image with fact.

In any case, the bottom line was that people trusted Grant's character. Hamilton Fish, for instance, when questioned by a Mississippian about certain promises attributed to Grant's opponent, could say with confidence: "Mr. Greeley is in a position where he or friends for him may and do promise all sorts of things. General Grant is a very different man from Mr. Greeley; he will make no promise that he does not think he can execute."[20]

Coupled with Dana's negative items about Grant were positive stories on Greeley. A September headline in the *Sun* read:

THE VOICE OF A STATESMAN
Magnificent Speeches of
Dr. Horace Greeley

Ohio and Kentucky
Boiling Over With Enthusiasm[21]

The *Tribune*, now edited by Whitelaw Reid, also did its best to help the Greeley cause, asking voters if they were willing to retain an administration of "plunder, waste, and corruption."[22] Such things helped Greeley to remain cheerful, even as he sensed the campaign was sagging. Optimistically, he said: "The money and office-holding power arrayed against us are fearfully formidable; but we *ought* to win, so I guess we shall."[23]

In the other camp, Republicans called themselves "the party that saved the Union" and went on the offensive. A main speaker was the handsome, charismatic Roscoe Conkling, who cursed the "traitors" who had bolted the Republican Party. Their faction, he said, included "every thief and cormorant and drone . . . every baffled mouser for place and plunder . . ."

The *New York Times* added its support to Grant, referring to Greeley as an impossible theorist and calling Grant a man of enormous "common sense."[24] While Conkling and others were active on his behalf, Grant stayed on the sidelines, spending much of his time at the family cottage in Long Branch, New Jersey. Early on he had said he'd do no campaigning: "It has been done, so far as I remember, by but two presidential candidates heretofore, and both of them were public speakers and both were beaten. I am no speaker and I don't want to be beaten!"[25]

He wasn't going to be. By October, returns from key states showed that Grant had solid support. That only caused the *Sun* to step up its attacks. One headline read:

Despotism Ahead
The Plot to Overthrow the Republic
Honest Election Stifled by Fraud

———

*Great Speech of the Hon. B. Gratz Brown
in Belleville, Ill.*[26]

In truth, Greeley's running mate wasn't being much help. Benjamin Gratz Brown, a former governor of Missouri, was mostly being noticed for getting drunk at political events. (At one picnic he was seen spreading butter on a piece of watermelon he'd mistaken for bread.) An even worse moment came at Yale, when he addressed a 25th reunion of his graduating class. Drunk almost to the point of incoherence, he told his classmates he didn't think much of Yale, didn't know why he'd gone there, or even how he'd managed to graduate. As for Greeley, he admitted he had never much liked the man, but he urged the group to vote for him anyway because "I believe he has the largest head in America."[27]

Suddenly Greeley received shocking news. In late October his daughter Ida sent word that her mother, back at their farm in Chappaqua, New York, was gravely ill. Actually, Mary Greeley had long been ailing, and for reasons of health had spent much of her time in Europe. She and Horace had somehow drifted apart over the years, and Greeley, busy with his campaign, hadn't seen her for weeks. Now filled with remorse, he canceled his final speaking engagements and hurried to Mary's side.

"My sky is darkened in many ways," he wrote a friend, "but more especially in my home. My wife is going at last. . . . I am glad the election will soon be over. My home trouble is enough to make me forget it."[28]

Greeley might have given up, but Dana had not. There had been many acts of malfeasance, Dana charged, both in Congress and in the Executive Branch, and every bad deed was attributed to Grant personally. Money was missing from a trust fund set up for the Rawlins family. Grant was a trustee of the fund, so the *Sun* implied he was personally responsible.[29] Only a week before the election, the *Sun* charged, with no evidence to support the claim, that money had been stolen from the

Freedmen's Savings and Trust Company and used for Grant's campaign.[30] In the words of historian Candace Stone: "Only Dana's hatred for Grant can explain these unjustified libels."[31]

Greeley moved Mary in to New York to be near good doctors, staying with her at the home of their friend, publisher Alvin Johnson. It was no use. On October 30, Mary Greeley died. Five days later, and with the election only 2 days away, a distraught Greeley wrote his longtime friend Margaret Allen: "I am not dead, but wish I were. My house is desolate, my future dark, my heart a stone. I cannot shed tears; they would bring me relief. Shed tears for me, but do not write again till a brighter day, which I fear will never come."[32]

On election day the country went overwhelmingly for Grant. Particularly satisfying was the margin of victory, which in both the popular vote and the Electoral College was significantly greater than it had been 4 years earlier.

Crowds of people came to the White House to congratulate Grant. After thanking them all, he said that "apart from the political issues involved, he was gratified that the people had vindicated his private character, which had been assailed during the campaign."[33]

Charles Dana, it must be said, was *not* a good loser. While other papers were hailing Grant's victory, the *Sun's* headline read:

GREELEY DEFEATED
FOUR MORE YEARS OF FRAUD
AND CORRUPTION[34]

At one point Greeley had looked defeat in the eye and joked about it, saying, "While there are doubts as to my fitness for President, nobody seems to deny that I would make a capital beaten candidate."[35]

Now, though, he *was* beaten, and the reality began to sink in. All his life he had loved the game of politics. As he now renounced that game forever, there seemed little reason to go on living. The bottom had dropped out of everything. He had lost an election; he had lost his wife of 36 years; maybe he'd also lost the *Tribune*.

In anguish and sounding more than a little paranoid, he wrote: "I am far beyond tears. Nor do I care for defeat, however crushing. I dread only the malignity with which I am hounded, and the possibility that it may ruin the *Tribune*. My enemies mean to kill that; if they would only kill me instead, I would thank them lovingly."[36]

Greeley was drained physically, mentally, emotionally. Nevertheless, he dragged himself down to his old office and wrote a statement an-

nouncing his return to "the editorship of the *Tribune*, which he relin-
quished on embarking on another line of business six months ago. . . .
Since he will never again be a candidate for any office, and is not now in
full accord with either of the great parties . . . he will be able and will
endeavor to give wider and steadier regard to the progress of science,
industry and the Useful Arts . . ."[37]

To his horror, Greeley read a staff writer's facetious, tasteless piece
that expressed satisfaction that the *Tribune* would no longer be in the
business of political patronage. For the past 12 years, it said, the
Tribune had kept, "for the benefit of the idle and incapable, a sort of
Federal employment agency . . . Every red-nosed politician who had
cheated at the caucus and bought at the polls, looked to the editor of
the *Tribune* to secure his appointment as gauger, or as army chaplain,
or as minister to France . . ."[38]

Greeley was outraged. He demanded a public apology and wrote out
a statement, which Reid refused to publish. A furious argument ensued,
during which, according to Reid, Greeley "whined and cried and went
on like a baby. He called himself over and over again 'a black fraud,'
said he was ruined, the *Tribune* was ruined, begged the trustees to turn
him out, turn Reid out, turn anyone out, to save the paper."[39]

Greeley was not only a sick man, he was a man who no longer
controlled the *Tribune*. Of a 100 total shares, he'd once held 50; he now
owned but 6. Although he was still called "editor," it was Reid who was
running things. Greeley began writing letters saying Reid had betrayed
him and was trying to seize control of the paper. Whether or not this
was true, it was enough to push Greeley over the brink.

A few days later, confused and dazed, he threw himself into bed and
called for a doctor. The next day, feverish, often delirious, he pulled
himself together long enough to write a somewhat coherent will. Then,
on *Tribune* letterhead, under the heading "Out of the Depths," he
scrawled: "I stand naked before my God the most utterly, hopelessly
wretched and undone of all who ever lived. I have done more harm
and wrong than any man who ever saw the light of day. And yet, I
take God to witness that I have never intended to wrong or harm
anyone . . . I pray God that he may quickly take me from a world
where all I have done seems to have turned to evil, and wherein each
hour has long been and henceforth must be one of agony, remorse,
and shame."[40]

Greeley did not deserve those words, and one can hope that in his
right mind he would have known that. The eloquent Uncle Horace, a
journalistic giant, had been reduced to a figure of tragedy, and whatever

he was, he was never evil. He was, rather, a man of good intentions who in many ways achieved greatness, even nobility.

Greeley was taken to Dr. Choate's private home for mental patients in Pleasantville, New York, where the doctors diagnosed his illness as "brain fever." He lingered on, sometimes lucid, more often delirious. His daughters Ida and Gabrielle were with him on November 28 when he sank into a coma. The next day, only 3 weeks after the election, Horace Greeley died. He was 61.

Although Greeley had left instructions for a simple funeral it was decided that he deserved a final, grandiose tribute. Three preachers officiated at the funeral service on Fifth Avenue. Several eloquent eulogies were delivered, the most moving by Greeley's longtime friend, the Reverend Henry Ward Beecher. Charles Dana was in attendance, as was Chief Justice Salmon P. Chase, several governors, the mayor of New York, and the president of the United States.

The funeral cortege passed down Fifth Avenue, heading for Greenwood Cemetery in Brooklyn. At Madison Square, people stood 20 deep to pay their last respects to Uncle Horace. They also saw, in the first carriage behind the family mourners, Ulysses S. Grant, who, putting aside past differences, had come to honor one of the most unforgettable Americans of the 19th century.[41]

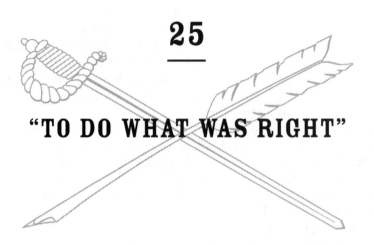

25

"TO DO WHAT WAS RIGHT"

THE SUN'S attacks had been unrelenting—sometimes clumsy, sometimes witty, always cruel. "It is announced," said a typical item, "that Mrs. Grant will receive every Tuesday afternoon during the winter . . . President Grant will receive anytime and anything whenever anything is offered."[1]

Now, with a decisive (276 to 66) Electoral College victory, Grant felt vindicated, both as general and as president. In his second inaugural, the "quiet man" spoke with uncharacteristic emotion. Doing so, he revealed how much the personal attacks had hurt and how greatly he appreciated the people's response: "Throughout the war, and from my candidacy for my present office in 1868 to the close of the last Presidential campaign, I have been the subject of abuse and slander scarcely ever equalled in political history, which today I feel that I can afford to disregard in view of your verdict, which I gratefully accept."[2]

He *had* been given a vote of confidence, and many believed that, like others before him, he had "grown" in office. Earlier, the once-skeptical Roscoe Conkling had said Grant "made a better President than . . . we had any right to expect, and he is a better President every day than he was the day before."[3]

Some had even proposed that Greeley electors cast their votes for Grant and thereby "lift the Administration out of partisanship."[4] The suggestion was ignored, and the ill feelings persisted. A *New York*

Tribune editorial would concede only that Grant was sincere, calling his inaugural address "the utterance of a man of the best intentions profoundly desirous to govern wisely and justly and profoundly ignorant of the means by which good government is secured."[5]

Upon Greeley's death, Dana had published a full-page eulogy, saying in part that "people always seemed to cherish toward Mr. Greeley a warmer personal regard than toward any other distinguished citizen." It was a beautifully written tribute, awarding Greeley his rightful eminence. Added, however, was a snide reminder of the man's "personal ambition, which was very profound and never inoperative, [and] made him wish to be Governor, Legislator, Senator, Cabinet Minister, President, because such elevation seemed to afford the clearest possible evidence that he himself was appreciated . . ." Even when paying its respects, the *Sun* managed to sound malicious.[6]

For some reason Dana declined to serve on a committee hoping to erect a statue to Greeley. In fact, people who had contributed money for such a statue were asked to "call at the *Sun* office and get it back." When Greeley was alive, Dana had tormented him by mockingly proposing a statue in his honor. Now that Greeley was dead, Dana rejected the idea, even though it was something that would have pleased Greeley very much.[7]

It's hard to know what Dana really thought of Horace Greeley. When Greeley was the *Tribune*'s editor, Dana called it the "False Reporting Tribune" and charged it with "wilfully misrepresenting news." As soon as he left, however, Dana promptly attacked his successor, Whitelaw Reid, and yearned for the Greeley days, when a *Tribune* editor had "brains and integrity."[8] The flip-flop concerning Greeley was all too typical of Dana. Not only could the *Sun* abruptly switch positions, Dana might even brag about it. Allegedly, he once said, "No citizen in this town can go to bed at night with the certainty that he can foretell the *Sun*'s editorial course the next morning on any given topic."[9]

In his message to the new Congress, Grant listed some of the achievements of his first term, including peace with foreign powers, settlement of the *Alabama* claims (a major dispute with England over losses to British-made Confederate warships), reduction of the national debt, extension of railroads, and progress in agriculture and education.[10]

Overall, however, Congress remained hostile to Grant. Soon a committee was actively investigating the Credit Mobilier affair, apparently intending to implicate the president. Since the investigation took place while Grant was in office, historians have often listed it as another administration scandal. Nevertheless, while there was indeed corruption in high places, neither Grant, his associates, nor his champions in Congress were implicated in the investigation. Moreover, as pointed out by historian William Hesseltine, the "scandalous acts of Oakes Ames and the Credit Mobilier were all committed before the Grant Administration began."[11]

In March 1873, early in Grant's second term, Congress voted a pay raise for the president, the Supreme Court, senators, representatives, and cabinet members. The measure, introduced by Senator Ben Butler, was made retroactive for 2 years in its application to Congress. The *Sun* blamed Grant, Butler, and Congressman James Garfield for what it called the "salary grab." Mostly it focused on the president: "The man who is more responsible for the back-salary-robbery than anybody else is President Grant. He has no moral tone nor any high sense of honor to restrain him from openly making an urgent effort to have his own salary raised."[12]

It did little good to fight back, for the *Sun* always had the last word. On one occasion, Grant referred to a scurrilous attack by a man named Gary, calling it even "more bitter in its personality and falsehood than anything he had ever seen in the *New York Sun*." It gave Dana an opening, and he was delighted.

"It pains us to say the President's reference to the *Sun* was incorrect as well as wanton," Dana wrote. "Spitting against the luminary of the day is doubtless a harmless practice so far as the luminary is concerned, but the poor lunatic who indulges in it is liable to make of himself an unseemly spectacle. It is not agreeable to see a President in the business. The first gentleman of the land ought to be intellectually, if not morally, above it. We were astonished therefore, at the unmannerly and inconsequential squirt which the President made at us in the course of his frightful mouthing against Gary. . . ."

After piously saying the *Sun* never engaged in aimless attacks on personalities, Dana hinted that Grant harbored dark, immoral secrets: "If on the other hand, the President has been guilty of licentious practices of a private nature which affected him alone, and inflicted no corresponding evil upon the public, the *Sun* has borne no testimony and made no comment in regard to them. . . ."

"The *Sun* will not abandon its mission of regeneration. The President may expect new alarms and other exposures, as the public good requires them. We hear the mutterings of a fierce storm gathering over his stronghold—a storm which no rogue will think of escaping by taking refuge with his wounded patron—a storm before which even Grant will cower at last, helpless and dumb."[13]

Of course, Dana assailed not only Grant but also his appointees; it mattered not if that included former friends. Silas Hudson, for example, the Minister to Guatemala, had been on Grant's staff during the war and had known Dana well. The *Sun* characterized him as "a plucky, rough, ignorant, manly fellow about as fit for a foreign mission as a crowbar is for a cambric needle."[14] Elihu Washburne, Minister to France, once called the "very incarnation of retrenchment and economy," became a "great European tourist and a magnificent spender of money."[15] During the Vicksburg campaign, Dana frequently visited Adm. David Porter's flagship and called Porter "active, courageous, and fresh-minded." He now chastised Porter for having the Naval Academy work on Sunday, which he called an offense to the moral and religious sentiment of the country.[16] Whether or not the insults were true, readers often found them amusing. The *Sun* described Postmaster General A. J. Creswell as having been "on both sides of every issue, and whenever there was a third side, he managed to take that also."[17]

Inevitably, like modern-day tabloids, the *Sun* faced its share of lawsuits. When it made the charge (undoubtedly true) that Henry Cooke, governor of the District of Columbia, along with certain others, was guilty of fraud, the group sued Dana for libel and tried bringing him to Washington for trial. Dana feared the bias of a Washington courtroom, and to his relief, a judge refused to grant a change of venue. Eventually the charge was dismissed by a Federal District Court in New York.[18]

An earlier suit was brought by John Russell Young, a former *Tribune* managing editor. The *Sun* said Young had "stolen" Associated Press dispatches on behalf of a small Philadelphia paper in which he had a controlling interest. Demanding that Young be fired, the story said he had "fleeced and bled" numerous persons and betrayed his employer, Horace Greeley. After looking into the matter, Greeley had said the charges were false and wrote an article exonerating his managing editor. Undaunted, the *Sun* said all this had increased the circulation "not only of our blood but of our journal, deeply interests our readers and delights our counsel." It reprinted the evidence in full, and Young, after being driven "almost crazy," had dropped the suit.[19]

More serious, perhaps, was a charge that the *Sun* could be bribed. Although it's highly unlikely that Dana himself was involved, many, including Grant, believed he was. In December 1870, Grant told Hamilton Fish that Dana was a "blackmailer." He had learned this, Grant said, from Antonio Soteldo, a former *Sun* employee who allegedly had memoranda showing precise sums of "hush money" paid Dana on various occasions. One episode cited by Soteldo involved an attack on the notorious financial speculator Jim Fisk Jr. The Fisk item had been quashed, Soteldo claimed, upon payment of a $5,000 bribe. As a result, Grant said, Soteldo imagined himself in danger of violence from some of the men he had exposed.[20]

Supporting such charges was an anonymous pamphlet called the "Biter Bit," which mentioned Soteldo and claimed to be a "narrative of some of the blackmailing operations of Charles A. Dana's *Sun.*" Dana responded indignantly to those he called the "coward authors." A lengthy editorial said in part: "I never received or agreed to accept, or was promised a dollar or a penny, or any other valuable consideration from any person or source whatever, directly or indirectly, to influence the course of the *Sun* on any subject or in any manner."[21]

Dana was probably telling the truth, but the rumors are understandable. Payoffs had become almost a way of life for many journalists. A typical practitioner was the well-known Uriah Hunt Painter, who served as both a lobbyist and a freelance reporter. For the right price, it was said, Painter's clients could purchase favorable publicity, a well-timed silence, or even slurs on their enemies.[22]

As early as 1867, a disgusted cabinet member, Hugh McCulloch, was moved to say, "I have generally found that the Editors and Reporters of the New York journals are influenced fully as much by their own pecuniary interest as by their duty to their country."[23]

In the midst of all this, the *Sun*'s circulation continued to grow, doubling after 1 year and more than tripling after 6. It made Charles Dana a wealthy man, but at a price. Evidently, it was a price he was willing to pay. Over time, his unscrupulous tactics had cost him the respect of men like E. L. Godkin, editor of the respected *Evening Post* and one of the few who might be called Dana's intellectual equal. (A joke of the day, noting the *Post*'s stuffy respectability, said, "The *Sun* makes vice attractive in the morning, and the *Post* makes virtue unattractive in the evening.")[24]

At one point Godkin had attended evening receptions in Dana's home and was "glad to be invited."[25] By 1869 their paths had diverged, and Godkin, having taken the high road, would write a friend: "The *Sun*, Dana's paper, has been rivaling the *New York Herald*, in its worst days, in ribaldry, falsehood, indecency, levity, and dishonesty . . . He [Dana] is now an object of general execration. I think I have never seen such nearly unanimous condemnation of a rascal, which is a good sign."[26]

Dana had once called Godkin a "stupendous humbug," so even if he'd seen that letter, Dana might well have laughed, just as he did when the *Washington Chronicle* said, "The *New York Sun* is to journalism what the can-can is to dancing."[27] Indeed, Dana didn't seem to care that his paper was seldom found in the "better" homes, or that the *Century*, New York's preeminent men's club, refused to allow the *Sun* in its library. After all, it was said that people ashamed to read the *Sun* in public somehow managed to do so in private![28]

Dana *did* care, however, about the *Sun's* prose, which consistently maintained a level of excellence. Even as rival newsmen traded insults with Dana, they admired his journalistic genius. Editors might envy his financial success or carp at his policies; they united in praising the literary quality of his paper. Even the reporters, veterans as well as cubs, studied and tried to copy the *Sun's* lively style, brevity, and daring wit.

An Ohio editor would declare: "There is but one newspaper in the United States, and that is the *New York Sun*. In this opinion I am not alone, but in company with every newspaper in the country. . . . It is a great paper, and while occasionally wrong it is yet the paragon of papers in this country, if not in the world."

The *Washington Post* agreed, saying editorially: "The *Sun* is the best edited and the most thoroughly interesting paper in the United States."[29] Unfortunately, like later-day products of Hollywood and television, it was too often the pursuit of excellence in the service of triviality.

The president was finding both happiness and sorrow in his second term. In 1873 his father, Jesse, died, as did Julia's father 6 months later. The following year the Grants' daughter Nellie, not yet 19, was married in a White House ceremony to a young Englishman, Algernon Sartoris. When the couple moved to England, Grant felt the loss deeply.

Meanwhile the scandals continued to mount. Some of the offenders were men unknown to Grant who'd been appointed on someone's recommendation; too often, however, they were old friends in whom Grant mistakenly placed his trust.

Grant saw the role of the president like that of a general—select good people and let them do their jobs. Unfortunately, the right people were hard to find. Unlike the days of the Founding Fathers, few were entering politics from a sense of civic duty. Greed was pervasive, and ambitious knaves with sticky fingers had penetrated nearly every government office.

Even when good people were found, they might fail to be confirmed. That was the case with Richard Henry Dana, nominated by Grant as Minister to the Court of St. James. (In view of his cousin Charles's hostility to the administration, many were startled by Grant's magnanimity.) In any case, the Senate refused to confirm him. Grant was even more frustrated after the death of Chief Justice Salmon P. Chase. His first candidate refused the job and the next two were rejected by the Senate. Finally he was forced to name an acceptable mediocrity, Morrison R. Waite of Ohio. Begrudgingly, the New York Tribune said Waite was "an honest man and a fair lawyer," then added disparagingly, "that is as much as can be expected from Grant."[30]

In 1874, a major financial crisis caused the Congress to pass what was popularly, and correctly, called the "Inflation Bill." When it arrived at the White House for signature, it became what was perhaps Grant's toughest call. A veto would cause funds to dry up and prolong an already severe recession. Signing the bill would put the country on a dangerous path of fiscal recklessness. After much soul-searching, he decided to veto. James Garfield, admiring Grant's courage, said, "For twenty years no President has had an opportunity to do the country so much service by a veto message as Grant has, and he has met the issue manfully."[31] The New York Times agreed, saying, "Once more General Grant has deserved well of the country."[32]

In many ways, however, Grant continued to flounder, often exercising poor judgment when it came to people he trusted. This was certainly the case with his secretary, Orville Babcock. For years a widespread so-called Whiskey Ring had been cheating the government out of tax revenues. Millions of dollars had been spread among crooks at all levels, and some of the money had found its way to Babcock. When Treasury Secretary Benjamin Bristow brought Grant evidence of Babcock's involvement, Grant said, "let no guilty man escape" and assured his Attorney General, Edwards Pierrepoint, "if Babcock is guilty, there is no man who wants him so proven guilty as I do, for it is the greatest piece of traitorism to me that a man could possibly practice."[33]

In the long run, however, the wily Babcock convinced Grant of his innocence, making him believe it was a case of people trying to get at Grant by smearing a longtime subordinate. Grant ended up by backing Babcock, even writing a deposition that convinced a St. Louis jury to acquit. Sadly, in this case Grant's loyalty greatly exceeded his judgment. The Sun was particularly indignant over Babcock's exoneration and temporary return to a White House position.[34] The criticism was fully deserved, and it came not only from the New York Sun. Others echoed Dana's cry of "Turn the Rascals Out," which in time became as well-known as "On to Richmond!" had been in 1861.

As the problems continued, Republicans suffered an overwhelming defeat in the 1874 elections. Rejoicing in the results, and predicting an impeachment for Grant, the *Sun* said: "The indignation of the people as expressed through the ballot boxes yesterday has shivered Grant's administration to atoms. The overthrow is complete and terrific. . . . It is impossible to enumerate the names of the great mass of hypocrites, adventurers, and rogues which the work of Monday and Tuesday has put under the sod never to rise again."[35]

Despite all this, Grant was still popular with the people and the best candidate the Republicans had. Party leaders continued to talk of submitting his name for a third term. At least initially, Grant gave the movement tacit approval. Why would he consider a third term, prolonging a role that brought so much grief? One explanation might be his feelings for Julia, who fully enjoyed life in the White House. "I love the dear old house," she wrote in her *Memoirs*. Blissfully ignoring the torment to her beloved "Ulyss," she would say, "Eight happy years I spent there—so happy!"[36]

Grant's presidency, Julia once said, was "a bright and beautiful dream. I wish it might continue forever."[37] Her husband felt otherwise. On one occasion he told Julia, "I wish this was over. I wish I had this Congress off my hands. I wish I was out of it altogether. After I leave this place, I never want to see it again." Julia, who didn't believe it, just smiled: "Why, Ulyss, how you talk! I never want to leave it."[38]

When the third-term movement began losing steam, Grant was probably relieved. To this point he'd never "politicked" for anything, in either military or political life. Honors had always come without his asking, and if the people didn't *insist* on his running again, he'd make it easy for them.

On the eve of a Pennsylvania convention, Grant wrote the presiding officer repudiating any third-term desires: "I do not want it any more than I did the first. I would not write nor utter a word to change the will of the people. . . . I am not, nor have I ever been, a candidate for a renomination." That seemed to settle it.[39]

The *Sun* was gratified; the idea of a third term had always been abhorrent.[40] All the same, it continued to go after Grant. In the final months of his presidency, a scandal came to light concerning the selling of post traderships on Indian reservations. When it was shown to involve William Belknap, who had succeeded Rawlins as Secretary of War, Grant forced Belknap to resign immediately. The *Sun* nevertheless said, "Grant has a finger in the Pie," and printed an outlandish story saying, "The connection of Grant himself with the scandalous traffic in post traderships is plain enough." The fact that there was no evidence along those lines seemed to matter little.[41]

Meanwhile, other papers began to treat Grant more kindly. "Unpopular as the later years of his Administration have been," said the *Tribune*, "he will . . . go out of office amid general good will."[42]

Men who knew Grant best, including a frequent political foe, James Garfield, were also finding good things to say. Garfield told his diary: "I was again impressed with the belief that when his presidential term is ended, General Grant will regain his place as one of the foremost of Americans. His power of staying, his imperturbability, has been of incalculable value to the nation, and will be prized more and more as his career recedes."[43]

In December 1876, the time had come for Grant to deliver his final message to Congress. Secretary of State Hamilton Fish once said that Grant, the most truthful man he ever knew, "was incapable of any attempt to deceive anybody . . . and above all he was incapable of deceiving himself."[44] Accordingly, and as Fish would have predicted, the farewell message made no attempt to put a favorable "spin" on his presidency. (Although the term "spin" had not yet appeared, in 1876 the practice of shading the truth was both well-known and widely practiced.)

For his part, Grant delivered an awkward, poignant combination of apology and explanation: "It was my fortune, or misfortune," he said, "to be called to the office of Chief Executive without any previous political training. Under such circumstances it is but reasonable to suppose that errors of judgment must have occurred. . . . Mistakes have been made, as all can see and I admit . . . I have acted in every instance from a conscientious desire to do what was right . . . Failures have been errors of judgment, not of intent."[45]

"The message," commented the *New York Tribune*, "is that of a man who is weary of public life and tired of political strife."[46]

How right they were. Ulysses and Julia would soon leave the country and set off on a long-anticipated vacation, an extended trip around the world. Accompanying them was their son Jesse and a small group of people that included the writer John Russell Young, representing the *New York Herald*. One day Grant told Young: "I was never as happy in my life as the day I left the White House. I felt like a boy getting out of school."[47]

26

"MAN PROPOSES
AND GOD DISPOSES"

THE NEW PRESIDENT, Rutherford B. Hayes, was inaugurated on March 5, 1877, after winning an election that many believed was stolen. That included Dana, who called the balloting a "fraud" and an "event of dishonor." Public distrust of government was widespread, not only from the postwar scandals but from "the poisoned atmosphere" that a sensational, adversarial press had helped create.[1]

Through it all, Grant seemed both untainted and unperturbed. "There is something wonderful and grand," wrote a contemporary biographer, "in his perfect freedom from all animosity, while those who surrounded him were full of the bitterest hate."[2]

Soon after the inauguration, the Grants left Washington and headed west. They saw friends and relatives in Galena and Georgetown, also visited a number of cities where gala receptions were held in their honor. Wherever he went, people by the thousands turned out to see Ulysses Grant. The cheers were long and loud, and if there was disappointment in his handling of the presidency, the crowds gave no evidence of it. The hero of Appomattox was still the most popular man in America.

In May, the Grants sailed for England on the *Indiana*. It was the first time in 15 years, Grant remarked, that he didn't have a telegraph wire trailing him, and the sensation was both agreeable and unusual.[3] Grant strolled the deck, smoked his cigars, and generally relaxed. When he chatted with fellow passengers, they mostly wanted to talk about the war, not his time in the White House. It was a pattern that would be followed the rest of his life.

As always, Grant was willing to praise but reluctant to criticize. He spoke highly of Sherman and Sheridan, saying modestly that if anything had happened to him, either man could have taken his place and done just as well. He even made it a point to compliment Confederate general Joe Johnston. When one of the passengers mentioned the army failures of politicians Carl Schurz and Nathaniel Banks, Grant said, smiling: "Don't forget that they commenced as major generals."[4]

While on the trip, Grant tried to forget the abuse he'd suffered during the previous few years. One account of his travels, however, contains an evident reference to Dana, though not by name, and may well be based on something Grant said. During the war, said the writer, "an official of the War Department came down and spent some time in the camp. Grant took his measure at once, for he seemed to understand war better than the General. When this man applied for an important commission under the government, Grant refused the appointment, and has been heartily hated by that gentleman ever since."[5]

When the *Indiana* docked at Liverpool, Grant was greeted by a swarm of small boats and a vast cheering throng. Although their government had been generally sympathetic to the Confederacy, that was not true of the British people. Workers in particular had identified not only with the North but with Grant personally; they saw him as a man of the people.

In city after city the Grants were honored by lavish receptions, speeches, parades, all for a man treated not as an ex-president, or ex-anything, but as a distinguished head of state. Grant saw it as a welcome sign of Anglo-American friendship. In a letter to George Childs, publisher of the *Philadelphia Ledger*, he said: "The attentions I am receiving are more for our country than for me personally. I love to see our country honored and respected abroad, and I am proud to believe that it is by most all nations, and by some even loved."[6]

The English visit was indeed a triumph, both for Grant and for the United States. The highlight for Julia might have been the dinner at Windsor Castle hosted by Queen Victoria. For Ulysses it might have been the side trip to Southampton to visit daughter Nellie and her husband. Somewhat ironically, there was even an elaborate breakfast given in Grant's honor by George Smalley, special correspondent of his one-time adversary, the *New York Tribune*. The pretentious Smalley, ignoring fellow reporters, had invited literary figures such as Matthew Arnold, Robert Browning, and Anthony Trollope. All seemed delighted at the chance to meet the American hero.[7]

Amid all the pomp and pageantry, Grant remained unaffected—and the people loved it. A description in the *Chronicle* read: "Looking as much like an ordinary Tyneside skipper as possible, open-browed, firm-faced, blunt, bluff, and honest, and unassuming, everybody at once settled in his own mind that the General would do."[8]

From England the party went on to visit nearly every country in Europe, crisscrossing the Continent for over a year. Next came Egypt. In Cairo, Grant smiled as he saw two men he'd known as cadets: former Union officer Charles Stone and former Confederate Henry Loring. The two expatriates were senior officers in the Egyptian army. "Look," Grant said, "there is Loring, whom I have not seen in thirty years—there is Stone, who must have been dyeing his hair to make it so white." It was a warm, heartfelt reunion.[9]

Grant was fascinated by the Egyptian antiquities, and it was said he spent hours staring into the timeworn face of the Sphinx. "It looks," he later wrote, "as if it has kept on thinking through all eternity without talking too much." Grant could relate to that.[10]

From Egypt the Grants traveled to India, China, and Japan. It was an exciting adventure, perhaps the happiest time in Grant's life, and from beginning to end, the trip lasted more than 2 years. Each portion was duly chronicled by John Russell Young, and his copious dispatches to the *New York Herald* let the American public follow the trip step by step. It was a hectic schedule, with each day bringing new sights to see, new people to meet, more functions to attend. A tireless Grant seemed to thrive on it, and from Japan he was ready to head for Australia. Julia, however, perhaps anxious to see the children and grandchildren, said it was time to go home.

From Japan, the party crossed the Pacific to land in San Francisco, where yet another cheering crowd awaited Grant. As he traveled east, still more crowds gathered, making it obvious that America had not forgotten him. In Chicago, he attended a reunion of the Army of the Tennessee, where he was warmly greeted by Sherman and Sheridan and welcomed by a parade of 80,000 people.[11] Alongside Grant on the reviewing stand was Samuel Clemens, the renowned Mark Twain. The taciturn Grant and the outgoing Clemens, two very different men, somehow took an immediate liking to each other. Over the years a deep and lasting friendship would develop. Twain liked Grant for his modest, honest character, rare qualities in such a famous man. Grant liked Twain for many reasons, including the fact that Twain could always make him laugh.

Then it was on to Philadelphia, where the mayor declared a holiday. Schools, stores, and factories were closed, and an estimated 350,000 people lined the sidewalks to see a parade in Grant's honor that lasted some 4½ hours.[12]

Grant's popularity was not lost on Roscoe Conkling, who hoped to return him to the White House for a third term. Grant had been silent on the subject, and some people took it as a sign of interest. A week before the Republican convention, however, Grant wrote another letter saying he didn't want the job. Conkling apparently didn't believe him. On the fourth day of the convention, Conkling put Grant's name in nomination. Almost immediately, delegates rose and began cheering, whistling, stamping their feet in a thunderous ovation. At the end of the first ballot, Grant led all candidates with 304 votes, 75 short of victory. The count changed very little during successive ballots, and had Grant offered some political deals, or even made an overt move, he might have gone over the top. True to form, he remained silent.

For 6 days and through 35 ballots, the convention remained dead-locked. The frustrated delegates finally settled on a compromise candidate, James A. Garfield, who became the Republican nominee.[13] That fall Grant campaigned for Garfield against the Democrats' Winfield Scott Hancock. Garfield went on to win the election, only to be assassinated 4 months after his inauguration.

Politics was a thing of the past, and for the first time in years, Grant frankly needed a job. He had a modest income from his investments, but it wasn't enough to sustain the Grants' current lifestyle. Grant himself had little problem with stepping down socially. For his beloved Julia, however, who had suffered through years of privation, he hoped to provide something better.

In the spring of 1881, Grant accepted a position as president of the Mexican Central Railroad. It looked promising, not only for the salary but for the chance to help a country he had come to love as a young lieutenant. From an office on Wall Street, he did what he could to help the fledgling line. However, skeptics such as Whitelaw Reid suspected that Grant was just being used. Whatever the case, the line floundered and failed to obtain the necessary financing. By 1884 it was in bankruptcy.[14]

Meanwhile, Grant had tried to augment his income by going into business with his son Buck. This was the son, Ulysses Grant Jr., who had graduated from Harvard University and Columbia Law School, the one his proud parents saw as a financial genius. Some time earlier, Buck had formed a partnership with Ferdinand Ward, a bright Wall Street speculator whom the press called "the Young Napoleon of Finance."[15]

When the senior Ulysses was invited to join Grant & Ward as a partner, he readily accepted what he saw as a fine business opportunity. After selling his St. Louis properties, he put into the firm some $100,000, nearly everything he had. Others were doing the same, and in return were receiving handsome dividends. None of the investors, even those who were financially astute, realized that the conniving Ward was operating a giant Ponzi scam, using the investors' own money to create overly generous payouts. This required a constant stream of new cash, some of which was being provided by Ward's crooked accomplice, James Fish, president of the Marine National Bank.

Finally the bubble burst. Ward came to Grant, saying they had a temporary cash-flow problem. To stay afloat and maintain investor confidence, the firm had an immediate need for $150,000. Grant obtained a check for that amount from William Vanderbilt—a personal loan to Grant, not to the firm. It wasn't enough. The money disappeared, and the unscrupulous Ward fled the country.[16]

On May 7, 1884, a front-page story in the *New York Tribune* read: "The Marine National Bank suspended payment yesterday on account of the complications with the Stock Exchange firm of Grant & Ward, whose failure was announced subsequently."[17]

By the following day, the whole house of cards had collapsed. Under a headline, THE GRANT & WARD FAILURE, the *Tribune* said: "Disclosures were made yesterday to show that the failure of the Stock Exchange firm of Grant & Ward, of which the ex-president is a member, is even more complete than was first supposed. . . . The facts which are gradually leaking out regarding the operations and business methods of the suspended firm . . . whose collapse was coincident with the suspension of the Marine National Bank on Tuesday, exhibit the condition of the house in even a worse light than has been generally imagined." The article mentioned Vanderbilt's $150,000 loan to Grant; it also noted that one of the firm's victims was Jerome Chaffee, Buck's father-in-law. "It is not believed," the story concluded, "that the ex-president knew the state of the firm's affairs."[18]

Eventually, both Fish and Ward went to jail, and although no blame was attached to Grant personally, the sad affair left him feeling stupid and ashamed. And because no system yet existed for either government or military pensions, the affair also left him flat broke.

A few friends helped out, at least enough to keep bread on the table, but the situation was grim. When someone in Congress proposed that Grant be given a pension, Charles Dana promptly objected. Although he seldom wrote the *Sun*'s editorials himself, this time he made an exception. Dana's friend Wilson alleged that Dana sympathized with Grant's situation. However, Wilson wrote, "in an editorial doubtless from his own pen, [Dana] opposed the proposition that Congress should give him a pension . . . but proposed instead that the public sympathy should be manifested toward the unfortunate general by a great popular subscription to be limited to ten dollars from any subscriber, and that the proceeds should be put into the hands of trustees. . . . this should not be considered as the payment of a public debt, and that General Grant's great military services were no more than his duty required him to render to the country that had educated and honored him. . . ."[19]

Dana's suggestion would have placed Grant in the role of public beggar. Such a plan, as Dana well knew, would mean utter humiliation, leaving Grant with neither pride nor dignity. Perhaps that was the idea.

One can understand Dana, or any other journalist, doing his best to expose corruption. His personal assaults on Grant, however, amounting almost to an obsession, seem to have deeper psychological roots that he himself might not have understood. An analyst, given enough time, might have looked to Dana's early life for an explanation. His father, a financial failure, had sent Charles away to live with an uncle, who in turn had also failed. Time and again the youth was either abandoned or disappointed—by his father, by his uncle, by the Transcendentalists, by his editor boss at the *Boston Chronotype*, finally by Horace Greeley. After all that, he had latched on to Grant, a man of solid character to whom he could give unqualified support. Then, when Grant failed to give Dana the appointment he wanted, it was seen not only as disloyalty but as yet another betrayal.

Soon, as other appointments went to friends, relatives, and political gift givers, Dana's disappointment in Grant grew and festered. Whatever the explanation, the scurrilous attacks would continue, even when they cost Dana the respect of George Ripley, an esteemed friend from his days at Brook Farm. At times Dana the sophisticated intellectual could resemble a rebellious teenager.[20]

Some time earlier, Grant had written four articles on the war for *Century* magazine. Following this, the *Century* publishers urged him to write his full memoirs. Seeing it as a way to earn some much-needed money, Grant agreed. Although he'd not yet signed a contract, he started writing, and somewhat to his surprise, found he liked doing so. A friend asked if he really intended to do the writing himself. "Oh yes," Grant said, "I am going to do it myself. If I do not do it myself it will not be mine."[21]

Then an improbable guardian angel, one with wild hair and a bushy mustache, appeared. Mark Twain looked at the proposed contract and said in effect that Grant was being cheated. He had his own publishers, Twain said, and they'd give Grant a *proper* contract. When he saw what was proposed, Grant said he feared the offer was too generous. Mark Twain, however, knew what he was doing.

Grant had begun the book by quoting the *Imitation of Christ* of Thomas à Kempis: "Man proposes and God disposes." He was saying, it seemed, that some divine hand must have guided the humble tanner's son as he rose to high position. Steadily, faithfully, Grant continued to write, day after day scribbling away with a stubby pencil. His prose was clear, straightforward, and sprinkled with both insight and wit. Meanwhile, thousands of Twain's agents were traveling the country, signing up buyers for the contemplated memoirs. The response was overwhelming.

During the fall of 1884, Grant had begun to feel sharp pains in his throat. At first he ignored them. By the time he went to a doctor, it was too late. Countless cigars had taken their toll—he had advanced cancer of the throat, and there was little the doctors could do. In other words, Ulysses Grant had but a few months to live.

His writing became a race against time and a test of will. He must finish the book, not for himself, not for the historical record, but to provide financial security for his loved ones. By June 1885, the writing was well along, but it was increasingly difficult to work in the sweltering heat of New York City. The Grants moved to a cottage at Mount McGregor in upstate New York, where at least some cooling breezes might offer relief.

Word spread of Grant's condition, and Union army veterans, thousands of them, came to Mount McGregor to see Grant one last time. Sometimes they filed past in quasi-military formation, and when they did, Grant would acknowledge them with a nod or a wave of the hand. Mostly, though, they stood at a respectful distance, watching Grant as he sat on the cottage porch writing his memoirs. Also on hand were the New York reporters, keeping their morbid death watch. Unlike earlier days, the stories would all be kind and gentle.

On July 9, the *New York Tribune* reported: "The warm, clear weather tempted General Grant to go out of doors this morning, and he spent nearly an hour sitting with Mrs. Grant on the veranda." Among his visitors that day was the Reverend Edmund Didier, a Catholic priest from Baltimore. After inviting him to sit down, Grant took up a pad and wrote, "I regret very much that I cannot converse, not even in a whisper."

"We are all praying for you, General," said Father Didier.

"Yes, I know," Grant wrote, "and I feel very grateful . . . Catholics, Protestants, and Jews, and all the good people of the Nation, of all politics as well as all religions, and all nationalities, seem to have united in wishing or praying for my improvement. . . . All I can do is to pray that the prayers of all these good people may be answered so far as to have all of us meet in another and better world."[22]

That week the memoir was completed. With a grateful sigh, the dying Grant put his manuscript aside. He had written of a war that had threatened to tear the country apart. Now, in the final pages, he predicted that the nation would not only reunite fully but, having done so, would go on to still greater "peace, happiness, and prosperity."

"I feel that we are on the eve of a new era," Grant wrote, "when there is to be great harmony between the Federal and the Confederate. I cannot stay to be a living witness to the correctness of this prophecy; but I feel it within me that it be so. The universally kind feeling expressed for me at a time when it was supposed that each day would prove my last, seemed to me the beginning of the answer to 'Let us have Peace.'"[23]

Once, quoting the Psalms, Grant told his doctor: "Three times I have been down in the valley of the shadow of death." The doctor asked what his thoughts were at such times. His chief consolation, Grant said, was "that he had tried to lead a good and honorable life."[24]

Day after day, columns appeared describing every aspect of Grant's final battle. One story told of a religious service held nearby, where the Reverend Dr. Newman made reference to "the illustrious sufferer in yonder cottage" and made the topic of his sermon, quite appropriately, "The Value of Character."[25]

On July 22, the headline read: GEN. GRANT MUCH WORSE. The story quoted Fred Grant as saying he didn't believe his father would survive the night.[26]

Two days later, as people picked up their papers, they saw that the columns were edged in black:

GEN. GRANT'S STRUGGLE OVER
Death Comes to him Quietly—
Conscious Almost to the End

The *Tribune*'s entire front page, as well as its editorial page, were devoted to Grant's final hours. One poignant paragraph read: "At the last moment the grief stricken family were all near the bed-side. Colonel Grant sat in a chair near the head of the bed, now and then stroking his father's forehead . . . Directly opposite sat Mrs. Grant, holding the

General's hand tightly clasped in both her own, as if she could not let him go."[27]

Grant's two-volume work became a financial success, making Julia a wealthy woman. Moreover, as a military memoir it would rank alongside Caesar's Commentaries. In time, it would also be recognized for its graceful prose. Mark Twain, speaking in April 1887 at a reunion of the Army and Navy Club of Connecticut, called it "a unique and unapproachable literary masterpiece."

"This is the simple soldier," Twain said, "who, untaught of the silken phrase-makers, linked words together with an art surpassing the art of the schools, and put them into something which will still bring to American ears, as long as America shall last, the roll of his vanished drums and the tread of his marching hosts."[28]

By 1896, Charles Dana was a rich man with a magnificent home on Long Island. He was a wine connoisseur, owned a valuable collection of rare Chinese porcelains, and also dabbled in horticulture. Among his circle of friends were literary figures, musicians, and artists. In addition, he traveled extensively and maintained his fascination for language, on occasion even teaching private classes in Icelandic. Twice he'd gone abroad to pursue his study of Russian.

It was then 11 years since Grant's death, and Dana's *Sun* was eminently successful, even though its editorials had become so cynical that its readers often doubted their sincerity. Nevertheless, his paper was properly applauded for its fine writing, lively style, and sparkling wit. Also, Dana had assembled an outstanding staff that knew the public; a titillating society scandal would always be preferred to the remarks of a stodgy statesman. One city editor, John Bogart, is credited with the classic "When a dog bites a man, that's not news. But when a man bites a dog, *that* is news." Another *Sun* staffer, Frank Church, would also make newspaper history with the famed editorial "Yes, Virginia, there is a Santa Claus."

One thing, however, had been left undone. Dana had never written of his Civil War experiences. To correct this, and after much persuasion, he granted a series of interviews to the noted writer Ida Tarbell. During the winter of 1896–1897, Dana and Tarbell met several times, and Tarbell faithfully recorded Dana's reminiscences. Without her they would not have been written, but the thoughts were Dana's. The highly acclaimed *Recollections of the Civil War* became a memoir of that conflict second only to Grant's.

As he talked to Tarbell, Dana put himself back in time and spoke of the Grant he'd admired so much during the war. Perhaps he'd mellowed with age; or as he remembered Grant's true character, perhaps he realized how unfair he'd been to the man during his presidency and how much hurt he'd inflicted. In any event, one cannot read Dana's description of Grant without hearing both regret and apology. Speaking of their first meeting, he said the general was "straightforward, cordial, and unpretending."[29] Later, after spending months in Grant's company, he spoke of him as "the most modest, the most disinterested, and the most honest man I ever knew . . . Not a great man, except morally; not an original or brilliant man, but sincere, thoughtful, deep, and gifted with courage that never faltered."[30]

Whatever the intention of those words, they at least were uttered—and barely in time. The plan was to publish the *Recollections* serially in *McClure's* magazine. In the fall of 1897, the issue of the magazine containing the first chapter also carried a notice of Dana's death.

By any standard, Horace Greeley and Charles Dana were remarkable men who made newspaper history. Between them they wrote millions of words, publishing countless thousands of editorial columns and more than a dozen books. Today those books and columns are mostly forgotten, while ironically, Grant's single literary effort is justly considered an immortal American classic.

NOTES

1 "NEITHER FLINCHED, BEGGED NOR SURRENDERED"

1. Background of Jake Ammen, *Register of Graduates—United States Military Academy* (West Point, N.Y.: Association of Graduates, 1990), 257.
2. Lloyd Lewis, *Captain Sam Grant* (Boston: Little, Brown and Company, 1950), 49–51. Lewis wrote perhaps the best account of Jesse Grant's early life and of Ulysses Grant's boyhood.
3. *1990 Register of Graduates*, 257.
4. Lewis, *Captain Sam Grant*, 50.
5. Ibid., citing Reverend E. Cox, quoted in the *Cincinnati Gazette*, 9 August 1885.
6. Ibid., 7.
7. Ibid., 7–8.
8. Ibid., 9.
9. Ibid.
10. Ulysses S. Grant, *Personal Memoirs of U.S. Grant*, 2 vols. (New York: Charles L. Webster & Company, 1886), 1:20.
11. Lewis, *Captain Sam Grant*, 15.
12. Ibid., 14.
13. Ibid.
14. Ibid., 15.
15. Ibid., 17.
16. Ibid., 22.
17. Grant, *Memoirs*, 1:25.
18. Lewis, *Captain Sam Grant*, 24.
19. Ibid., 25.
20. Grant, *Memoirs*, 1:26.
21. Lewis, *Captain Sam Grant*, 39.
22. Grant, *Memoirs*, 1:29–30.
23. Hamlin Garland, *Ulysses S. Grant: His Life and Character* (New York: Doubleday and McClure, 1898), 12; Lewis, *Captain Sam Grant*, 42.

24. Lewis, *Captain Sam Grant*, 43.
25. Ibid., 42.
26. Ibid., 44.
27. Ibid., 52–53.
28. Grant, *Memoirs*, 1:25.
29. Ibid., 33–34.; Lewis, *Captain Sam Grant*, 45.
30. Lewis, *Captain Sam Grant*, 53.

2 "TALL, SLENDER, PALE AND PLAIN"

1. William Harlan Hale, *Horace Greeley, Voice of the People* (New York: Harper & Brothers, 1950), 26–27.
2. Ibid., 39.
3. Ibid., 40.
4. *New Yorker*, 1 April 1837.
5. Ibid., 3 June 1837.
6. Horace Greeley, *Recollections of a Busy Life* (New York: J. B. Ford & Co., 1869), 46.
7. Ibid., 38.
8. Ibid., 49–50
9. Ibid., 61–62; Hale, *Horace Greeley*, 8–10.
10. Greeley, *Recollections*, 81.
11. Ibid., 82.
12. Ibid., 84.
13. Ibid., 86.
14. Ibid., 87–88.
15. Ibid., 92.
16. Ibid., 93.
17. Hale, *Horace Greeley*, 26–27.
18. Ibid., 28–29.
19. Ibid., 29.
20. Ibid.
21. Greeley, *Recollections*, 103.
22. Ibid., 126.
23. Hale, *Horace Greeley*, 48.
24. Ibid., 54.
25. Greeley, *Recollections*, 134.
26. Ibid., 142.
27. Ibid., 141.
28. Hale, *Horace Greeley*, 71.
29. James Harrison Wilson, *Life of Charles A. Dana* (New York: Harper & Brothers, 1907), 40–41.

3 "VOLUMES HE COULD NOT BUY"

1. Wilson, *Chares A. Dana*, 9. Wilson wrote what is undoubtedly the most complete account of Dana's life. However, as Allan Nevins put it, it is undoubtedly "uncritically eulogistic." A good summary of Dana's life, written by Nevins himself, appears in the *Dictionary of American Biography*.
2. Wilson, *Charles A. Dana*, 2
3. Ibid., 6.
4. Ibid., 10.
5. Ibid., 10.
6. Ibid., 20.
7. From an address by Dana delivered at the University of Michigan, 21 January 1895.
8. Wilson, *Charles A. Dana*, 31–32.
9. Dana, Michigan address.
10. Hale, *Horace Greeley*, 98–99.
11. Greeley, *Recollections*, 155.
12. Wilson, *Charles A. Dana*, 7, writes: "Although I have read all the accounts I could find of the Brook Farm experiment, I have failed to discover any word from Dana indicating complete confidence in its success."
13. Wilson, *Charles A. Dana*, 51–56.
14. Edwin Haviland Miller, *Salem Is My Dwelling Place, A Life of Nathaniel Hawthorne* (Iowa City: University of Iowa Press, 1991), 9.
15. Wilson, *Charles A. Dana*, 50.
16. Dana, Michigan address.
17. Wilson, *Charles A. Dana*, 57.
18. Dana, Michigan address.
19. Wilson, *Charles A. Dana*, 58.
20. Hale, *Horace Greeley*, 73.
21. Ibid., 71.
22. Louis M. Starr, *Bohemian Brigade: Civil War Newsmen in Action* (Madison: University of Wisconsin Press, 1954), 4.
23. Hale, *Horace Greeley*, 21.
24. Description of Greeley's office: Hale, *Horace Greeley*, 79.

4 "SO FAR AWAY FROM FRIENDS"

1. John Y. Simon, ed., *The Papers of Ulysses S. Grant*, 22 vols. (Carbondale, Ill.: University of Southern Illinois Press, 1967–97), 1:4.
2. Ibid. Although Hamer apparently took the middle initial "S." from the mother's maiden name of Simpson, the appointment was not made in that name, and Grant never acknowledged it as a middle name. Upon gradu-

ation from the Academy, however, "Ulysses S. Grant" was adopted as the standard name.

3. Grant, *Memoirs*, 1:32.
4. Garland, *Ulysses S. Grant*, 30–31.
5. Grant, *Memoirs*, 1:38.
6. Ibid., 35.
7. Ibid., 33.
8. *New York Herald*, February 1839, multiple entries.
9. Lewis, *Captain Sam Grant*, 62.
10. Ingalls interview, *New York Herald*, 7 April 1885.
11. Grant, *Memoirs*, 1:39.
12. Ibid., 41.
13. Lewis, *Captain Sam Grant*, 86.
14. James B. Fry, *Military Miscellanies* (New York: Brentano's, 1889), 292 ff.; Lewis, *Captain Sam Grant*, 94.
15. Grant, *Memoirs*, 1:43–44.
16. Horace Greeley, *The American Conflict*, 2 vols. (Hartford, Conn.: D. D. Case and Company, 1864, 1866), 1:169.
17. Grant, *Memoirs*, 1:50.
18. Greeley, *American Conflict*, 1:164.
19. Longstreet interview, *New York Times*, 24 July 1885.
20. U. S. Grant to Julia Dent, 14 September 1845.
21. U. S. Grant to Julia Dent, 7 February 1846.
22. Greeley, *Recollections*, 208.
23. Grant, *Memoirs*, 1:68.
24. Ibid., 85.
25. Ibid., 94.
26. U. S. Grant to Julia Dent, 11 May 1846.
27. U. S. Grant to Bvt. Col. John Garland, August 1846.
28. Grant, *Memoirs*, 1:106.
29. Ibid., 110.
30. Lewis, *Captain Sam Grant*, 179.
31. Ibid., 177.
32. Simon, *Grant Papers*, 1:121.
33. U. S. Grant to Mrs. Thomas L. Hamer, December 1846.
34. Hale, *Horace Greeley*, 129.
35. Ibid.

5 "REPORTS ARE SOMEWHAT EXAGGERATED"

1. U. S. Grant to Julia Dent, 3 April 1847.

2. *1990 USMA Register of Graduates*, 256.
3. Grant, *Memoirs*, 1:133.
4. Robert Ryal Miller, ed., *The Mexican War Journal & Letters of Ralph W. Kirkham* (College Station: Texas A&M University Press, 1991), 25, 34.
5. George Washington Kendall, co-founder of the *New Orleans Picayune*, often called the first modern war correspondent, was one of the best known reporters of his day.
6. Miller, *Mexican War Journal*, 72.
7. U. S. Grant to Julia Dent, September 1847.
8. Lewis, *Captain Sam Grant*, 272.
9. U. S. Grant to unknown addressee, 22 August 1847.
10. U. S. Grant to Julia Dent, 4 August 1847.
11. Grant, *Memoirs*, 1:158.
12. Ibid.
13. Allan Nevins, *Ordeal of the Union*, 8 vols. (New York: Charles Scribner's Sons, 1947–1971), 1:38.
14. Grant, *Memoirs*, 1:180.
15. Ibid., 191.
16. Ibid., 124.
17. Ibid., 139.
18. Ibid., 99–100.
19. John G. Nicolay and John Hay, *Abraham Lincoln: A History*, 10 vols. (New York: 1886–1890).
20. Grant, *Memoirs*, 119.
21. Hale, *Horace Greeley*, 83.
22. Ibid., 83.
23. Wilson, *Charles A. Dana*, 62.
24. *New York Tribune*, 7 October 1848.
25. Ibid., 10 November 1848.
26. Hale, *Horace Greeley*, 86.
27. Ibid., 87.
28. *New York Tribune*, 20 September 1848.
29. Wilson, *Charles A. Dana*, 72.
30. Ibid., 73.
31. Ibid., 71.
32. Ibid., 86.
33. Lewis, *Captain Sam Grant*, 283, citing Emma Dent Casey, "When Grant Went a Courtin'," typewritten ms.
34. Ibid., 284.
35. Ibid., 284–85, citing Emma Dent Casey.
36. Ibid., 285.

6 "WHO CAN REASON WITH HIM?"

1. Lewis, *Captain Sam Grant*, 216–17.
2. Greeley, *Recollections*, 252.
3. Greeley, *American Conflict*, 1:198.
4. Greeley to Schuyler Colfax, 3 April 1848.
5. Greeley to Schuyler Colfax, 15 September 1848.
6. Greeley, *Recollections*, 216.
7. Ibid., 217.
8. Ibid., 219–20; Hale, *Horace Greeley*, 130–31.
9. Greeley, *Recollections*, 224.
10. Hale, *Horace Greeley*, 132.
11. Ibid., 130.
12. Ibid., 132.
13. Wilson, *Charles A. Dana*, 94.
14. Lewis, *Captain Sam Grant*, 288.
15. Grant, *Memoirs*, 1:193.
16. Ibid., 139–40.
17. U. S. Grant to Julia Grant (who was still at White Haven), 29 June 1851.
18. Lewis, *Captain Sam Grant*, 293.
19. Greeley, *Recollections*, 138–39.
20. Ibid., 269.
21. Hale, *Horace Greeley*, 148–50.
22. James M. McPherson, *Battle Cry of Freedom: The Civil War Era,* vol. 3, *The Oxford History of the United States* (New York and Oxford: Oxford University Press, 1988), 188. McPherson provides an excellent summary of the "Know-Nothing" movement.
23. Hale, *Horace Greeley*, 158.
24. Greeley to Schuyler Colfax, 12 February 1851.
25. Hale, *Horace Greeley*, 159.
26. U. S. Grant to Julia Grant, 5 July 1852.
27. Lewis, *Captain Sam Grant*, 307.
28. Grant, *Memoirs*, 1:203.
29. Lewis, *Captain Sam Grant*, 316.
30. U. S. Grant to Julia Grant, 15 June 1853.
31. Lewis, *Captain Sam Grant*, 323.
32. U. S. Grant to Julia Grant, 2 February 1853.
33. Lewis, *Captain Sam Grant*, 324.
34. Ibid., 330–31; Garland, *Ulysses S. Grant*, 127.
35. Lewis, *Captain Sam Grant*, 332.
36. Hale, *Horace Greeley*, 154–55.
37. Ibid., 155.

38. Ibid., 152.
39. Ibid., 167.
40. McPherson, *Battle Cry*, 126.
41. *New York Tribune*, 16 June 1854.
42. Hale, *Horace Greeley*, 166.
43. Ibid., 167.
44. Simon, *Grant papers*, 1:329–30.

7 HARDSCRABBLE

1. Bruce Catton, introduction to *The Personal Memoirs of Julia Dent Grant* (Carbondale, Ill.: Southern Illinois University Press, 1975).
2. Lewis, *Captain Sam Grant*, 339–41.
3. *New York Tribune*, 3 August 1854.
4. Hale, *Horace Greeley*, 171.
5. Ibid., 172.
6. Ibid., 175.
7. Ibid., 174.
8. Ibid.
9. *New York Weekly Tribune*, 14 June 1856.
10. Starr, *Bohemian Brigade*, 15–16.
11. Nevins, *Ordeal of the Union*, 2:465.
12. Lewis, *Captain Sam Grant*, 350.
13. Lewis, *Captain Sam Grant*, 351; Grant, *Memoirs*, 1:128.
14. U. S. Grant to Jesse Grant, 7 February 1857.
15. Pawn ticket, dated 23 December 1857; Simon, *Grant Papers*, 1:339.
16. *New York Tribune*, 25 December 1854.
17. Lewis, *Captain Sam Grant*, 360.
18. Hale, *Horace Greeley*, 203.
19. Ibid.
20. Ibid., 205.
21. Ibid., 206.
22. U. S. Grant to Jesse Grant, 23 September 1859.
23. T. Harry Williams, *McClellan, Sherman and Grant* (New Brunswick, N.J.: Rutgers University Press, 1962), 82.
24. John M. Taylor, *William Henry Seward: Lincoln's Right Hand* (New York: Harper Collins, 1991), 3.
25. Hale, *Horace Greeley*, 191, 221.
26. Ibid., 220, 223.
27. Taylor, *William Henry Seward*, 10.
28. Greeley, *American Conflict*, 1:327.
29. *New York Tribune*, 1 August 1860; Starr, *Bohemian Brigade*, 8.

30. *New York Tribune*, 17 November 1860.
31. Richard M. Ketchum, ed., *The American Heritage Picture History of the Civil War* (New York: American Heritage Publishing Co., 1960), 50.
32. Ibid.
33. *Chicago Tribune*, 18 April 1861.
34. Ibid., 26 April 1861.
35. *Missouri Weekly Democrat*, 28 May 1861.
36. Lewis, *Captain Sam Grant*, 424.
37. Ibid., 423.
38. Bruce Catton, *Grant Moves South* (Boston: Little, Brown and Company, 1960), 4.

8 "TO RICHMOND! TO RICHMOND!"

1. *New York Tribune*, 9 November 1860.
2. Nevins, *Ordeal of the Union*, 2:233; Hale, *Horace Greeley*, 174.
3. Starr, *Bohemian Brigade*, 34.
4. Ibid., 16.
5. Shelby Foote, *The Civil War: A Narrative*, 3 vols. (New York: Random House, 1958), 1:85.
6. *New York Tribune*, 23 July 1861.
7. *Philadelphia Press*, July 1861.
8. Hale, *Horace Greeley*, 248.
9. Greeley, *Recollections*, 402–3.
10. Hale, *Horace Greeley*, 249–50.
11. Ibid., 250.
12. *New York Times*, 25 July 1861, describing the Bull Run battlefield.
13. *Chicago Tribune*, 8 August 1861.
14. Grant, *Memoirs*, 1:255.
15. Ibid., 256.
16. Ibid., 257.
17. *Weekly Missouri Democrat*, 3 September 1861.
18. *New York Tribune*, 11 September 1861.
19. Ibid., 10 September 1861.
20. Ibid., 13 July 1861.
21. Starr, *Bohemian Brigade*, 69–70.
22. Ibid., 59–60.
23. Catton, *Grant Moves South*, 48.
24. *Weekly Missouri Democrat*, 10 September 1861.
25. *New York Tribune*, 7 September 1861.
26. *Chicago Tribune*, 7 September 1861.
27. Ibid., 8 September 1861.

28. Ibid., 9 September 1861.

29. Ibid., 11 September 1861.

30. Ibid., 16 September 1861. The article was signed "B," probably identifying Albert B. Bodman, who wrote for the *New York Herald* as well as the *Chicago Tribune*. He was also known to sign his articles "Bod."

31. Catton, *Grant Moves South*, 65, quoting a letter from Chetlain to Washburne dated 16 October 1861.

32. Ibid., 51–56.

33. *Chicago Tribune*, 24 September 1861.

34. *New York Tribune*, 11 September 1861.

35. Ibid., 19 September 1861.

36. Grant, *Memoirs*, 1:269.

9 "LIKELY AS NOT TO DO IT"

1. *New York Tribune*, 24 October 1861.

2. Ibid., 29 October 1861.

3. Catton, *Grant Moves South*, 71–72.

4. *New York Tribune*, 9 November 1861; Catton, *Grant Moves South*, 70.

5. Grant, *Memoirs*, 1:270.

6. Catton, *Grant Moves South*, 73.

7. Kenneth P. Williams, *Lincoln Finds a General*, 5 vols. (New York: Macmillan Company, 1949–1959), 3:81.

8. Catton, *Grant Moves South*, 75.

9. John H. Brinton, *Personal Memoirs* (New York: Neale Publishing Company, 1914), 77.

10. Grant, *Memoirs*, 1:279.

11. Charles W. Wills, *Army Life of an Illinois Soldier* (Washington, D.C.: Globe Printing Company, 1906), 43.

12. Ibid., 44.

13. Grant, *Memoirs*, 1:280–81.

14. J. Cutler Andrews, *The North Reports the Civil War* (Pittsburgh: University of Pittsburgh Press, 1955), 119.

15. *New York Tribune*, 9 November 1861.

16. *Weekly Missouri Democrat*, 12 November 1861. This first casualty report was highly inaccurate. Revised official returns from Belmont show Union losses of 120 killed, 383 wounded, and 104 captured or missing, totalling 607.

17. Catton, *Grant Moves South*, 85.

18. Andrews, *The North Reports*, 119.

19. *Weekly Missouri Democrat*, 12 November and 19 November, 1861.

20. *Cincinnati Gazette*, 11 November 1861. Reprinted in the *Missouri Republican*, 12 November 1861.
21. Williams, *Lincoln Finds a General*, 3:90.
22. *Chicago Tribune*, 9 November 1861.
23. Williams, *Lincoln Finds a General*, 3:90.
24. *Chicago Tribune*, 9 November 1861.
25. *New York Tribune*, 9 November 1861.
26. Ibid., 11 November 1861.
27. *Missouri Republican*, 12 November 1861.
28. *Weekly Missouri Democrat*, 17 December 1861.
29. U. S. Grant to Jesse Grant, 28 November 1861.
30. Clifton C. Edom, *Missouri Sketch Book* (Columbia, Mo.: Kelly Press, 1963), 95.
31. *New York Tribune*, 19 November 1861.
32. Catton, *Grant Moves South*, 93–98.
33. Ibid., 94.
34. Ibid., 95.
35. *New York Tribune*, 3 December 1861.
36. Ibid., 31 December 1861. Starr, *Bohemian Brigade*, 15, describes Dana as "by turns profane and charming."
37. *New York Tribune*, 31 December 1861.
38. Starr, *Bohemian Brigade*, 16.
39. *New York Tribune*, 24 December 1861.
40. *Louisville Journal*, 17 December 1861.

10 "AT ALL EVENTS WE CAN TRY"

1. Nevins, *Ordeal of the Union*, 5:396.
2. Ibid., 410.
3. *New York Tribune*, 21 January 1862.
4. Charles A. Dana, *Recollections of the Civil War* (Lincoln and London: University of Nebraska Press, 1996), 4–5.
5. *New York Herald*, 24 January 1862.
6. Dana, *Recollections*, 6.
7. Ibid., 157–58.
8. Grant, *Memoirs*, 1:287.
9. Catton, *Grant Moves South*, 134.
10. Grant, *Memoirs*, 1:288.
11. Andrews, *The North Reports*, 162.
12. *Chicago Tribune*, 4 February 1862.
13. Emmet Crozier, *Yankee Reporters* (New York: Oxford University Press, 1956), 196.

14. *Chicago Tribune,* 9 February 1862.
15. Andrews, *The North Reports,* 168.
16. *Chicago Tribune,* 8 February 1862.
17. Andrews, *The North Reports,* 163; Crozier, *Yankee Reporters,* 199–200.
18. *New York Tribune,* 14 February 1862.
19. Catton, *Grant Moves South,* 145.
20. Starr, *Bohemian Brigade,* 86.
21. *New York Herald,* 8 February 1862.
22. *Chicago Tribune,* 11 February 1862.
23. Ibid., 14 February 1862.
24. Catton, *Grant Moves South,* 145.
25. *Missouri Republican,* 8 February 1862.
26. *New York Herald,* 11 February 1862.
27. Catton, *Grant Moves South,* 161.
28. Ibid., 165–69
29. Charles A. Dana and James Harrison Wilson, *Life of Ulysses S. Grant, General of the Armies of the United States* (Springfield, Mass.: Gordon Bill & Co., 1868), 66.
30. Catton, *Grant Moves South,* 170–71.
31. Ibid., 176.
32. Ibid., 175.
33. Lewis, *Captain Sam Grant,* 338.
34. Catton, *Grant Moves South,* 175–76.
35. *Chicago Tribune,* 20 February 1862.
36. *New York Herald,* 18 February 1862.
37. Ibid., 21 February 1862.
38. Catton, *Grant Moves South,* 177.
39. Dana and Wilson, *Life of Grant,* 68.
40. *Chicago Tribune,* 20 February 1862.
41. *New York Times,* 18 February 1862.
42. *Missouri Republican,* 27 February 1862.
43. Catton, *Grant Moves South,* 195–97.
44. Grant, *Memoirs,* 1:327.
45. Catton, *Grant Moves South,* 205.

11 LIKE CURRIER WITHOUT IVES

1. Starr, *Bohemian Brigade,* 90.
2. Ralph L. Rusk, ed., *The Letters of Ralph Waldo Emerson* (New York: 1939), 5:56; Starr, *Bohemian Brigade,* 18.
3. Hale, *Horace Greeley,* 256–57.
4. James M. Trietsch, *The Printer and the Prince: A Study of the Influence*

of Horace Greeley Upon Abraham Lincoln as Candidate and President (New York: Exposition Press, 1955), 16.

5. Starr, *Bohemian Brigade*, 94–95.
6. Ibid., 96.
7. *New York Tribune*, 17 February 1862.
8. Starr, *Bohemian Brigade*, 88.
9. Dana, in *New York Sun*, 24 July 1885; Nevins, *Ordeal of the Union*, 6:27.
10. Dana, *Recollections*, 7.
11. Edwin M. Stanton to Charles Dana, 19 February 1862; Dana, *Recollections*, 8.
12. Dana, *Recollections*, 9–11.
13. Hale, *Horace Greeley*, 252.
14. Greeley to Wilkeson, 17 November 1861.
15. Hale, *Horace Greeley*, 184.
16. Ibid., 252.
17. Ibid., 185.
18. Charles J. Rosebault, *When Dana was the Sun* (New York: Robert M. McBride and Co., 1931), 62; Starr, *Bohemian Brigade,* 96. In his *Recollections*, Dana erroneously says this happened "early in April" rather than in late March.
19. Starr, *Bohemian Brigade*, 96.
20. Hale, *Horace Greeley*, 253.
21. Wilson, *Charles A. Dana*, 172.
22. Ibid., 174.
23. Catton, *Grant Moves South*, 276.
24. Ibid., 201–2.
25. Ibid., 222, 271.
26. Grant, *Memoirs*, 1:42.
27. Lewis, *Captain Sam Grant*, 174.
28. *Missouri Republican*, 29 March 1862.
29. *Chicago Times*, 30 March 1862.
30. *New York Tribune*, 31 March 1862.
31. *Chicago Tribune*, 2 April 1862.
32. *New York Herald*, 2 April 1862.
33. *New York Tribune*, 2 April 1862; Nevins, *Ordeal of the Union*, 6:83.
34. Catton, *Grant Moves South*, 220.
35. Nevins, *Ordeal of the Union*, 6:84.

12 "ALL HEARTS WERE STILLED"

1. *1990 USMA Register of Graduates*, 257; Lewis, *Captain Sam Grant*, 50.
2. Nevins, *Ordeal of the Union*, 6:80.

3. Catton, *Grant Moves South*, 223.

4. Ibid., 228.

5. The relationship between Grant and Buell was an odd one. Technically, as the senior of the two, Grant would be in charge when their forces joined. However, Halleck, their immediate superior, had never spelled this out. Moreover, both men knew that Halleck planned to take command in person. To complicate matters, Buell (who had been senior to Grant only 6 weeks earlier) tended to regard Grant as something of an "upstart." As a result, Grant sent "suggestions" to Buell rather than commands.

6. Andrews, *The North Reports*, 174.

7. Greeley, *American Conflict*, 2:63.

8. Catton, *Grant Moves South*, 227–29.

9. *Civil War Atlas to Accompany Steele's American Campaigns* (West Point, N.Y.: Department of Military Art and Engineering, United States Military Academy, 1941), 18.

10. McPherson, *Battle Cry*, 410.

11. J. F. C. Fuller, *The Generalship of Ulysses S. Grant* (London, 1929), 111–13; cited by Catton in *Grant Moves South*, 511.

12. Matthew Forney Steele, *American Campaigns* (Washington, D.C.: United States Infantry Association, 1943), 188.

13. Catton, *Grant Moves South*, 225.

14. Andrews, *The North Reports*, 175.

15. Catton, *Grant Moves South*, 235–39.

16. Ibid., 238; citing a speech by Reid at New York's Lotus Club, quoted in the *Chicago Tribune* of 21 November 1880. (Strange words from the man who was chief generator of the press abuse heaped on Grant soon after Shiloh!)

17. Grant, *Memoirs*, 1:349.

18. Catton, *Grant Moves South*, 241.

19. Grant, *Memoirs*, 1:351.

20. Official Union losses were given as 1,754 killed, 8,408 wounded, 2,885 captured or missing; a total of 13,047. The Confederates reported 1,728 killed, 8,012 wounded, 959 missing; a total of 10,699. However, Grant always believed (and with reason) that Southern casualties were far greater than reported. For example, Union burial parties, which interred the dead of both sides, estimated there were 4,000 Confederate bodies. Also, while Johnston left Corinth with 40,000 in his army, Beauregard could "put only twenty thousand men in battle on the morning of the 7th" (Grant, *Memoirs*, 1:367).

21. Andrews, *The North Reports*, 177.

22. *New York Herald*, 10 April 1862. The story also appeared on April 9 in what was perhaps the war's most famous "extra."

23. Andrews, *The North Reports*, 68.
24. *New York Herald*, 10 April 1862.
25. Ibid.
26. Ketchum, *American Heritage Picture History*, 492.
27. Two days later, the *Herald* "apologized" for having placed Halleck's biography first, "as if he were in command of the troops" (*New York Herald*, 12 April 1862).
28. *New York Herald*, 10 April 1862.
29. Ibid.
30. Catton, *Grant Moves South*, 251. Strangely, Carroll is ignored by both Andrews and Crozier in their fine histories of Civil War reporting. Bruce Catton, on the other hand, not only mentions Carroll but attributes to him the story sent by Chapman! Catton was confused on this point by a letter dated December 24, 1862, from Carroll to Congressman Washburne (now in the Washburne papers at the Library of Congress), in which Carroll bragged about having been first with the news of Shiloh. Catton apparently assumed that Carroll must therefore have written the "big" story, which he did not.
31. *New York Herald*, 9 April 1862. Island No. 10 in the Mississippi was captured on April 7. On April 9, the *Herald*'s regular edition treated this, rather than Shiloh, as the lead story, thus evidencing the lack of attention paid to Carroll's "beat."
32. Ibid.
33. Starr, *Bohemian Brigade*, 100.
34. *New York Tribune*, 10 April 1862.
35. *Chicago Times*, 10 April 1862.
36. *New York Herald*, 10 April 1862.
37. *Cincinnati Daily Times*, 10 April 1862, cited in Andrews, *The North Reports*, 175.
38. William E. Woodward, *Meet General Grant* (New York: Literary Guild of America, 1928), 255.

13 "JUDGED ONLY BY MY ACTS"

1. Private Edward "Teddy" Chase, *The Memorial Life of General Sherman* (Chicago: R. S. Peale and Co., 1891), 119.
2. Grant, *Memoirs*, 1:345.
3. *Chicago Times*, 10 April 1862; *Chicago Tribune*, 10 April 1962. Both papers mistakenly referred to Prentiss's division as a "brigade."
4. *Chicago Tribune*, 10 April 1862.
5. Foote, *The Civil War*, 1:372; Catton, *Grant Moves South*, 254.

6. *New York Herald*, 16 April 1862, reprinting the Reid story from the *Cincinnati Gazette*.
7. Grant, *Memoirs*, 1:341–42.
8. *New York Herald*, 18 April 1862.
9. Ibid., 22 April 1862.
10. *New York Tribune*, 14 April 1862.
11. Ibid., 15 April 1862.
12. Ibid., 16 April 1862.
13. Ibid., 18 April 1862.
14. Ibid., 21 April 1862.
15. Ibid., 3 May 1862.
16. Catton, *Grant Moves South*, 272.
17. Bruce Catton, *U. S. Grant and the American Military Tradition* (Boston: Little, Brown, and Company, 1954), 87.
18. *Cincinnati Commercial*, 2 May 1862. The letter also appeared in the *Chicago Times* and the *New York Herald*.
19. Catton, *Grant Moves South*, 260.
20. Ibid., 260–61.
21. *General Grant's Letters to a Friend* (New York: T. Y. Crowell and Company, 1897), 10–11. This letter, dated 14 May 1862, also reveals some of Grant's "unusual" spelling.
22. Catton, *Grant Moves South*, 261, citing a letter, Medill to Washburne, dated 24 May 1862.
23. Charles W. Wills, *Army Life of an Illinois Soldier* (Washington, D.C.: Globe Printing Company, 1906), 81–82. The "little" *Tribune* in Wills's letter was the one from Chicago, so-called to distinguish it from Greeley's "big" *Tribune*.
24. Ibid., 83–84.
25. McPherson, *Battle Cry*, 414.
26. Dana to William Huntington, 11 April 1862; Wilson, *Charles A. Dana*, 176.
27. Dana to Robert Carter, 18 April 1862; Wilson, *Charles A. Dana*, 172.
28. Wilson, *Charles A. Dana*, 182–83.
29. Dana, *Recollections*, 12. Perhaps the reference to "hysterical newspapers" was an unsubtle dig at his erstwhile employer.
30. Nevins, *Ordeal of the Union*, 6:111.
31. Catton, *Grant Moves South*, 267–68.
32. Ibid., 268.
33. Grant, *Memoirs*, 1:377, 381.
34. Foote, *The Civil War*, 1:542.
35. Ibid., 541–42.

36. Dana, *Recollections*, 11.
37. Ibid., 13.
38. Ibid., 15.
39. Wilson, *Charles A. Dana*, 192–93.
40. Foote, *The Civil War*, 1:544.

14 "THE PRAYER OF TWENTY MILLIONS"

1. Nevins, *Ordeal of the Union*, 6:204.
2. *New York Tribune*, 6 June 1862.
3. Ibid., 9 January 1862.
4. Ibid., 31 January 1862.
5. Harlan Hoyt Horner, *Lincoln and Greeley* (Urbana: University of Illinois Press, 1953), 211.
6. Trietsch, *Printer and Prince*, 201–2
7. *New York Tribune*, 17 July 1862.
8. Ibid., 20 August 1862.
9. Trietsch, *Printer and Prince*, 7–8.
10. *New York Tribune*, 25 August 1862.
11. *New York Times*, 25 August 1862.
12. Grant, *Memoirs*, 1:354.
13. *New York Tribune*, 3 July 1862.
14. Ibid., 7 and 8 July, 1862.
15. Catton, *Grant Moves South*, 302; Starr, *Bohemian Brigade*, 279.
16. *New York Tribune*, 2 September 1862.
17. Ibid., 3 September 1862.
18. Ibid., 5 September 1862.
19. Ibid., 10 September 1862.
20. McPherson, *Battle Cry*, 544.
21. *New York Tribune*, 23 September 1862; Nevins, *Ordeal of the Union*, 6:234.
22. Grant, *Memoirs*, 1:410.
23. McPherson, *Battle Cry*, 522–23.
24. *New York Tribune*, 2 October 1862.
25. Grant, *Memoirs*, 1:417.
26. *New York Tribune*, 7 and 8 October, 1862.
27. Grant, *Memoirs*, 1:418.
28. Ibid., 1:420.
29. Julia Grant, *Memoirs*, 104–5.
30. Catton, *Grant Moves South*, 297.
31. Ibid.
32. Ibid., 359–60.

33. Ibid., 321.
34. Grant, *Memoirs*, 1:421.
35. Dana, *Recollections*, 16.
36. Grant, *Memoirs*, 1:426.
37. Catton, *Grant Moves South*, 326; Foote, *The Civil War*, 2:60. See Trietsch, *Printer and Prince*, 231, for Greeley's suggestion concerning Chase.
38. Catton, *Grant Moves South*, 329.
39. Ibid., 329; Foote, *The Civil War*, 2:61.
40. Catton, *Grant Moves South*, 339.
41. Grant, *Memoirs*, 1:430–31.
42. *Richmond Dispatch*, 15 January 1863.
43. Greeley, *American Conflict*, 2:287–88.
44. Hale, *Horace Greeley*, 254–55.

15 "MR. DANA IS MY FRIEND"

1. Lloyd Lewis, *Sherman, Fighting Prophet* (Lincoln: University of Nebraska Press, 1993), 256. (Originally published: New York: Harcourt Brace, 1932.)
2. Ketchum, *American Heritage Picture History*, 268–69.
3. Williams, *Lincoln Finds a General*, 4:292.
4. Nevins, *Ordeal of the Union*, 6:385.
5. Lewis, *Sherman, Fighting Prophet*, 261.
6. Nevins, *Ordeal of the Union*, 6:387.
7. Dana, *Recollections*, 17–19.
8. Hale, *Horace Greeley*, 270; *New York Tribune*, 22 January 1863.
9. Nevins, *Ordeal of the Union*, 6:390.
10. Hale, *Horace Greeley*, 268.
11. Williams, *Lincoln Finds a General*, 4:304.
12. Catton, *Grant Moves South*, 376–77.
13. Greeley, *American Conflict*, 2:295.
14. Catton, *Grant Moves South*, 379.
15. Hale, *Horace Greeley*, 276.
16. Foote, *The Civil War*, 2:107.
17. Catton, *Grant Moves South*, 368.
18. Dana, *Recollections*, 20–22.
19. Ibid., 27.
20. Ibid., 28.
21. Simon, *Grant Papers*, 8:5.
22. U. S. Grant to Porter, 2 April 1863.

23. U. S. Grant to McClernand, 6 April 1863; Catton, *Grant Moves South*, 391.
24. Dana, *Recollections*, 61.
25. A. O. Marshall, *Army Life*, as quoted by Catton in *Grant Moves South*, 391.
26. Dana, *Recollections*, 30.
27. U. S. Grant to Halleck, 12 April 1863.
28. Dana, *Recollections*, 33.
29. Ibid., 37–38.
30. Ibid., 40–41.
31. Catton, *Grant Moves South*, 423. "Secesh," as used here by Sherman, was slang for "secessionists."
32. Grant, *Memoirs*, 1:458; U. S. Grant to Jesse Grant, 21 April 1863.
33. Grant, *Memoirs*, 1:480–81.

16 "YOU WERE RIGHT, AND I WAS WRONG"

1. Williams, *Lincoln Finds a General*, 4:337; McPherson, *Battle Cry*, 628.
2. Catton, *Grant Moves South*, 427–28.
3. Foote, *The Civil War*, 2:348.
4. U. S. Grant to Porter, 1 May 1863.
5. U. S. Grant to McClernand, 1 May 1863.
6. Williams, *Lincoln Finds a General*, 4:350.
7. *New York Tribune*, 11 May 1863.
8. Catton, *Grant Moves South*, 428–29. During the campaign, this same James Harrison Wilson became quite close to Dana. In later years he would not only write Dana's biography but, with Dana, would co-author a biography of Grant.
9. Julia Grant, *Memoirs*, 92, 113.
10. Dana, *Recollections*, 45.
11. Grant, *Memoirs*, 1:487.
12. Dana, *Recollections*, 45–46.
13. U. S. Grant to Halleck, 3 May 1863.
14. Dana to Stanton, 4 May 1863.
15. U. S. Grant to Sherman, 3 May 1863.
16. U. S. Grant to Sherman, 9 May 1863; Dana, *Recollections*, 29.
17. U. S. Grant to Halleck, 11 May 1863.
18. Catton, *Grant Moves South*, 440–42.
19. Dana, *Recollections*, 52.
20. *Richmond Whig*, 18 May 1863, quoted in *New York Tribune*, 22 May 1863.
21. *New York Tribune*, 25 May 1863.

22. Grant, *Memoirs*, 1:519–20.
23. *New York Tribune*, 30 May 1863.
24. Sylvanus Cadwallader, *Three Years With Grant* (Lincoln: University of Nebraska Press, 1983), 81.
25. Grant, *Memoirs*, 1:520–21.
26. Catton, *Grant Moves South*, 448.
27. Grant, *Memoirs*, 1:529.
28. Catton, *Grant Moves South*, 452–53.
29. Williams, *Lincoln Finds a General*, 4:391.
30. U. S. Grant to Halleck, 24 May 1863.
31. Williams, *Lincoln Finds a General*, 4:391.
32. *New York Tribune*, 3 June 1863.
33. Dana, *Recollections*, 73.
34. Catton, *Grant Moves South*, 463.
35. Ibid., 463; Cadwallader, *Three Years*, 102–110; Simon, *Grant Papers*, 8:322–25; Williams, *Lincoln Finds a General*, 4:439–51. "One must suspect," said Williams, "that his book was largely the effort of an obscure but artful man to turn himself into one of consequence."
36. Catton, *Grant Moves South*, 466–67; Williams, *Lincoln Finds a General*, 4:408–10.
37. *New York Tribune*, 16 June 1863.
38. Williams, *Lincoln Finds a General*, 4:416.
39. Catton, *Grant Moves South*, 470–71.
40. Grant, *Memoirs*, 1:558.
41. Dana, *Recollections*, 97
42. *New York Tribune*, 8 July 1863.
43. Ibid., 15 July 1863.
44. Catton, *Grant Moves South*, 477.
45. Ibid., 489.

17 "WET, DIRTY AND WELL"

1. Greeley, *American Conflict*, 2:350.
2. Nevins, *Ordeal of the Union*, 6:456.
3. *New York Tribune*, 29 June 1863.
4. Ibid., 3 July 1863.
5. Greeley, *American Conflict*, 2:316.
6. *New York Tribune*, 5 June 1863.
7. *New York Tribune*, 14 July 1863; Starr, *Bohemian Brigade*, 220–24; Hale, *Horace Greeley*, 273.
8. Dana, *Recollections*, 102.

9. Grant, *Memoirs*, 1:576–77.
10. Dana, *Recollections*, 74–75.
11. Ibid., 81–82.
12. Wilson, *Charles A. Dana*, 249.
13. Bruce Catton, *Grant Takes Command* (Boston: Little, Brown and Company, 1968), 7; Foote, *The Civil War*, 2:639.
14. Catton, *Grant Takes Command*, 4.
15. Ibid., 14.
16. Grant, *Memoirs*, 1:581.
17. Wilson, *Charles A. Dana*, 254.
18. Ibid., 258–59.
19. Dana, *Recollections*, 115.
20. Ibid., 118.
21. Ibid., 128.
22. Grant, *Memoirs*, 1:583; Catton, *Grant Takes Command*, 33.
23. Catton, *Grant Takes Command*, 33–34; Foote, *The Civil War*, 2:784; Wilson, *Charles A. Dana*, 276.
24. Wilson, *Charles A. Dana*, 277.
25. Dana, *Recollections*, 129–31.
26. Catton, *Grant Takes Command*, 38.
27. Horace Porter, *Campaigning With Grant* (New York: Century Company, 1897), 1–2.
28. Grant, *Memoirs*, 2:24.
29. Ibid., 37–38; Catton, *Grant Takes Command*, 51–54; Porter, *Campaigning*, 9–10; U. S. Grant to Halleck, 28 October 1863.
30. J. F. C. Fuller, *Decisive Battles of the U.S.A.* (New York: Beechhurst Press, 1953), 287; Grant, *Memoirs*, 2:42; Porter, *Campaigning*, 11.
31. Dana, *Recollections*, 137–40.
32. Nevins, *Ordeal of the Union*, 6:832.

18 "THE QUESTION ASTONISHES ME"

1. Dana, *Recollections*, 141.
2. Grant, *Memoirs*, 2:49.
3. Ibid., 51, 59.
4. Fuller, *Decisive Battles*, 278; Dana, *Recollections*, 142.
5. S. H. M. Byers, "Sherman's Attack at the Tunnel," from R. U. Johnson and Clarence C. Buel, ed., *Battles and Leaders of the Civil War*, 4 vols. (New York: 1887–1888), 3:712.
6. Dana, *Recollections*, 147.
7. Catton, *Grant Takes Command*, 76–77; Foote, *The Civil War*, 2:847.
8. Wilson, *Charles A. Dana*, 293.

9. Catton, *Grant Takes Command*, 79.
10. Dana, *Recollections*, 149.
11. Dana to Stanton, 26 November 1863. The *New York Tribune* printed this dispatch on 3 December 1863, not mentioning Dana, and saying only that the story was as "described by an officer in a report to the War Department."
12. Fuller, *Decisive Battles*, 284.
13. Philip H. Sheridan, *Personal Memoirs of P. H. Sheridan*, 2 vols. (New York: Charles L. Webster & Co., 1888), 1:321; Catton, *Grant Takes Command*, 81, 91–92.
14. Grant, *Memoirs*, 2:90.
15. U. S. Grant to Julia Grant, 30 November 1863.
16. Grant, *Memoirs*, 2:94.
17. *New York Tribune*, 8 December 1863.
18. Dana, *Recollections*, 155; Wilson, *Charles A. Dana*, 296.
19. Catton, *Grant Takes Command*, 95.
20. Grant, *Memoirs*, 2:98.
21. *New York Tribune*, 27 November 1863.
22. *New York Herald*, 28 November 1863; *New York World*, 26 November 1863; Catton, *Grant Takes Command*, 91.
23. Grant, *Memoirs*, 2:99.
24. U. S. Grant to Elihu Washburne, 9 December 1863.
25. *New York Herald*, 9 December 1863; Catton, *Grant Takes Command*, 103.
26. *New York Herald*, 15 December 1863.
27. *New York Tribune*, 18 December 1863.
28. Catton, *Grant Takes Command*, 107; William S. McFeely, *Grant: A Biography* (New York: W. W. Norton & Co., 1981), 162. Grant knew that many a man threw his hat into the ring by publicly "denying" his candidacy. By having his letter kept secret, he tried to prevent his name from surfacing and thereby insure that no one misinterpreted a definite no for a coy maybe. Despite this, Grant biographer William McFeely claimed that Grant's "classic attitude" of denial was "the one calculated to make it come true." The revisionist McFeely was consistent, never missing an opportunity to question Grant's motives. Similarly, when Julia Grant, in the spring of 1864, said emphatically that "her husband would not think for one moment of accepting a nomination," McFeely wrote she was being "political." People other than McFeely might say she was simply being honest!
29. Catton, *Grant Takes Command*, 110.
30. Ibid., 111.
31. Ibid., 112.

32. Wilson, *Charles A. Dana*, 311–12.
33. Nevins, *Ordeal of the Union*, 7:76.
34. John S. C. Abbott, *The Life of General Ulysses S. Grant* (Boston: B. B. Russell, 1868), 218.
35. Catton, *Grant Takes Command*, 121.

19 "ENOUGH OF THIS SHOW BUSINESS"

1. *New York Tribune*, 5 March 1864.
2. Ibid., 2 February 1864; Hale, *Horace Greeley*, 275–76.
3. *New York Tribune*, 12 December 1863.
4. Ibid., 14 December 1863.
5. Foote, *The Civil War*, 2:947–48.
6. Ibid., 940.
7. Wilson, *Charles A. Dana*, 297.
8. Ibid., 304; Catton, *Grant Takes Command*, 130. The ambitious Wilson, a talented soldier and writer, was also an astute opportunist. Cultivating Dana's friendship, he was rewarded with an assignment to the War Department and a general's star. Gen. W. F. "Baldy" Smith told his diary that Wilson had been "spoiled" by his rapid rise. In the spring of '64, Wilson left Washington to assume command of a cavalry division under Sheridan. He performed with great distinction, and by war's end, as a major general, he would be second only to Sheridan as a leader of Union cavalry.
9. Dana, *Recollections*, 168–70.
10. Porter, *Campaigning*, 23; Wilson, *Charles A. Dana*, 306; Catton, *Grant Takes Command*, 130. Wilson, Dana's closest confidant, was probably echoing Dana when he wrote: "In this respect [Stanton's lack of courtesy and self-control] Dana was vastly his superior, and . . . could have filled the office of secretary with great advantage to the army and the country at large."
11. Catton, *Grant Takes Command*, 122, 133; Foote, *The Civil War*, 2:965.
12. Catton, *Grant Takes Command*, 124; Porter, *Campaigning*, 22; Nevins, *Ordeal of the Union*, 8:7.
13. *New York Tribune*, 10 March 1864.
14. Grant, *Memoirs*, 2:117.
15. Catton, *Grant Takes Command*, 156.
16. Foote, *The Civil War*, 3:12.
17. Catton, *Grant Takes Command*, 152.
18. Dana, *Recollections*, 192.
19. Grant, *Memoirs*, 2:146.

20. Catton, *Grant Takes Command*, 155.
21. Ibid., 159.
22. Ibid., 177.
23. Ibid., 177–78.
24. Grant, *Memoirs*, 2:135.
25. Greeley, *American Conflict*, 2:566.
26. Porter, *Campaigning*, 47.
27. Brian A. Bennett, *A Regimental History of Patrick O'Rorke's 140th New York Volunteer Infantry* (Dayton, Ohio: Morningside House, 1992), 352.
28. Ibid., 362.
29. Ibid., 373–74.
30. Porter, *Campaigning*, 70.
31. Dana, *Recollections*, 187–89.
32. Grant, *Memoirs*, 2:208.
33. Foote, *The Civil War*, 3:189.
34. Ibid., 191.
35. Grant, *Memoirs*, 2:204.
36. Porter, *Campaigning*, 83.
37. Ibid., 98.
38. Grant, *Memoirs*, 2:226; Greeley, *American Conflict*, 2:571; Porter, *Campaigning*, 98; Catton, *Grant Takes Command*, 236.

20 "HOLD ON WITH A BULLDOG GRIP"

1. Greeley, *American Conflict*, 2:563.
2. *New York Tribune*, 10 May 1864.
3. *New York Herald*, 11 May 1864.
4. Porter, *Campaigning*, 43–44.
5. *New York Tribune*, 12 May 1864.
6. *New York Tribune*, 13 May 1864; Nevins, *Ordeal of the Union*, 8:30.
7. U. S. Grant to Julia Grant, 13 May 1864.
8. Grant, *Memoirs*, 2:237.
9. Porter, *Campaigning*, 131.
10. Grant, *Memoirs*, 2:242.
11. *New York Tribune*, 23 May 1864.
12. Ibid., 30 May 1864.
13. Foote, *The Civil War*, 3:279.
14. Dana, *Recollections*, 204.
15. Porter, *Campaigning*, 174.
16. Foote, *The Civil War* 3:291.
17. Dana, *Recollections*, 209.

18. Grant, *Memoirs*, 2:276.
19. Dana, *Recollections*, 222.
20. Ibid., 225.
21. Ibid., 229.
22. U. S. Grant to Halleck, July 1864; Geoffrey Perret, *Ulysses S. Grant, Soldier & President* (New York: Random House, 1997), 344.
23. Perret, *Ulysses S. Grant*, 345; Dana to John A. Rawlins, 14 July 1864.
24. *New York Tribune*, 14 July 1864.
25. Dana, *Recollections*, 235.
26. *New York Tribune*, 27 July 1864.
27. Hale, *Horace Greeley*, 280.
28. Ibid., 280–85. Hale's book contains an excellent account of the Niagara fiasco, demonstrating both Lincoln's shrewdness and Greeley's well-intentioned but fruitless efforts.
29. *New York Tribune*, 30 July 1864.
30. Trietsch, *Printer and Prince*, 276.
31. Ibid., 278–81; Hale, *Horace Greeley*, 288–89.
32. Grant, *Memoirs*, 2:315.
33. *New York Tribune*, 5 August 1864.
34. U. S. Grant to Elihu Washburne, 16 August 1864.
35. Ibid.
36. Porter, *Campaigning*, 279; Catton, *Grant Takes Command*, 354.
37. Dana, *Recollections*, 261. Petroleum V. Nasby was the pen name of David Ross Locke, an American political satirist and journalist. Locke's "Nasby" letters attacked the Southern pro-slavery cause by presenting Nasby as a stupid, corrupt, and hypocritical Copperhead preacher with an atrocious style of spelling.

21 "LET'S END THE BUSINESS HERE"

1. Greeley to Francis Preston Blair Sr., December 1864; Nevins, *Ordeal of the Union*, 8:140.
2. Nevins, *Ordeal of the Union*, 8:623.
3. *Richmond Sentinel*, 12 November 1864.
4. Porter, *Campaigning*, 387.
5. Ibid., 284.
6. Grant, *Memoirs*, 1:381.
7. Porter, *Campaigning*, 347.
8. Grant, *Memoirs*, 2:371.
9. Ibid., 379–80.
10. Ibid., 375–76. Grant was undoubtedly hurt when he learned that Rawlins had gone to Stanton behind his back. He wrote in his *Memoirs*: "I was in

favor of Sherman's plan from the time it was first submitted to me. My chief of staff, however, was very bitterly opposed to it, and, as I learned subsequently, finding that he could not move me, he appealed to the authorities at Washington to stop it."

11. Ibid., 395; Cotton, *Grant Takes Command*, 402–3.
12. Porter, *Campaigning*, 402.
13. Ibid., 403.
14. Greeley, *American Conflict*, 2:728. Although Greeley called the fort "Steedman," it was actually "Stedman."
15. Catton, *Grant Takes Command*, 437.
16. Ibid., 438–41.
17. Nevins, *Ordeal of the Union*, 8:284.
18. Greeley, *American Conflict*, 2:735.
19. Catton, *Grant Takes Command*, 437.
20. Grant, *Memoirs*, 2:459; Nevins, *Ordeal of the Union*, 8:305; *New York Tribune*, 10 April 1865.
21. Dana, *Recollections*, 263–64; Dana to Stanton, 6 April 1865; Nevins, *Ordeal of the Union*, 8:298.
22. Grant, *Memoirs*, 2:477–78.
23. Ibid., 478–81.
24. Ibid., 627.
25. Ibid., 485.
26. Greeley, *American Conflict*, 2:744.
27. Catton, *Grant Takes Command*, 464.
28. Ibid., 466; Porter, *Campaigning*, 479–80.
29. Grant, *Memoirs*, 2:496.
30. Williams, *Lincoln Finds a General*, 4:451.
31. Nevins, *Ordeal of the Union*, 8:314–15.
32. Grant, *Memoirs*, 2:495; Porter, *Campaigning*, 488.
33. Dana, *Recollections*, 271.
34. Julia Grant, *Memoirs*, 153.
35. *New York Tribune*, 14 April 1865.
36. Grant, *Memoirs*, 2:508; Catton, *Grant Takes Command*, 473.
37. Julia Grant, *Memoirs*, 156; Catton, *Grant Takes Command*, 475.
38. Dana, *Recollections*, 274–75; Grant, *Memoirs*, 2:508–9; Catton, *Grant Takes Command*, 476.

22 "LET US HAVE PEACE"

1. Starr, *Bohemian Brigade*, 348.
2. U. S. Grant to Gen. E. O. C. Ord, 15 April 1865.
3. Brooks D. Simpson, *Let Us Have Peace: Ulysses S. Grant and the Politics

of War and Reconstruction, 1861–1868 (Chapel Hill: University of North Carolina Press, 1991), 93; Nevins, *Ordeal of the Union*, 8:337.

4. Catton, *Grant Takes Command*, 479.
5. *New York Tribune*, 19 April 1865.
6. Lloyd Lewis, *Sherman, Fighting Prophet* (Lincoln: University of Nebraska Press, 1993), 549–56; Grant, *Memoirs*, 2:514–15; Catton, *Grant Takes Command*, 481–86; *New Haven Journal*, 27 April 1865.
7. Lewis, *Sherman, Fighting Prophet*, 562.
8. Porter, *Campaigning*, 510.
9. McFeely, *Grant*, 234.
10. Greeley, *American Conflict*, 2:9; Dana, *Recollections*, 403.
11. Wilson, *Charles A. Dana*, 370.
12. Grant, *Memoirs*, 2:510–11.
13. Simpson, *Let Us Have Peace*, 132.
14. Ibid., 106–8.
15. Porter, *Campaigning*, 385.
16. Simpson, *Let Us Have Peace*, 122–23.
17. Ibid., 126–27; *New York Tribune*, 23 December 1865.
18. Mark Wahlgren Summers, *The Press Gang: Newspapers and Politics, 1865–1878* (Chapel Hill: University of North Carolina Press, 1994), 29; Hale, *Horace Greeley*, 320.
19. Grant, *Memoirs*, 2:510–12.
20. Summers, *Press Gang*, 56–57.
21. Ibid., 45, 70.
22. Wilson, *Charles A. Dana*, 377.
23. Ibid., 388.
24. Ibid., 374–375.
25. Hale, *Horace Greeley*, 322.
26. Greeley, *Recollections*, 415–16.
27. Wilson, *Charles A. Dana*, 381; *New York Sun*, 27 January 1868.
28. Wilson, *Charles A. Dana*, 385.
29. Simpson, *Let Us Have Peace*, 149.
30. Ibid., 139.
31. Ibid., 191.
32. Ibid., 233–34. Andrew Johnson claimed that Grant had lied about their conversation concerning the surrender of the Secretary of War's office. Johnson might have thought that, since that is what he *wanted* to believe, but it seems clear that he misstated what Grant actually said. According to Greeley: "In a question of veracity between U. S. Grant and Andrew Johnson, between a soldier whose honor is as untarnished as the sun, and a President who had betrayed every friend, and broken every promise, the country will not hesitate." (*New York Tribune*, 17 January 1868).
33. *New York Tribune*, 25 and 30 July, 1867.

34. Simpson, *Let Us Have Peace*, 236.
35. Ibid., 244.
36. Ibid., 246.
37. *New York Sun*, 30 July 1868.
38. Ibid., 4 September 1868.
39. Ibid., 30 October 1868.
40. Ibid., 4 November 1868.
41. Simpson, *Let Us Have Peace*, 251.

23   "A FOOL NOT TO GIVE IT"

1. William B. Hesseltine, *Ulysses S. Grant, Politician* (New York: Frederick Ungar Publishing Co., 1935), 98.
2. Ibid., 93.
3. Ibid., 141; Perret, *Ulysses S. Grant*, 383.
4. *New York Tribune*, 10 November 1868.
5. *New York Sun*, 22 May 1868.
6. Simpson, *Let Us Have Peace*, 307.
7. Perret, *Ulysses S. Grant*, 384.
8. Hesseltine, *Ulysses S. Grant*, 120. A commanding general sees firsthand the wastefulness of war. It's not suprising that another general, Dwight Eisenhower, made reducing military expenditures an early campaign theme.
9. Perret, *Ulysses S. Grant*, 386.
10. Wilson, *Charles A. Dana*, 407.
11. Ibid., 338–39.
12. Ibid., 415.
13. Candace Stone, *Dana and the Sun* (New York: Dodd, Mead & Company, 1938), 91.
14. *New York Sun*, 1 March 1885.
15. *New York Tribune*, 10 March 1869; Hesseltine, *Ulysses S. Grant*, 147.
16. *New York Tribune*, 6 March 1869.
17. *New York Sun*, 6 March 1869.
18. Ibid., 22 May 1868.
19. Ibid., 17 April 1869.
20. Allan Nevins, *Hamilton Fish: The Inner History of the Grant Administration* (New York: Dodd, Mead & Company, 1936), 582.
21. *New York World*, 23 March 1869; Hesseltine, *Ulysses S. Grant*, 154.
22. Hesseltine, *Ulysses S. Grant*, 185.
23. Ibid., 156.
24. Ibid., 169.
25. Hale, *Horace Greeley*, 330.
26. *New York Sun*, 30 August 1869.
27. Perret, *Ulysses S. Grant*, 391.

28. Ibid., 392–93.
29. *New York Sun*, 23 September 1871.
30. Hale, *Horace Greeley*, 326.
31. Stone, *Dana*, 115–16.
32. Perret, *Ulysses S. Grant*, 393–400.
33. Ibid., 401.
34. Summers, *Press Gang*, 152–53.
35. *New York Tribune*, 2 January 1871.
36. Hale, *Horace Greeley*, 330.
37. Hesseltine, *Ulysses S. Grant*, 269–70; Perret, *Ulysses S. Grant*, 295; Hale, *Horace Greeley*, 324–25. Reid's reference to "a man of Grant's calibre" is revealing. He seems to have been a bit of a snob, like Charles Dana's affluent cousin Richard Henry Dana. When the latter saw Grant in March 1864, he ridiculed the newly appointed commander of the Union armies as "rather scrubby" and having "a slightly seedy look, as if he was out of office on half pay, and nothing to do but hang around . . . cigar in mouth."
38. *New York Times*, 20 January 1872; Hesseltine, *Ulysses S. Grant*, 269.
39. Hesseltine, *Ulysses S. Grant*, 270–71.
40. Perret, *Ulysses S. Grant*, 418; Hale, *Horace Greeley*, 333–36; Hesseltine, *Ulysses S. Grant*, 273–74.
41. Hale, *Horace Greeley*, 337.
42. Ibid.

24 "SHED TEARS FOR ME"

1. Hale, *Horace Greeley*, 337.
2. Nevins, *Hamilton Fish*, 597–98.
3. Hale, *Horace Greeley*, 338.
4. Ibid.
5. *New York Sun*, 13 July 1872.
6. Hale, *Horace Greeley*, 342–43.
7. Ibid., 342.
8. Stone, *Dana*, 104; *New York Sun*, 25 June 1872.
9. *New York Sun*, 5 April 1872, 24 July 1872.
10. Ibid., 12 June 1872, 24 August 1871, 30 October 1871.
11. Ibid., 17 June 1872.
12. Ibid., 13 July 1872.
13. Ibid., 2 August 1872.
14. Rosebault, *Dana*, 149.
15. Stone, *Dana*, 102.
16. Hesseltine, *Ulysses S. Grant*, 285.
17. Nevins, *Hamilton Fish*, 609.
18. Hesseltine, *Ulysses S. Grant*, 301–2.

19. Andrews, *The North Reports*, 182. It's noteworthy that while examining countless hundreds of Civil War newspapers, the author failed to find a single mention of Grant's drinking. Only once was there such an allusion, and it was so veiled that it might have been my imagination. After Shiloh, Greeley's *Tribune* (21 April 1862) spoke of "the incapacity and criminal negligence of the Generals." We know a whispering campaign had already started to the effect that Grant was drunk on the first day of the battle. Was Greeley implying the same thing with the word "incapacity"?
20. Hamilton Fish to Edward S. Baker, 26 October 1872, quoted in Nevins, *Hamilton Fish*, 598.
21. Hale, *Horace Greeley*, 344.
22. *New York Tribune*, 19 August 1872.
23. Hale, *Horace Greeley*, 345.
24. Ibid., 344; *New York Times*, 13 June 1872.
25. Hesseltine, *Ulysses S. Grant*, 288.
26. *New York Sun*, 26 October 1872.
27. From an essay, "Would You Vote for These Men?" in *Civilization* magazine, October-November 1996, cited in the "Notable and Quotable" section of the *Wall Street Journal*.
28. Hale, *Horace Greeley*, 346.
29. *New York Sun*, 14 October 1872.
30. Ibid., 31 October 1872.
31. Stone, *Dana*, 114.
32. Hale, *Horace Greeley*, 346–47.
33. *New York Herald*, 7 November 1872; McFeely, *Grant*, 384.
34. *New York Sun*, 6 November 1872.
35. Hale, *Horace Greeley*, 345.
36. Ibid., 347–48.
37. Ibid., 348.
38. Ibid.
39. Ibid., 349.
40. Ibid., 351–52.
41. Ibid., 353.

25 "TO DO WHAT WAS RIGHT"

1. Summers, *Press Gang*, 64.
2. Nevins, *Hamilton Fish*, 613.
3. Hesseltine, *Ulysses S. Grant*, 261.
4. *New York Tribune*, 10 December 1872.
5. Ibid., 5 March 1873.
6. *New York Sun*, 5 December 1872.
7. Ibid., 18 December 1872; Stone, *Dana*, 124.

8. *New York Sun*, 26 June 1881; Stone, *Dana*, 128.
9. Stone, *Dana*, 115.
10. Hesseltine, *Ulysses S. Grant*, 309.
11. Ibid., 309–10.
12. *New York Sun*, 15 May 1873.
13. Ibid., 11 April 1874.
14. Ibid., 14 April 1869.
15. Ibid., 22 October 1869.
16. Dana, *Recollections*, 85; *New York Sun*, 17 November 1869.
17. *New York Sun*, 30 June 1874.
18. Ibid., 1 December 1882; Stone, *Dana*, 105.
19. *New York Sun*, 28 April 1869; Stone, *Dana*, 125.
20. Nevins, *Hamilton Fish*, 582.
21. *New York Sun*, 6 January 1871; Stone, *Dana*, 390.
22. Summers, *Press Gang*, 110.
23. Ibid., 122.
24. Ibid., 64.
25. Stone, *Dana*, 127.
26. Ibid., 391.
27. *Washington Chronicle*, 26 February 1875; Summers, *Press Gang*, 62.
28. Stone, *Dana*, 392; Rosebault, *Dana*, 185.
29. *Toledo Journal*, 28 May 1889; *Washington Post*, 10 May 1885; Stone, *Dana*, 393.
30. *New York Tribune*, 20 January 1874.
31. Hesseltine, *Ulysses S. Grant*, 336.
32. *New York Times*, 23 April 1874.
33. Hesseltine, *Ulysses S. Grant*, 384.
34. Perret, *Ulysses S. Grant*, 441–42; Nevins, *Hamilton Fish*, 612.
35. *New York Sun*, 4 November 1874.
36. Julia Grant, *Memoirs*, 174.
37. *Chicago Sunday Tribune*, 14 December 1902; Perret, *Ulysses S. Grant*, 429.
38. Perret, *Ulysses S. Grant*, 444.
39. Hesseltine, *Ulysses S. Grant*, 377–78.
40. Stone, *Dana*, 114.
41. *New York Sun*, 7 March 1876, 19 March 1876; Perret, *Ulysses S. Grant*, 437.
42. *New York Tribune*, 25 August 1876.
43. Hesseltine, *Ulysses S. Grant*, 411.
44. Nevins, *Ordeal of the Union*, 8:18.
45. Hesseltine, *Ulysses S. Grant*, 416–17.
46. *New York Tribune*, 6 December 1876.
47. *Chicago Tribune*, 1 September 1885; Perret, *Ulysses S. Grant*, 446.

26 "MAN PROPOSES AND GOD DISPOSES"

1. Wilson, Charles A. Dana, 444; Summers, *Press Gang*, 159.
2. J. T. Headley, *The Life and Travels of General Grant* (Philadelphia: Hubbard Brothers, 1879), 245.
3. J. F. Packard, *Grant's Tour Around the World* (Philadelphia: H. W. Kelley, 1880), 36.
4. Ibid., 38.
5. Ibid., 30.
6. Ibid., 65.
7. Ibid., 76.
8. Headley, *Travels*, 61.
9. Ibid., 114.
10. *New York Tribune*, 6 September 1885; Perret, *Ulysses S. Grant*, 454.
11. Perret, *Ulysses S. Grant*, 458.
12. Ibid., 460.
13. Ibid., 464.
14. McFeely, *Grant*, 487.
15. Perret, *Ulysses S. Grant*, 468.
16. McFeely, *Grant*, 491–92; Perret, *Ulysses S. Grant*, 469.
17. *New York Tribune*, 7 May 1884.
18. Ibid., 8 May 1864.
19. Wilson, *Charles A. Dana*, 469.
20. Ibid., 453. Dana's anti-Grant feelings might have been accompanied by a general animosity toward the army. Its strength, he said, should be reduced to no more than 10,000 or 12,000, since the United States "was no longer threatened by aggressive neighbors." Perhaps he recalled Horace Greeley's once saying the army should be eliminated altogether!
21. Perret, *Ulysses S. Grant*, 471.
22. *New York Tribune*, 9 July 1885.
23. Grant, *Memoirs*, 2:553.
24. *New York Tribune*, 26 July 1885.
25. Ibid., 13 July 1885.
26. Ibid., 22 July 1885.
27. Ibid., 24 July 1885.
28. *Hartford Courant*, 28 April 1887.
29. Dana, *Recollections*, 15.
30. Ibid., 61. Dana's *Recollections*, while autobiographical, were nevertheless "as told to" Ida Tarbell. Their credibility therefore rests on Tarbell's competence and integrity as a writer and as a historian. Those who know her work have consistently given her high marks on all counts.

BIBLIOGRAPHY

Anderson, Nancy S., and Dwight Anderson. *The Generals: Ulysses S. Grant and Robert E. Lee*. New York: Alfred A. Knopf, 1987.

Andrews, J. Cutler. *The North Reports the Civil War*. Pittsburgh, Pa.: University of Pittsburgh Press, 1955.

Cadwallader, Sylvanus. *Three Years with Grant*, ed. Benjamin P. Thomas. Lincoln, Nebr.: University of Nebraska Press, 1955.

Catton, Bruce. *Grant Moves South*. Boston: Little, Brown and Co., 1960.

————. *Grant Takes Command*. Boston: Little, Brown and Co., 1968.

Crozier, Emmet. *Yankee Reporters*. New York: Oxford University Press, 1956.

Dana, Charles A. *Recollections of the Civil War*. Lincoln, Nebr.: University of Nebraska Press, 1996. (Originally published by D. Appleton Co., New York, 1898.)

————, and James H. Wilson. *The Life of Ulysses S. Grant*. Springfield, Mass.: Gordon Bill and Co., 1868.

Edom, Clifton C. *Missouri Sketch Book*. Columbia, Mo.: Kelly Press, 1963.

Foote, Shelby. *The Civil War: A Narrative*. 4 vols. New York: Random House, 1958.

Fry, James B. *Military Miscellanies*. New York: Brentano's, 1889.

Garland, Hamlin. *Ulysses S. Grant: His Life and Character*. New York: Doubleday and McClure, 1898.

Granberg, Wilbur J. *Spread the Truth: The Life of Horace Greeley*. New York: Dutton, 1959.

Grant, Ulysses S. *Personal Memoirs*. 2 vols. New York: Charles L. Webster and Co., 1885–1886.

Greeley, Horace. *Recollections of a Busy Life*. New York: J. B. Ford and Co., 1869.

————. *The American Conflict*. 2 vols. Hartford, Conn.: O. D. Case and Co., 1864, 1866.

Hale, William H. *Horace Greeley, Voice of the People*. New York: Harper and Brothers, 1950.

Headley, J. F. *The Life and Travels of General Grant.* Philadelphia: Hubbard Brothers, 1879.

Hesseltine, William B. *Ulysses S. Grant, Politician.* New York: Frederick Ungar Publishing Co., 1935.

Horner, Harlan H. *Lincoln and Greeley.* Urbana, Ill.: University of Illinois Press, 1953.

Keller, Morton, ed. *The Art and Politics of Thomas Nast.* New York: Oxford University Press, 1968.

Ketchum, Richard M., ed. *The American Heritage Picture History of the Civil War.* New York: American Heritage Publishing Co., 1960.

Maihafer, Harry J. "U.S. Grant and the Northern Press." Master's thesis, University of Missouri at Columbia, 1966.

———. "Grant in Panama," *America's Civil War* 1, no. 2, (July 1988).

———. "The Partnership—Grant and Foote," *Naval Institute Proceedings* 93, no. 5 (May 1967).

McFeeley, William S. *Grant, a Biography.* New York: W. W. Norton and Co., 1981.

McPherson, James M. *Battle Cry of Freedom: The Civil War Era,* vol. 3, *The Oxford History of the United States.* New York and Oxford: Oxford University Press, 1988.

Miller, Edwin H. *Salem Is My Dwelling Place: A Life of Nathaniel Hawthorne.* Iowa City: University of Iowa Press, 1991.

Miller, Robert R., ed. *The Mexican War Journal & Letters of Ralph W. Kirkham.* College Station, Texas: Texas A&M University Press, 1991.

Nevins, Allan. *Ordeal of the Union,* 8 vols. New York: Charles Scribner's Sons, 1971.

———. *Hamilton Fish: The Inner History of the Grant Administration.* New York: Dodd, Mead and Co., 1936.

Packard, J. F. *Grant's Tour Around the World.* Philadelphia: H. W. Kelley, 1880.

Perret, Geoffrey. *Ulysses S. Grant, Soldier & President.* New York: Random House, 1997.

Porter, Horace, *Campaigning with Grant.* New York: Century Co., 1897.

Richardson, Albert D. *A Personal History of Ulysses S. Grant.* Hartford, Conn.: O. D. Case and Co., 1868.

Rosebault, Charles J. *When Dana Was the Sun.* New York: Robert M. McBride and Co., 1931.

Rusk, Ralph L., ed. *The Letters of Ralph Waldo Emerson.* New York: 1939.

Simon, John Y. *Ulysses S. Grant: One Hundred Years Later.* Springfield, Ill.: Illinois State Historical Society, 1986.

———, ed. *The Papers of Ulysses S. Grant.* Carbondale, Ill.: Southern Illinois University Press, 1967–1990.

Simpson, Brooks D. *Let Us Have Peace*. Chapel Hill, N.C.: University of North Carolina Press, 1991.

Smith, Gene. *Lee and Grant*. New York: McGraw-Hill, 1984.

Starr, Louis M. *Bohemian Brigade*. Madison, Wis.: University of Wisconsin Press, 1987.

Stone, Candace. *Dana and the Sun*. New York: Dodd, Mead and Co., 1938.

Summers, Mark W. *The Press Gang: Newspapers and Politics, 1865–1878*. Chapel Hill, N.C.: University of North Carolina Press, 1994.

Taylor, John M. *William Henry Seward: Lincoln's Right Hand*. New York: Harper Collins, 1991.

Trietsch, James H. *The Printer and the Prince: A Study of the Influence of Horace Greeley upon Abraham Lincoln*. New York: Exposition Press, 1955.

Wert, Jeffry D. *General James Longstreet: The Confederacy's Most Controversial Soldier*. New York: Simon and Schuster, 1993.

Wheeler, Richard. *The Siege of Vicksburg*. New York: Thomas Y. Crowell Co., 1978.

Williams, Kenneth P. *Lincoln Finds a General*. 5 vols. New York: Macmillan Co., 1952.

Wills, Charles W. *Army Life of an Illinois Soldier*. Washington, D.C.: Globe Printing Co., 1906.

Wilson, James H. *The Life of Charles A. Dana*. New York: Harper and Brothers, 1907.

Woodward, William E. *Meet General Grant*. New York: Literary Guild of America, 1928.

NINETEENTH-CENTURY NEWSPAPERS

Chicago Times

*Chicago Tribune**

Cincinnati Commercial

Cincinnati Gazette

Galena (Illinois) Advertiser

Hartford Courant

Louisville (Kentucky) Journal

*New Yorker**

Philadelphia Press

*(St. Louis) Missouri Democrat**

*(St. Louis) Missouri Republican**

New Haven Journal

*New York Herald**

*New York Sun**

*New York Times**

*New York Tribune**

New York World

Providence Journal

Richmond Dispatch

Richmond Sentinel

Richmond Whig

Toledo Journal

Washington Chronicle

Washington Post

---

*Primary

INDEX

ABOUT THE AUTHOR

Harry J. Maihafer, a retired U. S. Army colonel, West Point graduate, and former banker, holds a master's degree in journalism from the University of Missouri. He is the author of *From the Hudson to the Yalu: West Point '49 in the Korean War; Oblivion: The Mystery of West Point Cadet Richard Cox* (Brassey's, 1996); and *Brave Decisions: Moral Courage from the Revolutionary War to Desert Storm* (Brassey's, 1995). His articles have appeared in the *Wall Street Journal, Military History, Naval Institute Proceedings, America's Civil War, Military Review,* and other publications. He and his wife, Jeanne, make their home in Nashville, Tennessee.